EMERGING ADULTHOOD

EMERGING ADULTHOOD

The Winding Road from the Late Teens
Through the Twenties

Second Edition

JEFFREY JENSEN ARNETT

OXFORD
UNIVERSITY PRESS

Oxford University Press is a department of the University of
Oxford. It furthers the University's objective of excellence in research,
scholarship, and education by publishing worldwide.

Oxford   New York
Auckland   Cape Town   Dar es Salaam   Hong Kong   Karachi
Kuala Lumpur   Madrid   Melbourne   Mexico City   Nairobi
New Delhi   Shanghai   Taipei   Toronto

With offices in
Argentina   Austria   Brazil   Chile   Czech Republic   France   Greece
Guatemala   Hungary   Italy   Japan   Poland   Portugal   Singapore
South Korea   Switzerland   Thailand   Turkey   Ukraine   Vietnam

Oxford is a registered trademark of Oxford University Press
in the UK and certain other countries.

Published in the United States of America by
Oxford University Press
198 Madison Avenue, New York, NY 10016

© Oxford University Press 2015

Library of Congress Cataloging-in-Publication Data
Arnett, Jeffrey Jensen.
Emerging adulthood : the winding road from the late teens through the twenties /
Jeffrey Jensen Arnett.—Second Edition.
pages cm
Includes bibliographical references and index.
ISBN 978–0–19–992938–2 (pbk. : alk. paper)   1. Young adults.   I. Title.
HQ799.5.A72 2014
305—dc23
2014022210

1 3 5 7 9 8 6 4 2
Printed in the United States of America
on acid-free paper

CONTENTS

PREFACE TO THE SECOND EDITION

When I first became interested in 18–29-year-olds about 20 years ago, it was a pretty solitary area of research, for a psychologist. Research on human development within psychology has always been skewed toward the early years of life, and psychologists had devoted little attention to 18–29-year-olds. True, there were innumerable studies of college students, but mainly in social psychology studies, based on the dubious assumption that American college students in introductory psychology courses could be taken to represent all humanity. Few of these studies considered how young people in this age group might be distinct from adolescents or from older adults. Sociology devoted more attention to 18–29-year-olds, but mainly in studies looking at the timing and consequences of transition events such as leaving home, finishing education, finding employment, marriage, and parenthood.

I was interested in far more than this—their relations with parents, their love lives, their aspirations for work, their religious beliefs, their views of adulthood, and their hopes for the future. It was solitary work at first, my research on 18–29-year-olds, but that was what had drawn me to it and what made it so exciting. It felt like an uncharted continent, full of surprises and discoveries. For a long time, every time I interviewed people they taught me something I had not known before. It was exhilarating.

In the course of the 1990s I interviewed over 200 18–29-year-olds, in Columbia, Missouri (where I was a junior professor at the University of Missouri) and in San Francisco (where I spent a sabbatical year during 1996–1997). Graduate student research assistants interviewed nearly 100 more, mainly Latinos in Los Angeles and African Americans in New Orleans. We interviewed young people of all socioeconomic backgrounds, from high school dropouts to people with graduate degrees, and from a wide range of ethnic groups, including Whites, African Americans, Latinos, and Asian Americans.

For nearly a decade, I published little of it. I was excited about what I was discovering in the interviews with 18–29-year-olds, but it took me years to reach a point where I believed I had learned enough to write about them with authority. Furthermore, I wasn't sure what to call them. Were they "late adolescents"? That is what I assumed going in, because, like adolescents, most had not found stable long-term work or entered marriage and parenthood. However, I soon dropped this assumption, as they were far more mature and insightful than the adolescents I had interviewed previously, and less dependent on their parents. Nor did they seem like "young adults," because this implied a more settled life stage than most of them were experiencing. It was obvious to me that it made no sense to think of them as being in a stage of "young adulthood" that would stretch from age 18 to age 40.

Eventually I concluded that they were neither adolescents nor young adults but something in-between, something that required a new term and a new conceptualization. They were taking longer to grow up than young people had in the past, as measured by their entry to stable adult roles as well as their own self-perceptions of not-fully-adult status. To understand their development, I decided it would be helpful to propose the addition of a new stage to the normal life span of people in developed countries. After considering (and rejecting) "post-adolescence," I proposed that we call it *emerging adulthood*.

I presented an outline of the theory of emerging adulthood in 2000, in an article in *American Psychologist*.[1] Although it was a brief article, offering only a sketch of the theory, the term and the idea were quickly embraced by many psychologists and practitioners. I think that there were many people who, like me, had concluded that we needed a new way of understanding 18–29-year-olds, and some way of distinguishing them from adolescents or young adults. As of early 2014, that article has been cited over 4,500 times, according to googlescholar.com.

The Rise of Emerging Adulthood

One of my goals, or at least hopes, in proposing the theory of emerging adulthood, was that giving a new name to the 18–29-year-old age period would inspire other researchers to devote attention to it. As I stated in that 2000 *American Psychologist* article:

> [T]he dearth of studies among young people in their twenties... arises from the lack of a clear developmental conception of this age group. Scholars

have no clearly articulated way of thinking about development from the late teens through the twenties, no paradigm for this age period, so they may not think about young people at these ages as a focus for developmental research. Emerging adulthood is offered as a new paradigm, a new way of thinking about development from the late teens through the twenties, especially ages 18–25, partly in the hope that a definite conception of this period will lead to an increase in scholarly attention to it.[2]

Fourteen years later, this hope has come to fruition. There is now a Society for the Study of Emerging Adulthood (SSEA; see www.ssea.org) with over 400 members (as of June 2014). The SSEA sponsors a thriving journal, *Emerging Adulthood* (see http://eax.sagepub.com/). Six conferences on emerging adulthood have been held, and a seventh is in the works for 2015. Research on emerging adulthood is taking place all over the world—not just in psychology but in sociology, education, anthropology, and many other fields. Paradigms matter. Proposing a new life stage of emerging adulthood drew attention to the possibilities for research on 18–29-year-olds, and those possibilities are being energetically pursued by a wide range of talented people.

My Scholarship Since the First Edition

In the first edition of this book, I laid out a more fully developed theory of emerging adulthood, proposing that it is characterized by five distinctive features: identity explorations, instability, self-focus, feeling in-between, and possibilities/optimism. Drawing upon the interviews that I and my students had conducted in the previous decade, I sought to cover all the key aspects of the lives of 18–29-year-olds.

In the decade since the first edition, a substantial part of my scholarship has been devoted to continuing to develop the theory of emerging adulthood and to building up emerging adulthood as a field of scholarship. With Jennifer Tanner, I edited a book, published in 2006, that included contributions by eminent scholars from diverse fields, on topics ranging from identity development to sexuality to mental health.[3] I have published book chapters examining the international scope of emerging adulthood.[4] I have defended emerging adulthood theory from its critics, most notably in a 2011 book with Marion Kloep, Leo Hendry, and Jennifer Tanner, *Debating Emerging Adulthood*.[5] I have defended emerging adults, too, from critics who are all too eager to fling unfounded negative stereotypes at them.[6]

In my research over the past decade, I conducted interviews and surveys with emerging adults in Denmark as a Fulbright Scholar during 2005–2006. I also supervised a student, Marie Krog Overgaard, who interviewed Italian emerging adults the next year.[7] With Elizabeth Fishel, I surveyed and interviewed parents of emerging adults for a book we co-authored in 2012, *Getting to 30: A Parent's Guide to the Twentysomething Years.*[8]

Most notably, I have had the opportunity in recent years to direct several national surveys, funded by Clark University, where I am a research professor, and the results of these surveys are abundantly represented in this tenth anniversary edition. In 2012, the Clark University Poll of Emerging Adults surveyed over 1,000 18–29-year-olds across the United States, from diverse regions, ethnic groups, and socioeconomic backgrounds. In this tenth anniversary edition I use the results of this survey to examine national patterns on many of the questions I examined in the first edition, and also to provide national data on new topics, including media use and mental health. In 2013, the Clark University Poll of Parents of Emerging Adults surveyed over 1,000 parents of 18–29-year-olds, again comprising a diverse, nationally representative sample. Results from this poll have added substantial new information to Chapter 3, on relations with parents. Finally, the 2014 Clark University Poll of Established Adults surveyed over 1,000 persons ages 25–39, in order to gain insights into development after emerging adulthood. This survey was conducted just before the publication of this tenth anniversary edition, so few of the findings were available yet for inclusion in this book, but Chapter 1 contains data from this survey regarding features of emerging adulthood. Reports on all three of the Clark polls can be found at http://www.clarku.edu/clark-poll-emerging-adults/.

New Chapters in the Tenth Anniversary Edition

Over the 20 years I have been interviewing, thinking about, and writing about emerging adults, I would say there has been more stability than change in what I have found. I began my research in 1993, as the United States was coming out of a recession, and as I publish the tenth anniversary edition of this book, in 2014, we are again coming out of a recession. In-between was the boom of the late 1990s and then the stagnation of the early years of the twenty-first century. Throughout these economic ups and downs, I have found that emerging adults always struggle to find a place in a labor market that is vast, complex, and nearly always rewards people who have more experience and expertise than emerging adults have. Those emerging adults who have not obtained education and training beyond high school especially struggle, as the economy moves steadily away from manufacturing and toward services that require higher-level skills and credentials. But even among emerging adults who have obtained a college degree, the transition from school to work is often rough. Across educational levels, emerging adults seek work that will not only pay well but that will be challenging, rewarding, and self-fulfilling. That is an aspiration that is elusive for all.

The biggest change from 20 years ago in the lives of emerging adults is the explosion of media technology and the increasingly prominent place it has in their lives. Twenty years ago, the Internet, e-mail, and cell phones were still a novelty. Even 10 years ago, when the first edition was published, there was no Facebook, Twitter, or Instagram. Now, most emerging adults can scarcely imagine life without a constant connection to their electronic worlds. Consequently, it was essential to add a chapter on media use (Chapter 8) to this tenth anniversary edition.

I have added two other chapters to this edition, on social class issues (Chapter 10) and on problems (Chapter 11). The topic of social class has been a contentious one since I first proposed the theory of emerging adulthood. Although I have always included young people from diverse social class backgrounds in my research, and one of my reasons for proposing the theory in 2000 was to draw attention to 18–29-year-olds who were not college students,[9] critics of the theory have nevertheless claimed that it applies only to the college-educated middle class. Consequently, I felt it was essential to address this claim directly in this edition of the book. Fortunately, the 2012 Clark poll allows for a test of claims related to social class, because it was composed of a nationally representative sample of Americans ages 18–29, from all social class backgrounds.

The chapter on problems also seemed like a necessary addition. There are some kinds of problems, such as substance use, that peak during the emerging adult years. Furthermore, emerging adulthood is a complex period with respect to mental health, because feelings of depression and anxiety are strikingly high, even as most people are also optimistic and regard their current time of life as fun and exciting. Those complexities are now explored in Chapter 11.

The focus of the book remains on young Americans, rather than emerging adults worldwide. I consider myself a cultural psychologist, and I always seek to add a cultural context to my observations on development during emerging adulthood. However, except for the small studies on Danish and Italian emerging adults mentioned above, all my research has been on young Americans. They are the population I know best. This book contains a number of international comparisons, and mentions research from other countries, but it is mainly on American emerging adults. I am delighted that researchers around the world are now examining the forms that emerging adulthood may take in their countries, and my own perspective will continue to be expanded by their findings.

Acknowledgments and Dedication

It has been a pleasure to write the tenth anniversary edition of this book. In the course of updating the previous chapters and adding the three new chapters, I have been amazed to observe how much has been learned over the past 10 years about emerging adults. I am grateful to all the scholars who are working in emerging adulthood research and have enhanced my understanding of this new life stage.

I also wish to thank the people of Oxford University Press, especially Sarah Harrington, who immediately supported the idea of a tenth anniversary edition when I proposed it. In my view, OUP consistently publishes the most compelling, important academic books in the world, and it is an honor to be among their authors.

Finally, I wish to thank all the people who were inspired by the first edition of this book, and have let me know it. This includes not only my fellow scholars, but also therapists, educators, policymakers, parents, and emerging adults themselves. It was your enthusiasm for the first edition that drove me to create the new edition and to make it as good as I could. This tenth anniversary edition is dedicated to you.

Jeffrey Jensen Arnett
Worcester, Massachusetts

PREFACE TO THE FIRST EDITION

The origin of this book dates from about ten years ago, when I was a junior professor at the University of Missouri. As is often the case for those of us who do research in psychology, my interest in the topic was drawn from my own experience. At that point in my life, after many of years of education, I finally had a job that I expected to be in for a long time to come. After many years of dating, I had finally met and was living with the person I hoped to marry. After years of moving around from one place to another every year or two or three in pursuit of new opportunities and experiences, I was ready to stay in one place for a while and put down some roots. I felt at last that I had reached adulthood.

I began to wonder, how and when do other people feel they have reached adulthood? It occurred to me that there is no social or communal ritual in American society to mark that passage. Instead, it is left to each of us to determine when the threshold to adulthood has been reached, and what signifies it.

I had been doing research on adolescence for several years at the time, so it was easy for me to turn the focus of my research to the question of what it means to move from adolescence to adulthood. I soon learned that there was not much in psychology that had explored the topic, but there was a great deal of research in sociology on what was called "the transition to adulthood." Sociologists defined the transition to adulthood in terms of distinct transition events, specifically: leaving home, finishing education, entering full-time work, marriage, and parenthood. This seemed perfectly reasonable to me. My own sense of reaching adulthood had been marked by entering full-time work and, if not marriage, at least feeling ready for marriage.

I was quite surprised, then, when I began to ask college students about what they believed marked the transition to adulthood and found that for them entering full-time work and marriage had nothing to do with it. Nor did the other sociological transitions. In fact, the sociological transitions ended up rock bottom when I surveyed college students about possible criteria for adulthood. Instead of the sociological transitions, the most important criteria for adulthood to these college students were more intangible and psychological: accepting responsibility for one's actions, making independent decisions, and becoming financially independent.

Well, I thought, maybe that's because they're college students, and being in college leads them to think in more abstract and psychological terms. Maybe people in the same age group who were not in college would see the transition to adulthood more in terms of transition events, like the sociologists did. But when I surveyed and interviewed them, I came up with the same results as I had for the college students, and there were very few differences by educational level or socioeconomic background

By now I was thoroughly intrigued, and wanted to know more about what was going on in the lives of people experiencing the transition to adulthood. I started a study in Missouri of young people in their twenties, including both college and non-college participants, and asked them a broad range of questions—on their family lives, on love and sex and marriage, on their college and work experiences, on what they value most and what they believe about religious questions, and more. I spent a year in San Francisco and continued my research, focusing on Asian Americans and African Americans. I had graduate students conduct interviews on Latinos in Los Angeles and African Americans in New Orleans.

The more research I did, the more I talked to people in their twenties, the less satisfied I became with describing their development in terms of the transition to adulthood. Yes, the transition to adulthood takes place during this period, but that term does not begin to cover all that is going on in their lives from the time they leave high school to the time they reach full adulthood. Calling it "the transition to adulthood" seemed to diminish it, as if it were merely a transition connecting the two more important periods of adolescence and young adulthood. And it lasts so long, at least from age 18 to 25 and usually longer, as long or longer than any stage of childhood or adolescence, why shouldn't it be regarded as a distinct period of life in its own right?

I looked for existing theories that would provide a framework for understanding the transition to adulthood as a separate developmental period, but could not find anything satisfying. The most commonly discussed idea was

Kenneth Keniston's idea of "youth," but "youth" seemed to me a dubious choice of terms for this age period, because it was already used in so many other ways, to describe people as young as middle childhood and as old as their thirties. Besides, Keniston's ideas on "youth" were based mainly on the college student protesters of the 1960s, an atypical group at an unusual time in American history, and seemed to me to have little application to the present.

So, I decided to create my own theory of development from the late teens through the twenties, and this book is the result of those efforts. Already I have published numerous articles in scholarly journals outlining the theory, but this is my first attempt to present a comprehensive account of it, based on my research over the past decade. I hope scholars will find it compelling and persuasive, but I regard this book as the beginning of forming an understanding of emerging adulthood, not the last word. Already many other scholars are conducting research using the theory of emerging adulthood, and it is a field of study that is growing rapidly. The first scholarly conference was held at Harvard University in November of 2003, and there will certainly be more. A group of scholars has been formed to share information and support in studying emerging adulthood. Now that we are beginning to develop a shared language for talking about this age period, there are surely many exciting discoveries to come.

This is a book not just for scholars but for anyone interested in this topic and this age period. I hope many emerging adults will find it provocative and informative, and their parents as well. It was my goal to write a book that would make an important contribution to scholarship on emerging adulthood but that most people could read and would find engaging whether they were scholars or not. So, there are no complex statistical analyses, and most of the information comparing my results to other studies on the age period can be found in the Notes rather than in the main text of the book. What I have focused on instead is the voices of emerging adults, that is, what they say about their lives on a wide range of topics.

I present some questionnaire results, but mainly I present the results from the interviews, because that is where I learned the most about emerging adults. Questionnaires have a useful place in research, but in my experience as a researcher there is simply no substitute for sitting face-to-face with someone and talking to them about what they have experienced and what it means to them. I believe that in all psychological research it is important to listen to how people describe and interpret their lives—OK, except infants—but it may be especially important in emerging adulthood, because it is a highly self-reflective time of life, a time when they think a lot about who they are and what they want out of life. And it's fun to listen to them, as you'll see in the course of this book. No matter what their educational background, they are remarkably articulate, often funny, sometimes moving.

I have many people to thank for their support in making this book possible. Although I did most of the interviews myself, I had assistance from numerous students along the way, including Katie Ramos and Diane Rutledge in Missouri and Los Angeles, Terrolyn Carter in New Orleans, and Gretchen Cooke, Colleen O'Connell, and Megan O'Donnell in San Francisco. Several of my colleagues read part or all of the book before publication and provided comments and suggestions, including Jim Côté, Bill Damon, Wyndol Furman, Steve Hamilton, Hugh McIntosh, Mike Shanahan, Shmuel Shulman, Jennifer Tanner, and Niobe Way. Special thanks goes to my wife Lene Jensen, who read many a draft without complaint and always offered insightful and helpful comments. Thanks also to Catherine Carlin, psychology editor at Oxford University Press, for understanding what I was aiming for in this book and enthusiastically supporting it. Finally, I wish to thank the hundreds of emerging adults who opened up their lives to me in the interviews that are the foundation of this book. You taught me an immense amount, and I am grateful for it.

Jeffrey Jensen Arnett
University Park, Maryland

EMERGING ADULTHOOD

Chapter 1

A Longer Road to Adulthood

In the past half century a quiet revolution has taken place for young people in American society, so quiet that it has been noticed only gradually and incompletely. As recently as 1960, the typical 21-year-old was married or about to be married, caring for a newborn child or expecting one soon, done with education or about to be done, and settled into a long-term job or a role as full-time mother. Young people of that time grew up quickly and made serious enduring choices about their lives at a relatively early age. Today, the life of a typical 21-year-old could hardly be more different. Marriage and parenthood are at least six years off. Education may last several more years, through an extended undergraduate program—the "four-year degree" in five, six, or more—and perhaps graduate or professional school. Job changes are frequent, as young people look for work that not only pays well but will be enjoyable and fulfilling.

For the young Americans of the twenty-first century, the road to adulthood is a long one. They leave home at age 18 or 19, but most do not marry, become parents, or find a long-term job until at least their late twenties. From their late teens to their late twenties they explore the possibilities available to them in love and work, and move gradually toward making enduring choices. Such freedom to explore different options is exciting, and this is a time of high hopes and big dreams. However, it is also a time of anxiety, because the lives of young people are so unsettled and many of them have no idea where their explorations will lead. They struggle with uncertainty, even as they revel in being freer than they ever were in childhood or ever will be once they take on the full weight of adult responsibilities. To be a young American today is to experience both excitement and uneasiness, wide-open possibility and confusion, new freedoms and new fears.

The rise in the ages of entering marriage and parenthood, the spread of education and training beyond secondary school, and prolonged job instability during the twenties reflect the rise of a new life stage for young people in the United States and other economically developed countries, lasting from the late teens through the mid- to late twenties. This period is not simply an "extended adolescence," because it is very different from adolescence—much freer from parental control, much more a period of independent exploration. Nor is it really "young adulthood," since this term implies that an early stage of adulthood has been reached, whereas most young people in their twenties have not made the transitions historically associated with adult status—especially marriage and parenthood—and most of them feel they have not yet reached adulthood. It is a new and historically unprecedented stage of the life course, so it requires a new term and a new way of thinking. I have proposed that we call it *emerging adulthood.*

For some time, Americans have noticed the change in how young people experience their late teens and their twenties. In the 1990s "Generation X" became a widely used term for people in this age period, inspired by Douglas Coupland's 1991 novel of that title. More recently, a generation of "Millennials" born in the years before 2000 has been claimed to share certain characteristics, such as an obsession with social media. However, the characteristics of today's young people are not merely generational. The changes that have created emerging adulthood are here to stay. There seems to be little reason to doubt that the young people of the twenty-first century will experience an extended period of exploration and instability in their late teens and twenties. For this reason, I believe emerging adulthood should be recognized as a distinct new life stage that will be around for many generations to come.

In this book I describe the characteristics of emerging adults, based mainly on my research over the past 20 years, plus a synthesis of other research and theories on the age period. In this opening chapter I provide some historical background on the rise of emerging adulthood and describe the period's distinctive features. I also explain why the term *emerging adulthood* is preferable to other possible terms. At the end of the chapter I discuss cultural variations in emerging adulthood. Because most of my research has taken place in the United States, most of this book focuses on American emerging adults, but emerging adulthood is an international phenomenon.

The Rise of Emerging Adulthood: Four Revolutions

Emerging adulthood has been created in part by the steep rise in the typical ages of marriage and parenthood that has taken place since the middle of the twentieth century. As you can see in Figure 1.1, in 1960 the median age of marriage in the United States was just 20.3 for women and 22.8 for men. Even as recently as 1970, these ages had risen only slightly. However, since 1970 there has been a dramatic shift in the ages when Americans typically get married. By 2010 the typical age of marriage was over 26 for women and over 28 for men, a six-year rise for both sexes in the span of just four decades—and still rising every year.[1] The age of entering parenthood followed a similar pattern, although far more first births take place outside marriage now (48% as of 2010) than was true in 1960.[2]

Later ages of marriage and parenthood have created a space between the late teens and the late twenties for the new life stage of emerging adulthood. But these later ages were not causes of the new life stage in and of themselves. Rather, they were reflections of other vast changes taking place in modern societies. Four revolutionary changes took place in the 1960s and 1970s that laid the foundation for the world as we know it today, including the new life stage of emerging adulthood: the Technology Revolution, the Sexual Revolution, the Women's Movement, and the Youth Movement.

By the Technology Revolution, I do not mean iPads and iPhones but the manufacturing technologies that transformed the American economy. Because of extraordinary advances in technology, machines became able to perform most of the manufacturing jobs that were once the main source of employment in developed countries. (Manufacturing production in the United States is actually six times higher now that it was in 1950, but

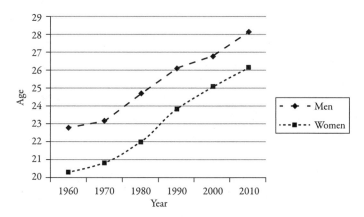

Figure 1.1 Median Marriage Age, United States, 1960–2010.
Source: Stritof & Stritof (2014).

new technologies have made that possible with far fewer jobs.)[3] As a consequence of this revolution, the United States and other developed countries have shifted from a manufacturing economy to a service economy that requires information and technology skills. In the early twentieth century, most work entailed *making things* in factory-based manufacturing jobs. By the early twenty-first century, most work involved *using information* in service-based work such as business, finance, insurance, education, and health. Figure 1.2 shows how the service sector has replaced the manufacturing sector as the primary basis of economic activity in the United States since the mid-twentieth century.[4]

The new service economy emphasizes information and technology, and therefore requires postsecondary education and training for most jobs, especially for the jobs with the highest pay and status. Consequently, an exceptionally high proportion of young Americans, nearly 70%, now continue their education beyond high school. This is a higher proportion than ever before, as Figure 1.3 shows.[5] Most young people wait until they have finished school before they start thinking seriously about making adult commitments such as marriage and parenthood, and for many of them this means postponing those commitments until at least their late twenties.

A second change was the Sexual Revolution, which was sparked by a technological change: the invention of the birth control pill in 1964. The ease and availability of "the Pill" led directly to the Sexual Revolution

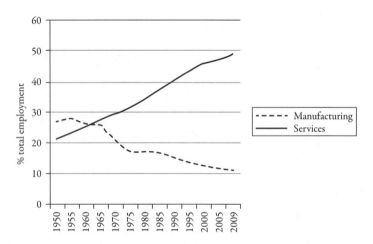

Figure 1.2 The Rise of the Service Economy.
Source: McGill & Bell (2013).

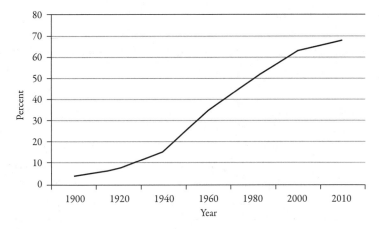

Figure 1.3 College Enrollment, 1900–2010.

Sources: Arnett & Taber (1994), National Center for Education Statistics (2013).

that began in the late 1960s, including less stringent standards of sexual morality. It became widely (if somewhat grudgingly) accepted that young people no longer had to enter marriage in order to have a regular sexual relationship. Today most young people have a series of sexual relationships before entering marriage,[6] and most Americans do not object to this, as long as sex does not begin at an age that is "too early" (whatever that is) and as long as the number of partners does not become "too many" (whatever that is). Although Americans may not be clear, in their own minds, about what the precise rules ought to be for young people's sexual behavior, there is widespread tolerance now for sexual relations between young people in their late teens and twenties in the context of a committed, loving relationship.

The third major change of the 1960s and 1970s that shaped the lives of today's young people was the Women's Movement. As a consequence of the Women's Movement, young women's options have expanded in ways that make an early entry into adult obligations less desirable for them now, compared to 50 years ago. The young women of 1960 were under a great deal of social pressure to catch a man.[7] Remaining single was simply not a viable social status for a woman after her early twenties. Relatively few women attended college, and those who did were often there for the purpose of obtaining their "M-r-s" degree (in the joke of the day)—that is, for the purpose of finding a husband. The range of occupations open to young women was severely restricted, as it had been traditionally—secretary, waitress, teacher, nurse, perhaps a few others. Even these occupations were supposed to be temporary for young women. What they were really supposed to be focusing on was finding a husband and having children. Having no other real options, and facing social limbo if they remained unmarried for long, their yearning for marriage and children—the sooner the better— was sharpened.

For the young women of the twenty-first century, all this has changed. At every level of education, from grade school through graduate school, girls now surpass boys. Fifty-seven percent of the undergraduates in America's colleges and universities are women, according to the most recent figures.[8] Young women's occupational possibilities are now virtually unlimited, and although men still dominate in engineering and some sciences, women are equal to men in obtaining law, business, and medical degrees. With so many options open to them, and with so little pressure on them to marry by their early twenties, the lives of young American women today have changed almost beyond recognition from what they were 50 years ago. And most of them take on their new freedoms with alacrity, making the most of their emerging adult years before they enter marriage and parenthood.

The fourth tectonic shift of the 1960s and 1970s was the Youth Movement, which denigrated adulthood and exalted being, acting, and feeling young. "Never trust anyone over 30" and "I hope I die before I get old" are phrases that remain familiar to anyone who was around during that era. As a consequence of the Youth Movement, there has been a profound change in how young people view the meaning and value of becoming an adult and entering the adult roles of spouse, parent, and employee. Young people of the 1950s were eager to enter adulthood and "settle down."[9] Perhaps because they grew up during the upheavals of the Great Depression and World War II, attaining the stability of a secure job, marriage, home, and children seemed like a great achievement to them. Also, because many of them planned to have three, four, or even five or more children, they had good reason to get started early in order to have all the children they wanted and space them out at reasonable intervals.

The young people of today, in contrast, see adulthood and its obligations in quite a different light. In their late teens and early twenties, marriage, home, and children are seen by most of them not as achievements to be pursued but as perils to be avoided. It is not that they reject the prospect of marriage, home, and children—eventually. Most of them do want to take on all of these adult roles, and most of them will have done so by the time they reach age 30. It is just that, in their late teens and early twenties, they ponder these obligations and think, "yes, but *not yet*." Adulthood and its commitments offer security and stability, but also represent a closing of doors—the end of independence, the end of spontaneity, the end of a sense of wide-open possibility.

Emerging adulthood lasts from roughly age 18, when most young people finish secondary school, to age 25, when most people begin to move toward making the commitments that structure adult life: marriage (or a long-term partnership), parenthood, and a long-term job. I sometimes use 18–25 to refer to emerging adulthood and sometimes 18–29, because the end of it is highly variable. Nothing magical happens at age 25 to end it. For most people the late twenties are a time of moving toward a more settled adult life, but there are many, especially the highly educated urban young, who continue their emerging adult lifestyle through their late twenties and into their early thirties. Age 18 to 25 is a conservative range to use when age ranges are required for referring to emerging adulthood, because relatively few 18–25-year-olds have crossed the major thresholds into a stable, established adulthood. However, 18–29 can be legitimately used as well, to include the many people who do not make the transition into established adulthood until closer to age 30. The 18–29 age range also makes most sense internationally, as median ages of entering marriage and parenthood are higher in all other developed countries than they are in the United States, usually around age 30.[10]

Although the rise of emerging adulthood is reflected in rising ages of marriage and parenthood, marriage ages were also relatively high early in the twentieth century and throughout the nineteenth century, especially for young men.[11] What is different now is that young people are freer than they were in the past to use the intervening years, between the end of secondary school and entry into marriage and parenthood, to explore a wide range of different possible future paths. Young people of the past were constricted in a variety of ways, from gender roles to economics, that prevented them from using their late teens and twenties for exploration. In contrast, today's emerging adults have unprecedented freedom.

Not all of them have an equal portion of it, to be certain. Some live in conditions of deprivation that make any chance of exploring life options severely limited, at best.[12] However, as a group they have more freedom for exploration than young people in times past. Their society grants them a long moratorium in their late teens and twenties without expecting them to take on adult responsibilities as soon as they are able. Instead, they are allowed to move into adult responsibilities gradually, at their own pace.

What Is Emerging Adulthood?

Emerging adulthood is defined primarily by its demographic outline. Longer and more widespread education, later entry to marriage and parenthood, and a prolonged and erratic transition to stable work have opened up a space for a new life stage in between adolescence and young adulthood, and "emerging adulthood" is what I have proposed to call that life stage.[13] These demographic changes have taken place worldwide over the past half century, and so the rise of emerging adulthood is an international phenomenon, true of developed countries across the globe and increasingly of developing countries as well.[14] Wherever there is a substantial number of years between the time young people reach the end of adolescence (around age 18) and the time they enter stable adult roles in love and work, emerging adulthood can be said to be present. However, young people's experience of emerging adulthood is likely to vary considerably across national, cultural, and socioeconomic contexts. It is best to think of it as one stage, with distinctive demographic characteristics, but with many possible paths through that stage, in terms of how emerging adults experience their education, work, beliefs, self-development, and relationships.

My research has taken place mainly in the context of American society, first in the 300 interviews that were the basis of the first edition of this book, and since then in a variety of other studies. In the course of this research, I have sought to distinguish the features of American emerging adulthood that make it distinct from adolescence or young adulthood, and I will present these features in this section.

I do not claim that these are "universal" features of 18–29-year-olds, regardless of their background. On the contrary, I fully expect that other features will be found to be more important in other cultural and economic contexts around the world. The five features presented her represent my current conclusions as to the distinctive features of American emerging adults, based on my research over the past 20 years. They are proposed as *distinctive* to emerging adulthood but not *unique* to it. That is, they may be experienced in other life stages as well, but I propose that they are more prevalent and prominent in emerging adulthood than in other stages.

So, what are the distinguishing features of emerging adulthood in the United States? What makes it distinct from the adolescence that precedes it and the young adulthood that follows it? There are five main features:

1. *Identity explorations:* answering the question "who am I?" and trying out various life options, especially in love and work;
2. *Instability,* in love, work, and place of residence;
3. *Self-focus,* as obligations to others reach a life-span low point;
4. *Feeling in-between,* in transition, neither adolescent nor adult; and
5. *Possibilities/optimism,* when hopes flourish and people have an unparalleled opportunity to transform their lives.

Let's look at each of these features in turn.

Identity Explorations

Perhaps the most distinctive feature of emerging adulthood in the United States is that it is a time when young people explore the available options for their lives in a variety of areas, especially love and work. In the course of these explorations, emerging adults develop an *identity,* that is, they clarify their sense of who they are and what they want out of life. The late teens and early to mid-twenties offer the best opportunity for such identity explorations. Emerging adults have become more independent of their parents than they were as adolescents and most of them have left home, but they have not yet entered the stable, enduring commitments typical of adult life, such as a long-term job, marriage, and parenthood. During this interval of years when they are neither beholden to their parents nor committed to an assortment of adult roles, they have an exceptional opportunity to try out different ways of living and different possible choices for love and work.

Of course, it is adolescence rather than emerging adulthood that has typically been associated with identity formation. In 1950, Erik Erikson proposed identity versus role confusion as the central crisis of the adolescent stage of life,[15] and in the decades following his articulation of this idea the focus of research on identity has been on adolescence. However, Erikson also commented on the "prolonged adolescence" typical of industrialized societies, and the *psychosocial moratorium* granted to young people in such societies, "during which the young adult through free role experimentation may find a niche in some section of his society."[16]

Decades later, this observation applies to many more young people than when he first wrote it. If adolescence is the period from age 10 to 18 and emerging adulthood is the period from (roughly) age 18 to 25, most identity exploration takes place in emerging adulthood rather than adolescence. Although research on identity formation has focused mainly on adolescence, this research has shown that identity achievement has rarely been reached by the end of high school and that identity development continues through the late teens and the twenties.[17]

In both love and work, the process of identity formation begins in adolescence but intensifies in emerging adulthood. With regard to love, adolescent love tends to be tentative and transient.[18] The implicit question is, "Who would I enjoy being with, here and now?" In contrast, explorations in love in emerging adulthood tend to involve a deeper level of intimacy, and the implicit question is more identity-focused:[19] "What kind of person am I, and what kind of person would suit me best as a partner through life?" By becoming involved with different people, emerging adults learn about the qualities that are most important to them in another person, both the qualities that attract them and the qualities they find distasteful and annoying. They also see how they are evaluated by others who come to know them well, and learn what others find attractive in them—and perhaps distasteful and annoying!

In work, too, there is a similar contrast between the transient and tentative explorations of adolescence and the more serious and identity-focused explorations of emerging adulthood. Most American adolescents have a part-time job at some point during high school, but most of their jobs last for only a few months at most.[20] They tend to work in low-skill service jobs—at restaurants, retail stores, and so on—that are unrelated to the work they expect to be doing in adulthood, and they tend to view their jobs not as occupational preparation but as a way to obtain the money that will support an active leisure life—concert tickets, restaurant meals, clothes, cars, travel, and so on.

In emerging adulthood, work experiences become more focused on laying the groundwork for an adult occupation. In exploring various work options, and in exploring the educational paths that will prepare them for work, emerging adults explore identity issues as well: "What kind of work am I good at? What kind of work would I find satisfying for the long term? What are my chances of getting a job in the field that seems to suit me best?" As they try out different jobs or college majors, emerging adults learn more about themselves. They learn about their abilities and interests. Just as important, they learn what kinds of work they are *not* good at or *do not* want to do. In work as in love, explorations in emerging adulthood commonly include the experience of failure or disappointment. But as in love, the failures and disappointments in work can be illuminating for self-understanding.

Although emerging adults become more focused and serious about their choices in love and work than they were as adolescents, this change takes place gradually. Many of the identity explorations of the emerging adult years are simply for fun, a kind of play, part of gaining a broad range of life experiences before "settling down" and taking on the responsibilities of adult life.[21] This is common enough among emerging adults today to have earned a popular acronym, YOLO: You Only Live Once. Emerging adults realize that they are free in ways they will not be during their thirties and beyond. For people who wish to have a variety of romantic and sexual experiences, emerging adulthood is the time for it, when parental surveillance has diminished and there is as yet little normative pressure to enter marriage. Similarly, emerging adulthood is the time for trying out unusual educational and work possibilities. Programs such as Teach for America, AmeriCorps, and the Peace Corps find most of their volunteers among emerging adults, because emerging adults have both the freedom to pull up stakes quickly in order to go somewhere new and the inclination to do something unusual. Other emerging adults travel on their own to a different part of the country or the world to work or study for a while. This, too, can be part of their identity explorations, part of expanding the range of their personal experiences prior to making the more enduring choices of adulthood.

Instability

The identity explorations of emerging adults and their shifting choices in love and work make this life stage not only exceptionally full and intense but also exceptionally unstable. Emerging adults know they are supposed to have a Plan with a capital "P," that is, some kind of idea about the route they will be taking from adolescence to adulthood,[22] and most of them come up with one. However, for almost all of them, their Plan is subject to numerous revisions during the emerging adult years. These revisions are a natural consequence of their explorations. They enter college and choose a major, then discover the major is not as interesting as it seemed—time to revise the Plan. Or they enter college and find themselves unable to focus on their studies, and their grades sink accordingly—time to revise the Plan. Or they go to work after high school but discover after a year or two that they need more education if they ever expect to make decent money—time to revise the Plan. Or they move in with a boyfriend or girlfriend and start to think of the Plan as founded on their future together, only to discover that they have no future together—time to revise the Plan.

With each revision in the Plan, they learn something about themselves and take a step toward clarifying the kind of future they want. But even if they succeed in doing so, this does not mean that the instability of emerging adulthood is easy. Sometimes emerging adults look back wistfully on their high school years. Most of them remember those years as filled with anguish in many ways, but in retrospect at least they knew what they were going to be doing from one day, one week, one month to the next. In emerging adulthood the insecurities of adolescence diminish, but instability replaces them as a new source of disruption.

The best illustration of the instability of emerging adulthood is in how often they move from one residence to another. As Figure 1.4 indicates, rates of moving spike upward beginning at age 18 and reach their peak in the mid-twenties, then sharply decline. This shows that American emerging adults rarely know where they will be living from one year to the next. It is easy to imagine the sources of their many moves. Their first move is to leave home, often to go to college but sometimes just to be independent of their parents.[23] Other moves soon follow. If they drop out of college, either temporarily or permanently (as many do), they may move again. They often live with roommates during emerging adulthood, some of whom they get along with, some of whom they do not—and when they do not, they move again. They may move in with

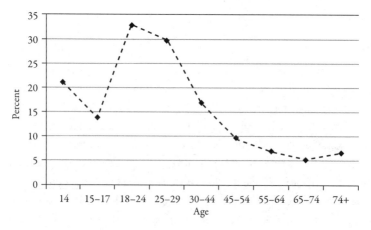

Figure 1.4 Change of Residence in Past Year, by Age.

Source: US Bureau of the Census (2011).

a boyfriend or girlfriend. Sometimes cohabitation leads to marriage, sometimes it does not—and when it does not, they move again. If they graduate from college they move again, perhaps to start a new job or to enter graduate school. For about 40% of American emerging adults, at least one of their moves during the years from age 18–25 will be back home to live with their parents.[24]

All this moving around makes emerging adulthood an unstable time, but it also reflects the identity explorations that take place during the emerging adult years. Many of the moves that emerging adults make are for the purpose of some new period of exploration, in love, work, or education. Exploration and instability go hand in hand.

Self-Focus

There is no time of life that is more self-focused than emerging adulthood. Children and adolescents are self-focused in their own way, yes, but they always have parents and teachers to answer to, and usually siblings as well. Nearly all of them live at home with at least one parent. There are household rules and standards to follow, and if they break them they risk the wrath of other family members ("Who left their towel on the bathroom floor?!"). Parents keep track, at least to some extent, of where they are and what they are doing. Although adolescents typically grow more independent than they were as children, they remain part of a family system that requires responses from them on a daily basis. In addition, nearly all of them attend school, whether they like it or not, where teachers set the standards and monitor their behavior and performance.

By age 30, a new web of commitments and obligations is well established, for most people. At that age the majority of Americans have married and have had at least one child.[25] A new household, then, with new rules and standards. A spouse, instead of parents and siblings, with whom they must coordinate activities and negotiate household duties and requirements. A child, to be loved and provided for, who needs time and attention. By age 30, most Americans also have the first job that they will remain in for at least five years.[26] An employer, then, in a job and a field they are committed to and want to succeed in, who holds them to standards of progress and achievement.

It is only in-between, during emerging adulthood, that there are few ties that entail daily obligations and commitments to others. Most young Americans leave home at age 18 or 19, and moving out means that daily life is much more self-focused. What to have for dinner? You decide. When to do the laundry? You decide. When (or whether) to come home at night? You decide.

So many decisions! And those are the easy ones. They have to decide the hard ones mostly on their own as well. Go to college? Work full-time? Try to combine work and college? Stay in college or drop out? Switch majors? Switch colleges? Switch jobs? Switch apartments? Switch roommates? Break up with girlfriend/boyfriend? Move in with girlfriend/boyfriend? Seek someone new, and if so, how and where? Even for emerging adults who remain at home, many of these decisions apply. Counsel may be offered or sought from parents and friends, but many of these decisions mean clarifying in their own mind what they want, and no one else can really tell them what they want.

To be self-focused is not necessarily to be selfish, and to say that emerging adulthood is a self-focused time is not meant pejoratively. There is nothing wrong about being self-focused during emerging adulthood; it is normal, healthy, and temporary. By focusing on themselves, emerging adults develop skills at daily living, gain a better understanding of who they are and what they want from life, and begin to build a foundation for their adult lives. The goal of their self-focusing is to learn to stand alone as a self-sufficient person, but they do not see self-sufficiency as a permanent state. Rather, they view it as a necessary step before committing themselves to enduring relationships with others, in love and work.

Feeling In-Between

The exploration and instability of emerging adulthood give it the quality of an in-between period—between adolescence, when most people live in their parents' home and are required to attend secondary school, and young adulthood, when most people have entered marriage and parenthood and have settled into a stable occupational path. In-between the restrictions of adolescence and the responsibilities of adulthood lie the explorations and instability of emerging adulthood.

It feels this way to most emerging adults, too—like an age in-between, neither adolescent nor adult, on the way to adulthood but not there yet. When asked whether they feel they have reached adulthood, their responses are often ambiguous, with one foot in "yes" and the other in "no." For example, Lillian, 25, answered the question this way:

"Sometimes I think I've reached adulthood and then I sit down and eat ice cream directly from the box, and I keep thinking 'I'll know I'm an adult when I don't eat ice cream right out of the box anymore!' That seems like such a childish thing to do. But I guess in some ways I feel like I'm an adult. I'm a pretty responsible person. I mean, if I say I'm going to do something, I do it. I'm very responsible with my job. Financially, I'm fairly responsible with my money. But sometimes in social circumstances I feel uncomfortable, like I don't know what I'm supposed to do, and I still feel like a little kid. So a lot of times I don't really feel like an adult."

The reason why so many emerging adults feel in-between is evident from the criteria they consider to be most important for becoming an adult. Their top criteria are gradual, so their feeling of becoming an adult is gradual, too. In a variety of regions of the United States, in a variety of ethnic groups, across social classes, in studies using both questionnaires and interviews, people consistently state these as the top three criteria for adulthood:[27]

1. Accept responsibility for yourself.
2. Make independent decisions.
3. Become financially independent.

The "Big Three" criteria are gradual, incremental, rather than all-at-once. Consequently, although emerging adults begin to feel adult by the time they reach age 18 or 19, most do not feel completely adult until years later, sometime in their mid- to late twenties. By then they have become confident that they have reached a point where they accept responsibility, make their own decisions, and are financially independent. While they are in the process of developing those qualities, they feel in-between adolescence and full adulthood. The Big Three have been found to be prevalent not only in the United States but around the world, as we will see in more detail in the final chapter.

Possibilities/Optimism

Emerging adulthood is the age of possibilities, when many different futures remain possible, when little about a person's direction in life has been decided for certain. It tends to be an age of high hopes and great expectations, in part because few of their dreams have been tested in the fires of real life. Emerging adults look to the future and envision a well-paying, satisfying job, a loving, lifelong marriage to their "soul mate," and happy children who are above average. The dreary, dead-end jobs, the bitter divorces, the disappointing and disrespectful children that some of them will find themselves experiencing in the years to come—none of them imagines that this is what the future holds.

Another aspect of emerging adulthood that makes it the age of possibilities is that it offers the potential for changing dramatically the direction of one's life. A simple but crucial feature of emerging adulthood in this respect is that typically emerging adults have left their family of origin but are not yet committed to a new network of relationships and obligations. This is especially important for young people who have grown up in difficult conditions. A chaotic or unhappy family is difficult to rise above for children and adolescents, because they return to that family environment every day, and the family's problems are often reflected in problems of their own. If the parents fight a lot, they have to listen to it. If the parents live in poverty, the children live in poverty, too, most likely in dangerous neighborhoods with inferior schools. If a parent is addicted to alcohol or other drugs, the disruptions from the parent's addiction rip through the rest of the family as well. However, with emerging adulthood and departure from the family home, an unparalleled opportunity begins for young people to transform their lives. For those who have come from a troubled family, this is their chance to try to straighten the parts of themselves that have become twisted. We will see some examples of dramatic transformations in Chapter 12.

Even for those who have come from families they regard as relatively happy and healthy, emerging adulthood is an opportunity to transform themselves so that they are not merely made in their parents' images but have made independent decisions about what kind of person they wish to be and how they wish to live. During emerging adulthood they have an exceptionally wide scope for making their own decisions. Eventually, virtually all emerging adults will enter new, long-term obligations in love and work, and once they do, their new obligations will set them on paths that resist change and that may continue for the rest of their lives. But for now, while emerging adulthood lasts, they have a chance to change their lives in profound ways.

Regardless of their family background, all emerging adults carry their family influences with them when they leave home, and the extent to which they can change what they have become by the end of adolescence is not unlimited. Still, more than any other period of life, emerging adulthood presents the possibility of change. For this limited window of time—seven, perhaps ten years—the fulfillment of all their hopes seems possible, because for most people the range of their choices for how to live is greater than it has ever been before and greater than it will ever be again.

Research on the Five Features

How have these five features fared in research since I first proposed them a decade ago? Alan Reifman developed a measure to examine the five features, the Inventory of Dimensions of Emerging Adulthood (IDEA), and tested it in five studies.[28] Consistent with the theory, participants in their twenties were higher than younger or older participants on the subscales representing the five features: identity explorations, negativity/instability, self-focus, feeling in-between, and experimentation/possibilities. Since the publication of the IDEA in 2007, it has been used in many other studies, but usually focusing on a sample in the emerging adult age range rather than comparing participants of different ages.[29]

My own research in the past decade has included a national study in 2012, the Clark University Poll of Emerging Adults, that contained items pertaining to the five features.[30] As shown in Table 1.1, all five features were supported by a majority of 18–29-year-olds. The feature with the lowest level of support, feeling in-between, varied substantially by age, as shown in Figure 1.5. Overall, 45% of the 18–29-year-olds responded "in some ways yes, in some ways no" to the question, "Do you feel that you have reached adulthood?" However, in the course of the twenties, feeling fully adult steadily rises, and feeling in-between steadily falls.

There were age differences on other features as well. The 18–25-year-olds were more likely than 26–29-year-olds to agree with the items pertaining to identity explorations, instability, and self-focus.[31] These findings are important, because, as noted earlier, different age ranges have been used for emerging adulthood, sometimes 18–25 and sometimes 18–29. The findings here suggest that 18–25 is the heart of the age range for emerging adulthood in American society. However, for most people there is nothing about reaching age 25 that results in a sudden and definite transition to adulthood, so, in some ways for some people, emerging adulthood may last through the twenties. Either 18–25 or 18–29 may be an appropriate age range for emerging adulthood, depending on the topic or question being addressed.

Table 1.1 The Five Features of Emerging Adulthood: Percent Agreement in a National (American) Sample

Feature of Emerging Adulthood	%
Identity Explorations	
This is a time of my life for finding out who I really am.	77
Instability	
This time of my life is full of changes.	83
Self-Focus	
This is a time of my life for focusing on myself.	69
Feeling In-Between	
Do you feel that you have reached adulthood?	
No	5
In some ways yes, in some ways no.	45
Yes	50
Possibilities	
At this time of my life, it still seems like anything is possible.	82

Source: Arnett & Walker (2014).

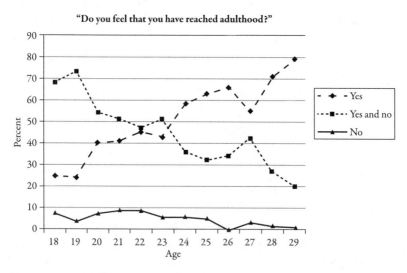

Figure 1.5 Feeling "In-Between": Changes With Age.

Do the five features vary by gender, ethnicity, or socioeconomic status (SES)? In the results of the Clark poll, there were few notable differences by gender or ethnicity.[32] The comparisons pertaining to SES are especially worthy of attention, because the most contentious issue surrounding the theory of emerging adulthood since it was proposed is the claim, by critics, that the five features apply only to the middle class and above, and do not reflect the harsh realities of life for young people in lower SES levels.[33] In 2011, I devoted an entire book (as co-author) to this question. With Jennifer Tanner, I took the view that emerging adulthood theory applies across SES, whereas Leo Hendry and Marion Kloep disputed this vigorously.[34] Consequently, it is notable that in the 2012 Clark poll, on a representative national sample that included all SES levels, there were no significant differences in any of the five features by SES.[35] Nevertheless, the experience of the emerging adult years differs in many other ways by SES, as we will see throughout the book and especially in Chapter 10.

In 2013 and 2014, I added national samples in Clark polls pertaining to 40–65-year-olds and 25–39-year-olds, respectively, allowing for age comparisons on the five features. For all five features, 18–29-year-olds were more likely than 30–65-year-olds to agree, although agreement was substantial across all age periods.[36] The age patterns are illustrated in Figure 1.6. These results provide support for the theory's proposal that the five features are most prominent during the emerging adult years.

I wish to underscore that, just because the majority of American emerging adults agree that the five features apply to them, and 18–29-year-olds are more likely than older adults to support the five features, this does mean I am in any way claiming that these are universal features of emerging adulthood. They probably do not apply even to all groups within American

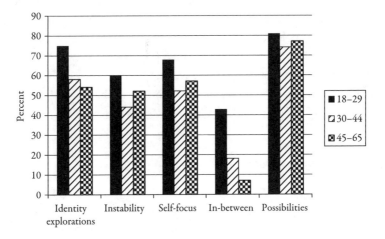

Figure 1.6 The Five Features, by Age Group.

Source: Arnett & Schwab (2014).

society, which is highly diverse, ethnically and economically. Other patterns will surely be found among other groups, nationally and internationally. For example, recent research in China by my student Juan Zhong showed that young women factory workers retained a strong sense of family obligation even after leaving their rural villages for city life, and "learn to care for parents" was their most important marker of reaching adulthood (in contrast to "accept responsibility for one's self" and other individualistic markers most favored by Americans).[37] Another example of variation is that, within Europe, northern Europeans generally leave home around age 18 or 19, whereas southern Europeans tend to stay home until they enter marriage around age 30, a pattern that suggests less instability in the lives of emerging adults in the south than in the north.[38] The field of emerging adulthood is new, and one of its challenges for the century to come is to chart the diversity of paths within emerging adulthood, among developed countries and also in developing countries as emerging adulthood expands there. "One stage, many paths" should be the guiding principle.

Who Needs Emerging Adulthood?

Who needs emerging adulthood? Why not just call the period from the late teens through the mid-twenties "late adolescence," if it is true that people in this age group have not yet reached adulthood? Why not call it "young adulthood," if we decide to concede that they have reached adulthood but wish to distinguish between them and adults of older ages? Maybe we should call it "the transition to adulthood," if we want to emphasize that it is a transitional period between adolescence and young adulthood. Or maybe we should call it "youth," like some earlier scholars of this age period.

I considered each of these alternatives in the course of forming the concept of *emerging adulthood*. Here is why I concluded that each of them was inadequate and why I believe *emerging adulthood* is preferable.

Why Emerging Adulthood Is Not "Late Adolescence"

In 1992, the first time I taught a college course on human development across the life span, when I reached the section on adolescence I told my students that, in social science terms, nearly all of them were "late adolescents." Social scientists defined adulthood in terms of discrete transitions such as finishing education, marriage, and parenthood. They were students, so clearly they had not finished their education, and few of them were married, and fewer still had become parents. So, they were "late adolescents."

They were outraged! Okay, they conceded, they had not really reached adulthood yet, not entirely, but they were *not* adolescents, whatever the social scientists might say.

At the time, I was surprised and bewildered at their objections. Now, I realize they were right. Adolescence, even "late adolescence," is an entirely inadequate term for college students or anyone else who is in the age period from the late teens through the twenties that I am calling *emerging adulthood*. True, adolescents and most emerging adults have in common that they have not yet entered marriage and parenthood. Other than this similarity, however, their lives are much different. Virtually all adolescents (ages 10–18) live at home with one or both parents. In contrast, many emerging adults have moved out of their parents' home, and their living situations are extremely diverse. Virtually all adolescents are experiencing the dramatic physical changes of puberty. In contrast, emerging adults have reached physical maturity. Virtually all adolescents attend secondary school. In contrast, many emerging adults are enrolled in education or training, but nowhere near all of them. Unlike adolescents, their educational paths are very diverse, from those who go straight through college and then on to graduate or professional school to those who receive no more education after high school, and every combination in-between. Adolescents also have in common that they have the legal status of minors, not adults. They cannot vote, they cannot sign legal documents, and they are legally under the authority and responsibility of their parents in a variety of ways. In contrast, from age 18 onward American emerging adults have all the legal rights of adults except for the right to buy alcohol, which comes at age 21.

In all of these ways, emerging adults are different from adolescents. As a result, "late adolescence" is an inadequate term for describing them. Emerging adulthood is preferable because it distinguishes them from adolescents while recognizing that they are not yet fully adult.

Why Emerging Adulthood Is Not "Young Adulthood"

If not "late adolescence," how about "young adulthood"? There are a number of reasons why "young adulthood" does not work.[39] One is that it implies that adulthood has been reached. However, most people in their late teens and early to mid-twenties would disagree that they have reached adulthood. Instead, they tend to see themselves as in-between adolescence and adulthood, so *emerging adulthood* captures better their sense of where they are—on the way to adulthood, but not there yet. *Emerging* is also a better descriptive term for the exploratory, unstable, fluid quality of the period.

An additional problem with "young adulthood" is that it is already used in diverse ways. The "young adult" section of the bookstore contains books aimed at teens and preteens, the "young adult" group at a church or synagogue might include people up to age 40, and "young adult" is sometimes applied to college students aged 18–22. Such diverse uses make "young adulthood" confusing and incoherent as a term for describing a specific life stage. Using *emerging adulthood* allows us to ascribe a clear definition to a new term and a new life stage.

To call people from their late teens through their mid-twenties "young adults" would also raise the problem of what to call people who are in their thirties. They are certainly not middle-aged yet. Should we call them "young adults," too? Or "not-so-young adults"? It makes little sense to lump the late teens, the twenties, and the thirties together and call the entire 22-year period "young adulthood." The period I am calling *emerging adulthood* could hardly be more distinct from the thirties. Most emerging adults do not feel they have reached adulthood, but most people in their thirties feel they have. Most emerging adults are still in the process of seeking out the education and training and job experiences that will prepare them for a long-term occupation, but most people in their thirties have settled into a more stable occupational path. Most emerging adults have not yet married, but most people in their thirties are married. Most emerging adults have not yet had a child, but most people in their thirties have at least one child.

The list could go on. The point should be clear. Emerging adulthood is superior to young adulthood as a term to refer to young people from the late teens through the twenties.

Why Emerging Adulthood Is Not "the Transition to Adulthood"

Another possibility would be to call the years from the late teens through the twenties "the transition to adulthood." It is true that most young people make the transition to adulthood during this period, in terms of their perceptions of themselves as well in terms of their movement toward stable adult roles in love and work. However, "the transition to adulthood" also proves to be inadequate as a term for this age period. One problem is that thinking of the years from the late teens through the twenties as merely the transition to adulthood leads to a focus on what young people in that age period are *becoming*, at the cost of neglecting what they *are*. This is what has happened in sociological research on this age period. There are mountains of research in sociology on "the transition to adulthood," but most of it focuses on the transitional events that sociologists assume are the defining criteria of adulthood—leaving home, finishing education, finding stable work, entering marriage, and entering parenthood.[40] Sociologists examine the factors that influence the age at which young people make these transitions and explain historical trends in the timing of the transitions.

Much of this research is interesting and informative, but it tells us little about what is actually going on in young people's lives from the late teens through the twenties. They leave home at age 18 or 19, and they marry and become parents sometime in their late twenties or beyond. But what happens in-between? They finish their education and find a job? Is that *all?* No, of course not. There is so much more that takes place during this age period, as we have seen in this chapter and as we will see in the chapters to come. Calling it "the transition to adulthood" narrows our perception of it and our understanding of it, because that term distracts us from examining all the changes happening during those years that are unrelated to the timing of transition events. Research on the transition to adulthood is welcome and is potentially interesting, but it is not the same as research on emerging adulthood.

Another problem with "the transition to adulthood" is that it implies that the period between adolescence and young adulthood is brief, linking two longer and more notable periods of life, hence better referred to as a "transition" rather than as a life stage in its own right. This may have been appropriate 50 or 60 years ago, when most people finished school, married, and had their first child by their very early twenties. However, today, with school extending longer and longer for more and more people, and with the median ages of marriage and parenthood now in the late twenties, referring to the years between adolescence and full adulthood as simply "the transition to adulthood" no longer makes sense. Even if we state conservatively that emerging adulthood lasts from about age 18 to about age 25, that would be a period of seven years—longer than infancy, longer than early or middle childhood, and nearly as long as adolescence. Emerging adulthood is a transitional period, yes—and so is every other period of life—but it is not merely a transition, and it should be studied as a separate life stage.

Why Emerging Adulthood Is Not "Youth"

One other possible term that must be mentioned is "youth," which in the late twentieth century was perhaps the most widely used term in the social sciences for the period from the late teens through the twenties.[41] There are a number of reasons why "youth" does not work. "Youth" has a long history in the English language as a term for childhood generally and for what later came to be called adolescence, and it continues to be used popularly and by many social scientists for these purposes (as reflected in terms such as "youth organizations"). Also, like "young adulthood," "youth" has been applied to people across a wide age range, from middle childhood through the twenties and thirties. A term that can mean so many things does not really mean anything.

None of the terms used in the past is adequate to describe what is occurring today among young people from their late teens through their twenties. There is a need for a new term and a new conception of this age period, and I suggested *emerging adulthood* in the hope that it would lead both to greater understanding and to more intensive study of the years from the late teens through the twenties.

The Cultural Context of Emerging Adulthood

Emerging adulthood is not a universal part of human development but a life stage that exists under certain conditions that have occurred only quite recently and only in some cultures.[42] The Four Revolutions have been experienced mainly in developed countries, although the consequences are being experienced worldwide.[43] As we have seen, the Four Revolutions have led to the rise of emerging adulthood, reflected in a relatively high median age of entering marriage and parenthood, in the late twenties or beyond. Postponing marriage and parenthood until the late twenties allows the late teens and most of the twenties to be devoted to other purposes.

So, emerging adulthood exists today mainly in the "developed countries" of the West, along with Asian countries such as Japan and South Korea. One reflection of this is in the timing of marriage across countries. Table 1.2 shows the median marriage age for females in a variety of developed countries,

Table 1.2 Median Marriage Age (Females) in Selected Countries

Developed Countries	Age	Developing Countries	Age
United States	26	Egypt	21
Canada	28	Ethiopia	17
Germany	30	Ghana	21
France	30	Nigeria	18
Italy	30	India	18
Japan	29	Indonesia	21
Australia	28	Guatemala	19

Source: United Nations (2009).

contrasted with developing countries. (The marriage age for males is typically about two years older than for females.)

Ages of marriage and parenthood are typically calculated on a country-wide basis, but emerging adulthood is a characteristic of cultures rather than countries. Within any given country, there may be some cultures that have a period of emerging adulthood and some that do not, or the length of emerging adulthood may vary among the cultures within a country. For example, in the United States, members of the Mormon Church tend to have a shortened and highly structured emerging adulthood.[44] Because of cultural beliefs prohibiting premarital sex and emphasizing the desirability of large families, there is considerable social pressure on young Mormons to marry early and begin having children. Consequently, the median ages of entering marriage and parenthood are much lower among Mormons than in the American population as whole, so they have a briefer period of emerging adulthood before taking on adult roles.

Variations in socioeconomic status and life circumstances also determine how a young person may experience emerging adulthood, even within a country that is affluent overall.[45] The young woman who has a child outside marriage at age 16 and spends her late teens and early twenties alternating between government dependence and low-paying jobs has little chance for self-focused identity explorations, nor does the young man who drops out of school and spends most of his late teens and early twenties unemployed and looking unsuccessfully for a job. Because opportunities tend to be less widely available in minority cultures than in the majority culture in most developed countries, members of minority groups may be less likely to experience their late teens and early twenties as a period of identity explorations, at least in the domain of work. However, as noted earlier, social class may be more important than ethnicity, with young people in the middle class or above having more opportunities for the explorations of emerging adulthood than young people who are working class or below. And yet, as we will see in Chapter 12, for some young people who have grown up in poor or chaotic families, emerging adulthood represents a chance to transform their lives in dramatic ways, because reaching emerging adulthood allows them to leave the family circumstances that may have been the source of their problems.

As noted earlier in the chapter, it may be most useful to think of emerging adulthood as one stage with many possible paths within it. That is, most young people in developed countries experience emerging adulthood, defined as a life stage in-between adolescence and the stable commitments of adulthood, but they experience it in a wide variety of ways depending on their culture, social class, gender, personality, individual life events, and other circumstances. This is the key point: *Emerging adulthood can be said to exist wherever there is a gap of at least several years between the time young people finish secondary school and the time they enter stable adult roles in love and work.* The five features presented in this chapter apply to most American emerging adults, but other features may apply in other cultural contexts. There is not one universal and uniform emerging adulthood, but many emerging adulthoods that vary by cultural, economic, and personal context.[46]

Currently in economically developing countries, there tends to be a distinct cultural split between urban and rural areas. Young people in urban areas of countries such as China and India are more likely to experience emerging adulthood, because they marry later, have children later, obtain more education, and have a greater range of occupational and recreational opportunities than young people in rural areas.[47] In contrast, young people in rural areas of developing countries often receive minimal schooling, marry early, and have little choice of occupations except agricultural work. Thus, in developing countries emerging adulthood may be experienced often in urban areas but rarely in rural areas.

However, emerging adulthood is likely to become more pervasive worldwide in the course of the twenty-first century, with the increasing globalization of the world economy. Table 1.3 shows an example of how globalization is affecting the lives of young people, by making tertiary education (that is, education or training beyond secondary school) a more common experience worldwide. Between 1980 and 2010 the proportion of young people in developing

Table 1.3 Changes in Tertiary Enrollment in Selected Developing Countries, 1980–present

| | % Enrolled 1980 | | % Enrolled latest year | |
	Males	Females	Males	Females
Poland	75	80	98	97
Argentina	53	62	73	81
Egypt	66	41	83	73
China	54	37	74	67
Turkey	44	24	68	48
Mexico	51	46	64	64
India	39	20	59	39
Nigeria	25	13	36	30

Source: UNESCO (2013).

countries who were enrolled in tertiary education rose sharply. The median ages of entering marriage and parenthood rose in these countries as well.

These changes open up the possibility for the spread of emerging adulthood in developing countries. Rising education reflects economic development. Economic development leads to a rise in the median ages of entering marriage and parenthood. As societies become more affluent, they are more likely to grant young people the opportunity for the extended moratorium of emerging adulthood, because their need for young people's labor is less urgent, and their young people need more education to prepare themselves for the developing economy. Thus it seems likely that by the end of the twenty-first century, emerging adulthood will be a normative period for young people worldwide. However, even as the service economy rises around the world, and the Technology Revolution spreads as machines continue to replace manufacturing workers, this transition will not necessarily be accompanied by a Sexual Revolution, Women's Movement, or Youth Movement. Consequently, there will continue to be many emerging adulthoods, because it is likely to vary in length and content both within and between countries.

The Plan of This Book

The challenges, uncertainties, and possibilities of emerging adulthood make it a fascinating and eventful time of life. In the following chapters, my intention is to provide a broad portrait of what it is like to be an emerging adult in American society. We start out in Chapter 2 by looking in detail at the lives of four emerging adults, in order to see how the themes described in this first chapter are reflected in individual lives. This is followed in Chapter 3 by a look at how relationships with parents change in emerging adulthood. Then there are two chapters on emerging adults' experiences with love, including Chapter 4 on romantic and sexual issues and Chapter 5 on finding a marriage partner. Chapter 6 discusses the diverse paths that emerging adults take through college, and Chapter 7 examines their search for meaningful work. In Chapter 8 we examine emerging adults' media use, and in Chapter 9 their religious beliefs and values. Chapter 10 focuses on the question of social class in relation to emerging adulthood. Chapter 11 is devoted to the most prominent problems faced by emerging adults. Then Chapter 12 highlights emerging adulthood as the age of possibilities by profiling four young people who have overcome difficult experiences to transform their lives. Finally, in Chapter 13 we consider the passage from emerging adulthood to young adulthood, focusing on the question of what it means to become an adult.

The material in the chapters was originally based mainly on over 300 in-depth structured interviews that I and my research assistants conducted in Missouri, San Francisco, Los Angeles, and New Orleans during the 1990s (hereafter "my original study"). We interviewed young people from age 20 to 29 from diverse backgrounds, about half of them White and the other half African American, Latino, and Asian American.[48]

Since the first edition of this book was published 10 years ago, I have continued my scholarship on emerging adulthood. In recent years this has included three national surveys: in 2012, the Clark University Poll of Emerging Adults, a survey of 18–29-year-olds (hereafter, "the national Clark poll"); in 2013, a survey of parents of 18–29-year-olds (hereafter, "the Clark parents poll"); and in 2014, a survey of 25–39-year-olds.[49] I have incorporated the results of these new surveys into this edition of the book. In addition, I use statistics and insights from other studies that include 18–29 year olds.

I present a variety of statistics in the course of the book, but I also rely strongly on excerpts from my interviews to illustrate my points.[50] When I first began studying this topic, the interview approach seemed appropriate to me for exploring a period of life that had not been studied much and on which not much was known. Also, emerging adults are a diverse group in terms of their life situations, and the interview approach allows me to describe their different situations and perspectives, rather than simply stating that they are "like this," based on an overall statistical pattern.

Finally, the interview approach is valuable in studying emerging adults because they are often remarkably insightful in describing their experiences. Perhaps because emerging adulthood is often a self-focused period of life, the young people we interviewed possessed a striking capacity for self-reflection, not only the ones who had graduated from college but also— perhaps especially—the ones who had struggled to make it through high school. Presenting excerpts from the interviews allows for a full display of their everyday eloquence. What they have to say about their lives and experiences is illuminating, moving, and often humorous, as you will see in the chapters to come.

Chapter 2

What Is It Like to Be an Emerging Adult?

Four Profiles

Douglas Coupland's 1991 novel *Generation X* can be credited with first drawing widespread attention to the fact that something new was happening in the lives of young people in their twenties. The novel follows the lives and musings of Andy, Claire, and Dag as they wander through their late twenties together. None of them has been able yet to find enjoyable work, and they refuse to settle into jobs that may pay well but involve "endless stress" and meaningless work "done grudgingly to little applause." As for love, none of them is close to getting married, but as Andy says, "I *do* at least recognize the fact that I don't want to go through life alone." Their feelings about entering adulthood are summed up in the title of one chapter, "Dead at 30 Buried at 70." As good novels often do, *Generation X* not only describes the lives of individual characters but, in doing so, also provides vivid insights into what it is like to live in a certain place at a certain time.

My aim in this book is different from Coupland's, of course, and not just because it is nonfiction rather than fiction. I want to describe common patterns in the lives of emerging adults, not just individual characters, and to illustrate these patterns I will take quotes from various interviews and weave them together, in addition to presenting survey results. However, there is also much to be gained from describing individuals, so that we can see what a complete life looks like in emerging adulthood. If we only combined isolated parts from the interviews, we would never see how all the parts fit together.

By describing several people in detail, we can gain a full sense of what it is like to be an emerging adult, in all its complexity.

In this chapter we will look at the lives of four emerging adults. The persons I chose for these profiles represent a broad range of backgrounds and experiences in emerging adulthood. Two are male and two are female, two are White and two are members of ethnic minorities, two are college graduates and two are not, and they grew up in several different parts of the United States. They range in age from 21 to 27. Together they provide a taste of the diversity that exists among emerging adults, as well as some of the qualities that are common to many of them.

Although the persons in the profiles are diverse, they were not chosen to be representative of all persons in my original study, much less all persons in their twenties. None of them is married and none of them has children. None of them is firmly settled into a career path. Rather, the persons in the profiles were chosen because they exemplify the five features that characterize emerging adulthood as a distinct life stage in American society: identity explorations, instability, self-focus, feeling in-between, and a sense of possibilities. The profiles presented in this chapter will serve to illustrate the features of emerging adulthood described in Chapter 1, by connecting them to the real lives of emerging adults. The profiles also preview many of the themes of the chapters to come.

Rosa: "Choking Life for All It's Got"

I arranged to meet Rosa, 24, at a coffee shop near the University of San Francisco, and I had no trouble spotting her when she walked in. She had told me over the phone that her mother was Chinese and her father was Mexican, and in her face I could see clearly the unusual, striking blend of features from both sides of her family. She had just come from her job at an Internet software company, and she was dressed in casual professional clothes, white pants and a sweater that matched the jet black of her shoulder-length hair.

We started out by talking about her work. Her current job requires a variety of skills, including editing, accounting, and human resources management, because it is a small company with only 17 employees. She likes the variety, because it gives her a chance to increase her knowledge and explore possibilities for where she might want to focus her efforts in the future. "I want to be able just to bounce around and learn as much as I can from each of the departments, so I just started doing editing. I want to kind of touch the marketing side, too. Just to see what I want to do."

Working for an Internet company was not what she had in mind when she graduated from the University of California–Berkeley two years ago. An English major in college, she planned to become a teacher in the Oakland school system that she had attended as a child. "I really thought I wanted to go into education," she said. "I graduated from college and I started running an after-school program at a very low-income school because I thought if I was going to teach, I was going to teach where I was needed the most. I didn't want to teach in any district but Oakland, because I grew up in Oakland and I wanted to give back to the city."

However, she soon became disillusioned and depressed with what she witnessed in the schools. "Some of the kids didn't eat all day. A lot of their parents were on crack. A lot of them lived with their grandmother one week, their aunt the next week; they really just floated. They were cruel to themselves and cruel to each other, just because they needed the attention." Her grim experiences at work seeped into the rest of her life. "I really got attached to my kids, and I couldn't snap out of it when I left the school. Like, I would still be in that zone when I got home, and I'd take it out on my boyfriend."

So she soon left the school for her current job. But she doesn't see this job as permanent. "I still don't think I'm a business person. Eventually I think I'm just going to open my own bakery. That's what I really want to do." She is also considering other possibilities. "I will probably end up taking a career more in editing. I can see myself in front of a computer, writing whatever, because I love to write. But I can also see myself in hard-core marketing for a big corporation, because I do like to work with people and I do like fast-paced, stressful work." For now, she is happy to do some temporary exploring during her emerging adult years. "I mean, this is cool for now. I'm just going to hop around for a while."

She is more settled in love than she is in work. She has been seeing her current boyfriend, Mark, for three years, and she expects they will marry, although she is not sure when. "I know that if he proposed to me today, I would say yes. Oh, I love him to death. We've been through so much. I know we can get through anything that came in our way. We communicate really well."

Before Mark, she had another boyfriend for four years. Like many emerging adults with immigrant parents from Asia or Latin America, she never embraced the American way of having a series of short relationships and "hook-ups" in adolescence and emerging adulthood before settling down. Still, now that she is in a relationship that may lead to marriage, she finds herself wondering if she shouldn't explore her options a bit more. As much as she loves her boyfriend, there are also what she calls her "distractions," other men she feels attracted to. "Sometimes there's these little things that happen on the side, or people you meet, and you just kind of wonder, 'God, would this be cool for now?' Because I haven't had very much experience with other people. And sometimes I question if I really want to be in a relationship right now."

She also feels a need to develop her own identity more clearly before she enters marriage, by having a period of being self-focused. "I think I want to get more in touch with myself. I want to be a little selfish for a while, and selfishness and marriage don't seem to go hand in hand. I'd like to be able to experience as much as I can before I get married, just so I can be well-rounded."

This sense of not being ready to commit to marriage, being "wishy-washy," as she puts it, makes her feel that she has not yet fully reached adulthood. But in other ways, she does feel like an adult. "I think the way that I care about people is very adult. The way I express myself is very adult. For the most part I think I'm adult. It's just the wishy-washy part that I don't know about." Overall, then, like many emerging adults, she feels in-between, on the way to adulthood but not there yet. "Maybe I am an adult. I don't know. I'm a kid a lot of the times."

Becoming independent from her parents has not been a big issue for her in marking her progress to adulthood. She lived with her parents all the way through college, and enjoyed it. She has always gotten along well with them, except for a brief period in her early adolescence when she often tangled with her mom. "I think I had it bad with her probably 6th, 7th, and 8th grade. But I went through it early, and then after that I was cake."

Her father travels around the world doing maintenance and repair on large ships, and her mother is an optician—solid, respectable middle-class jobs, by most standards, yet Rosa sees their career paths as examples to avoid. "I knew I wanted to be somewhere that I would grow as a person, and I don't see them growing as individuals. I mean, my mom is an optician, and you don't grow doing those things. That's why I kind of chose the high tech path, because there's always new software to learn. And with my dad, I didn't want to have a job that beat up my body. I knew I wanted to be able to grow, and I didn't want to be broken by the time I was 40, you know. I think that's what I took from their jobs."

Although she has always had a good relationship with her parents, family life in their household has not always been easy. Rosa said her parents "almost divorced a few times" during her childhood. Her father resented her mother for working long hours and for making more money than he did; her mother complained that he drank too much. They get along somewhat better now, but it is hardly an ideal marriage.

There was additional tension in the household because of the problems of Rosa's brother, who is 18 months older. "My brother and I have always hated each other," she said bluntly. "We don't really talk. We don't talk at all actually." He had various problems in childhood, then in high school "he went into the drug thing," she says. "I don't know. He got bent somewhere." She gets along much better with her sister, who is eight years younger. "My sister and I were never close until I moved out. Now I love her to death. She's 16 and she acts like it, but I love to be there for her. She's my baby sister."

Rosa sees the problems her parents and her brother have had as rooted partly in the unusual ethnic mix of Chinese and Mexican in the family. Each of her parents' families regarded the other with suspicion and hostility, which generated conflict between her parents. Her brother was often ridiculed and beat up by other kids simply for looking Asian. Rosa has felt her own share of ethnic prejudice. When she goes to the mostly White suburbs, "I feel sometimes that we're looked at like, 'Why are you here?' Definitely like 'There are too many of you here.'" It's not only Whites who look at her that way. "The Blacks, too. And I sense a lot of hostility from Mexican people. I just don't have the connection. And I *am* Mexican! But I don't look like it."

Nevertheless, she has embraced her ethnicity with enthusiasm, especially her Chinese side. When she was young her mother immersed her in Chinese culture, whereas her dad showed little interest in making her familiar with Mexican culture. "I grew up very Chinese. I hung out in Chinatown, and I always saw my mom's family every weekend. My mom spoke Chinese to us." Rosa has always had mostly Asian friends, and her only two boyfriends have been Asian.

Now that she is in emerging adulthood, Rosa feels bad about letting the Mexican side of her background lapse. "I feel it's really unfair to my father. The only thing I know about my Mexican culture is that I'm Catholic, and I can cook the food. I'd like to learn more because I love my father to death." Her hope is that her children will have more of a Mexican identity than she does. "I'm going to have my dad teach them their Mexican side. My dad already said 'When you have kids, they're going to call me "Buppa,"' which is grandpa in Spanish. So hopefully he'll be able to pass on a lot to them. I just think it's a nice thing to know. You know, you're not just 'an American.' You have a beautiful, long history to your name."

However, the Catholic faith is one part of her Mexican heritage that Rosa does not want to pass on to her children. Although she was raised "strictly Catholic," she now says, "I don't like Catholicism. I don't care for it at all. I don't think it applies to modern day society at all. I'm not going to raise my kids Catholic." As an emerging adult she has become a deist, a person who believes in God in a general way, unattached to any specific religion. "I don't think my god has a religion—it's just God. There's just God. And that's the only thing I don't question. I know there's a god. I think it's the same god that Jews have, that Muslims have, they just all have a different name."

Perhaps influenced by her mother's Buddhist beliefs, she is inclined to believe in reincarnation. "I believe I was a cat before because I love to lay in the sun. Seriously! Every time I go home, I have my mom scratch my head or scratch my back." However, she adds that her focus is on this life, not the past ones or the next one. "I don't really give an afterlife much thought because it's not really that important to me. When I'm gone, I'm gone."

For the future, Rosa has many dreams, of opening a bakery with her mother, of marrying Mark and having two children, of a lifetime of learning. "If I was rich, I'd be a lifetime student. I love to learn. I wouldn't go back to school because I would require it for my future, I would just go back because I want it for myself. Just for the fun of learning. I can really see myself going back for a Ph.D. in Lit or something. I love to read, I love to write."

By the end of her life, she would like to be able to say "that I was happy and I tried to make the people around me happy. Those are the most important things. I just want to know that I made the most of my time. I can't just sit and watch TV. I believe in just taking life and choking it for all it's got."

Steve: "Who Knows What's Going to Happen?"

Steve, 23, flashes his ironic smile often, as if he wants to make sure you can see that he doesn't take himself too seriously. His brown eyes peer out from underneath dark eyebrows, which contrast with his short light brown hair. When I met him for our interview in my office at the University of Missouri, he was wearing a green and maroon rugby shirt and casual light pants.

Although he currently lives in Missouri, he lived in a variety of places in the course of growing up. His family moved often to follow his father's work as a contract engineer; every time his father got a new contract, they moved. He grew to dislike moving around so much and vowed that he would put down roots somewhere once he left his parents' household. But as it turned out, he has moved around during emerging adulthood even more than he did with his family. "I always said that once I get out of high school and move away I'm going to stay in one place, but I've probably moved 15 times since I left home."

Missouri was one of the places his family lived for a while during his childhood, and he moved back there to go to the University of Missouri. However, he dropped out of school after a few semesters, feeling "kind of burnt out on it." Now, he waits on tables at a local restaurant. He is content with the money he is making. "I average about $16 an hour, so I mean, where else can I go right now and make that much money?" Nevertheless, he views his job like he views many things in his life, as temporary. "I'm just kind of lazy right now. I'm just taking it easy."

While he was in college Steve majored in fine arts because of his love of drawing. He continues now to do sketches and portraits, to make money in addition to his restaurant job, and because he enjoys it. However, he is doubtful that he could successfully build a career from his artistic talents. "If I could wing it and be an artist I'd do it, but it's one of those things where you have to be great or you're working in advertising," and advertising does not appeal to him. "I'll probably end up doing art as a hobby," he says.

What route will he take, then, in terms of work? It's pretty clear he doesn't know at this point. One moment he says, "I'll probably end up being an engineer. My dad's an engineer, so I'll probably end up doing that. I'm really good at math and I know I could pick up on it real easy." Yet when I ask him a few minutes later what he sees himself doing 10 years from now, engineering has nothing to do with it. "I'll probably be living in Colorado. I would want to say owning a restaurant, but probably in some kind of management position because I've been in the restaurant business for eight years so I know a lot about it. I cook, I've waited tables, I've bartended. I've pretty much done it all and that's what the criteria is to be a manager. I'm sure I could get a job, and just to be able to ski all the time would be great." But right now he is doing little to bring this dream to fruition, unless you count the job as a waiter. "I'm just kind of 'treading water,' as my mom says."

With regard to love, Steve has been involved for about two months with Sandy, who is a waitress at the restaurant where he works. They get along well and spend most of their time together. They would like to live together, but hesitate because of the objections of her parents, especially her father. "That's like his last little grip before he lets her go," Steve says resentfully. He'd like to move in with her for practical reasons, not because he feels they may marry eventually. "It would totally cut our expenses in half."

He is in no hurry to get married, to Sandy or anyone else. In his view, there is a lot less pressure to get married by a certain age today than in the past. "Any more nowadays, it's not even really an issue. If it happens, it happens, and if not, not. It's not as big of an issue as it was like in the fifties." He's still not sure what qualities he would like to find in the person he marries. "I haven't really narrowed it down yet. I guess when I find her I'll know."

Steve is as uncertain and unsettled in his beliefs as he is in love and work. As he was growing up, his parents made little attempt to teach him a set of religious beliefs. He says they told him, "If you want to believe it, fine. But if you don't, that's fine too. We'll support you either way." Now, at age 23, he seems to have reached a few conclusions. "I believe in a creator. Obviously, we couldn't have just sprouted from the earth." Reincarnation also seems plausible to him. "I always thought that there was obviously reincarnation." But as he talks further, it turns out that none of his beliefs is really so "obvious" after all. "I mean, none of us really know. There's no proof-positive to any of it. You have to have the facts and really I have none so I can't really make an educated guess yet."

Given his uncertainties about love, work, and beliefs, it's not surprising that he does not feel like he has entirely reached adulthood. "Mentally I'm still trying to grab a hold of it," he says. He explains that what he means is that he doesn't yet accept the adult requirement of having to decide where his life is going. "I just don't look at it in an adult point of view. I just don't really buy into the whole system, you know. I'm like 'I'm confused right now,' and everybody's like, 'You've got to make a decision,' and I'm like, 'Well, no, I don't.'"

Another way he feels he has not entirely reached adulthood is that he drinks more alcohol than he thinks an adult should. "I'm still in the party mode," he says. Still, his alcohol use has gone down from what it was a year or two earlier. "I don't really necessarily drink as much as I used to. Most of all it's because it's expensive to go out anymore." He has grown tired of the local bar scene. "You can only go out to so many bars without them getting kind of boring." He has also grown tired of the effects of heavy drinking. "I don't like puking and I don't like being hung over." Not to mention the insurance bills. "I got a DWI and I had a couple of rear-ends where I wasn't watching. I mean, my insurance is like, outrageous. That's why I kind of stopped drinking so much." But he still drinks enough to see it as a reason why he has not become an adult.

Nor do Steve's parents view him as having reached adulthood. "When I get a job they will," he says. A job other than waiting on tables, that is. "We call it a 'real job.' 'When you get a real job.'" Nevertheless, his relationship with his parents has changed in recent years to more of a relationship between equals. Now he is "a little more open with them I guess. The way I talk to them and the way they talk to me, it's more on an adult level."

His parents have been successful in both their professional and personal lives. His dad has been successful as an engineer, and his mom, after devoting herself to raising Steve and his brother when they were young, now owns an antique store. Their marriage has been a relatively happy one. "I can't even remember them ever fighting once," Steve says. "They've got a pretty good sense of humor with each other and they know how to communicate in kind of a funny way and still get the point across." They seem to have good relationships with their children, as well. Steve says he was "very close" to his parents growing up, and it is clear that he remains fond of them.

Yet despite their success, and despite the instability of his life at age 23, Steve believes that his life will be better than his parents' lives have been. The reason for this is that he has been allowed to have an emerging adulthood with years of freedom to try out different possible paths, whereas his parents did not. "My dad, when he was 15, moved out and basically had to find a way to support himself and eventually his family, and I'm not having to go through that. My dad is in a position where he can help me out more than he got helped."

Eventually, Steve expects to have everything his parents have and more, all the best that adult life has to offer: satisfying and well-paying work, a happy marriage, a couple of children, living in an area he loves. For now, however, he is happy being "very nomadic. I've got so little stuff I can just move it around. I don't like to sign a lease, so usually I just try to do it month-by-month." He wants to be ready to hit the road in case a promising opportunity comes along. "Who knows when I'll find a job in Colorado? I've got to be ready to go! I don't want to owe anybody $1,000 on a lease when I'm not going to be living there. Who knows what's going to happen?"

Charles: "I'm Highly Portable"

You could tell by looking at Charles, 27, that there was something different about him, something out of the ordinary, even by San Francisco standards.

His hair was in dreadlocks, and his black beard was trimmed short and looked striking against his brown skin. He wore a black T-shirt under a brown leather vest, and a silver earring. A black necklace with a gold pendant shone from his neck. But most striking were his eyes—large, alert, and intense, shining with energy.

He looked like he might be in the arts, and he is, as a songwriter and singer, part of an *a cappella* group called the House Cats, which he described as "a rock band without instruments." He also works for an advertising agency, writing and editing advertisements, but even though he has been working there for a year, he describes himself as a "temp," meaning that he has an understanding with the agency that he can leave at any time, for short periods or long, as opportunities come up for the band. Right now he and the band are recording a CD, so they have all taken temporary jobs to support themselves until the CD is finished and they can go on tour promoting it.

Charles graduated from Princeton, an elite Ivy League college, with a major in psychology, and he thought seriously about becoming either a psychologist or a lawyer. By then, however, he realized that "music is where my heart is," and he decided that "I didn't want to regret not going for something that would ultimately bring me more satisfaction" than psychology or law. His unfettered, self-focused status as an emerging adult has given him the opportunity to pursue his dream of devoting himself to music. "I'm single, I don't have a car or a house or a mortgage or a significant other that's pulling me in another direction, or kids or anything. I'm highly portable, and I can basically do whatever I want as long as I can support myself."

In the future, Charles sees himself pursuing other avenues of creative expression in addition to music: writing novels, plays, and perhaps screenplays, or designing games, like the card game he recently invented. He expects to have a full life, and sees no reason why he should not be able to fit many different things into it. "I would basically like to set up my life in such a way that the things that I wish to do are the things that I'm doing. Now, obviously, you can't do everything you want to do all the time, but you can work in ways so that you're able to consistently do pieces of things that you want to do."

Charles grew up in Shaker Heights, Ohio, an affluent suburb of Cleveland. His parents are attorneys, his mother in labor law and his father in personal injury. He got along well with them during childhood and adolescence, and he still does. Once or twice a year they "whisk me away," he says, for an exotic vacation—southern Spain, Belize, Saint Martin.

Still, the privileges of his upbringing have not protected him from the wounds inherent in growing up as an African American. He recalls, "The first day of first grade, a White kid hit me in the nose and gave me a bloody nose all over my new shirt." When Charles returned to school the next day, he gave the offending boy a bloody nose of his own, "with my parents' blessing. I told them about it, and my dad said, 'You can't let him do that to you.'" The following year, he heard for the first time the epithet that nearly all Black children have thrown at them eventually. "I was at a sports camp in the summer and a kid called me a nigger. I'd never heard the word before, so I went home and asked my parents, 'What does this mean?' And they said, 'He called you that?' And I said, 'Yeah.' My dad said, 'If he calls you that again, hit him.' So within two or three days, we were in tennis class, and he said it to me again, 'Nigger.' So I hit him in the head with the tennis racket, and he never called me a nigger again."

In adolescence, several times Charles had the experience shared by many young African American men, of being pulled over for "Driving While Black." "My parents always had reasonably nice cars since I've been able to drive. And seeing a Black youth driving a nice car at night is grounds enough for many a police officer to pull that person over, regardless of whether or not there's any sort of violation."

However, these experiences have not prevented Charles from having many good relationships with Whites. His friends in high school were the smart kids, White as well as Black. Many of his friends at Princeton were White. He has dated Whites as well as Blacks and Asian Americans. The person at Princeton who persuaded him to lead the *a cappella* group there that sparked his enthusiasm for music was an older White student who "took me under his wing," Charles recalls. And the House Cats are two Black guys and four White guys.

As an emerging adult, being African American is definitely part of his identity. "I'd be silly to try and say that none of my experiences have been at least somewhat based on or influenced by the color of my skin." He believes that opportunities in American society are restricted in some ways for African Americans. "My parents told me at an early age that 'You're a Black kid, and you're going to be Black all your life. And that means you're going to have to work twice as hard to get half as much.'" Nevertheless, he believes that his talents and the advantages of his background will allow him to succeed at whatever he tries. Opportunities may not be entirely equal in American society, but "I think it's getting closer."

His parents, highly educated themselves, always encouraged him to excel academically. He says the message they gave to him was that "you are gifted with good genes because we gave them to you, and we know that you're bright. We know that you can make straight A's. We're not going to ride you and make you get straight A's because we don't think that's necessarily best for you. But we don't ever want you to think in any course you take that you can't get an A because that is bullshit.'"

The messages from his peers were more mixed. His best friends all did well in school themselves, and supported each other in doing well. But he was aware that there were some Black kids who believed that "[i]f you were in AP [Advanced Placement] classes, that was a strike against you," because most of the students in those classes were White. "Who you were in classes with determined who you would become friends with, so if you were in AP classes with almost all White kids and you were friends with almost all White kids, then they would say you're stuck-up." He also recalls that when he was accepted at Princeton, the reaction of one of his Black acquaintances was not "Congratulations" but "I can't believe that, man. What the fuck is a nigger doing in the Ivy League?" However, Charles always shrugged off such views, and never allowed his own pursuit of educational success to be affected by them.

He feels he has "definitely" reached adulthood, ever since he moved out to the Bay Area after college. He was alone, with no one to rely on but himself, and that made him feel adult. "I had found my own living space, using my own contacts and my own initiative, and had gotten two jobs out here and was paying rent, you know, doing that whole thing. I felt that I had gotten off the ground in terms of starting a life out here. Not that it was my ideal life. I was working for a financial software company in a non-exciting capacity, and I was working at a nice restaurant in Berkeley, busing tables. But I felt that I had set my foot on the road, you know, 'Okay, I'm an adult now, and I'm walking.'" Staying on his feet, learning to stand alone.

Even though Charles is confident that he has reached adulthood, his life shows a substantial amount of the identity explorations and instability that are two of the defining characteristics of American emerging adulthood. In work, he has made a clear choice of pursuing a career in music, but the nature of that pursuit is still very much up in the air. He says that in 10 years "I think I will still be doing music in some way, shape or form," but he adds, "I couldn't say exactly how." Perhaps with his current group, if they are successful, but perhaps as a guitarist or bass player, perhaps as a record producer, perhaps as a songwriter, perhaps some combination of these possibilities. Of course, there is also the writing of novels and plays to fit in, and the game designing. And then there is that Princeton degree to fall back on, perhaps leading to further education and a career in psychology or law. So, at this point, Charles is a young man full of possibilities, but it is difficult to predict which ones will be fulfilled in his future.

In love his future is even more wide open. He has been seeing his current girlfriend for three years. She is half Asian and half White. They share a love for music—they met at a singing competition—and a high level of education (she is currently a Ph.D. student in language and literature). Yet he says they both see marriage as something that is "not a realistic possibility anytime soon." His musical career is likely to take him on the road for extended periods. She has at least two more years of graduate school, and after that there is no telling where her career opportunities might take her.

His beliefs about religious issues also seem not yet settled, still in the process of forming. Although he grew up going to an Episcopal church with his parents, by adolescence he was "bored with Sunday School and bored with the service." Also about that time, he said he "realized that I was not being encouraged to think for myself." Even though the Episcopal church is relatively liberal in its doctrine, relatively tolerant of departures from orthodoxy, for Charles any organized religion is objectionable because it tells people what to believe rather than having them find out for themselves.

Now, he believes generally in a deity. "There's got to be something better than mankind in our universe, because we're too screwed up to be the best thing." However, he is more definite about what this deity is not than what it is. "I don't believe in a bearded White God or a bearded Black God or a non-bearded Black or White or Asian or Indian or Latino god or goddess sitting someplace, watching everybody." Buddhism appeals to him, especially the Buddhist belief in reincarnation. "I like the Buddhist idea of rebirth and that in each subsequent life you make mistakes but you're approaching perfection, at which point you can achieve nirvana. There is something that really appeals to me about the idea that you get another chance because everybody makes tons of mistakes in their life. It'd be nice to have another shot with some benefit from the experience you've been through." However, he hastens to add, "I am not a Buddhist."

He is more certain about what he believes about this world, here and now, and the values he wants to live by. "In terms of how I conduct myself with friends and with people who aren't even friends, I try to treat them the way that I would want to be treated. To a certain extent, that boils down to the Golden Rule, 'Do unto others. . . .'" He also believes in being true to himself, following his heart, and doing what he really wants to do with his life. "It concerns me that of the many gifted people that I went to school with, so few of them are actually doing what they really want to do. And so many people say to me, 'You are an inspiration to me because you are doing what you want to do. You have not yet sold out and said, "I got a fancy degree, I'm just gonna go to business school or law school and make lots of money."'" Although Charles is 27 years old, an age when many of his peers are moving out of emerging adulthood into more settled lives, he has maintained his zeal for identity explorations, and he easily tolerates the instability that goes along with it.

Angela: "I Want to Get My Life in Order"

Angela, 21, has a job in landscaping, and you might have guessed that from looking at her. She is deeply tanned and her long hair is sun-bleached to a blondish light brown. She is quite tall, probably six feet, and quite slender. Her face is cheerful; she smiles a lot. You can see both vulnerability and hope in that smile, especially after you have talked to her for a while.

She returned to Missouri a year ago after spending two years at Michigan State, where she was majoring in horticulture therapy, which entails teaching people to cultivate plants as a way of dealing with psychological problems. Going away to college was a key event in making her feel like she was reaching adulthood, because it meant "being away from my parents and everything and being independent." She loved being on her own, and she would have liked to finish her bachelor's degree at Michigan State. However, she decided she wanted to change her major from horticulture therapy to "just plain horticulture," and when university officials resisted she dropped out. She plans to finish her degree gradually at a local college. Meanwhile, she is working at her landscaping job.

Angela has known since high school that she wanted to pursue a career in horticulture. "I've always been an outdoors person and I took a class in high school in horticulture. They had a greenhouse and stuff, and my teacher, I really liked her and she kind of showed me where some schools were and stuff, and that's why I went over there to Michigan State." She feels "a little bit disappointed" that she didn't graduate when she had intended, but she knows she is not alone. "It sounds like a lot of my friends aren't going to graduate, either. A lot of them have dropped out."

Toward the end of her time at Michigan State she was feeling exhausted from working full-time in addition to carrying a full load of classes. "I was burnt out on school I think, so I'm kind of glad I took some time off." Now she can finish school gradually as she works in a job in her field. She is learning a lot about landscaping through her job. "We do all the planting and design of flowers and shrubs, and we do irrigation, we mulch, we cultivate, fertilize, all kinds of stuff. I enjoy it."

Although Angela is glad she chose horticulture and glad she went to Michigan State for two years, she is concerned about the debt she has taken on in order to finance her education. "I've got loans and I'm worried about that. How am I going to pay off my loans? I'm in debt probably about $15,000 now." Her mother and father are both well-off financially, but neither of them supported her college education. "My parents could have helped me pay, you know. They say they can't afford it or something, but I mean, they both have nice houses and my mom has a condo down in Florida and on and on and on, and they didn't help me at all." Why didn't they? "I don't know why. I don't know if they were trying to teach us responsibility or whether they're just self-ish or what. I don't know what the deal is." She feels burdened by her debts. "It's kind of depressing. I wish I could win the lottery!"

Angela's parents divorced when she was four and her mother remarried two years later, so she mostly grew up in the household of her mother and stepfather, along with her older brother (now 24) and younger sister (now 16). Her mother is a medical technician, her stepfather a professor of astronomy. She has always gotten along well with her mother, but she has never liked her stepfather. "I stayed away from him, basically. He was just a jerk." His alcohol use was a source of conflict between him and her mother, and still is. "He gets to drinking and she says 'Don't drink a lot' and they start bickering back and forth. It's ridiculous." All the conflict made for a difficult environment to grow up in. "When I look back, it wasn't the best childhood, I think."

As for her father, he is a professor of medicine at a college in South Carolina, where he remained after her parents divorced, and Angela has seen him rarely since then. In fact, she hasn't seen him at all for the past seven years. Her reasons for why she hasn't seen him in so long sound more persuasive for explaining seven weeks or months than seven years. "It seems like there's never any time because he's busy all the time, and with me going to school and working I don't know when is the last time I had a vacation." But she talks to him a couple of times a month on the phone. "I don't know him as well as I would like to, but we talk about a lot of stuff."

With regard to her own love relationships, Angela got a late start because she was taller than virtually all of the boys. In high school, she says, "I went out with a few people but never dated anybody for a long period of time because I was tall and the guys were all short and they didn't want to ask me out. They were really intimidated. I was kind of paranoid about it." She still finds that some men are intimidated by her height, but her own view of it has changed in emerging adulthood. "It doesn't bother me now. It meant more what your friends thought then and it was more the peer thing that was so big, and you had to fit in."

At Michigan State she dated a young man for two years. They shared a love for sports and the outdoors, and they got along well. But they broke up a year ago, shortly after he graduated. "He was wanting to get married and I think that scared me off. I think that's why we broke up." At age 21, she doesn't feel anywhere near ready for marriage. "I just can't get married until I'm about 26 or so, because I want to get my life in order, like have a good job, be set financially. I don't want to depend on a man."

Angela met her current boyfriend shortly after returning to Missouri last year. It is clear she has a lot of reservations about their relationship. He drinks too much. "He's got a drinking problem and I just don't want to deal with it." The difference in their educational levels makes it hard for them to understand each other. "Tom doesn't have a degree, so he does construction, and I think we just have two levels of thinking that just kind of conflict." He is older, 29, divorced, and has a son, and Angela thinks he is a poor father. "He has no patience. He just can't handle him, basically." Her boyfriend expects her to take over the child care when the boy visits, which she resents. "I'm 21 years old. I don't want to be a mother right now."

How did she get herself into such an unpromising relationship? That's what she wonders. "I think I've been insane here for the last year. I lost my mind." She has noticed that her relationship with her boyfriend bears a disturbing resemblance to her mother's relationship with her stepfather, which alarms her. "My mom puts up with a lot of crap and I don't know why she does, so I'm looking at my relationship now and I'm like 'Boy, this is the exact relationship as they have,' and I'm going, 'What is going on?' I don't know how I got myself into this situation but I need to get out of it!"

Despite Angela's concerns about her boyfriend, they are currently living together. "That's another thing I can't believe I did," she says regretfully. She moved in with him strictly for practical reasons. "I didn't want to live at home anymore because they drove me nuts, and everybody else already had apartments, and some of my friends were living at home and they didn't want to move out because they couldn't afford it. So I figured I might as well try it." But she doesn't plan to try it for much longer. "The lease is up here at the end of July and I think I'm going to say 'See you later' then."

Angela hopes to marry someone who shares her interest in the outdoors, as her former boyfriend did, but even more important is finding someone with the right personal qualities. "Someone sweet, honest, who can be my friend, who's not temperamental all the time, who can be happy. Because I'm a happy person and I just want to have a good time and not worry."

She also looks forward to having children, eventually. "I think it'll be neat having a kid." She hopes that by waiting until at least her late twenties to marry, she'll improve her chances of having a successful marriage, unlike her parents. "I don't want to have kids until my upper twenties and I really don't want to be married until after 25 or 26. No hurry. Because my parents are divorced and it's just a pain in the butt."

If you look at Angela's life right now, as it is, you might not see much in her favor. She has dropped out of college, and she is working at a job she enjoys but that doesn't pay well and doesn't offer much in the way of long-term prospects. She is living with a boyfriend she doesn't respect and certainly doesn't want to marry. Yet she is reasonably happy with her life, less for what it is now than for what she believes it will be in the future. Ten years from now, she sees herself in a successful career doing something she enjoys. Ten years from now, she sees herself married to a man she loves, raising happy children with him. Although the fulfillment of these goals is far from imminent, she is confident that eventually she will be successful and happy. At age 21, even if she is currently adrift in many ways, all her hopes are alive and well.

Conclusion: Themes and Variations in Emerging Adulthood

Four lives, each of them unique, each with its own history and its own prospects. Yet they share certain common characteristics as well, characteristics that are also common to many of their American peers in this age period. In their lives we can see the themes laid out in Chapter 1, of emerging adulthood as a time of identity explorations, instability, self-focus, feeling in-between, and a sense of wide-open possibilities.

All four of them are engaged in identity explorations in love and work. They have some sense of what they would like to do in the way of work, although their ideas range in clarity from Charles's devotion to music to Steve's vague hopes of managing a restaurant. But none of them has settled into a definite work pattern yet. Rosa likes her job in the Internet company, but she views it only as a way of gaining a broad range of experience on the way to something else, she is not sure what. Steve's position as a waiter is a long way from owning or managing a restaurant, and he concedes that he is only "treading water" right now. Charles is committed to a career in music, but the precise form of that career remains to be determined, and he has many other options besides music. Angela loves horticulture, but she has not decided yet how this love will translate into a career. All of them are still in the process of answering the identity questions, "what do I enjoy most, what am I best at, and how does that fit with the options available to me?"

In their love lives, the same process of exploration is evident. Steve, Charles, and Angela are all in relationships that seem unlikely to last. None of them has any desire to marry any time soon. Charles's first priority is his music, Angela and her boyfriend seem poorly matched, and Steve's life is too up in the air to include commitment to anything right now, including his girlfriend. Rosa is the most settled of the four in terms of love, but even she wants to wait a while before entering marriage, and she wonders if it wouldn't be a good idea to explore her options a bit more. All of them are still pondering the question of who should be their partner for life.

For all of them, the identity explorations of emerging adulthood go in tandem with instability. Exploring in love and work means that they may change direction at any time, as new possibilities come along. Steve is the extreme example of this, with his determination to sign only month-to-month leases so that he can take off on short notice. But none of them knows exactly what life will be like a year from now, much less 10 or 20 years from now. With the possible exception of Rosa, none of them knows who their intimate partner will be a year from now. But instability doesn't trouble them much. They accept it as part of the process of exploring, as a reflection of the fact that they are still in the process of deciding what form they want their adult lives to take.

Their concentration on identity explorations makes emerging adulthood a self-focused time. Rosa is the most explicit about this, when she says "I want to be a little selfish for a while," but it is an undercurrent for all of them. Steve and Charles don't want to commit themselves to a love relationship because they want to be free to go where their wishes take them, on their own. Angela doesn't feel ready for marriage or children for many years yet, not until she has had enough time to focus on her own life and achieve self-sufficiency. All of them want to commit themselves to others eventually, but for now, during their emerging adult years, they want to focus on personal goals and self-development.

They are aware of being in a period of exploration, of not yet having made the choices that will provide the foundation for their adult lives, and this awareness makes them feel in-between, no longer in adolescence but not yet fully adult. They feel like they have reached adulthood in some ways, but in other ways they feel like they are "still trying to grab a hold of it," as Steve said. Of the four, only Charles feels he has definitely reached adulthood, and even Charles realizes that he is in a temporary period of being "highly portable," prior to taking on the enduring commitments of adult life.

Although there is a lot of exploration and instability in their lives right now, all four of them are confident they will get what they want out of life. Everything seems possible for them, and their hopes are high. They expect to have a happy marriage, and they expect to find meaningful work and to be successful in it. At this age, there is nothing to impede their dreams. Angela may have her career in horticulture, Steve may have his restaurant, Rosa may have her bakery, Charles may turn his musical ambitions into reality. All of them may find a lifelong love. Or maybe not. But here in emerging adulthood, no dreams have been permanently dashed, no doors have been firmly closed, and every possibility for happiness is still alive. This is what is heartening as well as poignant about emerging adulthood, that it is the age of possibilities, the age of unvanquished hopes.

Not all emerging adults are like the ones profiled in this chapter. Some make enduring decisions relatively early, and have settled lives by their mid-twenties. Others find their opportunities for identity explorations restricted by poverty, poor schooling, or family chaos. We will explore their stories, too, in the following chapters. However, we will see that most emerging adults resemble Rosa, Steve, Charles, and Angela in having lives characterized by exploration and instability, and in focusing on self-development as they seek to translate their possibilities into realities.

Chapter 3

From Conflict to Companionship

A New Relationship with Parents

"When I was a boy of 14," Mark Twain famously remarked, "my father was so ignorant I could hardly stand to have the man around. But when I got to be 21, I was astonished at how much he had learnt in seven years." Although written over a century ago, Twain's wry observation is an apt description of the changes that take place today in relationships with parents from adolescence to emerging adulthood. Conflict with parents tends to be high for adolescents, who often view their parents as ignorant and worse. But in the course of emerging adulthood, most people come to see their parents in a much more sympathetic and benevolent light, as persons and not merely as parents.

Twain's jest about how much his father had "learnt" in seven years is true in a sense, because parents do change as their children move from adolescence to emerging adulthood. For the most part, parents adapt to their emerging adults' growing maturity and treat them differently than they did in adolescence. Just as emerging adults come to see their parents as persons and not merely parents, so parents come to see their children as persons and not merely their children. These changing perceptions on both parts allow parents and emerging adults to establish a new relationship, as near-equals.

Still, this change does not take place overnight but occurs gradually through emerging adulthood. The feeling of in-betweenness that so many emerging adults have, that feeling of being no longer adolescent but not yet fully adult, is rooted in the changes taking place in their relationships with their parents. Recall from Chapter 1 that emerging adults see the Big Three cornerstones for becoming an adult as *accepting responsibility for yourself, making independent decisions*, and *becoming financially independent*. Each of these criteria has connotations of independence, specifically of independence *from parents*. Learning to accept responsibility for yourself means taking over responsibilities that had previously been assumed by your parents, and no longer expecting your parents to shoulder the responsibility for the consequences of your mistakes. Making independent decisions means no longer having important decisions about your life made by your parents. Becoming financially independent means no longer having your parents pay some or all of your bills. Emerging adults are on the way to achieving independence in all three of these respects, but they are in-between, not there yet. They still rely on their parents in ways they expect will not continue once they become fully adult, especially for money but also for advice and emotional support.

In this chapter we take a look at the many facets of emerging adults' relationships with their parents. First we look at the overall outline of relations with parents in emerging adulthood, which shows a remarkably positive picture. Then we examine the changes that take place when emerging adults move out of their parents' household, as well as the experiences of emerging adults who move back in again and those who remain at home. Next we look at the shift that often takes place in emerging adulthood from a parent-child relationship to a new relationship as friends and companions. Finally, we look at the enduring repercussions of parents' divorce and remarriage—how emerging adults recall these events and how they believe they have been shaped by them.

Closeness and Harmony, Most of the Time

Although moving through emerging adulthood involves becoming more independent from parents, most American emerging adults remain closely connected to their parents throughout their twenties. In the national Clark poll, over half (55%) of 18–29-year-olds reported being in contact with their parents "every day or almost every day."[1] The younger the emerging adults, the more contact with parents they reported, but even at ages 26–29, 51% were in daily contact.

This frequency of contact with parents is far greater than parents remember experiencing when they were young.[2] The technological advancements of the past 20 years have made contact cheaper and easier than ever before. When parents were young, calling home was expensive, which made it rare.

Now, cell phones with unlimited calling and texting plans allow people to contact whomever they want, whenever they want, without worrying about the cost.

It has been observed that today's emerging adults are "digital natives," having grown up with personal computers, mobile phones, Facebook, iPods and iPads.[3] Their parents, in contrast, are "digital immigrants" who are not quite as comfortable with the new technologies as their kids are. This divide is reflected in their preferences for how to keep in contact with each other. According to the national Clark parents poll, parents generally prefer the phone (73%).[4] Emerging adults were more likely than their parents to prefer texting (45% to 19%), but even for them digital natives though they may be, the phone was preferred by 48%, slightly higher than texting.[5] Newer technologies, including e-mail, social networks (such as Facebook), and video calling (such as Skype), were preferred by only a few percent of parents or emerging adults. Apparently the old-fashioned phone still allows for greater closeness and more effective communication than any of the new technologies.

Frequent contact with parents during emerging adulthood is motivated not only by the cheapness and ease of the technology. It also reflects the closeness and harmony that typically characterizes emerging adults' relations with their parents. Both sides see their relationship as having improved greatly since the throes of adolescence. In the national Clark poll, 75% of emerging adults ages 18–29 agreed that they get along a lot better with their parents now than they did in their mid-teens.[6] Similarly, in the Clark parents poll, two-thirds (66%) of parents agreed that they get along better with their 18–29-year-old now than when the child was in the mid-teens.[7]

Parents observe a variety of specific ways their relationship with their child has strengthened and improved from adolescence to emerging adulthood, according to the Clark parents poll.[8] Asked to compare the relationship now to when the child was age 15, over 80% of parents agree that they have more adult conversations with their child, nearly 80% enjoy their time together more, and only 16% say that they have more conflict now (Table 3.1). Parents' reports of positive changes grow more pronounced in the course of the emerging adult years. Three fourths (74%) of parents of 18–21-year-olds name "we enjoy our time together more" as a change that has taken place since the child was age 15, but this rises to 83% for parents of 26–29-year-olds. Nearly half (49%) of parents of emerging adults ages 18–21 say they have become more like friends now than at age 15, but the

Table 3.1 Parents' Reports of Changes Since Their Emerging Adult Was 15 Years Old

Which of the following changes have taken place in your relationship with your child since he/she was 15 years old?	Percent "yes"
We have more adult conversations.	86
We enjoy our time together more.	78
He/she is more respectful toward me.	71
We have become more like friends.	55
He/she sees me more as a person rather than a parent.	49
We are not as close.	20
We have more conflict now.	16

Source: Arnett & Schwab (2013).

proportion is even higher (64%) for parents of emerging adults 26–29 years old. Parents of 26–29-year-olds are also more likely to believe that their child now "sees me more as a person rather than a parent" (55%) compared to parents of younger (18–21) emerging adults (43%).

Although relations between parents and emerging adults are remarkably positive overall, family relations are always more complex than "happily-ever-after." For a substantial proportion of emerging adults, their parents are a bit too close. In the national Clark poll, 30% of 18–29-year-olds agreed that their parents are more involved in their lives than they really want them to be.[9] There were notable ethnic differences in responses to this item: 41% of Latino and 39% of African American emerging adults agreed, compared to 24% of Whites. The cultural traditions of family closeness and mutual support among Latinos and African Americans have this drawback, in the eyes of many emerging adults, but there are benefits, too, as we will see shortly.

Moving Out, Moving Back In, Staying Home

Cultural customs about the appropriate timing of moving out vary widely around the world, from leaving at age 18 or 19 (northern Europe) to staying home through the late twenties or early thirties (southern Europe) to never leaving the family household and even bringing a marriage partner to live there, too (young men in rural Asia). In the United States, the typical age of moving out is 18 or 19, but not all move out at that age, and among those who do, some come back again.

Moving Out

Most Americans first move out of their parents' household at age 18 or 19, usually either to go away to college or simply to be independent.[10] Moving out means more freedom, but also more responsibilities. Emerging adults may find it tough to run their own household and pay their own bills. They might miss having their parents take care of many of the annoying but essential details of daily life—the laundry, the grocery shopping, the toilet cleaning. However, for most of them it is worth taking on these responsibilities in order to feel like they have control over their own lives, without their parents peering over their shoulders. In the national Clark poll, nearly three-fourths (74%) of 18–29-year-olds agreed that "I would prefer to live independently of my parents even if it means living on a tight budget."[11]

As long as they live at home, their parents are likely to be part of their lives every day, noting when they leave and when they return, inquiring in a subtle or not-so-subtle way about their job or their school progress or their love life, offering subtle or not-so-subtle advice. Most emerging adults prefer to avoid this much involvement with their parents, if they can afford to live on their own. In the national Clark poll, emerging adults were more likely to agree that "my parents are more involved in my life than I really want them to be" if they lived with their parents (36%) than if they had moved out (27%).[12]

It's not that they stop loving their parents, or that they do not value their parents' advice and assistance. It's just that by no longer living at home they have more control over how much involvement their parents have in their lives. They can call on their parents when they wish and see them when they like, but the rest of the time they are free to make their own, independent decisions. Carrie put it succinctly: "I don't have to talk to them when I don't want to, and when I want to, I can."

Perhaps because moving out means seeing their parents only when they choose, emerging adults tend to get along better with their parents after they leave home. Numerous studies have found that emerging adults who have moved out feel closer to their parents than emerging adults who have remained at home and have fewer negative feelings toward them. For example, in one study of 21-year-olds,[13] emerging adults who had moved at least an hour's drive away felt closest to their parents and valued their opinions most highly. In contrast, emerging adults who were living at home had the poorest relations with their parents, and those who had moved out but remained within an hour's drive were in-between the other two groups. Similarly, in the Clark parents poll, parents whose kids had moved out were more likely than parents whose kids were still at home to describe their relationship as "mostly positive."[14] In my original study, Rich's comments were typical: "I don't live under their roof anymore. They don't see me as often and I don't see them as often, so we're friendlier for the most part."

Apparently, absence makes the heart grow fonder toward parents, for many emerging adults. Simply put, it's a lot easier to be fond of someone you do not see very much. Living with other people almost inevitably entails some degree of friction over household responsibilities and the collision of different habits and preferences—the dirty dishes someone left on the counter, the music one household member loves and another loathes, the question of who ate the last donut. Moving out means avoiding all that day-to-day friction. Once they leave home, emerging adults can visit their parents for a day or a weekend, enjoy a few good meals, and leave while everybody is still smiling.

As long as they are still living at home, their parents might feel obliged to comment on how they eat, how they spend their money, and when they come home at night. Once they move out, their parents no longer know the details and so are less likely to meddle in things that emerging adults feel are none of their business. If absence makes the heart grow fonder, that's at least in part because ignorance is bliss. Lynn said that she gets along much better with parents now that "I don't let them know what I'm doing a lot of the times. The less they know the better, because otherwise they'd bicker or talk to me and try to influence my life. I don't want to hear their advice. I want to be able to do what I want to do." Karen has found that she gets along better with her parents in emerging adulthood than she did in adolescence because she tells them less and they ask her less: "In high school, I went out of my way to avoid conversations with my parents because I felt that a lot of things they wanted to know about didn't concern them. I find now that my parents know less about my life because I'm not at home. They don't ask me as many questions, so I enjoy having conversations with them."

Although today's emerging adults generally expect to leave home shortly after high school, leaving home as early as age 18 or 19 is a new phenomenon in the United States.[15] Up until the 1970s, the most common reason for leaving home was marriage, which usually meant staying at home until one's early twenties. Young women, especially, did not typically leave home to live on their own before marrying. However, in recent decades it has become uncommon for young people to remain at home until marriage. Now, the most common reason that emerging adults give for leaving home is simply "to be independent."[16] Also, more young people now than in the past attend college, so leaving for college has increased as a reason for leaving home.

For some, reaching emerging adulthood gives them the opportunity to liberate themselves from a family environment they find intolerable. Adolescents, because they are financially and legally dependent on their parents, do not have much choice but to live at home. Unless their parents' treatment reaches the extreme of abuse or neglect, they are legally required to remain in their parents' household. Some adolescents run away from home, of course. However, there are many others who would not take that drastic step but who nevertheless find their home lives unpleasant and look forward to leaving. Ron said that when he was in high school he and his mother fought "several times a day, seven days a week." Leaving for college came as a welcome relief. Time and distance have helped him understand his mother better, well enough to know that the best way for him to have a decent relationship with her is to see her rarely. "I've learned a great deal about my mother over the last four years, when I have not been at home. She can be sweet and kind of normal—you just have to stay away from her."

Moving out enabled Jill to escape a family situation that had taken a turn for the worse. Her parents got along "fairly well" as she was growing up. However, when she was 19, her father's sister committed suicide, and "he began drinking after that." He became an alcoholic, in fact, and the relationship between her parents deteriorated. But she was old enough that she could escape the worst of it by leaving home and being selective about when and how much she saw her parents. "I was old enough that I could go to college, I could get my own apartment and I could choose the times I came back to visit. I could choose times that I knew would be good times."

But even for emerging adults who come from relatively healthy home environments, leaving home often improves their relationships with their parents. Parents and their emerging adults value their time together more once they have to make an effort to have contact with each other. As Emily put it, "In high school they took me for granted because I was always around. Now I'm rarely around, so they appreciate me more." For Warren, the appreciation goes both ways. "Since leaving home last year, my relationship with my parents has been a lot closer because we miss each other more."

Sometimes emerging adults are surprised to discover the intensity of the attachment they have to their parents. While they were home they may not have realized it in the course of daily life, or their love for their parents may have been buried under the petty conflicts and resentments generated by living together. Especially when they first move away, emerging adults may realize more than ever how much their parents mean to them. Ellen, now a junior in college, recalled, "My first two semesters away at school I was extremely homesick. I called my mom and dad every single day. I started to rely on their voices to make it through until my next break. I probably had more conversation time with my parents my first year at college than my entire high school career. I found myself telling them things I would never have dreamed about telling them, and they also shared many things with me."

Parents, too, often feel a sense of loss when their kids leave home. A large majority of parents (84%) in the Clark parents poll said that they miss their kids who have moved out.[17] Nevertheless, parents also perceive a variety of positive consequences when emerging adults move out, as Table 3.2 shows. Nearly all parents are happy that their child is becoming more independent (90%). Furthermore, the parents' own lives improve in many ways when kids move out, with 61% of parents saying that the change allows them to enjoy having more time with their spouse or partner and 60% welcoming the chance to have more time for themselves.[18]

Moving Back In

Moving out is not necessarily forever. Early in the twentieth century, when marriage was the main reason for moving out and divorce was rare, young people usually did not return home once they had left. The rate of returning home was about 20% in the 1920s, which is as far as records go back.[19] Now,

Table 3.2 When Kids Move Out: How Parents Respond

If your child has lived outside your household, how did you feel about your child leaving home?	Percent agree
I was happy that he/she was becoming independent.	90
I missed him/her.	84
I enjoyed having more time with my spouse or partner.	61
I welcomed the chance to have more time for myself.	60
I was concerned that he/she was not ready to be independent.	37
It was a relief because we had less conflict.	31
I felt we were not as close emotionally.	27

Source: Arnett & Schwab (2013).

with leaving for college or for independence the main reasons for leaving home, moving home again has become quite common, experienced by just over 40% of today's emerging adults.[20]

For those who left home for college, moving back home may be a way of bridging their transition to post-college life after they graduate or drop out. It gives them a chance to decide what to do next, be it graduate school, a job near home, or a job in another place. For those who left home for independence, some may feel that the glow of living on their own dims after a while as the freedom of doing what they want when they want becomes outweighed by the burden of taking care of a household and paying all their own bills. Moving back in after an early divorce or a period of military service are other reasons that emerging adults give for returning home.[21] Under these circumstances, too, coming home may be attractive to young people as a transition period, a chance to get back on their feet before they venture again into the world.

Emerging adults and their parents react in a range of ways when grown kids "return to the nest." For most, the return home is welcome and the transition is managed easily. Nancy, a social worker, recently moved back home while she is between jobs. She was apprehensive at first but pleasantly surprised when things went well. "I was scared, not how they would react, but just what it was going to feel like for all of us. We talked quite a bit about it before I moved back, and they were very supportive. 'Oh, move back home! We'd be happy for you to move back home while you look for a job.' So I mean, they made it really easy and they basically just let me do my own thing."

Nancy's experience is not unusual. The pop culture stereotype that parents groan when their grown kids move back home and immediately begin scheming to get them out again could not be further from the truth. In the Clark parents poll, of the parents who had an 18–29-year-old son or daughter living with them, 61% described their feelings about it as "mostly positive" and only 6% described it as "mostly negative."[22] When emerging adults live at home, parents' lives are certainly disrupted in various ways, but they are more likely to see benefits than burdens. In fact, they are more favorable about the move home than emerging adults are, and see it as strengthening their relationship and making them closer. As Table 3.3 shows, the top three consequences that parents in the Clark parents poll observed from having their grown kids at home were all positive, with 67% of parents saying they feel closer to their child emotionally, 66% saying they have more companionship with their child, and 62% noting that their emerging adult helps with household responsibilities. None of the negative consequences were nearly

Table 3.3 A Grown Kid at Home: How Parents Respond

If your child is living at home or has moved back in, which of the following are consequences of your child living with you now?	Percent agree
I feel closer to my child emotionally.	67
I have more companionship with my child.	66
My child helps with household responsibilities.	62
I have more financial stress.	40
I worry more about my child.	40
I have less time for myself.	29
I have less sexual freedom with my spouse or partner.	27
I have more conflict with my child.	25

Source: Arnett & Schwab (2013).

as common, but it is notable that 40% of parents say that they have more financial stress and worry more about their children when living with them. Having an emerging adult living at home means witnessing every up and down of daily life, from an argument with a boyfriend or girlfriend to a bad day at work, and witnessing it all magnifies parents' concerns.

The key to a successful transition back home is for parents to recognize the change in their children's maturity and treat them as adults rather than adolescents. Darren, like many college students, returns home for the summer, and has found that his parents monitor him much less than they did when he was an adolescent. "I still live at home during the summer but the atmosphere is very different. In high school they always wanted to know where I was going, what I was doing, when I was coming home, and so on. Now I have almost total independence even at home. I come and go as I please and they don't question me. Because of the freedom they allow me I feel closer to them. It's like they treat me as an equal even though I'm their son."

For others, however, the return home is a bumpy transition. Parents may have come to enjoy having the nest all to themselves, without children to provide for and feel responsible for.[23] Emerging adults may find it difficult to have parents monitoring them daily again, after a period when they had grown used to managing their own lives. After Mary moved back home at age 22, she was dismayed to find that her mother would wait up for her when she went out with her boyfriend, as if it were high school all over again. They did not argue openly about it, but it made Mary feel "like she was sort of 'in my territory' or something." Annie moved home at age 20 as a single mother and has found that living at home makes her feel "like a kid with a kid. They boss me around, they boss her around, and then they tell me what to do with her, so it's like I'm her sister rather than her mother." Nevertheless, she appreciates the freedom that living at home allows. "Whenever [my daughter] goes to bed and if they're home, I can go do what I want. Eight o'clock comes and I'm at the mall!" For many emerging adults, moving back home results in this kind of ambivalence. They are grateful for the support their parents provide, even as they resent returning to the subordinate role of a dependent child.

Staying Home

Of course, there are also many cases of families who get along fine even as the emerging adults remain in their parents' household. This is true in the United States, and it appears to be even more common in Europe. Emerging adults there tend to live with their parents for longer than American emerging adults do, especially in central and southern Europe. For example, in Germany the typical age of moving out is 22.[24] There are some practical reasons for this. European universities typically do not have dormitories or other on-campus housing, and for college and non-college emerging adults alike, apartments in urban areas are scarce and expensive. But also important is that European emerging adults are often able to enjoy the financial and emotional support of their parents within the household while maintaining an independent life of their own.

Italy provides a good case in point. Ninety-four percent of Italians ages 15–24 live with their parents, the highest percentage in the European Union (EU). Yet only 8% of young Italians view their living arrangements as a problem—the *lowest* percentage among EU countries.[25] This suggests that many young Italians remain at home contentedly through their twenties, by choice rather than by necessity. Many young Europeans find that they can enjoy a higher standard of living by staying home rather than moving out, and still live as they wish. Perhaps because southern European societies are somewhat less individualistic than American society, young Europeans in these countries may feel less compelled than young Americans (or northern Europeans) to demonstrate that they can stand alone in emerging adulthood by living independently of their parents.

Several European societies have coined terms to describe young people in this extended state of living at home. In Sweden, the term is *mamboende*, roughly translated as "those who live with mama," applied to anyone who stays or returns home after age 18.[26] In Italy, the term is *mammoni*, which means "mama's boys," applied to men who live at home past their early twenties.[27] These terms have a pejorative, sarcastic tone, as if it is somewhat socially disapproved to be an emerging adult living at home. At the same time, the prevalence of living at home during emerging adulthood in these societies suggests social acceptance of the practice. Especially in southern Europe, parents as well as emerging adults usually see no reason why the kids should leave home until marriage, unless an educational or occupational opportunity takes them elsewhere.[28]

In the United States, although most emerging adults move out of their parents' home in their late teens, some stay home into their early twenties.[29] With staying home as with returning home, one of the primary reasons for living with parents is economic. Emerging adults ages 18–24 who live with their parents are more likely to be in school and less likely to be working full-time, and if they work they make less money than those who have moved out.[30]

Staying at home was once more common among young Latinos, African Americans, and Asian Americans than among White Americans, but the most recent data show no ethnic differences in the likelihood of living at home.[31] However, there may be ethnic differences in the reasons for living at home.[32] Economic reasons may be especially important for young Latinos and African Americans, who are more likely to be unemployed during emerging adulthood than Whites (or Asian Americans) are. Another reason in ethnic minority cultures may be greater emphasis on family closeness and interdependence, and less emphasis on being independent as a value in itself.[33] Rosa (who was profiled in Chapter 2) lived with her Chinese American mother and Mexican American father throughout her college years. She enjoyed the way staying home allowed her to remain in close contact with them. "I loved living at home. I respect my parents a lot, so being home with them was actually one of the things I liked to do most. Plus, it was free!"

For Latinos and Asian Americans, an additional reason for staying home is specific to young women, and concerns the high value placed on virginity before marriage. Some parents in these ethnic cultures prefer to have their daughters stay home until marriage in order to reduce the likelihood that they will have opportunities for sexual experiences. Jenny, a 28-year-old Korean American who is now married, said that when she was single "I wasn't allowed to go and live with roommates or friends. They basically said, 'You're living at home until you get married.'" Her brother, in contrast, never lived at home again after leaving for college. Although sexual issues were never discussed directly, it was clear to Jenny that sex was behind her parents' pressure for her to live at home. If she had decided to cohabit with a partner, she said, "I think my parents would have strangled me!"

Despite their parent' restrictions, many emerging adults from ethnic minority families view living at home as desirable, perhaps because of the values of family closeness they have learned in their cultures. However, there is considerable diversity in each minority group, and many emerging adults in minority groups leave home for reasons similar to Whites, especially leaving for college and for independence.[34] For Latinos and Asian Americans, the more generations their families have been in the United States, the closer their home-leaving patterns resemble those of Whites.

Is it possible to be an emerging adult while still living at home? If emerging adulthood is the period between dependence on parents and taking on new family obligations, does living at home imply remaining dependent on parents and therefore remaining in adolescence rather than entering emerging adulthood? It is certainly true that if you live at home, you are more dependent on your parents than you would be if you had moved out. However, the demographic outline of emerging adulthood—longer education and later ages of entering marriage and parenthood—applies no less to those living at home than to those who have moved out. In fact, as noted earlier, 18–24-year-olds living at home are more likely to be enrolled in school than their peers who have moved out.

Specifically in the American context, if we consider the five features of emerging adulthood—identity explorations, instability, self-focus, feeling in-between, and a sense of possibilities—there is no reason that they could not apply to young people who live at home. It is possible to live at home and still explore various possibilities in love and work. The instability of emerging adulthood, in the form of changes in love relationships, educational paths, and jobs, can take place while living at home as easily as while living independently—maybe even easier, because those who live at home are not as compelled to stay with an unsatisfying job just to pay the bills for rent and food. There is no reason that someone in his or her twenties could not be self-focused, feel in-between, and feel a wide-open sense of possibilities while living at home.

Also, like emerging adults who move back home, emerging adults who stay at home have more autonomy from their parents than they had as adolescents. Some parents feel obligated to keep close tabs on their children as long as the children are in their home, no matter how old they are, but most parents adjust to the new stage of life that their emerging adults have entered by letting them lead their own lives, with little interference. Belgians use the term "hotel families" to describe the arrangements between parents and their emerging adult children, implying that in such homes the parents provide a room, food, and laundry services, but otherwise the young people go their own way.[35] Many American emerging adults and their parents reach a similar kind of understanding. Aaron still lives at home, "but it's pretty much up to me. I go and do my own thing and if I'm not coming home I'll call them so they know. They just want to know if I'm not going to be there for a day or two at a time."

From Parent and Child to Near-Equals

Adolescence is often a difficult time for family relations.[36] Conflict rises, as adolescents press for more autonomy while parents continue to feel responsible for protecting their children from potential harm. Closeness declines, as adolescents begin to have experiences, especially involving sexuality and romantic relationships, that they feel uncomfortable discussing with their parents and would much rather discuss with their friends. From age 10 to 18, adolescents spend an increasing amount of time with their friends and a decreasing amount of time at home.[37]

Relations improve once the adolescent becomes an emerging adult, as we have seen in this chapter. This positive trend results in part from leaving home, but there is more to the changes in relationships with parents in emerging adulthood than simply the effect of moving out. Emerging adults also grow in their ability to understand their parents. Adolescence is in some ways an egocentric period, and adolescents often have difficulty taking their parents' perspectives. They sometimes cast a pitiless gaze on their parents, magnifying their deficiencies and becoming easily irritated by their imperfections.

As emerging adults mature and begin to feel more adult themselves, they become more capable of understanding how their parents look at life. They begin to realize that their parents are neither the demigods they adored as children nor the bumblers they scorned as adolescents, but simply people who, like themselves, have a mix of qualities, merits as well as faults. Joseph, echoing the Twain quote that began this chapter, said, "I guess the old adage that 'the older you get, the smarter your parents get,' is really true. The things they said and did make a lot more sense to me now than they used to." Gerard said he hated his father as a teenager, but as an emerging adult the problems he has faced in his own life have made him more sympathetic. "I feel profoundly more forgiving towards my father since I've seen how life actually can be difficult, and so I respect him a lot more than I used to because he's really persisted and got through a lot of his own struggles."

For some, this new sense of seeing their parents as persons leads to remorse for how they behaved toward their parents as teens. Lisa said, "I treat them a lot better now than I did when I was a teenager. I look back and I go, 'Man, I was terrible to them. Why did I treat them like that?'" Matt recalled that "[i]n high school I was rude, inconsiderate, and got into many fights with my mom. Since coming to college I realize how much she means to me and how much she goes out of her way for me. I've grown to have a true appreciation for her."

For Diana, the change has been especially dramatic: "In high school, even starting in middle school, I had a terrible relationship with my parents. My mom and I rarely talked and my dad and I were in conflict almost every day. Looking back, it's almost frightening to think of all the things I put my parents through. I went through a wildly rebellious time where I would do the most horrible things without thinking twice. Stealing, lying, sneaking out, taking the car, even getting a tattoo were just some of the things I felt compelled to do. I was kicked out, I ran away—everything was so dramatic!

"Then somehow I managed to control myself and make it to college. I slowly started to make attempts at reconciliation towards my parents. Somehow in the course of four years I've managed to get to a point where I can hang out with my parents and really love them. It's weird how time and age can just change relationships like that. My relationship with my parents is now on a loving, mutually respectful kind of level."

For other emerging adults, what they learn about their parents as persons is disillusioning. Carla grew up thinking her parents had a good marriage, but discovered otherwise once she became an emerging adult. "They hid it very well until I got older and then, when I started developing a friendship instead of a parent-daughter relationship, I found out the real business—divorce threats, affairs, all this stuff that I had no idea was going on." Helen had a similar experience. Growing up, she said, "I admired my dad a lot. I think he gave me a lot of the qualities that I have that people like." Now, however, she has learned that "[p]arents aren't always perfect, you know. There's some things you find out." What she found out was that her dad has been having a series of affairs for many years. This included sending money to his lovers while telling her he did not have enough money to give any to her when she asked. As a result, "I almost hated him. And I had so much trouble dealing with it. It's still tough for me because it just makes me so upset." Doug now sees both his parents in a less flattering light: "I guess just growing up I can see how fucked up they are. I think I've come to probably resent them a lot more. They have no fun, and they penalize themselves. My mom is like a big martyr and my father is pretty solemn. When I was younger I didn't really perceive their feelings too much, but now I perceive their feelings and also their personalities and some of their hang-ups and stuff."

Parents change, too, in how they view their children and how they relate to them. Their role as monitor of their children's behavior and enforcer of household rules diminishes, and this results in a more relaxed and amiable relationship with their children. Nancy said, "They're still my parents, but there's more—I don't know if friendship is the right word, but like I go out with them and just really enjoy spending time with them, and they're not in a parental role as much. It's not a disciplining role, it's just more of a real comfortable friendship thing." Parents become less inclined to issue commands, and more inclined to take their children's point of view seriously. Paul said, "Now they look at me eye to eye, where before it was 'Do this, do that.' They give me a lot of leeway and a lot of respect and value my opinion a lot more." Similarly, Laurel observed that her parents "actually ask me what I'm going to do rather than tell me what I'm going to do, and that's sort of marked the change right there."

The changes in parents and their emerging adult children allow them to establish a new intimacy, more open than before, with a new sense of mutual respect.[38] Bonnie said that compared to adolescence, her relationship with her parents now is "completely different. I talk to them and stuff now. I can just be more honest. There isn't any of that feeling that I'm hiding something. I can be more honest with them about who I am. I feel they actually like me for who I am, and I like them." Luke has especially changed in his relationship with his father: "Over the past year I have become very close with my dad. To sit down with my dad and have a beer and exchange dirty jokes has been a weird experience. We have also been able to relate to each other when it comes to work, school, women, and so on. Before college there was a definite parent-child relationship with my father. Now he is more like a mentor or friend."

Not all emerging adults reach a near-equal relationship with their parents. Darrell, who was living with his parents again after some time living on his own, said they "treat me like a boy. 'You all right?' They worry about me. 'You're not getting into any trouble?' Just like parents. It's like when you go out or something, 'Where you goin'? You got money? You want a cold drink? You want this?' I'll be like, 'I got money, Mom.'" Darrell is African American, and as noted earlier, in the national Clark poll, agreement with the statement "my parents are more involved with my life than I really want them to be" was higher among African Americans and Latinos than among Whites. The closeness and interdependence common in American ethnic cultures sometimes feel a bit too close for emerging adults.

For some emerging adults, their parents' reluctance to let them go is mirrored by their own reluctance to take on the responsibilities of adult life. Cheryl, a recent college graduate, admits, "I'm not ready to accept responsibility for paying for my health insurance and blah, blah, blah right now. So I guess it's kind of like a double-edged sword thing. Like, I want them to think of me as being an adult and independent, but I also don't want to be fully independent." But Sharon is an exception. For the most part, both parents and emerging adults are able and willing to adjust to a new relationship as near-equals.

Are Parents Too Involved?

Parents and their 18–29-year-old children are closer today than in the previous generation.[39] This is due partly to the rise in the median marriage age. Once young people find a spouse or long-term partner, that person becomes their main companion and their closest confidant. Now that it is not until the end of the twenties or the early thirties that most people find their "soul mate," they rely more on their parents during their twenties than they did in the past, not just financially but emotionally.

Another reason for this closeness is changing views about parent-child relations. As part of the Youth Movement described in Chapter 1, young Baby Boomers sought to abolish the traditional hierarchy between parents and children. When they became parents, they strived to be closer to their children than they had been to their own parents, and they mostly succeeded. American parents today are rarely stern authority figures, as many (especially fathers) were in the past. Authority must be exercised sometimes as part of the parental role, but in general both mothers and fathers seek to be close to their kids as companions and friends.[40] Boomer parents also had fewer children than their parents did, which left them with more time and energy per child.

This closeness has been welcomed on both sides. As we have seen, emerging adults generally describe their relations with their parents as warm and harmonious, a crucial source of support as they enter an adult world that sometimes roughs them up. Parents, too, place great value on the relationship they have with their emerging adults. In the Clark parents poll, in response to the question, "Which of the following are current sources of enjoyment for you?," ranking number one was "relationship with my 18–29-year-old children," favored by 86% of respondents, a higher percentage than for watching TV (82%), travel (79%), and even "relationship with spouse or partner" (75%).[41]

But are parents and their emerging adults perhaps *too* close today? According to one popular narrative, for this generation of young people the dreaded "helicopter parent" is insistently hovering, intruding inappropriately on their decisions, small and large. In lurid media accounts, anecdotes are spread about zealous parents who allegedly harass their children's college professors over poor grades, pester their grown kids constantly with texts and calls, or accompany their children to job interviews. More sober academic investigations have warned of the dangers of "over-parenting" for college students, that is, of parents attempting to maintain an unhealthy level of involvement and control.[42]

Although the anecdotes can be misleading, there are certainly some parents who are over-involved in the lives of their emerging adults. As we have seen, nearly one-third of the 18–29-year-olds in the national Clark poll agree that their parents are more involved in their lives than they really want them to be. Similarly, in a study of college students, the National Survey of Student Engagement, 38% of freshmen and 29% of seniors reported that their parents had intervened on their behalf during their time at college.[43] That could mean a lot of things, but it seems likely that in some of those cases the intervention was unwarranted and unwanted.

In general, however, research strongly supports the conclusion that parental involvement in the lives of emerging adults has mostly beneficial effects.[44] The same National Survey of Student Engagement that found that many parents of college students "intervene" in some way in the lives of their children also found that those who reported parental intervention were more active in and more satisfied with their college experience. Other studies, too, confirm the value of parental support and assistance. For example, Karen Fingerman and her colleagues examined the outcomes related to parents' "intense support" involving multiple types of assistance (e.g., advice, lending a listening ear, financial or practical help) at least once a week.[45] Emerging adults who received such support reported higher life satisfaction and better adjustment than those who did not.

The sensible conclusion seems to be that the involvement of today's parents in the lives of their emerging adults is greater than the past, but that this increase should not be reflexively scorned. Their involvement mostly benefits their children. The kooky extreme should be avoided, of course, and usually is. Emerging adults generally do not want their parents peering over their shoulders all the time and offering advice, and most will not be shy about telling their parents to back off if they are overstepping the boundaries. Also, keep in mind that, with modern technology, emerging adults who find their parents to be overly involved have a simple solution available: turn off the phone, don't answer the e-mail, let the text go for a few days without a response. But most emerging adults want and need their parents' support into their twenties. The emerging adults who struggle the most are not the ones suffering from the invasion of helicopter parents, but the ones who cannot count on their parents' love and support even when they need them.

Money Is the Root of Most Conflict

One of the main signs that it takes a long time to grow up these days is in how long it takes to achieve financial independence. Nearly half (44%) of parents say they provide their 18–29-year-olds with either "frequent support when needed" or "regular support for living expenses," according to the Clark parents poll, and only 26% provide "little or none."[46] Figure 3.1 shows the pattern. As might be expected, the higher the parents' socioeconomic status, the more money they have available to share with their grown kids. Among parents with a four-year college degree or more, 43% provide their emerging adults with "regular support for living expenses," compared to only 23% of parents with a high school education or less.

Parents' financial support diminishes in the course of emerging adulthood, but remains surprisingly high even in the late twenties. According to the Clark parents poll, 56% of 26–29-year-olds receive at least occasional financial support from their parents—a decline from 89% at ages 18–21, but still substantial.[47] Other research has found that occasional financial support may take forms such as staying on the family cell phone plan, remaining in the parents' health insurance program, or receiving parents' help with a one-time expense such as a car repair or a security deposit on an apartment.[48]

According to parents, they provide a lot more financial support to their kids than they received from their own parents. As shown in Figure 3.1, only 14% of parents in the Clark parents poll said they were provided with either "frequent support" or "regular support for living expenses" when they were in their twenties, and 61% reported receiving little or no support, in sharp contrast to the more generous support they provide to their children. It is important to keep in mind that this is the parents' report, not an objective financial record. Perhaps parents have a rosier memory of their own progress

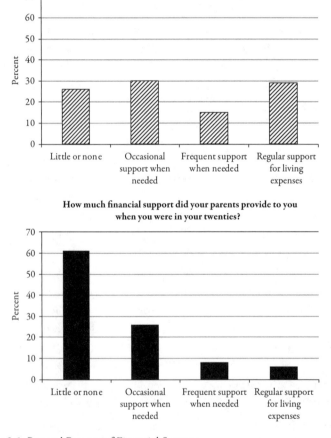

Figure 3.1 Parents' Reports of Financial Support.

Source: Arnett & Schwab (2013).

toward financial independence than was actually the case. However, it might be expected that parents would provide more financial help to their kids now than was true a generation ago, because more emerging adults stay in school for longer than ever before.[49]

Despite the many positive qualities in relationships between parents and their emerging adults, money is a major thorn among the roses. In fact, the number one source of strife between emerging adults and their parents is money, named by 42% of parents as a topic of conflict with their child in the Clark parents poll (Table 3.4). One of the central challenges of emerging adulthood in American society is moving toward independence and self-sufficiency, and money is a tangible representation of progress—or lack of progress—toward that goal.

Parents and emerging adults both experience a considerable amount of ambivalence over the money issues in their relationship. On one side, emerging adults realize that they need their parents' financial help in their late teens and early twenties, because they are often pursuing education, and if they are working, they are often not making much money—but they do not like being dependent on their parents, because taking money from them gives parents control over their decisions. As noted earlier in the chapter, in the national Clark poll, 74% of 18–29-year-olds agreed that "I would prefer to live independently of my parents, even if it means living on a tight budget." On the other side, most parents want to do what they can to support their children financially during the emerging adult years and help them reach their educational and occupational goals—but they also feel the drain on their own finances as they approach retirement age, and they feel it is quite reasonable to expect that if they are giving their kids money, they should have a say in how it is spent.

Table 3.4 Sources of Conflict Between Parents and Emerging Adults

What are the main topics of conflict with your child now, if any?	Percent "yes"
Money	42
Not always taking responsibility for his/her actions	37
His/her educational progress	34
His/her occupational progress	33

Source: Arnett & Schwab (2013).

Money issues are a source of concern as well as conflict in the relationships between parents and their emerging adults. Financial problems rank number one as the most common worry or concern that parents have about their son or daughter, higher than choosing the wrong romantic partner, lack of work progress, or lack of educational progress (Table 3.5). Additionally, half (50%) of all parents are "somewhat" or "very" concerned that their emerging adult is taking too long to become financially independent.[50]

Although kids rely on their parents for longer than in the past, parents realize they may need their kids' help someday, too. According to the Clark parents poll, over three-fourths (77%) of parents are confident that their child will be willing to help care for them in their old age if they need help, with 70% confident that their child will be able to help out financially.[51] Expectations of support from their kids is especially strong for African American parents, among whom 86% are confident that their child will help care for them in old age, while 74% of Latino parents and 76% of White parents express this confidence. A similar ethnic pattern applies for financial help, as 84% of African American parents are confident that their child will help out financially in the future, compared to 69% of Latino parents and 70% of White parents. Here again we find evidence of the greater value placed on family obligations and mutual support in American ethnic minority cultures.

The Multiple Legacies of Divorce

Americans, like people in most cultures, have a long tradition of extolling the joys of family life and idealizing family relations. "There's no place like home." "Home is where the heart is." As with most ideals, however, the reality of family life is much different and often falls considerably short of what we would like it to be. By emerging adulthood, many people have experienced

Table 3.5 Parents' Main Worries and Concerns About Their Emerging Adults

What are the main worries or concerns you have about your child?	Percent "yes"
Financial problems	38
Choosing the wrong romantic partner or partners	28
Lack of work progress	27
Lack of educational progress	26

Source: Arnett & Schwab (2013).

one or more of the crises that may afflict families and change irrevocably the course of family members' lives. In just the 300 interviews conducted in my original study, we heard about many varieties of family tragedy. Parents lose their jobs and/or their money, as a result of bad decisions or simple misfortune. A parent becomes injured or falls victim to a chronic illness. A parent dies young. A sibling dies in an accident. A father goes to jail. A parent suffers a psychological illness such as manic-depression. A parent slides into the mire of alcoholism or drug abuse.

But the number one affliction of family life, affecting more families than all of the others combined, is divorce. No account of the family lives of emerging adults would be complete without a discussion of their responses to their parents' divorces. With a divorce rate of nearly 50% in the United States, many young people have witnessed the demise of their parents' marriage by the time they reach emerging adulthood.

Overall, experiencing parents' divorce is related to an increased risk of a wide range of problems in childhood, adolescence, and emerging adulthood.[52] Compared to young people in nondivorced families, young people from divorced families have higher rates of using alcohol and other drugs. They are also more likely to be depressed and withdrawn, especially in the first year or two following the divorce. They tend to do less well in school and are less likely to attend college. Boys tend to be affected more deeply and for longer than girls are.

Nevertheless, the responses of emerging adults to their parents' divorce are complicated and various, and perhaps for this reason their responses are the subject of dispute among scholars. There has been a vigorous debate about the long-term effects of divorce on children, with some scholars arguing that the damage of divorce is evident into the twenties, while others argue that most children recover from divorce after a few years and lead reasonably contented and successful lives by emerging adulthood.[53]

However, argued in this polarized way, the debate misses the truth about the effects of divorce in the lives of emerging adults. Anything that happens to half of the population will not be experienced in one way but in a wide variety of ways, as the experience takes specific forms according to a vast range of circumstances. Some emerging adults recall responding to their parents' divorce with shock and sorrow, but others with relief or even happiness, because the divorce finally brought an end to years of conflict and tension in the household. Some of them have no memory of the divorce, because it happened when they were very young and they grew up with their parents living apart. For others, their parents divorced in recent years, after they had reached emerging adulthood and left the household, so they were little affected by it in their daily lives.

Thus the circumstances of the divorces vary tremendously. It matters how much conflict there was between the parents before the divorce, how old the children were when the divorce took place, how well or badly the parents got along following the divorce, how much the father remained in the picture, when and whether the parents remarried, and so on. As a result, there is not just one legacy of divorce but multiple legacies, with all the different circumstances filtered through the individual personalities of the persons who experienced the divorce. Let's examine these multiple legacies, focusing first on negative legacies, then on positive legacies, then on the further complications that parents' remarriage can bring.

Negative Legacies: Divorce as Tragedy

For some emerging adults, their parents' divorce is a wound that has never quite healed. Years later, they still vividly remember the pain of it, and they see it as a source of the problems they have as emerging adults. Ray said his parents fought a great deal, but for him their divorce when he was 10 years old was a turn for the worse. "I lost all will. I figured I don't have what the others have now. They got the mother, they got the father, they got the sisters. I just had my mother. That kind of made me feel that I lost my better half. You know? So, I didn't strive for the things I wanted. [If not for the divorce] I wouldn't have got in a lot of stupid things I got in."

Like Ray, Holly has compared her divorced family to nondivorced families and has felt distressed—then and now—at what she feels she has missed. "I was always jealous. My little cousin, I used to go stay with them and her dad would come home. She would run into his arms, you know, and yell 'Daddy!' and I was just so jealous when I'd go over there. And I'd see them, you know, they'd cook dinner and all that kind of family stuff, and I had never seen anything like it, because me and my mom would always have McDonald's or something and eat in front of the TV, every night. I was always jealous of that atmosphere, which I still am when I go over there. I mean, I can't wait to someday have that."

Christopher Lasch, who was a trenchant observer of American family life, argued that because of the decline in the stability of the family, children grow up learning "a certain protective shallowness, a fear of binding commitments, a willingness to pull up roots whenever the need arises, a dislike of depending on anyone, an incapacity for loyalty or gratitude."[54] Although it is by no means true for all emerging adults from divorced families, this effect is evident in the comments of emerging adults like Jerry, whose parents divorced when he was 11. Because his parents divorced, "I grew up on my own. I mean, my mom was there, but when you deal with things, you have to take care of yourself, and for a good number of years I didn't really feel like anybody cared about me. I went through a lot of counseling, and it wasn't until the past year or two that I actually trust people.... I always know that I can count on myself, and that's what it comes down to. You've got to be able to count on yourself, and then you can count on others."

Melissa has also grown more protective of her self-interest in the decade since her parents' divorce when she was 17. "It's not my problem, it's theirs. They got divorced. I'm not going to have two birthday parties and I'm not going to have two Christmases. It's their problem, and if they want to come to my birthday and if they want to come to my Christmas, they can come, and that's how I see it. That's how I've always seen it. And I know some people think that's really rude, but it's not my fault they got divorced and it's not my problem."

The Fading Father

After divorce the father's role in children's lives usually diminishes sharply. Even in nondivorced families, the father is usually less important in children's lives than the mother is. By adolescence, the father is often on the margins of the family's emotional life, a "shadowy presence," as one pair of scholars puts it.[55] But when parents divorce, the father's role in his children's lives usually becomes even more removed. By age 15, American adolescents in divorced families live an average of 400 miles away from their fathers, and almost half have not seen their father in over a year.[56]

There are a number of reasons why divorce pushes most fathers further out of their children's lives. Most obvious is that in about 90% of divorces the mother retains custody of the children and the father leaves the household.[57] As a result, he may see his children only every other weekend, plus an occasional holiday or vacation, and perhaps much less if the father or mother moves away after the divorce. But perhaps even more important is that the children's sympathies and loyalties tend to be with the mother rather than the father.

This imbalance exists even before divorce, as one reflection of the greater emotional closeness between mothers and children, but divorce skews it further. Despite the legal rhetoric, few divorces are "no-fault" in the eyes of the family members experiencing it. Perhaps because marriage is the most intimate of relationships, divorce often generates emotions that are fierce and deeply painful.[58] Ex-husbands and ex-wives each tend to see themselves as the injured party, and their children are under implicit or explicit pressure to side with one or the other. Because they are already closer to the mother before the divorce, most children tend to side with her. Christy recalled that after her parents divorced "there was a lot of resentment there. My poor mother had to pretty much raise her children while her ex-husband was finding himself. I listened to her crying a lot at night, wondering who was going to pay the heating bills and the food bills. There was a lot of bitterness there." Now, although she says that she and her father "get along fine," she also says, "His wife is only 3 years older than I am. I mean, there's tension there, and I don't choose to be involved with that family, and that really hurts his feelings." The hurting is quite deliberate, on her part. Although she is now 27 and the divorce took place when she was 16, she is still punishing him for "the way he pretty much shoved us all away and took this other woman into his life and created another family. He can't regain the things that he lost. And I know that bugs him and deep down I think I really want it to bug him. I want him to know the consequences of his actions."

The remarks of Christy and others show how the reverberations of divorce continue in emerging adulthood even when the divorce took place years earlier, especially in relationships with fathers.[59] Theresa, recalling her reaction to her parents' divorce when she was seven, said, "I was like 'Why did you leave my mom?' I went through a very angry stage. I'm just now working through the anger with my father. He's one subject that's really hard to talk about. I can't see myself sitting down and having a father-daughter talk with him. I don't feel like he can say anything to me because he was never there." Divorced fathers who try to reconcile with their emerging adult children may face a reluctant audience. Corey's parents divorced when he was five, and he saw little of his father until he was 20. In the past five years his father has tried to develop a relationship with him, but Corey feels it is too late. "When I needed a father growing up, he wasn't there, and now it seems like I really don't need him anymore. It's kind of hard to forgive."

The question of whether or not to forgive their fathers for the divorce is a key issue for emerging adults from divorced families, and one that is not easy for them to resolve. Forgiving the father can seem like betraying the mother. Bob's parents divorced when he was nine. Every summer for the past 15 years he has gone to live with his father. But he still harbors anger toward his father for being unfaithful to his mother and for leaving them both, and he is reluctant to relinquish this anger, despite his father's entreaties. "He has kind of reached the point where he thought, well, I should have totally forgiven and totally forgotten all this. But I couldn't do that and I told him as much, and we had severe fights about it because I could not just completely block that out. I really believe when that sort of thing happens, you should forgive, but not forget, because forgetting is stupid."

Some emerging adults are more open to reconciliation with their fathers but find it difficult to recover the lost years. Cleo was just three when her parents divorced, and she did not see her father from age five to 18. He was "a drug addict, and he sold drugs. He was a basic idiot. He was a loser, and my mom didn't want me around him." Now that she has reached emerging adulthood she has begun to see her father again, and they have grown quite close, although both mourn the years they have lost. "He'll feel bad about it, and he'll be like, 'Why didn't your mom let me see you?' I told him, 'You'd lie to me. You wouldn't come through on things, and my mom was sick of me being disappointed. So I couldn't see you. But I loved you every day. I thought of you every day.' He may not have been there physically, but his spirit was there." Despite the sadness of growing up without her father, Cleo understands and supports her mother's decision to cut off contact. "If I had kids and that was the situation, I'd do the absolute same thing."

Not all emerging adults have experienced a fading relationship with their fathers after their parents divorced. For some, the mandatory time together in their weekly visits resulted in more time actually talking and doing things together than when the father was still at home. Leah said, "Actually, I became closer to my father afterwards because, it's ironic, but I spent more time with him after they got divorced than when he was living in our house." Calvin echoed Leah's comments: "I actually saw my father more when they were divorced. I spent the whole weekend with him so I saw him more." Other emerging adults with divorced parents lived with their fathers rather than their mothers after the divorce, and now feel closer to their fathers. Still others had difficult relationships with their fathers after the divorce but managed to reconcile with them in emerging adulthood. Nevertheless, the most common pattern is that emerging adults with divorced parents recall the divorce as a crucial turning point—for the worse—in their relationship with their father, and in emerging adulthood they continue to feel ambivalent.

Positive Legacies: Divorce as Relief

Divorce may be a tragedy when placed next to the ideal of a happy, stable family, but it looks quite different when the alternative is a household full of chaos and conflict. It is the latter that typically precedes divorce; after all, if the parents were happy with each other they would not be divorcing. In the months or perhaps years preceding most divorces, the parents' unhappiness with each other is often displayed vividly before their children in frequent battles, which the children respond to with anguish and distress as they find themselves unable to stop the fights and unable to escape them.

When this is the case, the parents' divorce may come as a relief to their children, because the daily fighting in the household finally comes to an end. Chalantra, whose parents divorced when she was 11, recalled that "I was very happy. Because I got tired of the noise waking me up every day, and I am the type of person that'll cry and get emotional, so me and my brother would hide in the closet together until they stopped fussing. So I was happy they got divorced." Like Chalantra, Christy was fed up with years of fighting by the time her parents divorced. "They had been fighting for 20 years and it was just a relief to get it off. In fact, when my mother said, 'Your dad and I are splitting up,' all I said was 'Good,' and that's the last thing I said about it." Similarly, Tammy recalled, "My parents divorced when I was 12, and up to that point, it was kind of a 'stay out of the way of flying objects' kind of thing. It was horrible, pretty much. I really am glad they got divorced, because they were just killing each other, they really were."

Sometimes, when their parents' divorce does not take place until after they have left home, emerging adults are able simply to shrug it off as something that is more their parents' business than their own. Barry, whose parents divorced when he was 18, said, "I guess I was happy for them, because I think they were happier people. And I was gone by that time, so its effects on me I think are subtle. I think there may be nostalgia for the way things were or a sense of loss in a way, but I don't feel traumatized or anything like that." Keith also took it in stride. "I thought it was a good thing. I wasn't really spending a lot of time at home, so when they were apart it really didn't make any difference to me either way. I'm just like, 'Okay, you do what you have to do.'"

But for some who experience their parents' divorce in emerging adulthood, the blend of thoughts and emotions that results is more complicated, more ambivalent. Allen's parents are in the process of divorcing after separating for the third time, and he views it with complex feelings—detachment, because he is no longer living with them, happiness, because he believes they will be happier apart, and wistfulness, because they will no longer be together: "It's very odd, you know 'cause I'm so far away from the whole situation. It's not in my face like it was before. And my dad, he's a lot happier, and I'm happy to see him happy, and I know my mom will be fine. So in that sense it's almost a relief in a way. It's just kind of twisted, 'cause you know, I want to see my parents together. I don't want to see my parents getting divorced, but I want to see them happy."

Doug experienced similar ambivalence when his parents announced their divorce just after he left for college: "I had just arrived at Stanford and I was like totally detached. It was my first time out of New England and I was so psyched to finally be at the college I wanted to be at, and meeting all these great people and doing these things. And so at first I was like, 'Gosh, you know, maybe if they're happy it's fine with me. I'm happy, so hopefully they can be happy.'" As his first semester went on, however, and his college experience became more stressful, he regretted not having his former family home to go back to. "I came home for Christmas and I needed to take some time off and needed my parents to be together, like, I would really have liked them to be on some kind of united front. They were both going through a lot of difficulties. And so when my life like kind of fell apart for a second there, it really hurt. You know, it was too bad they weren't together."

In sum, parents' divorce can leave a positive legacy in the lives of emerging adults, in the sense that many of them feel it was a relief from the alternative of living in an unhappy household where conflict or the threat of conflict was a constant presence. Also, the more they come to see their parents as persons, the better they understand and accept that their parents would wish to leave an unhappy marriage, and the more they support their parents' wishes to pursue happiness by dissolving the marriage. Nevertheless, for some emerging adults there remains a sense of loss, a certain ambivalence, as they reflect that even after they have reached their twenties, left home, and established their own independent lives, there are times when it is "too bad they weren't together."

Out of the Frying Pan: The Multiple Legacies of Remarriage

As complex as the legacy of divorce is, for most children it is not the end of the changes in their family situation. Most people who divorce remarry,[60] so most children who experience their parents' divorce also experience the remarriage of one or both parents. For emerging adults from divorced families, this means their current relationships with their parents are affected not only by the lingering legacy of divorce but often by the enduring complexities that result from remarriage.

Like divorce, parents' remarriage is correlated with a variety of negative outcomes for children and adolescents, including depression, anxiety, poor school performance, and conduct problems.[61] However, like divorce, parents' remarriage happens to many children, and they respond in a variety of ways. Some emerging adults describe their parents' remarriage with pure enthusiasm and approbation, and their stepparent as someone they like and value. Theresa said, "My stepfather is wonderful. I'm probably closer to him than I am my father." Rachel said her father's remarriage "has actually been probably the best thing for him. And it helped me a lot, too, because during that time, I was living in his house when he got married. Since Dad was really strict, [my stepmother] made it a lot easier. She could be kind of like a go-between. Everybody got along a little bit easier." Tory's mother remarried when he was 17, and he says of her new husband, "He's great. He's probably the best thing that's happened to her. He's really nice." His own relationship with his stepfather is described with similar enthusiasm. "I love him. He's a great guy. I mean, it's more like a friend, not really a stepfather. I talk to him about everything. And he knows that he's more than welcome to come over or call me or whatever."

More commonly, however, relationships between stepparents and stepchildren are fraught with difficulty and bad feelings.[62] For a variety of reasons, the deck is stacked against the likelihood of a happy relationship between them. The stepparent may be viewed as a usurper, taking the place that rightfully belongs to the displaced parent. This is especially likely if the stepparent had an affair with the parent prior to the divorce. Also, the remarriage brings to an abrupt end any fantasies the children may have harbored that their parents would reunite.

There is also the blunt fact that the decision to marry the stepparent is made by the parent, not by the children. Presumably, the parent chooses the stepparent because they love each other and get along reasonably well, but the children come along for the ride without ever signing up for it, whether they want to or not. Doug put it succinctly: "There's people that you get along with and there's people that you don't, and my dad just happened to marry somebody I don't get along with." Stepparents may, in turn, view their stepchildren as an annoyance, an unavoidable but regrettable part of marrying their new spouse.

But by far the biggest issue of contention between stepparents and stepchildren is the extent of the stepparent's legitimate authority.[63] Stepparents, especially stepfathers, often feel compelled to take a role of authority in the household, setting and enforcing rules, and exercising discipline just as they would if they were a "real" parent. However, with no history of mutual affection and attachment between the stepparent and the children, and with possible resentment and dislike for the reasons just described, stepparents' attempts at exercising authority are often fiercely resisted by their stepchildren, especially if they enter the household when the children are in or near adolescence. Terry, whose mother remarried when she was 12, recalled that during her teen years, "when I'd get in trouble, he'd yell at me and I'd get mad, like, 'You're not my dad,' you know." Joel said that when he was 14 years old and his stepfather moved in, "he set down a bunch of stupid rules. I had to be home before dark if I went to a friend's house. I couldn't go out with my friends unless it was a weekend." The result was a kind of cold war within the household. "He would say something to me and I'd ignore him because I felt he didn't have the right to tell me what to do." Leanne had difficulty accepting her stepfather's entry into the household when she was 10 years old—"it had just been me and mom all that time and I didn't like somebody else coming in"—and resisted his attempts to assert authority: "For a while he tried, I always call it 'tried to be my dad,' you know, but it wasn't in a good way, it was in a bad way. I felt like he was trying to boss me around or something, and I didn't feel he had any right to. So I guess right from the beginning, as soon as he started acting like that, we just never really got along. We kind of avoided each other as much as possible."

The silver lining in the generally dismal relations between stepparents and stepchildren is that things often improve once the children reach emerging adulthood. Just as with their parents, emerging adults often get along better with their stepparents once they no longer live with them and no longer have to rub shoulders with them on a daily basis. And just as with their parents, as emerging adults mature they often come to see their stepparents in a different light, as persons rather than merely as stepparents. Sheila said that when her mother first married her stepfather, "I resented him because he tried to be my father and he wasn't. But now, I love him." Eventually, his patient good will won her over. "I was a terrible teenager. I was absolutely terrible, and he loved me and stood by me no matter what. Yeah, we've had our fights, you know, the 'I hate you' kind of thing, but he's loved me and supported me through everything, regardless of whether it was right or wrong. So we're very close."

Lillian recalled that in the years following her mother's remarriage when she was nine years old, she and her stepfather were in constant conflict. "It was a hard time. Boy, we did not get along well at all, and it was very stressful for my mom and for me. I didn't like him very well for a long time." She deeply resented the new rules he and her mom laid down for her and her brother. "They were very, very strict. I mean, we couldn't have sleepovers. There were very set curfews. I had a bedtime of 10:00 even when I was in high school." But now, from the perspective of her twenties, she sees things much differently. "It's all worked out very well now. I very much appreciate everything they did. But I was horrible in high school to them, and I apologize all the time. But they never missed a basketball game or a volleyball game or anything I ever did. They were always there, which I look on now and think, 'Wow. That's really amazing.'" Her view of her stepfather has changed dramatically from adolescence to emerging adulthood. "He's a very wonderful man. He always has been, but we just didn't appreciate him. But I think that would be the same for any kid. Really, I don't know that you appreciate your parents until you're older and can look back and think, 'Wow. They were pretty incredible.'"

Conclusion: The Enduring Importance of Parents

Becoming independent from parents is a key transition for emerging adults in American society. The process begins in adolescence, but it accelerates during emerging adulthood. When they move out of the household, emerging adults experience a dramatic shift in the balance of power in their relationship with their parents. No longer do they inevitably see their parents every day. No longer do their parents know the details of their daily lives—what they eat, what they wear, how much they spend, how much they drink, and so on. Instead, they can see their parents as much, or as little, as they wish. They can tell their parents as much, or as little, about their lives as they wish them to know. As a result, typically they get along with their parents much better than they did before moving out. What their parents do not know cannot become a source of contention.

Although emerging adults are more independent than they were as adolescents, in some ways they become closer to their parents. The hierarchy of parent as authority figure, child as dependent and subordinate, fades away. What remains, in most cases, is the mutual affection and attachment they have for one another on the basis of many years of shared experience. They learn to see each other as persons, as individuals, rather than being defined for each other strictly by their roles as parent and child. They talk about a wider range of subjects than they did before, and more openly, more as friends. Still, there is a limit to their openness, and a limit to the extent that their transformed relationship is like a friendship. One of the reasons they get along better is that emerging adults edit their lives when talking to parents, withholding information that might be a source of conflict, and parents learn not to inquire too much.

For those who have experienced their parents' divorce, emerging adulthood is a time for reassessing the legacy of that experience. Some move toward reconciliation with a parent from whom they have long been estranged. Some continue to feel bitter and resentful toward the parent they believe was in the wrong, usually the father. Some see their divorced parents or their stepparents in a new and more benevolent light, now that they have greater insight into human relationships than they did in childhood or adolescence. In any case, for emerging adults who have experienced their parents' divorce and remarriage, these changes have left an enduring mark that has helped to shape their personalities, their identities, and their own approach to intimate relationships. This is a topic we will return to in Chapter 5.

Whether their parents divorced or not, whether their family life growing up was happy or unhappy, whether they have stayed at home or moved away, for virtually all emerging adults their relationships with their parents remain emotionally charged. The nature of the emotions varies tremendously: Love, with roots all the way back to infancy and childhood. Gratitude, from a new perspective of appreciation they have gained in emerging adulthood. Acceptance, as they relate to their parents on a new, adult level. And darker emotions are present as well. Resentment, for how they believe their parents have failed them in one way or another. Disillusionment, when they come to realize in emerging adulthood that their parents have flaws that had been concealed from them. Wariness, as they strive to keep their parents from meddling in their lives. Even outright hatred, especially as the residue of a bitter divorce. Emerging adults' relationships with their parents may involve blends of any of these emotions, but together, the emotions are nearly always among the strongest they have for anyone in their lives. For better and worse, their parents have contributed mightily toward shaping the persons they have become in emerging adulthood.

Chapter 4

Love and Sex

New Freedoms, New Problems

Consider this letter, which appeared in a widely read advice column: "Two years ago, I met the most wonderful guy in the world. We are both in college and plan to marry. 'Darryl' is saving up for my engagement ring. The problem is, he is my first and only boyfriend. All my dating experience has been with him. My friends and family members have said, 'Don't marry the first guy you date. You need to have fun and get more experience.' They ask, 'How do you know it is love when you have nothing to compare it with?'"

The letter goes on, but this much is enough to illustrate that the expectation for emerging adults today is that they will have a number of love partners in their late teens and early twenties before settling on someone to marry. With marriage delayed for most people until at least their late twenties, the late teens and early twenties become a time for exploring their options, falling in and out of love with different people, and gaining sexual experience. They clarify for themselves what kind of person they would like to marry by having involvements with a variety of people and learning what they *do not* want in a relationship as well as what they want most.

In fact, as the letter suggests, finding a love partner in your teens and continuing in a relationship with that person through your early twenties, culminating in marriage, is now viewed as unhealthy, a mistake, a path likely to lead to trouble in the long run. Those who do not experiment with different partners are warned that they are limiting their options too narrowly by staying with one person, and that they will eventually wonder what they are missing, to the detriment of their marriage. Emerging adults believe that they *should* explore different love relationships, that such exploration is both normal and necessary in order to prepare for committing to a marriage partner. But most emerging adults don't need to be encouraged. They are eager for the opportunities that emerging adulthood provides for having a variety of love relationships.

Like emerging adulthood itself, the current norm of pursuing variety in love and sex before settling down to marriage is a new phenomenon. Early in the twentieth century, the main pattern of middle-class courtship in American society was "calling."[1] A young man would call on a young woman, at her invitation, by visiting her at her home. There he would meet her family, and then the two young people would be allowed some time together, probably in the family parlor. They would talk, perhaps have some refreshments she had prepared for him, and she might play the piano. All of this seems innocuous enough, even superficial, but the underlying meaning of it was entirely serious. A young man did not call on just any girl, or on a variety of girls. Calling was considered a statement of serious intentions, potentially leading to marriage.

Needless to say, very little sex went on in that parlor. There was a strong taboo on premarital sexual relations. A young woman's virginity was her highly prized "jewel," a "treasure" that she would bestow on her beloved only on her marriage night.[2] The pressure on men to remain chaste until marriage was not as intense, and some men had premarital sex with a prostitute or with a woman who did not observe the taboos. Nevertheless, for both young women and young men, courtship was tightly structured through the custom of calling, and sexuality was restricted until marriage.

Norms changed dramatically in the 1920s, as calling declined and dating arose.[3] In contrast to calling, dating meant *going out* to take part in a shared activity. This moved the location of courtship out of the home and into the public arena—restaurants, theaters, dance halls, and so on. It also removed the young couple from the watchful eyes of the girl's family and gave them opportunities for sexual experimentation in the automobiles that were now widely available. The 1920s are sometimes called a period of "the first sexual revolution" because the strict taboo against premarital sexual activity faded and it became acceptable to engage in necking and petting before marriage. However, sexual explorations were supposed to stop short of intercourse, and usually did.

From the 1920s to the 1960s, the norm continued to be dating and sexual play up to intercourse. The most notable change during this period was that the age of marriage declined. For men, the median marriage age declined from 24.6 in 1920 to 22.8 in 1960; for women, from 21.2 in 1920 to 20.3 in 1960.[4] As a consequence of the drop in the age of marriage, dating became more serious at an earlier age. By the 1950s, it was not uncommon for young people to become engaged in high school and marry shortly after graduating.

For the increasing proportion of young people who attended college, the campus became the setting not only for education but for finding a mate. Few young people remained unmarried past their early twenties. Although premarital intercourse became somewhat more common—about 40% of college students at mid-century reported having sexual intercourse at least once[5]— the majority of young people continued to save intercourse for marriage.

The period that set the stage for love and sex as emerging adults experience it today was the 1960s and 1970s. Dating became much less formal as distinctions in gender roles came under fire by the Women's Movement, and the traditional dating pattern—where the young man asks the young woman out, chooses the event, and pays for everything—began to be viewed as sexist. A new Sexual Revolution took place, and previous restrictions on sexual activity before marriage now seemed repressive and unhealthy. The invention of the birth control pill made it easier for young women to have premarital sex without becoming pregnant.

By the mid-1970s, the proportion of American college students who reported having premarital sexual intercourse rose to 75%.[6] The median marriage age reversed its decline and began to rise, beginning a steady ascent that has continued into the twenty-first century.[7] With so many years—a decade or more—stretching between the time they first begin dating and the time they start thinking about marriage, few young people now give much thought to marriage in high school or even college. Instead, through their teens and early twenties they pursue a pattern of what sociologists call "serial monogamy"—a series of exclusive love relationships, usually including sex.

Although serial monogamy may be the norm for emerging adults today, marriage is the ultimate goal for virtually all of them. In a variety of studies, over 90% of emerging adults plan to marry eventually.[8] But "eventually" may be a year, five years, or even ten years or more down the line. Meanwhile, they gain experience through a variety of romantic and sexual relationships.

In this chapter we examine many aspects of love and sex in the lives of emerging adults. First, we look at the ways American emerging adults meet potential love partners. This includes a discussion of the role that ethnic background plays in love choices. Then we look at sexuality, including emerging adults' reflections on the age at which sexual activity becomes acceptable, their use (or not) of contraception, the threat of sexually transmitted infections (STIs), and uses of pornography. Finally, we explore the experiences of emerging adults who are gay or lesbian.

Meeting Someone

Emerging adults meet potential love partners in a wide variety of ways: through friends and relatives, at bars, parties and church functions, in the workplace, or on the Internet.[9] School is an especially fertile setting for love. Colleges and universities place young people of similar ages in close proximity on a daily basis, which gives them plenty of opportunities to meet, get to know each other, and arrange to see each other later. Many emerging adults met their current love partner in college or graduate school—at parties, in dormitories, or in classes. Perry's experience is a little unusual, but nevertheless provides a good illustration: "To tell you the truth, we met in a graveyard. It was during what we called 'the summer field exercise' with the geography department. I was on the same team as her, and we were looking at the cultural geography of the area by looking at names on tombstones."

Once they are out of school, meeting someone becomes a little more challenging for emerging adults now that they are no longer in a setting where there is a concentration of other people their age. But most of them manage, one way or another. Friends, family members, or coworkers introduce them to someone. They keep their eyes out: Tracy met her boyfriend when "I was driving down the street and he was the passenger in the car next to me. He asked me to pull over and I did." They go to bars and nightclubs—most bars and nightclubs are filled mainly with people who are young and single, looking for love or something like it. However, emerging adults tend to regard the people they meet in these settings as potential partners for flirtation and perhaps casual sex rather than as potential love partners.[10]

Most of the ways that emerging adults meet someone have been around for a long time. School, friends, work, and family have long been sources of connections to potential love partners. One relatively new method is through the Internet. According to a 2009 survey, 22% of couples who began their relationship during 2007–2009 met through the Internet, up from 3% just a decade earlier.[11] Because emerging adults spend so much time connected to technology, sometimes an opportunity comes across the screen. Katy met her current boyfriend when "we started talking through e-mail. We chatted back and forth for about a week, and finally said 'we've got to meet.'" Ian met his girlfriend in a similar fashion: "I was fiddling around on the computer and I got on the Internet and met her. And I drove up just to meet her. There was a whole bunch of people that I'd talked to on the Internet and that she'd talked to and we were all going to meet. The rest of them couldn't make it, and I'm like 'Well, I can still make it.' So I went up. The wonders of technology!"

Some emerging adults like Ian meet potential dating partners just in the course of "fiddling around" on the Internet, but in recent years there has been a boom in Internet dating services. The most popular Internet dating websites have tens of millions of subscribers and are adding tens of thousands more every week.[12] There are also sites designed for specific groups, such as Asian Americans, Catholics, Jews, and gays and lesbians. Some sites are free, but most charge a monthly fee. Subscribers provide personal information such as educational background, leisure activities, and what they are most looking for in a partner. Some sites require applicants to take a personality test. Most have the option of including a photo. The site's computer then matches the subscriber up with persons who have similar characteristics, and the dating adventures begin.

Does this work any better than the old-fashioned ways of meeting? Certainly Internet dating services provide emerging adults with an easy way to meet new people. However, although the technology is different, the basic idea behind Internet dating is not really new. Internet dating services offer little more than a high-tech personal ad, with all the advantages and liabilities of personal ads: yes, it's a way to meet more potential love partners than you are likely to meet in the course of everyday life, but chances are high that you will meet a lot more frogs than princes or princesses, however royal they may have appeared in their web self-description. Even with photo (and personality test) included, most people are likely to make themselves appear a lot more appealing and wart-free in cyberspace than they are in real life, so the great majority of meetings through Internet dating services are likely to begin with great expectations and end in disappointment.[13] Nevertheless, the fact that 22% of new relationships now begin through the Internet indicates that many people find romantic success through this method, even if it may take them many attempts.

Another recent change in emerging adult dating patterns is that young women are more likely to take the initiative, to do the "asking out." In the old days of "calling," women did the asking; a man would have been seen as rude and unmannerly if he asked to call on her. When calling declined and dating arose, men became the initiators—they did the asking, arranging, and paying. A woman could not ask a man out without appearing too aggressive, too "forward," potentially "loose."

Most of the onus is still on boys and men to do the asking, arranging, and paying, but the rules are not as rigid as they used to be.[14] It is no longer frowned upon for young women to do the initiating, so many of them do. Kay met her husband at a dance, where "we started dancing and we just danced the rest of the night, and I got his phone number and I called him the next day, and the rest is history." Brock recalled that he met his girlfriend when "I had her in a class and she came up during class and asked me out." Corey and his girlfriend met at the liquor store where he worked. "She used to come in and flirt with me a lot, and I'd flirt back with her, and a lot of times she'd ask me to go out and finally I decided to go ahead and go."

Another way the rules of courtship have become less rigid for the current generation of emerging adults is that often young men and women become friends first, then gradually move toward love.[15] They may not even "date," per se, but just do things together, perhaps as part of a group of friends, and gradually become intimately involved. For example, Mandy and her boyfriend "started doing stuff together just on a friendship basis, going to church and having dinner and stuff like that. And then eventually it became more."

Becoming Partners

After they meet, what is it that leads two emerging adults to fall in love? Sexual attraction is certainly at the heart of it.[16] Even when emerging adults such as Mandy have been friends with their love partner for a long time before dating, they usually say they were attracted to their partner from the beginning.

Beyond sexual attraction, similarity between the two partners often forms the basis for love.[17] Opposites rarely attract; on the contrary, birds of a feather flock together. A long line of sociological studies has established that emerging adults, like people of other ages, tend to have romantic relationships with people who are similar to them in characteristics such as personality, intelligence, social class, ethnic background, religious beliefs, and physical attractiveness.[18] Sociologists attribute this to what they call *consensual validation,* which means that people like to find in others a match, or *consensus,* with their own characteristics. Finding this consensus reaffirms, or *validates,* their own way of looking at the world. The more similar your love partner is to you, the more likely you are to reaffirm each other, and the less likely you are to have conflicts that spring from having different views and preferences.[19]

Similarity also brings potential love partners together in settings that give them the opportunity to meet and initiate a relationship. Students taking the same class may have a common interest in the subject that reflects other common interests as well. Emerging adults attending the same church or temple or mosque are probably similar in their religious views. There were numerous examples in our interviews of this kind of similarity bringing two emerging adults together. For example, Charles (who was profiled in Chapter 2) met his girlfriend at a singing showcase in which they both competed, reflecting their common interest in music. Arthur, who is Chinese American, met his girlfriend in a class on Asian American films. He confessed that his motivation for taking the class "was not purely educational!"—that is, he'd taken it for the purpose of meeting girls with an ethnic background similar to his own.

Similarity of ethnic background is one of the most influential determinants of whether two emerging adults will become involved. The long, troubled history of race relations in the United States continues to cast its shadow on this generation of emerging adults. Up until fairly recently, marriages between persons of different racial backgrounds were actually forbidden by law in many states. It was only in 1967 that the Supreme Court ruled that such laws were unconstitutional, forcing 16 states to rescind them.

In some respects, the United States has come a long way since those days. The number of interethnic marriages has surged over the past half century.[20] It is no longer unusual to see interethnic couples on the streets of most American cities. About 15% percent of new marriages in the United States are now between partners of different ethnic groups, up from just 7% in 1980. However, there is substantial diversity among ethnic groups in their rates of intermarriage. Native Americans have the highest rate of marrying outside their ethnic group, at slightly over 50%. Asian Americans are next highest, at about 28%, followed by Latinos at 26%, African Americans at 17%, and Whites at 9%.

Despite the increase in interethnic marriages, for the most part, people still choose love partners from within their own ethnic group. One reason for this is that emerging adults often find love partners from their social circle, and their social circle usually consists mainly of people from their own ethnic group. Figure 4.1 shows that in my original study of 300 emerging adults, a majority in all four major ethnic groups said that "all" or "most" of their friends come from their own ethnic group.

This corresponded to their choices in dating partners, as Figure 4.2 shows: for all ethnic groups except Asian Americans, a majority of emerging adults said that "all" or "most" of their dating partners come from their own ethnic group. Notice how these findings on dating partners match the patterns from national statistics on interethnic marriage, with Asian Americans most likely to find partners outside their ethnic group, Whites least likely, and African Americans and Latinos in-between.

Latisha, a 20-year-old African American, described her ethnic pool of friends and romantic partners like this: "If I met a really nice guy that wasn't [Black] I wouldn't like shun him or anything. I guess I just [date Black men] because those are the people that seem to be around, like if I go to a party, those are the kind of people that I meet. So it just kind of happens like that." Just as emerging adults with a particular interest in music, religion, or the outdoors are likely to seek out groups of other people with similar interests and may find love partners from within those groups, so emerging adults with a common ethnic background tend to form groups of friends and then find their love partners within those groups.

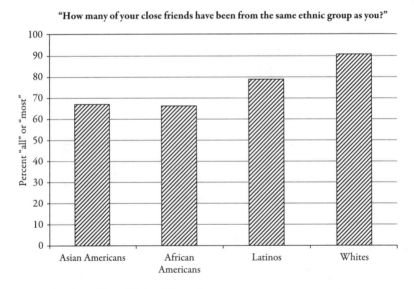

Figure 4.1 Friendships Within Ethnic Groups.

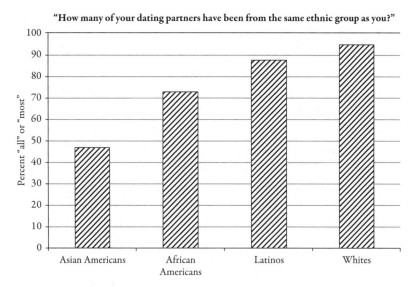

Figure 4.2 Dating Partners Within Ethnic Groups.

A second reason for finding a love partner within one's own ethnic group arises from an awareness of cultural differences between ethnic groups and a feeling of being more comfortable with what is familiar. Rhonda, who is African American, said she prefers to date African American men "because we have the same background and the same ideas and goals. It's not that I have anything against people who are not African American, but we tend to have the same outlook on things. And it's easier to communicate with someone who you're in sync with." Arthur, the Chinese American who met his girlfriend in a college class on Asian American films, said he prefers Chinese women because "I want to be with someone who can understand me without me having to go through an entire explanation of why I think that way about a certain thing. Without having to educate them. I feel like I do that enough with just people at large, and I don't want to do that with the person I'm going to spend the rest of my life with." Emerging adults with immigrant parents also usually believe their parents will be more comfortable with someone within their ethnic group, especially if their parents speak limited English.

Racism stops some from dating and marrying outside their ethnic group. No emerging adults admitted to such views themselves, but many of them freely admitted that their parents had made their prejudices clear in conveying to them that they should not marry outside their ethnic group. Sophie, who is Chinese American, said her parents had explicitly told her "this is the order: Chinese American, Chinese, and then any Asian, and then White, but I don't think they would want me to marry an African American or Hispanic person. *[They wouldn't? Why is that?]* Because of what they see in the media—how they're always in trouble, how it seems like whoever's getting arrested is African American or Hispanic." Cleo, who is African American, said that if she became involved with a White man her mother would "flip her lid" and her father "would disown me." Becky, who is White, said she had once dated an African American, a "wonderful man" with whom she "just clicked and everything was there." But when she told her mother about him, "my mom said, 'Now don't you go liking him.' Because he was Black! I mean, she was being a racist saying that. I said, 'Mom I can't believe you!'" Becky's relationship with him did not last long, in part because of her mother's opposition.

This finding is supported by other studies showing that young Americans are much more accepting of interracial marriage than older Americans are. For example, in one national study, 85% of 18–29-year-olds said they would have no objection to a family member marrying someone of a different ethnic background.[21] As shown in Figure 4.3, the percentage who were accepting of intermarriage declined steadily with age, to just 38% for persons age 65 and over. Emerging adults generally believe it is the qualities of the person that matter most, not their ethnic background. For example, Leonard, a 20-year-old African American, said that to him a prospective love partner's ethnic background "doesn't matter.... It's the person, the heart, not the skin color. I mean, everybody's human." Amelia, a White 22-year-old, summed it up this way: "If

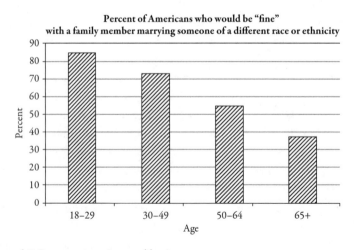

Figure 4.3 Intermarriage Approval by Age.
Source: Wang (2012).

I really loved someone it wouldn't bother me. I mean, I think I realize that it might make my life harder in some ways because not all people are accepting of, you know, that type of thing. But I also think in order to overcome that type of thinking in our society we need to get beyond that, and if I really want to do something I'm not gonna think, 'Well, this might make my life hard so I'm not gonna marry someone who I love and think is a great person."

Sex: New Freedoms, New Problems

The Sexual Revolution of the 1960s and 1970s demolished what was left of the long-standing expectation that young women would remain virgins until marriage. That expectation had been under pressure since the earlier sexual revolution of the 1920s, when some degree of sexual play before marriage became common. But between the two sexual revolutions, sexual intercourse remained the boundary that young people, especially young women, were not supposed to cross. Young lovers learned to enjoy each other within what the novelist John Updike described as the "large and not laughable sexual territory...within the borders of virginity, where physical parts were fed to the partner a few at a time, beginning with the lips and hands."[22]

Since the 1960s, virginity until marriage has ceased to exist as an ideal for most emerging adults.[23] Angela reflected the norms of her generation and her times when she observed, "I mean, I don't know anybody who waits for marriage anymore. I think that's probably gone out of style." According to various national surveys, over 80% of 18–23-year-olds have had sexual intercourse, and about 95% of Americans in our time have their first experience of sexual intercourse before marriage.[24] Although only 15% of American adults believe it is acceptable for two 16-year-olds to have premarital sex, a majority (55%) believe it is acceptable if the hypothetical partners are 18 years old.[25]

We can see how American society has become more liberal in its views on premarital sex by looking at changes in the policies of American colleges.[26] Until the late 1960s, college officials were expected to act *in loco parentis*, "in place of parents." This meant monitoring students closely, especially female students, and enforcing rules that discouraged sexual activity. The rules included nightly curfews in women's dormitories. Repeated violations might prompt a letter from college officials to parents, or the threat of expulsion from the school. Even during daylight hours, most colleges allowed no young men in the women's dormitories. Those that did stipulated that the young woman's door must remain open at all times while she had a male visitor.

Today's emerging adults would find it hard to imagine such restrictions on their social and sexual behavior. They are intent on making their own decisions without adult interference, including decisions about their sexual behavior. Nor would today's adults wish to play the role of enforcing restrictions on emerging adults' sexual behavior, as adults did in the past. They, too, believe that by the time young people reach their late teens and early twenties they deserve a wide scope of personal autonomy that adults have no right to infringe upon.

The old rule about remaining a virgin until marriage is passé, but it's unclear exactly what the new rules are. It's OK to have sex before marriage, but at what age does it become OK to begin? It's OK to have partners other than your future spouse, but how many partners? There are no clear guidelines in American society for answering these questions, so young people must muddle their way to the answers as best they can.

Despite headlines about a supposed "hook-up culture" among today's young people, most of them are not sexual adventurers. In a national study of 18–23 year-olds, the most common pattern, reported by close to half, was one sexual partner in the past year.[27] Some, about one-third, had two or more partners during that time, but one-fourth had no sexual relations at all in the past year. These variations reflect the volatility of relationships during the emerging adult years. Most sexual activity takes place between committed partners, but relationships tend to be short, and at any given point there is a substantial proportion of emerging adults who do not have a partner. Those who currently have no romantic partnership either have no sex at all or occasional sex with a temporary partner.

"Hooking up"—meaning sexual relations between two people who are not involved in a romantic partnership—is most common between exes, who *used to be* romantically involved.[28] They know each other well, they once loved (or at least liked) each other, and they are attracted to each other, so it's easy to slip back into bed together occasionally, especially if neither has yet moved on to another relationship.

When hooking up with a casual partner does take place, it is often fueled by alcohol. Use of alcohol, including "binge drinking" (five or more drinks in a row for a man, four or more drinks in a row for a woman), peaks in the early twenties. Not coincidentally, this is when casual sex episodes peak as well. In various studies, from one-fourth to one-half of emerging adults report having consumed alcohol before their most recent sexual encounter, and emerging adults who drink often are more likely than others to have had multiple sexual partners.[29]

One variation on hooking up is a "friends with benefits" relationship, in which partners have sex on a regular basis but are not romantically involved.[30] These relationships usually prove to be complicated before long.[31] Partners typically avoid talking about the relationship, which leads to uncertainty and misunderstandings. One partner may assume that the relationship is monogamous, whereas the other may not. One partner, but not the other, may be expecting or at least hoping that a romantic relationship will develop. Partners are often unclear about what to call the relationship, how to maintain it, and the future of the relationship, and they are often concerned that their sexual involvement risks their friendship.

Despite greater gender equality today, views of sex in emerging adulthood remain somewhat different for men than for women. For example, in a national survey of unmarried 20–29 year-olds, 65% of men but only 41% of women agreed that there are people they would have sex with even though they have no interest in marrying them.[32] Similarly, in the national Clark poll, 52% of young men ages 18–29 agreed that "[i]t is OK for two people to have sex even if they are not emotionally involved with each other," compared to just 33% of young women.[33] Both men and women seek a soul mate in marriage, almost unanimously, but prior to marriage young men often have a more recreational attitude toward sex, whereas young women are more likely to enjoy sex if it is in the context of an emotionally intimate relationship. Jessica, now engaged, looked back at her previous relationships and observed, "Maybe it's my Catholic roots, but the sex I could have done without. It wasn't until finding a man I truly loved and trusted that I felt comfortable enough to learn about myself physically." Of course, some women also have a recreational attitude toward sex in emerging adulthood, but in general they are more likely than men to prefer the combination of love and sex.

How Young Is Too Young?

The question about when it becomes acceptable for young people to have their first sexual intercourse is especially problematic. As noted, only 15% of American adults believe that premarital sex is OK for 16-year-olds, but if the partners in question are 18, that proportion rises to 55%.[34] This seems nonsensical at first glance. How could just two years make such a difference in the acceptability of premarital sex? But a lot happens during those two years for most young people. Perhaps the majority of American adults have an intuitive sense that most 16-year-olds would not be ready to handle sex, psychologically and socially, whereas most 18-year-olds would be. To put it another way, most American adults recognize that adolescents are different, developmentally, from emerging adults. And sex is something that emerging adults are ready for, but adolescents are not.

This conclusion matches the personal accounts of emerging adults in my original study, when they recalled their first experience of sexual intercourse. Most of them had sex for the first time when they were adolescents, from age 14 to 17. This is consistent with other studies. According to the Centers for Disease Control (CDC), the median age of first sexual intercourse in the United States is 17.1.[35] However, over 70% of the emerging adults in my original study now believed that their first intercourse had taken place when they were "too young."

Their feeling of being too young that first time is due to a belief that premarital sex is "wrong" for adolescents, not so much in a moral or religious sense as in a psychological sense. Many emerging adults regret their teenage premarital sex because they realize now that they were too immature at the time to appreciate the significance of what they were doing. Emerging adults do not believe that in adolescence they were capable of making such a profound decision wisely. Learning to make independent decisions is something they view as an important part of becoming an adult, and when they look back to adolescence they shake their heads at what they now see as foolish sexual decisions. Mindy had sex for the first time at age 14, and at 25 feels that was "way too young." The basis of her decision to have sex seems immature to her now. "I was just curious, and I don't think that's why you should do it. I was just too young to make that decision."

Some see their unreadiness for making the decision to have sex reflected in their failure to appreciate the possibility of pregnancy and the necessity of contraception. Leah, who had sex for the first time at age 17, now recalls: "I wasn't even in tune with my own body, you know, and I was terrified. It didn't hit me until afterwards, then 'Oh my God! What if I get pregnant?' That never even crossed my mind. I was just young and stupid." Similarly, Jean, who also had sex for the first time at age 17, says now: "I think I was probably too young because I didn't prepare for it the first time. It was with my first boyfriend and I don't think I was making logical decisions at that time in my life." Larry had a similar view, from a male perspective, of his first sex at age 15: "It was too young for me, I think. I mean, you tell yourself you know what you're doing, but you don't. You know, you're not mentally ready for all the implications, like what if she got pregnant? You'd be like 'Oh my God, I'm 15 years old, and she wants to keep it!' "

In contrast, the emerging adults who have no regrets about their first sex tend to recall themselves as making the decision at a later age and in a more mature, careful manner. When Martin and his girlfriend had sex for the first time at age 18, they decided on it together and bought condoms so they would be well prepared. "It was a very rational decision, because my girlfriend and I had discussed it for about two or three weeks prior and we finally set it up."

Also important to having good memories of that first episode of intercourse is that it took place in the context of a loving relationship. For example, Gabriella said she had no regrets about her first partner at age 16 because "[h]e was a good guy and I really cared about him. I felt like I was old enough to handle it and I felt like he was the right person for it to be with." Similarly, Christy had sex for the first time at 17 and now believes that was "probably about the right age." Then she adds, "I don't think the age was so much the issue. I was in a relationship that was healthy and I was with someone that sex wasn't just sex. It was emotional, and that was really important to me." But age does matter, because the older people are when they have their first episode of intercourse, the more likely they are to make a careful decision about it. Although the majority of the emerging adults in my study believed they were too young when they had their first intercourse, no one who waited until age 18 or older expressed regrets.

Having their first intercourse within the context of a loving relationship is especially important to young women. In a national survey, one-half of women said their main reason for having intercourse the first time was love for their partner, compared to one-fourth of men.[36] For young men, including the emerging adults in my study, their first intercourse is more likely to be recalled as an adventure, a rite of passage. Rocky glowed with nostalgia as he described his first time: "On my 16th birthday. First day with my license. In my first car. That was a big day! A friend threw me a party and I walked in the room and a girl grabbed my hand. I had no idea who in the hell she was. I wasn't even there long enough to get drunk. It was more like, I walked in, people say 'Happy Birthday,' she grabs my hand and we go out to the car and drive off to have sex! It was a trip!"

Contrast this with the experience of Mindy, who had her first sexual intercourse at age 14 with a neighbor boy she knew but did not love. Because it was loveless she regretted it so much she became depressed. "I never felt like committing suicide, but I felt really bad about myself." She also swore off sex for years to come, because of the unpleasantness of the experience. "I hated it. I thought 'This is not what it is on TV. I don't want to do this anymore.' And I waited until after I was out of high school to even try sex again." These two experiences reflect the general patterns: studies indicate that boys generally respond to their first intercourse with feelings of excitement, pride, and happiness, while girls are usually more ambivalent, more likely to feel guilty, worried, and regretful.[37]

Some young people look back with regret on their teenage sex because they wish they had saved the first time for their true love, the special person they intend to spend the rest of their life with. Although the majority of emerging adults see no problem with nonmarital sex as long as the persons involved are mature enough and in love with each other, there are some who still maintain the traditional belief that sex should take place only in the context of marriage. This belief is nearly always grounded in religious principles. Most emerging adults believe that sexual intercourse is best reserved for a special relationship, but only those with conservative religious beliefs think the special relationship must be marriage.[38]

For example, Nate is "still a virgin" at 25 and says this is due to "my religious beliefs. I believe in commitment and that sex is a gift for marriage." Also, Nancy said, "I have a real strong feeling about not having sex until I'm married. It's because of my religious beliefs and my upbringing that I feel that way." Now 28, as she has passed through her twenties she has felt increasing pressure on her beliefs, from boyfriends as well as from society at large. "It's hard, it's really hard now. There was a time when it would be easier to say 'This is what I believe and this is how I'm going to lead my life,' and it wasn't as hard to follow through with it." However, she has a group of friends who share her beliefs and who have provided mutual support, and now she has a boyfriend who also values virginity before marriage. "Fortunately, I think I've found one of the few guys out there that shares the same belief and is the same age. It's been really refreshing to find someone who shares that belief because in at least a couple of my relationships that's been a problem." Not all emerging adults with conservative religious beliefs stay virgins until marriage, of course, but they are more likely to believe that virginity until marriage is an ideal worth striving for.[39]

Contraceptive Use, Some of the Time

Although virgins like Nate and Nancy still exist, they are now the rare exception rather than the norm. As noted earlier, about 95% of Americans in our time have their first experience of sexual intercourse before marriage. For most, their "first time" takes place in their late teens, a decade or more before they will enter marriage.

This has never happened before, ever, in any human society. You could say that young people today are part of a novel social experiment, living out the question, "What happens when you decouple sexuality from marriage?" Every human society has marriage as an adult institution that almost everyone joins, and until now marriage and sexuality have been closely connected. Young people of the past reached puberty later than they do now, because their nutrition was poorer and they had little or no medical care. They reached physical and sexual maturity in their late teens, and within two or three years they were ushered into marriage. In some cultures young men have had to wait longer, until they showed they could support a family economically, but girls have almost always been married by their late teens, until modern times in economically developed societies.[40]

Early marriage, shortly after reaching sexual maturity, made practical sense for most of human history. Marrying early would make the most of a woman's reproductive years, which was important because, given high rates of infant and child mortality, she would need to have six or eight children in order for even two or three of them to be likely to survive to adulthood. Early marriage was also a way that cultures acknowledged that once young people reach sexual maturity they experience sexual desire, and marriage was necessary as a social arrangement for protecting and caring for the babies that would be conceived as a consequence of that desire.

But what happens to these traditional arrangements when technological advances make it possible for sexual activity to take place without babies as a result? We are in the process of finding out. In one sense, emerging adulthood is what happens. That is, once young people can have an active sex life without reproduction, they tend to wait until their late twenties or early thirties to get married and have their first child, all over the world, which opens up the late teens and most of the twenties for other purposes. Waiting until the late twenties or early thirties to take on the weighty responsibilities of marriage and parenthood means that the late teens and early to mid-twenties can be devoted to pursuing education, trying out different possible career paths, hanging out with friends, traveling, and other self-focused experiences.

Yet the social consequences of contraceptive technologies turn out to be not quite that simple. It's true that the invention of the Pill had an enormous impact on views of sexuality, on fertility rates, and on women's roles. You could argue persuasively that the Pill was a key instigator of both the Sexual Revolution and the Women's Movement. It is also true that the invention of the Pill is a key event in the rise of emerging adulthood as a new life stage in the late twentieth century.

Alas, having the capacity to use contraceptive technologies to avoid reproduction, even with an active sex life, and actually using those technologies effectively for this purpose, have turned out to be two quite different things. Among unmarried 18–23-year-old Americans, only 72% used any kind of contraception in their most recent experience of sexual intercourse, according to a national study.[41] More generally, only 51% say they use contraception "all the time," whereas 37% report using it "most" or "half" or "some of the time," and 12% "none of the time." In sum, half of the unmarried 18–23-year-olds who are sexually active are risking an unintended pregnancy.

So why don't they use contraception more consistently? There are lots of reasons, according to a wide range of studies.[42] For all the wonders of the Pill, many women have negative physical or emotional responses to its hormonal effects. Condoms are viewed as reducing sexual pleasure, especially by young men, and they may not be available when the mood strikes. Sex in emerging adulthood is more likely than adult sex to be unplanned and infrequent, and both these factors work against consistent contraceptive use. As noted, a substantial proportion of emerging adult sex takes place under the influence of alcohol, and that is not the best condition for taking the precautions necessary to avoid pregnancy.

These considerations apply across countries, but there is something distinctively American about this problem; more than emerging adults in other developed countries, young Americans fail to use contraception responsibly. Consequently, Americans have higher rates of both nonmarital births and abortions.[43] Figure 4.4 shows rates of abortion in a range of developed countries.

Why are unintended pregnancies relatively high in the United States? There may be many reasons, but one key reason seems to be the distinctly American ambivalence about nonmarital sex. If you look at other developed countries around the world, they fall into two broad categories on this topic: those that still strongly prohibit premarital sex (Japan, South Korea), and those that view premarital sex as normal, healthy, and acceptable (Europe, Canada, Australia, New Zealand).[44] Nonmarital pregnancies are rare in the

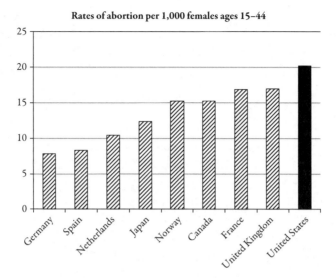

Rates of abortion per 1,000 females ages 15–44

Figure 4.4 Abortion Rates, Selected Developed Countries.
Source: UN data (2014).

first case because premarital sex is relatively rare (although it certainly happens and is more common now than in the past). Nonmarital pregnancies are rare in the second case because young people are taught even before they reach sexual maturity how to avoid them, and when they become sexually active contraception is routine, widely available, and free or inexpensive.

The United States is unique in taking the middle ground: Americans don't forbid premarital sex, but don't exactly accept it, either. Premarital sex is controversial and *morally contested* in the United States in a way that it is not in other developed countries. Our unique status on this issue is in turn related to our status as by far the most religious of the developed countries. Most of the opposition to premarital sex, including opposition to access to contraception, comes from highly religious Americans and from religious authorities.[45] So, the Catholic hierarchy in the United States fights bitterly against the government mandate that all healthcare plans must include contraceptive services, for married and unmarried persons alike. The conservative Protestant authorities encourage their young members to pledge never to have sex before marriage, exalting the value of remaining a virgin until the wedding night. Mormons and Orthodox Jews urge their young adherents to marry early, recognizing that the longer they wait, the more difficult it will be to maintain premarital chastity.

No other developed country has such diverse, well-organized, vehement opposition to premarital sex. It is true that the opponents of premarital sex remain a minority, even when all are added together. The majority accepts, or at least tolerates, premarital sex, as long as it takes place in the context of a loving relationship and does not begin too young.[46] But the minority is large and vocal, and believes deeply that premarital sex is wrong and should be prohibited.

With respect to preventing unwanted premarital pregnancies, then, young Americans have the worst of both worlds: on the one hand, most of them believe that there is nothing wrong with premarital sex between two loving partners, and once they reach emerging adulthood they expect that sex will be part of their romantic relationships.[47] But they are also aware that there are many in their society who oppose premarital sex and consider it a grave moral violation, perhaps including religious authorities they have been taught to respect, perhaps including their own parents. And they find their access to contraception restricted and impeded by these same opponents. Seen in this light, it is not surprising that nonmarital pregnancies are higher in the United States than in other developed countries.

Even in other developed countries, tens of thousands of unintended nonmarital conceptions take place every year. Enough is known by now about how to prevent unintended pregnancies so that from a purely scientific, technological standpoint the number could be, effectively, zero. Even when neither the Pill nor condoms nor other contraceptive options are used prior to sexual contact, there are now highly effective methods of "emergency contraception," or "the morning-after pill," that prevent implantation of a fertilized ovum. Yet large numbers of unintended pregnancies take place among emerging adults nevertheless, across developed countries.

Our social practices are running behind our technologies, in this respect. The decade-long gap between reaching sexual maturity and entering marriage is still new, historically, and we are still adapting to it, culturally. In the decades to come, further technological and cultural changes are sure to take place in this area. Contraceptive methods will become even easier to use and more effective than they are now, with few or no side effects. It is easy to imagine a world where effective means of contraception are used routinely from the beginning of each person's sexual experiences, and unintended pregnancies are virtually unknown. But we are a long way from that now, especially in the United States.

In any case, even if this were to come to pass, there would still be the problem of sexually transmitted infections, as we will see next.

The Specter of STIs

Because they are more independent of their parents than adolescents are, and because there is not as strong a social stigma against them having sex as there is for adolescents, emerging adults have less reason to be furtive and anxious about sex. Most of them passed through the awkwardness of their first experiences of intercourse during adolescence, and as emerging adults they are more comfortable with their sexuality, more knowledgeable about the emotional and physical experience of sex. Except for the deeply religious ones just described, they more or less assume that sex will be a part of any love relationship they become involved in.

However, one source of anxiety surrounding sex for emerging adults is the threat of sexually transmitted infections (STIs), especially HIV/AIDS. Sexual explorations take place for emerging adults under the specter of potentially becoming infected with a deadly virus for which there is no cure.

Today's emerging adults are not the first generation of young people to face such a grim threat. Syphilis carried a similar threat for centuries, until the development of penicillin in the 1940s, and syphilis is contracted much more easily than HIV. However, strict social codes against nonmarital sex made the prospect of syphilis remote for most people. In contrast, AIDS arose at a time when the taboo against nonmarital sex had faded, in the aftermath of the Sexual Revolution. Emerging adults today grow up in a society in which the normative expectation is that they will have a series of sexual relationships before marriage. But this freedom to engage in sexual explorations now collides with the terrible prospect of contracting a deadly disease.

Emerging adults respond to this situation in a variety of ways. Some view AIDS as a threat to other people but not themselves. Brady dismissed AIDS by remarking, "I don't know anybody who has it, so I don't really think about it." Jake said, "I'll admit that I never thought something like that would happen to me. That's not very smart, but I just never did." Casey said his reading had convinced him that "the odds of me getting AIDS from a woman are so incredibly remote. I can get AIDS from another man, and I can get AIDS from a needle. Those are two of the highly possible ways. So I think technically, doing what I do, the odds are incredibly low for me, anyway."

Some young men view AIDS as a legitimate danger, but accept that risk as the price of pursuing sexual pleasure. Benny admitted that although he is aware that unprotected sex leaves him at risk for AIDS, "I haven't been careful at all. I guess you could say I've been rolling the dice. It's kind of hard to say, but putting on a rubber is like turning on the cold water, you know, it just don't happen. And I want [sex] to happen enough that I would even blow off all the worries and scariness about it and end up doing the deal." Keith sometimes worries about AIDS, but the threat of it "hasn't stopped me. I've always been willing to suffer the consequences of my actions. If something like that ever came about, I mean, I'm sure I would be quite upset because I was going to die—who wouldn't be?—but all you can do is say 'Well, I got what I deserved. I took my chances and knew what the possibilities were. Tough luck.'"

Some emerging adults, however, say that fear of AIDS is the framework for their sexual consciousness, deeply affecting their attitudes about sex and the way they approach sex with potential partners. Bridget insisted her boyfriend get tested before she would have sex with him. "I was like 'we're not going to do it until we find out.'" He resisted, but eventually agreed when she held firm. "He had problems with it, but it was kind of like 'If you don't want to wear your raincoat, you can't play in the rain,' you know. So I was like, 'It's your choice, buddy.'" Sam took a similar view: "Today, you basically want the blood test before you go to bed with somebody." Gabriella asserted, "I don't think I would ever have unprotected sex, meaning without a condom. I've always known a lot about AIDS. I certainly wouldn't want to put my life in jeopardy for something like that." Bruce said his "awareness and consciousness" of AIDS is "really intense." A rock musician, he often has sexual opportunities when on the road that he passes up for fear of AIDS. "I don't want to roll the dice with somebody I don't even know."

Studies confirm that young people's sexual behavior has changed since the rise of AIDS. Use of condoms has increased sharply since the late 1980s among both high school and college students. According to the National Center for Health Statistics, reported condom use at last sex among 15–19 year-olds rose from 31% in 1988 to 55% in 2006–2008 among women, and from 53% in 1988 to 79% in 2006–2008 among men.[48]

Nevertheless, although many young people are quite responsible about their sexual behavior, a substantial proportion of them take at least occasional risks. As noted in the previous section, only about half of emerging adults say they use contraception of any kind consistently. An opportunity comes along, the mood is right—often enhanced by alcohol—and they take their chances. Communication about contraceptive use tends to be limited or nonexistent among emerging adults, until they have a committed relationship, which may not happen until sex has been occurring for some time—or may not happen at all.[49] They are sometimes inhibited from talking about contraception by embarrassment, or by fear that doing so will break the mood. It may seem ironic that two people could be unembarrassed enough to have sex with each other yet too embarrassed to talk about contraception, but that is often the way it is between emerging adults.

Few emerging adults match Bridget and Sam in requiring a clean blood test from their partner before having sex. The typical pattern is for a couple to use condoms in the early phase of a relationship, then switch to reliance on birth control pills after a few months.[50] The transition to birth control pills is not inspired by any mutual certainty that neither has HIV or any other STI, or even by a conversation about STIs, but simply by knowing each other better and trusting each other more. As their relationship develops and they become more committed to each other, they each decide that their partner is "not the kind of person" who would have HIV. Wilson put it this way: "I've had a girlfriend for a while, and I've never been tested but I don't feel the need to be safe. I trust her and she trusts me. I know that's sort of unsafe, but now we're both only having sex with each other and that's it. So I think we're doing all right."

Even for some emerging adults who have been on the conservative side in their sexual behavior, AIDS is part of their consciousness. Helen has been with the same boyfriend for the past five years. "I know I don't have anything," she said. Yet: "I do think about it sometimes. You know, if something popped up on my body that's kind of weird-looking, you'll think about AIDS a lot of times. I'm glad I know the symptoms so I can look out for those."

They realize that even if they have been careful in their sexual behavior, their partners may not have been, and that puts them at risk. Vernon said, "One of the girls I dated, I found out she had sex with one of these [male stripper] guys. And I started doing the math and I was like 'Holy cow! I had sex with California just now!' And that made me nervous, you know."

Gay men are at especially high risk for HIV/AIDS, because the risk of HIV transmission is much higher through anal sex than through vaginal sex. Two-thirds of HIV infections in the United States occur as a consequence of male-to-male sexual contact, and men in their twenties have the highest rates of HIV infection.[51] During the 1990s, the threat of HIV led to steep declines in unprotected sex among young gay men. However, in the past decade the fear of HIV has waned somewhat in this population, perhaps because more effective methods of treatment now mean that a diagnosis of HIV is not necessarily a death sentence. In recent years, rates of HIV infection have gone up among men ages 20–29 even as they have declined among older men.[52] Today, use of condoms—or not—is negotiated between gay partners, and depends on their preferences, risk perceptions, and relationship commitment.[53]

HIV/AIDS is the most formidable source of anxiety in the sex lives of emerging adults, but other STIs also present risks during an age period where people typically move from one sexual partner to another for several years. The most common STI among young Americans is human papilloma virus (HPV). Most Americans acquire HPV at some point in their lives, and about half of new infections are among 15–24-year-olds.[54] In over 9 out of 10 cases, the infected person has no symptoms, and usually the virus fades within a few months. However, in a small percentage of cases the virus persists and genital warts develop, which result in itching and bleeding. Various treatments are available for the warts, but none of the treatments kills the virus, so recurrences are common. Women who have HPV are at increased risk for cervical cancer, even though it may take 5 to 25 years to develop. Nearly all cases of cervical cancer resulting from HPV can be prevented if detected in the precancerous stage through regular gynecological checkups. A vaccine for HPV has been developed and is being vigorously promoted by health authorities, which may make HPV risk lower for emerging adults in the next generation than it is now.[55]

The next most common STI among young people is chlamydia.[56] Symptoms include pain during urination and during intercourse, although sometimes there are no symptoms at all. It can be treated effectively with antibiotics, but if left untreated in women it can lead to pelvic inflammatory disease (PID), which in turn causes infertility; in fact, chlamydia is the leading cause of female infertility. It is also highly infectious; 25% of men and nearly three-fourths of women contract the disease during a single episode of intercourse with an infected partner.

That was Holly's unfortunate fate. "I slept with this one guy one time—one guy, one time—and we actually didn't use anything, and I don't know why. We were both being stupid." She had no symptoms afterward, but about a month later she had her annual pelvic exam. "They called me and said I was positive for chlamydia. That just shook me up because I couldn't believe that would happen to me." She was treated immediately, but the experience made her realize that "it could happen. Anything could happen." She won't forget the experience.

Nor will her friends. "My two good friends, they say 'You know, every time we hear that word 'chlamydia,' we think of you.' And I'm like, 'Thanks.'"

Herpes simplex virus II is a third common STI among emerging adults. Like chlamydia, it is highly infectious; 75% of persons who have sexual contact with an infected partner contract the disease.[57] Symptoms usually appear from one day to one month after infection. First there is a tingling or burning sensation in the infected area, followed by the appearance of sores. The sores last three to six weeks and can be painful. Other symptoms include fever, headaches, and fatigue. Treatment within four days of infection reduces the chances of recurring outbreaks of sores, but there is no cure for herpes. Once people are infected the virus remains in their bodies for life, and the chance of a recurrent episode is ever present.

This can't be an easy thing to break to a prospective lover, as Freda found out. She contracted herpes at age 17, from the first person she ever had sex with. She noticed sores on his genitals, but did not recognize them as symptoms of herpes. "I remember a day when he had a sore or something and I didn't even think about it. I remember going 'What's that?' and he said 'Oh, nothing.'" When she found out she was infected, the news was devastating. "It affected me a lot. A *lot*. It just really threw me for a loop. I was just like, 'Okay, scarred for life.'"

She has had only two episodes of sores in the four years since then, and she has learned to live with it. But she dreaded having to tell her current boyfriend about it when they became involved. Herpes is most infectious when sores are present, but it can also be transmitted through repeated unprotected sex over a long period of time. So, she had to tell him that she was infected and that there was a risk of him becoming infected unless they always used a condom. "It was very difficult for us. I had to be so honest and try to be careful about not freaking him out to the point of no return, you know. I was just kind of like, 'Well, I have to tell you this.'" He did not take it well at first, but eventually accepted it. At least it wasn't HIV. "He was pretty freaked out, but I think he started to realize that there's worse things you can get." Still, she continues to resent her misfortune in getting herpes. "I feel really cheated somehow, but at the same time I'm going to have to live with it. That's just the way it is."

Pornography: New Technologies, Old Questions

Because they have reached sexual maturity, emerging adults' interest in sex is understandably high. Yet, as we have seen, actual sexual activity in emerging adulthood varies, and may be low or nonexistent. Many emerging adults are not currently sexually active, and nearly all of them have occasional periods when they have no regular partner. Even for emerging adults who have a partner, the frequency of their sexual activity is generally lower than it is for married adults.[58] And as we have seen, some cultures, and some cultural groups within American society, strongly prohibit nonmarital sex.

Perhaps for these reasons, pornography has long been appealing to sexually mature but unmarried young people, especially males. For over a century, pornographic photographs and magazines have displayed naked women in sexual poses, and for decades pornographic movies have shown various sex acts. In recent years, with the spread of Internet access, pornographic material has suddenly become much easier to obtain, and viewing Internet pornography is now normative among young American males. In one study of college students at six sites around the country, 87% of young men and 31% of young women reported viewing Internet pornography.[59] Frequent use was far higher among men; nearly half reported watching porn weekly, compared to just 3% of women.

What are the effects, if any, of viewing pornography on emerging adults' perspectives on sexuality and relationships? Studies on the topic consistently find regular pornography use to be related to several attitudes and beliefs about sex:[60]

- Overestimating the prevalence and pleasure of unusual forms of sexual behavior, such as anal intercourse;
- Believing that monogamy is unrealistic and uncommon;
- Holding cynical attitudes regarding love and marriage.

However, as in all studies of media use, correlations like this should be interpreted with caution. Does viewing pornography cause people to have these beliefs and attitudes about sex, or are people who view pornography already more likely to hold these beliefs and attitudes? It is impossible to tell, since people are not randomly sorted into "pornography viewing" and "no pornography viewing" groups. They make choices about how often to view pornography, based on beliefs and attitudes they already hold.

There is no doubt that viewing pornography has become more common among emerging adults now that the Internet makes access to it so easy. So, if pornography actually causes changes in people's sexual beliefs and attitudes, by now it could be expected that these changes would be evident in their behavior. One could predict, for example, that today's emerging adults would be less likely than their counterparts of 20 or 30 years ago to use condoms (which are rarely used in pornographic episodes), as well as less likely to have monogamous relationships, and that once they marry they would be more likely to divorce because staying sexually faithful would be harder for them after years of exposure to the decidedly unfaithful depictions of sex found in pornography. But there is no evidence that this is what has resulted so far. On the contrary, today's emerging adults are somewhat more conservative and responsible in their sexual practices than their age-mates of a generation ago. As noted earlier, due to greater awareness of the threat of STIs, they are more likely to use condoms. Rates of divorce have gone down (slightly) over the past 20 years, not up, including rates of early divorce.[61]

This is not to say that there's nothing to worry about regarding young men's consumption of pornography. Young women often regard pornography as threatening, or at least foolish and stupid, and with good reason.[62] There is no doubt, as many studies have shown, that pornography often dehumanizes women, exalts men's dominance over them, and portrays sex in a way that is loveless and exploitative.[63] No one who cares about emerging adults and how they view relationships could be unconcerned about their regular exposure to the brutish sex common in pornography. Emerging adults are often ambivalent about it themselves, even the young men who are frequent consumers. They see it as natural, normal, and inevitable, but not really a good thing... but not quite a bad thing, either.[64]

A useful analogy could be made to violent electronic games, which are also highly popular among emerging adult men, and which also arouse alarm and concern about the potential effects. In the same way that Internet pornography has exploded during a period when sexual behavior among emerging adults has become somewhat more conservative, use of violent electronic games has exploded during an era when violent crime among young men has declined.[65] Such patterns make it difficult to make a persuasive case against these types of media use, however distasteful or repellent they may be to outside observers.

With both pornography and violent electronic games, perhaps emerging adults are generally able to separate fantasy from reality and not allow their media use to corrupt the rest of their lives. They recognize that pornography is not a reflection of reality, it's a holiday from reality, or perhaps a temporary substitute. It is something that may provide relief to young people who have intense sexual desires but are not yet having the regular sex that usually goes along with marriage. But it is not satisfying in the long run as a substitute for sex, any more than watching lavish meals prepared on the Food Channel is an adequate substitute for a good meal. Virtually all emerging adults hope eventually to find a three-dimensional soul mate to love and cherish for life.

The New Homosexuality

Homosexuality has long been stigmatized in American society, as it is in many societies. In fact, until a 2003 Supreme Court decision, homosexual acts were against the law in many American states. Even now, many gays and lesbians are subject to ridicule and abuse, especially in adolescence and emerging adulthood.[66] Consequently, young gays and lesbians have higher rates of substance use, school difficulties, depression, and suicide than their peers. In one widely publicized case in 2010, a young man at Rutgers University was secretly filmed by his roommate during a sexual episode with another man. After the video clip was posted on the Internet, the young man committed suicide. This tragedy illustrates the shame still associated with homosexuality in American society.

Nevertheless, it is clear that there has been a dramatic cultural shift in attitudes toward lesbians, gays, and bisexuals (LGBs) in recent years. Gays and lesbians are stars of popular culture to such an extent that their sexual orientation hardly matters any more. LGBs have been elected to high political offices. Public support for same-sex marriage, adoptions by same-sex couples, and gay people serving openly in the military is higher than ever and still rising, and is highest of all among the young. For example, a March 2013 national survey found that 81% of 18–29-year-olds supported gay marriage, but support declined steadily with age, to 44% of persons age 65 and over.[67]

Consequently, LGB emerging adults are coming of age today at a time when homosexuality is still controversial in American society but is rapidly becoming more acceptable. They are less likely to be subject to homophobia than LGBs were a generation ago, or even a few years ago. Nevertheless, the degree of acceptance of LGBs today should not be overstated. The more conservative elements in American society continue to view homosexuality as morally wrong and a violation of the laws of God. The experience of being an LGB emerging adult depends greatly on where you live; the response is likely to be a lot more favorable in the urban Northeast than in the rural South.[68]

Emerging adulthood is a key time for gay and lesbian experiences. During this life stage, people are more likely than earlier or later to explore sexual variety. In a national study of 18–23 year-olds, 18% of young women and 7% of young men reported experiencing same-sex attractions, and 14% of young women and 5% of young men had had at least one same-sex sexual episode. However, only 1% of the women and 2% of men identified as lesbian or gay, respectively.[69]

Becoming aware of a gay or lesbian identity generally happens in adolescence or earlier. Most LGBs report feeling same-sex attractions beginning in early adolescence, and the process of "coming out" (disclosing their sexual identity to others) usually begins at around age 16, when they tell their closest friends. In the 1970s, the average age of coming out was around 21, and the decline since that time may be due to growing acceptance of LGBs.[70]

But coming out is a process, and even though most LGBs first tell their friends around age 16, coming out to parents tends to happen later, around age 19. Not coincidentally, this is an age by which most emerging adults have moved out of their parents' household. Young people often dread and fear their parents' response.[71] Even the most loving and liberal parents may receive the news that a child is LGB with mixed emotions. They may be distressed that their child will be following a path that is likely to subject them to the hostility of others. They may be disappointed that their child will be less likely to marry or have children (although same-sex marriages are becoming increasingly possible, and 20% of gay men and 30% of lesbians do have children).[72] They may be fearful of the increased risk of HIV and AIDS (for gay men). They may wonder how (or if) they are going to share the news with more conservative friends and relatives.

But parents may also feel gratified that their LGB child trusts them enough to disclose such an important part of themselves. Parents may feel relieved that openness has replaced secrecy, and admire their sons or daughters for wanting to live with honesty and integrity. Now they can enjoy getting to know their grown children's same-sex partners.

Tad, now 27, recalled that "I knew I was gay very young," when he realized that he was more attracted to the boys his age than to his seventh-grade girlfriend. It was not until years later that he came out to his parents. "I wanted to come out when I was comfortable with it myself," he explains. His Dad took it in stride; in fact, he had known for years. But with his Mom, "it was a little more complicated. It took her a while to adjust to it." He brought her along gradually. "I understand it's new for you," he told her. "I've been living with it for years, and it's not a phase."

It took some time for her to be comfortable enough to meet one of his boyfriends, but by his sophomore year in college they were able to go on a double date. "We all shared a giant martini, got a little drunk, and had a lot of fun," he remembers happily. "Any lingering weirdness was gone." That night was a turning point for more than their acceptance of his sexual orientation. "It was the beginning of a new framework for my relationship with my parents. I could stop viewing them as parents and now think of them as friends." Most important, they were friends who accepted him for who he is.

Conclusion: The Perils of Freedom

Emerging adults today have unprecedented freedoms in love and sex. Unlike previous generations, they are not constricted by gender roles that prescribe rigid rules for how they may meet and get to know each other. A man may take the initiative and ask the woman out, or a woman may be the initiator. They may share time together as friends and get to know each other well before they decide whether to cross the border from friendship into love, without anyone tut-tutting that they are doing something improper by spending time together.

Also unlike previous generations, they are not forbidden to fall in love with someone from a different ethnic background. Prejudices still exist, of course, but they are not inviolable—or illegal—as they once were. Most young people still find their love partners within their ethnic group, partly for reasons of shared social circles and shared cultural backgrounds, partly because of the lingering effect of ethnic prejudice. But increasingly, and more than ever before, emerging adults find love partners across ethnic lines. Similarly, LGB emerging adults are freer than ever before to find a same-sex partner, although homophobia still exists.

Sexually, too, emerging adults today have freedoms that would have seemed unimaginable half a century ago. Most of them have a series of sexual partners from their late teens until they get married. For the most part, their sexual partners are not people they have just met and barely know, but people with whom they have an ongoing intimate relationship. Few Americans see anything wrong with a young woman and a young man in their twenties having a sexual relationship in the context of their love relationship, even if they are unmarried. The new norms are especially striking for women, who in the past would have been scorned and ostracized if they were known to be sexually active before marriage, even with someone they loved. Likewise, most young people have no objection to their peers finding same-sex partners.

Yet the new freedoms of emerging adulthood are accompanied by new fears. Although they are allowed and even encouraged to have a variety of sexual experiences before marriage, many American emerging adults do not use contraception consistently, and high rates of unintended pregnancies are the predictable consequence. Furthermore, the spread of AIDS has added an undercurrent of anxiety to their sexual freedom. Few emerging adults will ever contract HIV, but for many of them AIDS has become part of their sexual consciousness. The threat of other STIs, nonfatal but nevertheless traumatic, also casts a shadow on their sex lives.

There are perils in their pursuit of love as well. They may be freer than generations past to seek a love partner without the restrictions of courtship or dating rules and without prohibitions against crossing ethnic boundaries, but that does not mean that finding the right love partner has become any easier. This is especially true when emerging adults begin looking for a love partner for life, someone to commit to in marriage. It is to this topic that we turn in the next chapter.

Chapter 5

Meandering Toward Marriage

To look at the titles of some of the books popular among emerging adult women, you might think that most of them could do without marriage. *Why Dogs Are Better Than Men. One Hundred and One Reasons Why a Cat Is Better Than a Man.* Even *Why Cucumbers Are Better Than Men.* As for emerging adult men, the cliché is that they are terrified of commitment, especially of the marriage variety. Humorist Dave Barry, in his *Complete Guide to Guys,* offers women a number of "relationship-enhancement tips," including *"Do not expect the guy to make a hasty commitment.* By 'hasty,' I mean, 'within your lifetime.' Guys are *extremely* reluctant to make commitments. This is because they never feel *ready.*....A lot of women have concluded that the problem is that guys, as a group, have the emotional maturity of hamsters. No, this is not the case. A hamster is much more capable of making a lasting commitment to a woman, especially if she gives it those little food pellets."

Yet few young women remain sufficiently satisfied with cats, dogs, or cucumbers in the long run, and few young men fear commitment so much that they stay single past their twenties. Over 80% of Americans get married by age 40, 65% by their early thirties.[1] Today's emerging adults spend more years single and dating around than young people in previous generations, but the great majority of them eventually make their way to the altar.

In the course of emerging adulthood, young people change in a number of ways that make them increasingly ready for marriage.[2] Emerging adults become more capable of enduring intimacy. They come to appreciate the rewards of staying with one person for a longer period of time and developing a deeper emotional closeness. They also come to desire more security and commitment in their relationships. Eventually it grows old to move from one partner to the next every few weeks or months and start all over. Most emerging adults come to desire the stability and comfort of developing a long-term relationship with a person who seems to fit them just right.

For nearly all of them, this means thinking about marriage and trying to find someone who will make a good marriage partner. They may wish to wait for marriage until they have finished school, or have become settled into a career, or have had sufficient opportunity to live independently and focus on their own development and desires for a few years. But they expect to commit themselves to marriage once they feel ready, and most of them, even the "guys," eventually do. They fear some things about marriage, but the dream of a true lifelong love outweighs those fears.

In this chapter, we first look at the qualities emerging adults hope to find in a marriage partner. Then we look at how they decide when they would like to marry, and the widespread sense, especially among women, of having an "age 30 deadline" for marriage. Next, we discuss issues of commitment, and examine different motives for cohabitation. We also examine the recent rise in single motherhood during the twenties and its consequences. Finally, we look at how the fear of divorce shapes marriage expectations.

In Search of a Soul Mate: Finding a Marriage Partner

When they talk about what they are looking for in a marriage partner, emerging adults mention a wide variety of ideal qualities. Sometimes these are qualities of the person, the individual: intelligent, attractive, or good sense of humor. But most often they mention interpersonal qualities, the qualities a person brings to a relationship, such as kind, caring, loving, and trustworthy. Emerging adults hope to find someone who will treat them well and who will be capable of an intimate, mutually loving, durable relationship.

In addition to looking for ideal qualities, emerging adults also seek a marriage partner who will be like themselves in many ways. Just as they look for similarities when considering another person as a potential dating partner, they look for similarities when considering potential marriage partners.[3] Mindy thinks that marriage prospects look good with her boyfriend because "we have the same interests, we like to do the same things, we can talk about things on the same level.... We both want pretty much the same thing out of life."

Similarity is more important for marriage in this generation than in the past, because married couples today usually expect to spend most of their leisure time together. Gone are the days when men would spend their evenings with other men at a pub or a men's club. Groups such as the Elks, the Lions, the Masons, and so on have all declined steeply in membership over the past 50 years.[4] Nor do today's young women have much use for women-only groups—garden clubs, bridge clubs, and so on. Young couples often expect to find their main leisure companion in one another, and this makes similarity in leisure preferences a key quality to look for in a marriage partner.

It is not that they expect to do *everything* together. They just want to have enough common interests so that they can enjoy shared activities. Perry said he'd like to find someone who "likes to do some of the things that I do, but then won't mind if there's some things I like to do and she doesn't. Just somebody that does have enough similar interests so that we can spend a lot of quality time together." Most emerging adults want to strike a balance and find someone whose companionship they will enjoy in doing things together but who will also allow them some time for independent activities.

Even more important than shared activities are shared beliefs and values, a similar way of looking at the world. Those who have strong religious beliefs emphasize the importance of finding someone who shares them.[5] Andrea said she's looking for "somebody who's got the same religious beliefs as I do, and values and all that." When emerging adults who are members of ethnic minority groups emphasize finding a marriage partner with the same ethnic background, it is often because they believe that similarity of ethnic background means similarity of worldview.

Gloria, a 22-year-old Latina, put it this way: "It would have to be someone who was of the same religion that I was and also the same ethnicity as me. And sometimes when I say that people take it that I'm prejudiced or something. But it's not necessarily that, because I have a lot of traditions and customs that I grew up with and I want someone who understands the same traditions and everything. So I've always looked for someone who was Latino. And I've always looked for someone who was Catholic because I'm Catholic."

Good interpersonal skills on both sides, and similarity of interests, beliefs, and values, together make up the ideal of compatibility that emerging adults envision when they think about marriage. This is the ideal emerging adults have in mind when they search for a "soul mate" as a marriage partner. When Annie thinks of her future husband, she imagines "someone you'd like to share your life with, your soul mate, the one you share everything with." Annie's dream is extremely common. In a national survey, 94% of single

Americans in their twenties agreed that "when you marry you want your spouse to be your soul mate, first and foremost."[6]

Add physical attractiveness and sex to this soul mate vision and you have a powerful ideal—but an elusive one. Ideals are not easy to find walking around in the flesh. Those who find their soul mate plus passion in their marriage are fortunate, but many will find that this is more than marriage can deliver. Given the loftiness of the ideal, many real marriages will seem inadequate in the long run. But before marriage, when emerging adults are still imagining who their future spouse will be, their hopes run high that they will be one of the lucky ones. In the same national survey reporting that 94% of single Americans in their twenties hope to marry their soul mate, 88% agreed that "there is a special person, a soul mate, waiting for you somewhere out there."[7]

Deciding When to Marry

Nearly all emerging adults want to get married eventually, but when? In the past, the answer was relatively clear. Men married when they became financially capable of supporting a wife and children, usually by their early twenties and rarely later than their mid-twenties. Women married when they were mature enough to assume the responsibilities of caring for a husband and children and running a household, often in their late teens and rarely later than their early twenties. Any woman who remained unmarried past her early twenties was relegated to the dreaded status of "old maid," applied to a woman who was viewed as past marriageable age and who would never marry. A 1953 *New York Times Magazine* article warned that "[a] girl who hasn't a man in sight by the time she is 20 is not altogether wrong in fearing that she may never get married."[8]

Emerging adults today have much greater freedom to decide for themselves when they should marry. The norms for what is considered the "right" age to marry have weakened.[9] Some young people still marry in their late teens or early twenties, but most wait until at least their mid- to late twenties, and it is no longer unusual for them to wait until their thirties. It is not just that the average marriage age has risen steeply since 1970 for both men and women, but that the whole range for when people marry has become spread out. Young people can marry in their early twenties, their mid-twenties, their late twenties, or their early thirties and still be considered "normal."

This is an important new freedom for emerging adults, since they may now marry according to the timing they feel best fits their individual personalities and circumstances, rather than rushing to get married because of the pressure of social expectations. However, like the other freedoms of emerging adulthood, this new freedom comes with a cost. Instead of being able to follow a clear cultural norm for when to marry, now the responsibility for deciding when to marry is on the emerging adults themselves. And it may not be easy.

In the views of most emerging adults, the early twenties are clearly too early. Marrying that early would cut off their opportunity to experience the independence and spontaneity that are such appealing qualities of the emerging adult years. It would restrict their possibilities during a time of life when they have unparalleled opportunities to do what they want to do when they want to do it.

Roy, age 23, described it this way: "It would kind of bum me out to be married. One day I was at work and my friend called me up from Florida and said 'What are you doing?' I'm like, 'Just working,' and he said 'Can you come down?' I'm like, 'When?' and he's like 'Tomorrow,' and I'm like, 'Well, let me see what I can do.' So I took a week off all of a sudden and went down to Florida. And I know I'd never be able to do that if I was married."

But emerging adults also wish to delay marriage for more substantial reasons. They want to get their own lives in order, as individuals, before they commit their lives and fates to another person. Some of this project is practical and concrete: finishing education, settling into a stable career. Other aspects of emerging adults' self-assessment of readiness for marriage are more intangible and internal. They look within themselves and ask themselves if they feel ready, if they feel mature enough, if they feel they know themselves well enough.

Financial reasons are often involved as well. In a national survey of 20–29-year-olds conducted by the National Marriage Project,[10] 86% agreed that "[i]t is extremely important to you to be economically set before you get married." However, in focus group interviews conducted as part of the same study, the researchers observed that emerging adults "believe that they have to take time to 'work on yourself and your own happiness.' Postponing marriage gives you time to grow up, experience life, and 'be happy with yourself.'" These results indicate that both economic preparation and identity explorations are important as precursors to marriage for emerging adults. Only after they have become financially independent and have formed a stable identity—they know themselves well enough and have learned to be happy with themselves—do they believe they are ready for marriage.

In Erikson's theory of human development across the life span, after the challenge of forming an identity, the next challenge is intimacy versus isolation, that is, finding someone with whom to build a lifelong intimate relationship, usually marriage.[11] According to Erikson, after forming a definite identity, young people are ready to take the psychological and emotional risks involved in intimacy. Emerging adults sometimes seem to be ordering their lives in the way Erikson described, waiting until they feel they have resolved identity issues before considering marriage as the next step. Bonnie has been living with her boyfriend for a year and a half. He would like to get married, but she says, "I don't know...I'm not sure. There's a part of me, I think, that still needs to find some things. Not that I couldn't if I was married, but I don't know if this is it, and if I'm ready. Because there's times I guess I just feel it would be too soon, right now. There's things I don't want to lose, and I'm not sure what they are."

Staying unmarried allows emerging adults to keep their options open, not just in terms of whom they might marry but in terms of who they might become and what they might decide to do with their lives. What if you decide you want to move across the country to train to be a helicopter pilot, as Carl is thinking of doing? What if you decide you want to join the Peace Corps and move to another part of the world for a while, as Maya is pondering? As long as you remain unmarried, those kinds of choices continue to seem possible.

It should be noted that not all emerging adults wait until their late twenties or early thirties to marry, even today. Currently, 14% of American 20–24-year-olds are married.[12] The likelihood of marrying early is higher among emerging adults who are White, live in the South, live in a rural area, are highly religious, are from a lower social-class family, and have parents who married young themselves.[13] But sometimes it is just a matter of having a relatively conservative personality and of finding "the one" at an early age. Not all emerging adults want to experience romantic and sexual variety before they commit themselves to one person. Some would prefer to avoid the whole mess, and if they find someone to love by their early twenties who feels the same way, they see no reason to wait.

The Age 30 Deadline

Although there may be no "right" age to marry for emerging adults, age 30 comes up often as the age by which they would like to be married.[14] For some,

30 is the age when they imagine that they will be finished with their identity explorations and ready to commit themselves to someone else. Scott chose age 30 as the upper limit for marrying because "I'd like to be focused by 30, be settled down and working in my long term job or whatever. I'd just like to be focused by that age."

Sheila also thought she would be done with her independent explorations by age 30 and ready to marry. "I hope to be married by the time I'm 30. I mean, I don't see it being any time before that. I just think I have a lot of life left in me, and I want to enjoy it. There's so much out there, not that you couldn't see it with your husband, but why have to worry 'Is he going to get mad at this?' Just go out and enjoy life and then settle down, and you'll know you've done everything possible that you wanted to do, and you won't regret getting married."

For many emerging adults, especially women, 30 is the deadline age because it fits with their Plan for the rest of their lives. If they get married by age 30, that gives them a while to enjoy time as a couple with their spouse and still be able to have a child or two before they pass their prime childbearing years. Nancy, who will be 28 in two months, said she'd like to get married to her boyfriend "ASAP!" but by age 30 at the latest, because "I feel very strongly about being married several years before starting a family, just in terms of getting to know each other, which much past 30 puts you into your mid-thirties to start a family, and that concerns me." Sandy voiced similar sentiments: "I'd like to be married before 30, but definitely by 30 because I'd like to have time to spend with my husband before we have kids, just to get to know each other better before the family thing. And once you get to a certain age, you just don't really have time for that."

So, in theory they can get married whenever they want, whenever they decide the time is right, but in practice age 30 is for many people a deadline age. It is the age they want to get married by, and it is also the age they feel that other people expect them to get married by. Emerging adults start to feel the pressure of these expectations as they cross into their late twenties. Often the pressure comes from parents. Sometimes this pressure is mild, as for Wendy, whose mother, "hinting around about grandchildren," helpfully suggested, "You should go to Alaska. There's a ratio of like 2 to 1 men to women."

Sometimes the pressure from parents is more direct, especially for Asian Americans. Because Asian American parents place a stronger value on family obligations than most other Americans do, they feel fewer qualms about telling their emerging adult children what they should be doing.[15] They often tell them explicitly that they have an obligation to keep the family line going. Greg, a 23-year-old Chinese American, said his parents tell him, "They really want to see grandchildren. I think it would provide them more of a sense of accomplishment if they saw that they had not only taken care of me but that they also provided for a new generation. And so they can rest assured that 'Our family moves on. It doesn't stop here. All that hard work paid off.'"

Asian American immigrant parents also sometimes bring traditional beliefs about gender roles from their home countries, specifically the belief that women should focus on finding a husband and having children. Vanessa, whose parents immigrated from Taiwan, said her mother "doesn't understand why I'm working so hard to get a master's degree. She thinks a husband is the most important part in your life. If you can find a nice husband to marry, even though you only graduated from elementary school, that would be enough."

Sometimes pressure to get married comes from friends. Emerging adults whose friends are marrying may find themselves the object of unwanted expectations. Tory said he and his girlfriend "went to nine weddings this year. We're the last ones left. So yeah, there's a lot of pressure. And she gets really mad when everybody goes, 'Well, when are you guys going to get married?' It's to the point now where she's tired of hearing it." Melissa, who has been with her boyfriend on and off for several years, said, "Our friends are getting married and that kind of puts pressure on you because everybody says 'Well, you'll be getting married next.' And then it'll be, 'When are you having kids?'"

Of course, then there are emerging adults such as Brock, who says, "To be honest with you, I look at all my friends who have gotten married and think they've made the hugest mistake of their life." Most emerging adults would probably agree with Kwame: "It's not when you get married, it's who you marry. That's the whole thing. If you find your happiness early, that's great. If you find your happiness later, that's great, too, 'cause the whole thing about it, you gotta make sure you're happy for yourself. Don't feel like you've been forced into any situation."

So, emerging adults may feel pressure to get married as they approach age 30, but most of them are intent on deciding for themselves when the time is right.

Commitment: His and Hers

Young men and women are more similar than different when it comes to deciding about marriage. Both want to find a "soul mate" who is similar to themselves in key ways and who is easy to live with. Both want to have a period of years in emerging adulthood to stand on their own, to make independent decisions, and to explore the possibilities available to them before committing themselves to marriage. Both get more serious about finding a marriage partner once they reach their late twenties and see the age 30 deadline looming only a few years off.

Less rigid gender roles than in the past make it possible for men and women to meet on more equal ground in their love relationships. Young women no longer need to feel that they have to marry as soon as possible in order to have a man who will support them and to have a legitimate, respected role in their society. Young men no longer need to worry that in order to marry they must first be capable of being the sole "breadwinner" for a wife and children. Young men and women can now, more than any time in the past, anticipate a marriage in which they will be equal partners and have a relationship as soul mates plus sex.

Still, it is unmistakable that women feel more pressure than men to find a marriage partner before age 30. They feel this pressure partly because they believe they face a biological deadline. If they wish to have children, as most of them do, they want to have them no later than their early thirties, because the risk of infertility and prenatal development problems rises substantially by the late thirties. But part of the pressure is also social and cultural. They fear that by the time they pass age 30, they will have missed their chance to marry because men their age will prefer younger women. The term "old maid" may be used rarely anymore, but the stigma it represents still lingers.

Men do not face a comparable social judgment, and they know it. In a national survey of unmarried 25–29-year-old men, 62% agreed that they were "not interested in getting married any time soon."[16] Jake was quite blunt in assessing the issue from a man's perspective: "I think men have a great advantage over women in that they can be at an older age when they get married, because it's acceptable for a man to marry someone of a younger age. Like, I could be 35 and marry someone who's 23. I mean, I've got all the time in the world."

To investigate the reasons why some young men are in no hurry to marry during their twenties, researchers at the National Marriage Project conducted focus group interviews in four American cities with 60 single men ages 25–33.[17] On the basis of the interviews, the researchers identified 10 reasons:

1. They can get sex without marriage more easily than in times past.
2. They can enjoy the benefits of having a wife.
3. They want to avoid divorce and its financial risks.
4. They want to wait until they are older to have children.
5. They fear that marriage will require too many changes and compromises.
6. They are waiting for the perfect soul mate and she hasn't yet appeared.
7. They face few social pressures to marry.
8. They are reluctant to marry a woman who already has children.
9. They want to own a house before they get a wife.
10. They want to enjoy single life as long as they can.

This difference between men and women in readiness to marry sometimes results in tension within couples who are in their late twenties and serious about each other but not engaged or married. She, believing that her time to marry is running out, is often eager to marry—although she realizes she has to be careful about seeming *too* eager, as it is no longer acceptable for women to be seen as trying to "catch" a husband. He, on the other hand, may feel like he has "all the time in the world," as Jake put it. He wants to stay involved with her, but he sees no need to hurry the decision about whether to marry her.

The views of Jean, 26, and Trey, 28, illustrate this difference. They have been seeing each other for two years, and living together for a year and a half. Jean says, "I'd like to be engaged before Christmas." If not by Christmas, well, then, at least "within the next year to two years." If not within the next year or two, okay, but "it would be nice to be married by the time I'm 30," even though "it's not going to kill me if I'm not."

Talk to Trey and you get a much different perspective. It becomes clear that Jean can forget about getting engaged by Christmas, and it's a good thing it's not going to kill her if she's not married by age 30. Trey says he might get married—"possibly someday." He is well aware that "my significant other would probably like it to be soon," but he says, "I'm not quite ready for that." Originally he thought he would be married by age 25, but "that's past. And then it was 30, and that's approaching and I don't think I'll feel too bad if that goes by either." For now he has decided that "I'm not ready to settle down. I'm more on the side of 'I've got plenty of time yet.'"

Jean was taking the delay in her marriage hopes pretty well at this point, but other young women express frustration at the difficulty they face in getting their young men to make a commitment to marriage. Twenty-seven-year-old Christy and her boyfriend have been seeing each other for three and a half years, and for all but the first year of that period he has been in medical school. She has been supportive of him during the stresses of his medical training. "I've been understanding. I've pretty much helped him through med school emotionally." But three months ago, he suddenly told her, "I don't think I'll ever get married." Surprised and dismayed, she told him, " 'Well, I'm sorry, but I'm going to leave you now' and we didn't talk for three weeks."

Then he called her and said he had reconsidered. He agreed to marry her—sort of. "He said 'I will marry you,' so I did get a verbal agreement from him," she said, sounding like someone trying to coax a reluctant client into signing a contract. He has told her they will talk about becoming officially engaged when he finishes medical school in a year and a half. Although she remains skeptical of his commitment to her, she figures, "I will only lose about 18 months at the most if I wait it out."

She is telling herself to be patient, because "men think of it differently. They don't want to feel like there's a time limit, where they're feeling like they're being coerced or rushed." But if he doesn't come through when medical school is over, "I'm fully prepared to leave, although it would be very hard."

I want to emphasize again that men and women are more alike than different in how they view marriage. Most people, men and women both, feel ready to enter marriage by the time they reach their late twenties. Like Joel, they "get tired of going home every night and looking at four walls by myself." Like Joseph, they anticipate that it will be nice "not to have to worry about who I'm going to be sleeping with or worry about what they've got or who they've been with, or even have to mess with the dating thing." Nevertheless, when there is a difference between partners in their feelings of readiness for marriage, it is usually the woman who feels ready and wants to get on with it while the man is reluctant and is dragging his feet.

One Foot In: Cohabitation

For emerging adults who do not feel ready to marry but who want to have many of the benefits of marriage—daily companionship, shared expenses, more frequent sex—there is the alternative of cohabitation. This is an alternative that was not as readily available in previous generations. Figure 5.1, adapted from a national study, shows how the proportion of American women who have cohabited with at least one person prior to marriage changed in the course of the past half century.[18]

For the generation that reached their twenties in the 1950s and early 1960s, cohabitation was extremely rare. Nearly everyone waited until marriage before living with a romantic partner. Even for young people in the late 1960s and early 1970s, the generation of the much-discussed Sexual Revolution, cohabitation remained relatively rare, practiced by only about 10% of young women. This was an increase from the previous generation, but cohabiters were still a small minority. However, by the 1990s, cohabitation was the norm, and over half of emerging adults lived with a romantic partner before marriage. In the past decade, rates of cohabiting have leveled out at between 60% and 70% of emerging adults.[19]

Cohabiting bears obvious resemblances to marriage, but it begins earlier, at an average of age 21 for women and 23 for men.[20] It is also less stable than marriage. Over half of cohabiting relationships dissolve within five

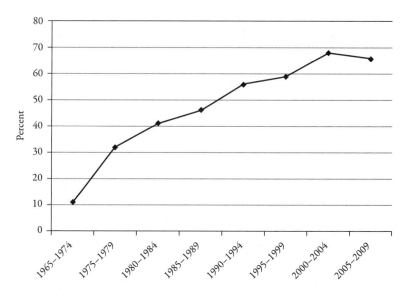

Figure 5.1 Changes in Cohabitation Rates, American Women Ages 19–44, 1965–2009.

Source: Manning (2013).

years.[21] Cohabiters tend to be less religious, less educated, and more politically liberal than their non-cohabiting peers.[22]

Although the rise in cohabitation has been dramatic, placing all cohabiters into one category is a bit misleading. There are three distinct kinds of cohabitation, very different from each other. The two most common types in the United States are *premarital cohabitation* and *uncommitted cohabitation*.[23] In premarital cohabitation, the couple has firm plans to marry. They may be officially engaged and may even have set a date for their wedding. In uncommitted cohabitation, however, the two emerging adults have made no long-term commitment to each other. One partner or the other may be hoping their relationship will lead to marriage eventually, but the fact that they are living together does not signify that marriage between them is imminent or even likely in the long run.

Premarital cohabiters often want to test their compatibility before they enter marriage.[24] Pete and his wife lived together for about a year before they married recently, and he's glad they did. "I don't see how people can do it without that. I wanted to make sure she doesn't throw her socks on top of the sink and if she puts the top back on the toothpaste and stuff. All those little things." Mindy and her boyfriend have been living together for five months. They are engaged, but before they married "we wanted to try it out and see how we got along, because I've had so many long term relationships. I just wanted to make sure we were compatible. And he'd been married before and he felt the same way."

As Mindy's comments suggest, premarital cohabiters often decide to live together in the hope that doing so will make it less likely that they will divorce. Indeed, in a national survey of emerging adults, 62% agreed that "living together with someone before marriage is a good way to avoid eventual divorce."[25] Emerging adults who have experienced their parents' divorce are especially likely to mention this as a reason for cohabiting. They have seen divorce up close, and they want to avoid it themselves if at all possible. By living together before marriage, they hope to improve their odds.

Jackie and her fiancé both have divorced parents; his mother has been divorced three times. Burned by divorce and wary of marriage, they decided to live together during their engagement to try to make sure it would work. "I'm not going to marry somebody and maybe have children and then have him walk out or me feel like this was a big mistake," she said. Unfortunately for Jackie and young people like her, living together does not enhance the likelihood that a marriage will endure. In fact, until recently the probability of divorce for young people who lived together and then married was higher, not lower, compared to their peers, although that effect seems to have faded in the past two decades.[26]

Premarital cohabiters also may have practical reasons for moving in together. He has a lease ending and cannot find a new roommate; she wants to escape a current roommate; they both want to save on their expenses. They will be getting married soon anyway—why not just move in? But even if they have practical reasons as well, premarital cohabiters are motivated to live together mainly because they are committed to each other and the momentum of their relationship is toward marriage.

In contrast, uncommitted cohabiters almost always move in together mainly or solely for practical reasons, because their relationship lacks a shared understanding that they are headed toward marriage. For Amelia and her boyfriend, their decision to live together was motivated primarily by high rental prices in San Francisco. They talk about marriage only "in an abstract sense, more like in a 'someday' type of thing or jokingly like, 'Oh yeah, we'll get married when I'm old,' you know, stuff like that." Living together is seen by both of them as likely to be temporary. "We both want to go back to school and want to do a lot things so it's sort of like…you know, there's a good chance we're gonna be apart for awhile, too, and so like we'll take that as it comes. But getting married right now? I don't feel like I'm ready to make that type of decision yet."

The third type, *committed cohabitation*, is essentially a stable—if often impermanent—substitute for marriage. Partners in this type of cohabitation are committed to each other, as premarital cohabiters are, but they have no intention of ever entering marriage. Leah has been living with her boyfriend for a year, and says, "I don't expect to get married to him or anybody. I don't view marriage as being very important. I mean, I basically consider myself to be married to him now. There's just not a legal document that says that we're married. I just don't believe that you need to have a piece of paper that ties you up with somebody like that."

In the United States, this view is unusual among emerging adults. Even among the uncommitted cohabiters, nearly all of them eventually want to get married, to someone if not to their current partner.[27] However, committed cohabitation is already quite common in northern Europe. For example, in the Scandinavian countries, over half of children are born to cohabiters, and only about half of these cohabiting parents have married five years after the birth.[28] But even in northern European countries, cohabiting relationships are less "committed" than marriage is—that is, cohabiting relationships are more likely than marriages to dissolve.[29]

What makes marriage different from cohabitation? Why don't more emerging adults take the committed cohabitation path of Leah and Brad and simply "consider themselves married" without obtaining the legal document, especially if they already live together? Marriage is different precisely because it requires the legal document, the ceremony, the public declaration of the intention to remain together " 'til death do us part." This makes marriage not only a private commitment between two people but a social commitment, backed up by the expectations of society, the power of tradition, and the force of law.

And marriage really is different from cohabitation in terms of the effects it has on the people involved. According to a substantial body of research, marriage has a variety of positive effects on psychological health, financial well-being, and emotional well-being that cohabitation does not.[30]

Each partner gains from marriage a sense of security, a promise that his or her partner is serious about staying together for the long run. This may seem ironic, given that nearly half of marriages in the United States end in divorce. But almost no one who enters marriage expects to end up among the half who divorce. In the national Clark poll, 86% of 18–29-year-olds agreed that "I expect to have a marriage that lasts a lifetime."[31] Upon entering marriage, partners at least have from one another a public declaration of their intention to remain together for life.

The relationship between Mike and Laurie illustrates some of these issues. They have been married for a year, after cohabiting for five years. Talking about the past year, Mike first says, "Being married wasn't a big change other than I have a ring on my hand now and a piece of paper that says we're married." But then he adds: "I take that back. It does make the relationship a little more comfortable to know that the escape hatch isn't standing open just waiting for you to walk out. Once you're married it kind of forces you to at least try to work things out before somebody packs up and goes."

For Laurie, the five years of living together were more fraught with anxiety, and marriage was more of a relief. "I think during that time I was really stressed, because I didn't know exactly whether or not I was going to be with him or if I was wasting that much time in my life." She felt that, as a woman, she was risking more by living with someone for so long without the commitment of marriage.[32] "I think it's always a major thing for a woman, whether or not they're going to find somebody." To her, living together unmarried even for as long as five years meant that they were "not really committed. You could leave at any time. There's always a chance that the other one is going to leave." Now that she and Mike are married, she feels liberated from that anxiety. "Once you get married, there's no turning back. You're bound for life."

We can see, then, that marriage is different from cohabitation not just legally but *psychologically*. The two partners are still living together after marriage, just as they were before. There is still the possibility that they will split up eventually, just as there was before. But once they move from cohabitation to marriage, it *feels different*. Whatever the future may actually hold, when they enter marriage they believe and hope they are making a permanent commitment, that they are "bound for life."

In addition to the desire for this psychological sense of permanence, what moves emerging adults from cohabitation to marriage is social pressure, especially from parents. Although there is no longer a deep social stigma for cohabiting in American society, there are many parents who have mixed feelings about it or who oppose it, especially when their own son or daughter is involved.[33]

Few emerging adults have any moral qualms about cohabiting. For them it is normal, typical, and perfectly acceptable, something that most people their age do at some point, and a smart strategy for avoiding current expenses and a future divorce. But for their parents, who grew up at a time when cohabiting was considered daring if not scandalous, the prospect of seeing their own child move in with a lover may not be something they welcome. Especially when the cohabitation is uncommitted, many parents are adamantly opposed to it. Grandparents, remembering a time when cohabitation was known as "living in sin," also sometimes register their opposition.

To avoid confronting their parents about the issue and facing their opposition directly, many emerging adults adopt a strategy I call *semi-cohabiting*, in which they maintain two residences even though they essentially live together at one or the other. As Taylor Swift sings in "Mine," it is common among emerging adult couples that "[t]here's a drawer of my things at your place." When I asked Steve if he and his girlfriend were living together, he said "lease-wise, no," meaning that "I have my own place and she has her own place but we basically spend most of our time together." Semi-cohabiting is a necessary strategy for them because her parents have told her she cannot move in with him. But it is a source of great irritation and unnecessary expense in his eyes. "We're paying two rents and two utilities and two of this and the other, and it doesn't make any sense to me."

It is interesting to note that semi-cohabiters may respond "no" to a simple yes-no question about whether they are cohabiting, as Steve did at first. This suggests that the proportion of emerging adults who cohabit before marriage may be even higher than the 60%–70% reported in surveys, because the surveys may miss those who are semi-cohabiting. It seems reasonable to count the semi-cohabiters as people who are cohabiting, since they are living together for all practical purposes except "lease-wise."

Besides stating their opposition to cohabiting, parents can also obstruct it by withholding resources from their emerging adult children. Leslie and her boyfriend Rich are 20-year-old college students. She says, "I think we both would prefer to live together, but his parents don't approve of that and they won't help him with school if he does." Rich says they have made this known to him "very blatantly." So he and Leslie are semi-cohabiting as long as they are still in school and he is financially dependent on his parents.

However, parents' power to obstruct cohabitation diminishes as emerging adults move into their mid-twenties and become less dependent on their parents financially as well as more intent on making their own decisions. When Ginny told her parents that she and her boyfriend were going to move in together, her mother threatened her "by just saying things like, 'Oh, you're not going to get any money from us.' You know, making it clear that money was directing a lot of her orders."

But Ginny was 24 by then and no longer depended on her parents financially. It was difficult nevertheless to defy her parents, but she was able to do so because she did not need the money they threatened to withhold. "I had always done everything they told me to do, and now I made my own decision. I said, 'You know, I really can't do what you want me to do this time because this is too important to me. This one I'm not going to compromise on.'" Financial independence allows emerging adults to make their own decisions about cohabiting, even if it means overriding their parents' objections.

First Comes Love, Then Comes...Baby? The Puzzle of Single Motherhood

Start sex at an average age of 17, place the median marriage age over a decade later, and add inconsistent contraceptive use, and it should not be surprising that a lot of nonmarital pregnancies take place during that decade-plus. Nevertheless, the statistics today regarding single motherhood in the United States are stunning and unprecedented. Overall, 48% of first births in the

United States are now to single moms. For births to moms under age 30, the figure is even higher: 53%.[34] This startling trend is a phenomenon of the twenties decade. Since 1990, teen pregnancies have actually plummeted by half. Meanwhile, nonmarital pregnancies in the twenties have soared. Currently, only 23% of all nonmarital births are to teen moms, whereas 60% are to women in their twenties. As the authors of a 2013 report on this topic put it, "If thirty is the new twenty, today's unmarried twenty something moms are the new teen mothers."[35]

As a result of the increase in rates of nonmarital births in the twenties, the median age of first birth for women is now lower than the median age of marriage. Historically, the first birth has taken place a year or two after marriage. However, around 1990, what the National Marriage Project calls the "Great Crossover" occurred: the median age at first birth for women fell below the median age of marriage, and has remained below ever since, even as the median ages of both first birth and marriage have risen, as shown in Figure 5.2.[36]

But the Great Crossover has not occurred for everyone. There is a gaping disparity by social class (as represented by educational attainment). Among college-educated women, there has been no Great Crossover, nor has there been much increase in their rates of single motherhood. On average they

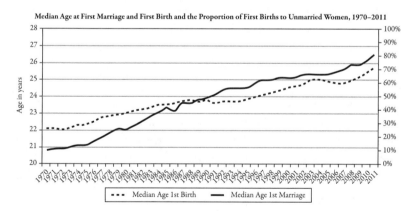

Median Age at First Marriage and First Birth and the Proportion of First Births to Unmarried Women, 1970–2011

Median Age 1st Birth ——— Median Age 1st Marriage

Figure 5.2 "The Great Crossover": The Median Age at First Marriage and First Birth.

Sources: National Center for Family & Marriage Research. Median age at first marriage, *Current Population Survey, 1970–2011* (March Supplement); Median age at first birth and percentage of first births to unmarried mothers, *National Vital Statistics Reports, 1970–2011.* Modified with permission from The National Marriage Project at the University of Virginia.

marry around age 27 and have their first child about three years later, around age 30. Only about 12% of their first births take place outside marriage. In contrast, among women with a high school degree or some college, their median marriage age is also around 27, but their median age of first birth is about 24 and a half. Over half (58%) of their first births occur outside marriage. For women who have not obtained even a high school degree, their median age of marriage is 25, their median age of first birth is just 20, and 83% of their first births are nonmarital.

In addition to these social class differences in nonmarital births, there are also stark ethnic differences.[37] The rate of nonmarital first births is just 8% among Asian Americans, but it is 37% among White women, 64% among Latinas, and a whopping 80% among African Americans. These ethnic differences are due partly to the educational differences just described, but not entirely. For example, among women without a college degree, the percent of women who have a nonmarital first birth is 55% for Whites, 69% for Latinas, and 87% for African Americans.

Clearly, a profound social change has taken place in rates of single motherhood in the twenties over the past several decades. What should we make of it? Most emerging adults think it's no big deal. In a survey by the National Campaign to Prevent Teen and Unplanned Pregnancy, 70% of young men and 77% of young women ages 18–29 agreed that "it is OK for an unmarried female to have a child."[38] This laissez-faire attitude is one aspect of the broader emerging adult values of individualism and tolerance for diversity, the same values that make them accepting of gay marriage and ethnic intermarriage: "Hey, if that's what will make you happy, go for it."

The problem is, it is not at all clear that having kids outside marriage makes people happy—not moms, not couples, and not kids. On the contrary, there is abundant evidence that the opposite is true, that single motherhood raises the risks of every kind of calamity for everyone involved.[39] For moms, it means lower educational attainment and lower incomes. For couples, it means lower likelihood that the relationship will last and that the father will be involved in the child's life in the long run. For kids, it means higher risks for school failure, behavioral problems, depression, drug use, and eventually being involved in nonmarital births themselves. Of course, there are exceptions to these patterns, and many moms, couples, and kids defy the odds and succeed in life. But overall, there is just no denying that the consequences of single motherhood are likely to be grim.

If it is true that nonmarital births raise the risk of unfortunate consequences in so many ways, why are the rates so high? Why aren't emerging adults waiting until they have established a stable marriage before having their first child, and why aren't they trying harder to avoid nonmarital births? One reason emphasized by many sociologists in this area is that young people from lower social classes—the ones described earlier, who do not have a college degree—do not see much payoff for postponing childbirth until after marriage.[40] According to this view, these emerging adults do not foresee a future in which they could achieve a college degree, become financially independent, then marry, then have their first child. Because they see no feasible route to middle class prosperity, and no career path ahead that would merit delaying motherhood, young women settle on single motherhood as the central source of meaning and structure for their lives.

This explanation has become the conventional wisdom in sociology for explaining high rates of single motherhood in populations where educational attainment is low. No doubt this scenario applies to some young women who do not have the benefit of a college education and have limited opportunities for developing a career. However, it may make single motherhood sound like a more rational decision than it usually is. If you have been unable to obtain a college degree and your job prospects are therefore limited, wouldn't it make more sense to have your first child later rather than earlier, so that you would have a longer horizon of time to get some kind of occupational training or at least develop some job experience and skills? Wouldn't it be even more important to wait for marriage before having a child, because with marriage the child would potentially have the benefit of two incomes rather than one, even if they might be low and erratic incomes? If you already have little in the way of education, occupational training, or family financial resources, doesn't becoming a single mom in your twenties make it all the more likely that you and your child will struggle financially and in every other way for years to come?

Often, young women are not asking these questions before they decide whether or not to become pregnant outside marriage, because becoming pregnant is not something they *decide* to do; it "just happens." It is estimated that 7 out of 10 of the births to unmarried women in their twenties are unintentional, but "unintentional" is not quite the right word.[41] Often, the pregnancy is not really intended, but it is not exactly unintended, either. The title of a report by the National Campaign to Prevent Teen and Unintended Pregnancy puts it well: *The Fog Zone: How Misperceptions,*

Magical Thinking, and Ambivalence Put Young Adults at Risk for Unplanned Pregnancy. In the survey that was the basis for the report, the authors found that half of unmarried 18–29-year-olds said they would like to have a baby now "if things were different," and even among those who agreed that it was important to avoid pregnancy right now, a third also agreed they would be "happy" if they got pregnant. So, they are not exactly planning to have a baby, but many are not exactly against the idea, either. It is easy to see how this ambivalence would lead to inconsistent contraceptive use or no contraception at all. Only half of the emerging adults in the survey used effective contraception every time—even though 90% said they believe pregnancy should be planned.

As mentioned in the previous chapter, this ambivalence is further propelled by the way that premarital sex and contraceptive use are morally contested in the United States, more than in most other developed countries.[42] Nearly all young Americans take part in premarital sex sometime in their twenties, and most of them view it as a normal part of a loving relationship, regardless of marriage. But many of their parents and grandparents disagree, and most major religious authorities are outspoken opponents of premarital sex and seek to obstruct access to contraception, believing that easy access to contraception would make premarital sex morally permissible. Once again, it is all too easy to see how the result of this ambivalence—this time on a societal rather than an individual level—would be that unmarried emerging adult partners would continue to have sex but might avoid communicating about it with their parents, their doctors, and even with each other so as not to have to confront moral barriers to continuing it.[43] Under this formula, unintended pregnancies are certain to result.

Societal ambivalence about premarital sex underlies not only inconsistent contraceptive use but lack of knowledge of contraception among young Americans. Because of the ambivalence, sex education is taught inadequately or not at all in most American states, and consequently American children fail to learn what they would need to know in order to avoid pregnancy.[44] The *Fog Zone* report revealed an appalling array of ignorance and misperceptions among emerging adults.[45] Nearly two-thirds of 18–29-year-olds said they know *little or nothing* about birth control pills. About half erroneously believed that the chance of getting pregnant while on the Pill is about 50% over the course of a year (the actual chance: 8%). About half believed (falsely) that the likelihood of cancer or other serious health risks is higher for women who take the Pill. Even among those who have relied on the Pill, nearly half (44%) incorrectly believed that a woman should "take a break" from the Pill every few years to preserve her health.

But it is not just the Pill that emerging adults misunderstand. Nearly one-third admit to knowing *little or nothing* about condoms. Among those who rely on the "rhythm method," 40% do not know that a woman's most fertile time is midway between her menstrual periods. Fifty-nine percent of women and 47% of men believe it is at least slightly likely that they are infertile (actual figure: 8%). The subject is ethnically charged, too: 44% of African Americans and 46% of Latinos agree that "the government is trying to limit blacks and other minority populations by encouraging the use of birth control." Given these head-shaking statistics, perhaps we should be surprised that rates of single motherhood are not even higher than they are.

Finally, the role of cohabitation has to be considered as part of the explanation for high rates of single motherhood in the twenties decade, because about half of all nonmarital births are to cohabiting couples.[46] As we have seen, cohabitation is now normative among young Americans, but, like single motherhood, it is especially common among those who do not have a college degree. When a young couple is cohabiting, and using contraception inconsistently or not at all, and a pregnancy results, what will they decide to do about it? If they are not strongly against the prospect of having a baby, and if they have no definite career ambitions that would be derailed, and if they believe having an abortion would be morally wrong—all views that are more common among the less-than-college-educated than among the college-educated—then they will often go ahead and have the baby. Since they are cohabiting, they often believe that it is likely they will marry eventually, anyway, so why not just have the child first and marry later? Actually, however, cohabiting couples in their twenties who have a child are three times more likely than married couples who have a child to split up by the time the child is five years old (39% to 13%).[47]

Can a single mother still be an emerging adult? Certainly the identity explorations of emerging adulthood are severely limited by the responsibilities of caring for a baby, with all of a baby's relentless needs. Many single moms continue to have high hopes in love and work and to believe they will achieve their educational and occupational goals.[48] However, the hard reality is that the prospects for succeeding in having a lifelong marriage and achieving a college degree and a middle class lifestyle diminish sharply for young women who have a child outside marriage. Because children require so much from their mothers for so long, it seems clear that having a child thrusts a person from emerging adulthood to the next life stage, ready or not. For young unmarried dads it is less true, but only because they often are no longer involved in the child's life within a few years.

"A Horrible Alone Feeling": The Shadow of Divorce

Although nearly all emerging adults eventually want to get married, and although they often have high hopes for the kind of marriage they will have, they realize that today in American society, marriage is often a temporary rather than a permanent bond. The ship of hopes they send out on their wedding day amid sunshine and celebration may, some years later, end up being dashed against the rocks. Divorce looms before them as the thundercloud on the horizon, carrying the storm they may already have seen claim the hopes of their parents, siblings, or friends.

Americans have among the highest divorce rates of any society in the world.[49] As sociologist Andrew Cherlin explains in *The Marriage Go-Round*, divorce rates are higher in the United States than in other countries not because Americans do not respect the institution of marriage, but because they idealize it so much that if it does not match up, they feel compelled to bail out and try for a happier match with someone else. Emerging adults share this ideal, as we have seen in their aspirations for finding a "soul mate." Although nearly all Americans are idealistic about marriage, in recent decades a sharp social class divide has developed in divorce rates. The risk that a marriage will end in divorce has continued to escalate in the lower social classes, whereas in the upper social classes the risk has actually declined. So, among women who never obtained a high school degree, one-third are divorced within five years of marriage. For those who have a high school degree, the rate is one-fourth, but for women who have a college degree or more, just 13% are divorced after five years.[50] There are ethnic differences, too, with overall rates of divorce among African Americans (70%) much higher than among Whites (47%). Nevertheless, across social classes and ethnic groups, the fear of divorce is pervasive. Even if they believe bravely that their own marriage will last a lifetime, emerging adults are well aware that nearly half of American marriages ultimately end in divorce.[51]

The fear of divorce, and the desire to avoid it, has contributed to the rise in the marriage age that has made emerging adulthood a distinct stage of life.

True, most emerging adults postpone marriage until at least their late twenties so that they can be free to pursue opportunities in school, work, and leisure, and so that they can gain experience with intimate relationships. But for some of them, postponing marriage also has fear as a motivation—fear of divorce and the desire to be as certain as possible that their marriage will succeed.

We have already seen how fear of divorce can be a motive for cohabiting. But even for many emerging adults who do not cohabit or who do so for other reasons, fear of divorce is often part of their thinking about marriage. It leads them to be wary of marriage and to delay it until they feel as confident as possible that they are making the right choice with the right person. Dana and her boyfriend have been seeing each other for five years and have been living together for two and a half years. They are engaged to be married this summer. They might have married years earlier, but "we wanted to make sure that we were doing what was best for both of us. I mean, we didn't want to get married and then get divorced two years later. We wanted to be sure." Wesley is 22 and doesn't see himself being married for many years yet. "I want to wait until I'm older because I know a lot of people who get married young and then there's a lot of fights and stuff. Personally I think I'd rather wait until I know myself a little bit better and probably the person I marry a little bit better so we're more secure with each other."

Sheila thinks her parents divorced because they married young and her father "felt trapped." So for herself, she wants to finish her emerging adult identity explorations before she thinks about getting married, in the hope that she will be less likely to divorce when she does marry. "I think everyone should experience everything they want to experience before they get tied down, because if you wanted to date a Black person, a White person, an Asian person, a tall person, short, fat, whatever, as long as you know you've accomplished all that, and you are happy with who you are with, then I think everything would be okay. I want to experience life and know that when that right person comes, I won't have any regrets."

As Sheila's comments suggest, emerging adults with divorced parents often take their cues from their parents in learning what *not* to do in a marriage. In the course of witnessing the breakup of their parents' marriage, they observed their parents behave in ways they hope not to repeat themselves. For Dana, her parents' divorce comes to mind whenever she and her live-in boyfriend have a disagreement, as a model of what to avoid. "When I see myself saying or doing something that I remember them saying or doing before they got divorced, I try to stop myself and back up."

Emerging adults are especially motivated by a desire to spare their future children the pain they experienced. Melissa, who has been living with her boyfriend for the past two years, said that before they decide to get married, "I think we both want to be really sure, because his parents are divorced and mine are, too. I don't want to go through what my parents did, and I don't want to have kids and put them through what happened to me, and he wouldn't either. So I think we're both real careful about that." Dan said that witnessing his parents' bitter divorce and problematic remarriages has made him "scared to death of divorce. It's hell. Divorce is so painful for everybody, you know, and when you get some kids involved, that's a big deal. So I've been really careful, and I know what I want and I wouldn't settle for anything."

Samuel Johnson wrote centuries ago that "[r]emarriage is the triumph of hope over experience." For today's emerging adults, especially those with divorced parents, even a first marriage often represents such a triumph. But with their heartfelt hopes and their determination about making their marriage last, how could it be that emerging adults whose parents have divorced have an even higher likelihood of divorce than those with nondivorced parents?[52] What happens to the emphatic resolutions of people like Melissa to be "really sure" before they enter marriage? Why don't the experiences of people like Dan, that have made them "scared to death of divorce" and vow to be "really careful" about marriage, make them any less likely to become divorced eventually themselves?

The explanation seems to be that even though witnessing parents' divorce is often horrifying and deeply painful, it also makes divorce seem more acceptable as an option when a marriage is unhappy.[53] For example, Rob's parents divorced recently after 25 years of a marriage that was not very satisfying for either of them. After long hesitating to marry his girlfriend, his parents' divorce inspired him to become engaged to her, because now he has "the knowledge that if it doesn't work out, you know, divorce is a way out of it, and it's acceptable. You're not trapped. I think their divorce now, for me, says 'Well, if you don't get along, it's okay. You can get divorced. It's not going to be the end of the world.'" Similarly, Jake saw his parents divorce when he was in high school, after years of being unhappy together, and concluded: "I don't think divorce is such a bad thing, because I don't think you should spend your time with somebody that you're not enjoying. It just doesn't make any sense. I think that's why divorces happen more often now, because people realize they should be happy, you know, it's not their job to make somebody else happy. I just don't think that's right."

It works the other way, too—emerging adults whose parents have had long, reasonably happy marriages see divorce as a less acceptable option. Maya said her parents' long marriage has taught her that "I don't feel like you can choose to get married and then choose to end it. I think you need to decide before you get married, and I think that if I married someone, even if I wasn't necessarily perfectly happy, I wouldn't divorce him." Terrell said his parents have impressed upon him that his marriage, like theirs, ought to be for life. "I was always raised to believe that when you get married, you stay married. So when you get married to somebody, you better know it's the right person. It's a lifetime commitment."

Even emerging adults whose parents are still together cannot help but witness many examples of marriages that have failed—brothers, sisters, friends, uncles, aunts, cousins, coworkers. Although they fervently hope their own marriage will last for life, they are all too aware of how common it is for once-hopeful couples to end their marriages in acrimony. Holly has been talking to a coworker who is in the process of divorce, and now the thought of divorce "just scares me to death, because I even asked him, 'Well, there must have been something good there once, a long time ago?' and he's like 'Well, I thought there was.' Well, everybody thinks there is. Nobody goes into it going, 'Someday we'll hate each other's guts.' So it just scares me to death." They try to keep their hopes up, even as they shudder to think what divorce would be like. Gabriella's comments sum it up: "I think it would be a horrible alone feeling. When I think of divorce I think of loneliness. I think it would be really hard to start all over again. Hopefully I'll find somebody that I will be with forever."

Conclusion: Marriage Hopes, Marriage Fears

Just as with love and sex, when it comes to marriage, emerging adults today have greater freedoms than the young people of the past. There are no longer any rigid expectations about the "right" age to marry that push young people to rush into marriage before they feel ready, with someone about whom they may have serious doubts. Most emerging adults want to marry by age 30, but that gives them the entire decade of their twenties to meet people, have different relationships, and find someone with whom they wish to commit themselves to a common future. Even for emerging adults who do not marry by age 30, their marriage prospects are by no means over. Enough young people are still unmarried when they reach age 30 that emerging adults who are in that group have plenty of company, and plenty of people left to choose from.

Flexible expectations for when to marry allow emerging adults to decide on the timing of marriage according to what fits best with the individual circumstances of their lives, rather than according to what other people are doing. For some, that means waiting until they have finished an extended period of education, or attained financial stability, or until they have tried various career paths and settled on one they believe suits them well. For others, it means waiting for less tangible changes, until they know themselves well enough and have a clear enough identity that they feel ready to commit themselves to another person.

For nearly all, it means waiting until they find someone who at least approximates the ideal they imagine, of a marriage partner who will be kind, loving, attractive, and similar to themselves in what they like to do and how they look at the world. Until they find their soul mate or someone close to it, they can have other relationships that involve love and sex. They are also free to cohabit with someone if they wish, in order to have daily companionship and save on their expenses without the binding commitment of marriage.

Yet, as with love and sex, the freedoms of emerging adults in their marriage decisions are tinged with fear and anxiety. It may seem like an advantage to have various love partners without being bound by the commitment and restrictions of marriage—unless you are the one who would like to have the commitment. You may be in love with someone, having sex with them, even living with them, and yet they may feel no long-term obligation to you. You may have given yourself to them, body, heart, and soul, yet they could walk out any time. Young women, especially, sometimes fear that they may use up their twenties in a relationship or a series of relationships that do not lead to marriage, only to find themselves at 30 feeling that their marriage prospects are sharply reduced. They are also far more likely than young men to find themselves becoming single parents in their twenties, with all the difficult challenges that condition presents.

For young men and young women alike, divorce lurks among their marriage hopes as a potential disaster. They are well aware that divorce is prevalent in American society. They do not need the statistics to tell them, because they have seen it happen to the people around them, if not to their parents, then to siblings, other relatives, friends, or coworkers.

They do what they can to try to avoid the same fate. Cohabiting is not just for convenience or companionship, but to see what it is like to live with that person, to try to detect any major problems so that an unhappy marriage and an unhappier divorce can be avoided. Waiting until at least their late twenties to get married is not just to allow years for exploration during emerging adulthood, but to allow them to reach a level of maturity and judgment that they hope will lead them to make the right choice in marriage.

Even then, of course, there is no guarantee they will make a choice they will not regret and that their marriage will work out as they wish. As Holly observed, nobody goes into marriage thinking, "Someday we'll hate each other's guts." Emerging adults look ahead to marriage as they look ahead to much of life, wary but optimistic, aware of the hazards before them but confident that they have it within their power to shape the future into something resembling their dreams.

Chapter 6

The Road Through College

Twists and Turns

These days, it is widely recognized that you must have some kind of education beyond high school in order to get a good job in American society. As many studies have shown, the number of years of *tertiary education* (any education or training beyond secondary school) is strongly related to future income and occupational status.[1] Emerging adults may not know the studies or the statistics, but they know, from what they have seen friends, neighbors, and family members experience, that tertiary education opens up a wide range of job possibilities, and that those who do not have it face more limited, less promising employment options. In the national Clark poll, 78% of 18–29-year-olds agreed that "[o]ne of the most important keys to success in life is a college education."[2] So, as they leave high school, 9 out of 10 young Americans expect to continue their education by attending a college, university, or vocational school.[3] About 70% actually enter tertiary education the year following high school.[4] Of these, about half enter a two-year school and half enter a four-year school.[5]

Participation in tertiary education has risen slowly and steadily for young men over the past half century, but among young women the increase has been truly revolutionary. In 1960, there were twice as many young men as young women among college students in the United States, but now there are more women than men, 57% to 43%.[6] This pattern has occurred worldwide. In a survey of 141 countries, there were more young women than young men in tertiary education in 83, including many developing countries.[7] Within the United States, the increase in obtaining tertiary education has taken place across ethnic groups, although entry to college following high school graduation remains higher for Asian Americans (90%) and Whites (71%) than for African Americans (60%) and Latinos (60%).[8]

Although education now continues after high school for most young Americans, the significance of schooling changes from adolescence to emerging adulthood. With some exceptions, most American adolescents do not take high school very seriously. They find it boring, except for the fun of seeing their friends.[9] They are rarely engaged in what is taking place in the classroom, and they rarely do much homework. They do not really expect to learn anything important in high school. Few adolescents believe that their high school education will provide the basis for an adult occupation. In my original study, only 35% of emerging adults agreed with the statement, "my high school education prepared me well for the work place."

In emerging adulthood, school takes on an entirely new significance. Now you have to think about how your education will propel you onto a career path. Instead of simply going to your local high school, you must choose from a wide range of possible colleges or occupational training programs. And once you enter college, it is not so easy to just show up and shrug your way through it, as you may have done in high school. If you are not engaged in the classroom and you do not finish your homework, your college professors are less likely simply to pass you through, as your high school teachers did. In college, you have to develop enough self-discipline to get yourself to class and do the work required, or you may find yourself flunking out. The stakes are also higher in college because somebody, probably you or your parents, is paying real money for you to go, money that will be wasted if you do not pass your classes. Thus school, like love, becomes more serious in emerging adulthood, more focused on laying the foundation for adult life.

Because tertiary education has become a requirement for obtaining the best jobs available in the new service/information/technology economy of the twenty-first century, participating in tertiary education has become normative among emerging adults across developed countries.[10] However, in sheer size the American system dwarfs all others. No other country in the world has a system of tertiary education as extensive as the United States, with over 4,400 colleges, universities, and community colleges.[11] The structure of the American tertiary education system supports an extended emerging adulthood, in which young people have abundant opportunities to explore a wide range of possible occupational futures. Young Americans are able to keep their work options open for a long time as they try out different college paths before choosing a specific direction. In Europe, young people who enter tertiary education must have their focus already decided; they do not take a mix of courses for a year or two while they decide on a major, as college students do in the United States, but take courses only in the area they have chosen to study before entering.

The percentage of today's emerging adults in tertiary education is higher than at any time in American history.[12] Until the middle of the twentieth century, tertiary education was mainly for the elite. In 1900 only 4% of 18–21-year-olds attended college, and by 1940 that proportion had risen only to 16%. But the percentage rose steadily through the second half of the twentieth century, as shown in Chapter 1, until college had become an experience shared by the majority of emerging adults in the early twenty-first century. In other countries, too, participation in tertiary education rose steadily over the past century as their economies became based less on agriculture and manufacturing and more on information, technology, and services.

In this chapter, we examine a variety of aspects of emerging adults' college experiences. First, we look at how emerging adults chart their course through college, including choosing a college major from among the many options available to them. This section also contains a look at emerging adults who succeed in college and those who flounder, and some reasons for the differences. Then we will take a critical look at the American system of allowing such widespread access to higher education, and compare it to the European system, looking at the pros and cons of each. In the second half of the chapter, we look at what undergraduates have to say about their college experiences, for better and worse. We will finish the chapter by looking at two possible future trends, MOOCs and gap years.

Charting a Route Through College

As they enter college in the fall following their graduation from high school, most American emerging adults have only the most general idea of what they want to study when they get there.[13] They know they want to get a college degree. They know that attending college is important for their future, because a person with a college degree has a wider range of employment options and is likely to make considerably more money than a person without one. They may look forward to the non-academic enjoyments of college life: meeting a variety of new people, having sexual adventures, falling in love, making new friends, getting drunk, and running their own lives independently of their parents. They may have made a tentative decision about a field of study. But few of them have made a firm choice of an occupation that will be the ultimate purpose of their college studies.

College in the United States is for finding out what you want to do. Typically, at four-year colleges you have two years before you have to make a definite decision by declaring a major. During those two years you can try out a variety of different possibilities by taking classes in areas you think might want to major in. And even after you declare a major, you can always change your mind—and many emerging adults do.

Their college meanderings are part of their identity explorations. In taking various classes and trying various potential college majors, they are trying to answer the identity question, "What kind of job would really fit me best, given my abilities and interests?" Many are waiting for something to click, hoping for that "aha!" moment when they know they have found their true calling. Some find it, some do not. But college at least gives them the opportunity.

Many of them have complicated tales to tell about their search for a college major that fits with their developing identity. For example, Barbara has changed her major four times since entering college six years ago. "I started out in chemistry actually. I wanted to go into pathology or radiology. And then I went through a stage where I wanted to be in pharmacy school and do some drug testing in space. Then I decided that that probably wasn't going to be realistic. I kept changing my mind. I went back to chemistry. And then I got into the business end of it, into accounting, but I decided that I did not want to sit in an office all day long. I wanted to be out seeing more people every day."

Now, she is majoring in "administration of athletics" and plans to get a job arranging advertising and promotion for athletic events. She grew up in an athletic family—her father was a professional athlete, and all the children were involved in sports—and athletics feels like the right fit to her. "I've just always enjoyed sports. It was just a love of sports more than anything" that eventually led her in this career direction.

Ken also followed a serpentine road during college, through four different degree programs. "The first major I got into was in communications and public relations, but I didn't really care for that one. So I switched to educational counseling psychology, leaning more towards teaching social studies. And then I went into physical education and was going to be a teacher and coach. Finally I ended up taking a physiology class and really liking it. Then one thing led to another and I ended up getting a degree in exercise physiology." It took him seven years to graduate, but he has no regrets about it. "I think when I finally ended up graduating, I had 140–150 hours of class work just because I'd changed so many times. There were a lot of things I enjoyed in terms of class work."

Some emerging adults, especially the younger ones, are still looking, still waiting for something to click. Elaine is about to enter her third year of college, but she still has not decided what she wants to study:

"I don't have a major right now. I'm undecided. And I have absolutely no idea. I mean, I have a lot of interests—that's the problem. I can't decide on just one to stick with for the rest of my college career. I'm interested in psychology. Also in sciences, like, any of the sciences. I guess mainly toward biology. I'm kind of interested in law. Law is kind of overwhelming thinking about it, but law. And arts. I love drawing. I'm not very good at it, but I think I'm kind of good at, like, designing things. I thought about maybe going to fashion school. Everyone I know is majoring in business, but it's not my thing. So I don't think I'm going to get into that."

So, she has narrowed it down to the arts, the sciences, psychology, law, or fashion design—pretty much anything but business! Clearly she still has a long way to go in her educational explorations before she finds the right identity fit, but she remains hopeful. "I guess to me the important thing is to be able to actually find that little niche and get there and be able to make lots of money and be happy and still have time for myself."

In general, the late teens and early twenties, the years that are the heart of emerging adulthood, are the main years of educational explorations for most people. Few people are still bouncing from one possible path to another by the time they reach their late twenties. In both love and work, most people make a transition by their late twenties from the explorations of emerging adulthood to more settled choices. They may obtain more education later in their twenties or beyond, but it is likely to be in the field they have already chosen.

Some emerging adults enter college with a major that has been influenced strongly by their parents, only to discover that it does not fit at all with their own identity. Rob was a pre-vet major his first year in college, following in the footsteps of his veterinarian father. However, he soon realized that "I really wasn't that interested in the chemistry and biology that I was taking." Trying to figure out what he really wanted to do, he thought about how "I've always been mathematically inclined," and he decided to take a few courses in accounting. It clicked, and he changed his major to business.

For Cindy, the influence from her parents was more explicit. "I have Asian parents, so every Asian parent's dream—especially if they've immigrated here—they want to live their dreams through their children because they never had the chance to go through education. So my parents' dream was always for us—there's three girls in my family—to pursue being a doctor or a lawyer. So I remember when I was little, my little sister said, 'I'll be a doctor,' and I said, 'Then I'll be a lawyer.'" She stuck with this resolve through childhood and entered the University of California–Berkeley intending to prepare herself for law school. But two years into her college studies, she still had not declared a major. Her advisor gave her a book with descriptions of 80 majors and told her to pick one by the same time next week. "So I looked through the whole book," Cindy recalled, "and I thought 'What do I really like doing? I mean, I know my mom wants me to go be a lawyer, but I only live once and I really want to do something that I really like doing.' So I thought 'There's something about being on stage that I really like' and I'd done a lot of shows as a model." She decided to major in dance—about as far away from law as it is possible to be. Now graduated from Cal, she is a model and actress, and her dancing is one of the skills she has to offer as an actress.

Succeeding and Floundering

Although 70% of American emerging adults enter college following high school, this does not mean that all of them follow a direct path to a college degree four years later. Quite the contrary. For most emerging adults, entering college means embarking on a winding educational path that may or may not lead to a degree. Only 59% of students who enter a four-year college or university have graduated six years later.[14] Among all 25–29-year-olds, just 30% have obtained a bachelor's degree. Even for emerging adults who do get a bachelor's degree, for most of them it takes five or six years to get their "four-year degree." Rates of dropping out are even higher for students who enter two-year schools.[15]

There are many reasons why students often sputter in their educational progress once they enter college. With some emerging adults, it is clear that they were not ready for college when they entered. They did not really know why they were there, they were not committed to it, and consequently they floundered. They may have come to college simply out of inertia, because it seemed like the thing to do, or because all of their friends were going and their parents expected them go, too. Cecilia went to college for a year and a half, but did poorly and dropped out. "I just wasn't ready. I wasn't really sure what I wanted to do. I wasn't studying." Instead, she spent her time "watching TV, going out, just anything but studying." Now, she is working as a cashier in a bookstore and trying to decide what to do next. She has a vague desire to enter a medical profession, but she says, "I'm not good at math and there's a lot of classes like chemistry where you have to do lots of math." She admits she has "no clue" what she will be doing in 10 years.

Some enter college because of their parents' wishes rather than their own, and fail as an act of defiance. This was the case with Danielle. "My mom made me come to the university and I didn't want to be there, so I was like 'Well, I'll blow off school if I want.'" She was soon expelled for poor grades, and spent three years drifting among low-wage jobs before she decided to re-enter college—her own decision, this time. Now she is studying to be a nurse.

Some enter college and find they lack the self-discipline to get themselves to class and do their coursework. They may enjoy the freedom of being away from home so much that they are easily distracted by the pleasures of the moment, which usually do not include studying. Jake nearly flunked out during his first two years of college, because he was too undisciplined and too busy with activities that diverted him from his schoolwork. "I slept too much, played too many computer games, partied too much—all that stuff." Eventually he did get his degree, in psychology, and he now works as a bank teller. Looking back, he now thinks he lacked the maturity to make the most out of his early college years. "I wasn't ready. I should have gotten a job for maybe a year and then decided what I wanted to do. I think I would have gained some perspective."

This is a common sentiment among emerging adults in their mid-twenties, that they were too immature at age 18 or 19 to apply themselves to educational goals in college, and consequently their early college years were wasted. They got caught up in what education critic Murray Sperber calls the "beer and circus" of college life—the parties, the drinking, the social life, the sports events.[16]

Not that there is anything wrong with these things in moderation, but for many emerging adults moderation is not the standard they live by in their early college years. On the contrary, the pursuit of excess may be part of the fun of college life, part of what students view as the full college experience. This is especially evident with regard to alcohol use. College students drink more than emerging adults who are not college students, and in national studies nearly half of college students in their late teens and early twenties report *binge drinking* (five or more alcoholic drinks in a row for men, four in a row for women) at least once in the past two weeks.[17]

All their lives, until they left home for college, their parents were around to exercise control on their behalf. Their parents made sure they got up in the morning to go to school, their parents kept track of how they were doing in their schoolwork, and their parents knew what they were doing after school and what time they came home at night. Sure, they were able to conceal some things from their parents, but they were always aware that their parents were keeping track of them. Once they leave home for college, their parents are no longer around to make sure they do things they are supposed to do—get up on time in the morning, go to class, do their homework—or to discourage them from doing the things they are not supposed to do—go out drinking several times a week, play electronic games or watch pornography or listen to music late into the night, sleep through their morning classes the next day.

Many college students manage to handle their new freedoms well. By the time they leave for college, they have developed enough self-control that they no longer need to have their parents monitoring them in order for them to behave responsibly. They manage their own schedule, they get their schoolwork done, they pass their classes. Although they may sometimes drink to excess, as long as they restrict their binges to the weekends they can still manage to get to class and do their schoolwork.

But for many others, the freedoms of college life prove to be too much for them to handle. With no one around to exercise control on their behalf, their own resources of self-control and self-discipline prove to be inadequate for the challenges of college life. They blow off their classes, they fail to do their coursework, they drink too much too often, and eventually they drop out or get kicked out.

The cost of college is another reason why many students drop out before obtaining a degree. Over the past 30 years, costs have risen at a steep rate, four times the rate of everything else.[18] As a consequence, 70% of full-time students now hold a job while they go to school, and 59% work at least 20 hours a week.[19] Despite working, many students go into debt during their college years.[20] Imagine a student attending college while working 20 or more hours a week, under constant pressure from juggling school and work, and sliding more deeply into debt with each semester. In this light, it is understandable that many of them decide to give up school before obtaining their degree. Especially for emerging adults who are undecided about a career path, staying in college may come to seem pointless under these conditions. Still, dropping out for financial reasons is a serious miscalculation of future costs and benefits. Although the payoff for obtaining a four-year degree is enormous (as we will see shortly), students who drop out before graduating have the burden of debt from the years they attended but not the financial reward in the workplace for having a degree—the worst of both worlds.

Students from relatively poor families are especially likely to report financial obstacles, as Figure 6.1 shows (with data from the national Clark poll). Using mother's education to represent family social class background, the figure shows that the lower the family's social class, the more likely emerging adults are to report that they have received less education than they need, due to financial reasons. Studies show that high-achieving high school students from poor families are often unaware of opportunities that exist for them to obtain college scholarships.[21]

College achievement rates are lower among African Americans and Latinos than among Whites.[22] This is partly because African Americans and Latinos tend to grow up in poorer areas and go to lower-quality schools than Whites, so they are less prepared for the academic demands of college. However, it is also because the financial strain of college tends to be greater for African Americans and Latinos. The poorer a student's family, the more likely he or she is to drop out of college, and African Americans and Latinos are more likely than Whites to grow up in poor families.

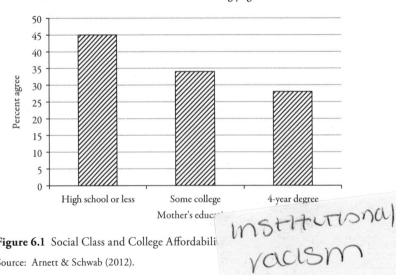

"I have not been able to find enough financial support to get the education I need."
% somewhat or strongly agree

Figure 6.1 Social Class and College Affordabili

Source: Arnett & Schwab (2012).

This predicament is evident in the life of Nicole. She is one of four children of a single mother with mental health problems who was on welfare for most of the time Nicole was growing up. Since she was very young, Nicole has had high educational goals, but so far those goals have been difficult for her to reach. She left home after high school after concluding that "I needed to experience living out of my mother's home in order to study," and has attended two community colleges. But she has found it hard to make progress in her education while also working full-time as a medical receptionist to support herself and also provide money for her mother and younger siblings. She has taken classes at night and is close to finishing an associate's degree, but "this semester, I took off. I said, 'I gotta get my funds together.' Hopefully by the time I'm 26, 27, I will have enough saved to go to school full time." She remains determined to achieve her ultimate goal of getting a Ph.D. and becoming a talk-radio psychologist, but the obstacles before her are formidable. We will hear more about Nicole's life in Chapter 12.

Some emerging adults know from an early age what kind of work they want to do, and they enter college already firmly established on a path toward their career goal. For them, no period of exploration is necessary in their first year or two of college to allow them to find the kind of work that best fits with their identity. The purpose of college is to obtain the skills and the credentials that will enable them to do the work they know they are cut out to do. Gloria is studying to be an elementary school teacher because "I just really like children and I've always wanted to work with them." Maya said, "I knew since I was five that I've wanted to do science," and now she is studying chemistry, planning to go to graduate school and eventually become a chemistry professor. Arnold remembers that "I was very, very strong in math, ever since the 3rd grade. I took an accounting class in high school and everything just started to click—the numbers started to flow and everything was fine." He majored in accounting in college and now works in an accounting firm.

Emerging adults like Gloria, Maya, and Arnold go straight through college in four years, because they know what they want to do when they enter college and they do not spend any time searching for the career direction that will fit them best. But they are the exception, not the rule. The influences that lead emerging adults to take a long time to finish their degree are the same ones that lead many of them to drop out—uncertainty over what to study, too much "beer and circus," and financial struggles.

Emerging adults are mixed in their feelings about taking five, six, or more years to finish their undergraduate education. On the one hand, many of them are frustrated by it. They expected to get their four-year degree in four years, and when it turns out to take longer than that, they feel a sense of inadequacy, like they have failed to meet the standard set out for them. In response to the interview question, "Are you satisfied with what you have achieved by this age?" the most common source of dissatisfaction stated by emerging adults in their mid-twenties in my original study was that they had not yet completed college.

Casey, 24, entered college intending to major in business, but soon discovered that he did not like it at all. "The accounting and the marketing and the econ [economics] classes, I just did not enjoy them. I was just like 'This isn't right.' It was a chore to get up and go to class." He dropped business and floundered for a year and a half, uncertain of what direction to pursue next. Then he decided to major in education, with the goal of being a math and science teacher in a high school and coaching the high school baseball team. He loves the area he has chosen and feels he has found the right fit, but he regrets that it took him so long to find it. When I asked him if he was satisfied with what he had achieved, he said, "No, I'm not satisfied at all. I'm very disappointed in myself. Just because of the education thing. I would have liked to have shown up in college and known what I wanted to do and graduated in four years."

More typically, however, emerging adults see their education as something they expect to continue through their twenties or even their thirties, combined or interspersed with work. The idea that college is mainly for persons aged 18–22 is rapidly fading. By the early twenty-first century, nearly half of undergraduate students were over 25 years old.[23] Furthermore, according to one national survey of college undergraduates, only about one-fourth said they planned to end their education when they obtained their bachelor's degree. Nearly 40% planned to get a master's degree, and nearly 30% planned to get a Ph.D., a medical degree, or a law degree.[24] And they are backing up their goals with their actions. From 1970 through 2011, according to the National Center for Education Statistics, there was a 50% increase in graduate program enrollment among men and a staggering 400% increase among women.[25]

There are a variety of reasons why so many emerging adults intend to continue their education through their twenties and thirties. First, they recognize that continued education is a way of improving their income. In most fields, the more education you have, the higher the salary you can command. A related incentive is that more education carries higher status. Being able to tell others you have a bachelor's degree, a master's degree, or a Ph.D. is something to be proud of in American society. But some emerging adults wish to obtain more education simply for the joy of learning. They like the classroom environment, they like learning new things, and they do not want that process to stop.

Evaluating the American System

In sum, most young Americans spend the early years of emerging adulthood taking college courses and using those courses to help them clarify what career path they want to pursue. Some succeed in their college courses and establish a clear direction to follow, others flounder and drop out, but for nearly all of them a college degree is one of their eventual goals, whether it takes them four years or far longer. The openness and flexibility of the American system of higher education makes it possible for emerging adults to take college courses on and off through their twenties and beyond if they wish, often in combination with a part-time or full-time job.

Is this a good system? Is it better to allow young people to take their time and explore various possible career directions in their late teens and early twenties, or would it be better to encourage or require them to decide while still in high school what career direction they will take? These questions arise because the European educational system is so different from the American system. In most European countries young people are separated into different schools by age 14 or 15, with some entering schools that will prepare them for university and others entering schools that will prepare them for a business job or a trade, such as electronics or auto mechanics. Those who enter tertiary education must decide before entering what they will study. Once they begin their tertiary education program, all their courses are in the field they have chosen.

So, which system is better? There is probably no simple answer to this question. In truth, each system has strengths and weaknesses. The strength of the European system is that many young people leave secondary school already on a path toward a well-paying job in a respectable trade. They devote their late teens and early twenties to making further progress in their chosen profession, rather than searching for a profession during those years, as Americans typically do. But the weakness of the system is that many young people may not be ready at age 14 or 15 to make a decision about what career path to follow for the rest of their working lives, because their identities are not yet developed enough to guide this choice. It is difficult for them to change their minds in their late teens or their twenties and pursue a different career path. The European system does not possess that kind of flexibility.

Similarly, for European emerging adults who enter university, the strength of the system is that students must know what they want to study when they enter, and they focus on that one area of study. Consequently, they do not spend two or three years meandering through the curriculum, waiting for inspiration to strike. But that strength is also a weakness. If they decide after entering university that they do not want to study that topic after all, it is difficult for them to switch tracks. The government pays most university education costs, allowing young Europeans to graduate with little or no debt, which is great—except that, since the government is paying the bill, the government can also set limits on how many times students can change their minds.

The strength of the American system is that young people have a longer period to try out different possible career directions. Few Americans have decided for certain what career path they will take by the time they leave high school. During emerging adulthood they try out various jobs and college courses in the process of clarifying for themselves what they "really want to do," what job would suit them best. But the weakness of this system is that for some emerging adults, this is more freedom and flexibility than they can handle. Rather than using their late teens and early twenties as a period of systematic exploration, many American emerging adults drift through that period, paying little attention to their college courses, drinking a lot of alcohol, learning little. They may find themselves in their mid-twenties with no college degree but with a large load of debt from their sporadic efforts to obtain one.

Maybe it is because I am American, but it seems to me that the American system offers young people more of an opportunity to find the educational and occupational path that will be the right fit for them. It is difficult for me to believe that most people can know themselves well enough at the age of 14 or 15 to make a decision about what career path to follow for the rest of their lives. It would be like asking them to decide at that age whom they want to marry—absurd! Most people simply have not developed their identity well enough by that age to make a permanent decision about love or work. Self-understanding is required for those kinds of choices, and for most people this quality develops gradually through their teens and early twenties, partly as a consequence of experiencing different possibilities.

Educational psychologist Stephen Hamilton, in comparing the American and European systems, makes a useful distinction between *transparency* and *permeability*.[26] *Transparency* is his term for how clearly the path is marked through the educational system leading to the labor market. In a transparent system the educational and training requirements for various occupations are clearly laid out and young people are well informed about them from an early age. *Permeability* refers to how easy it is to move from one point within the educational system to another. A permeable system makes it easy to drop one educational/career path and choose a different one.

Thus the American system is low in transparency and high in permeability. Even in emerging adulthood, most Americans have only a limited understanding of how to obtain the education or training that will lead to the job they want, but it is easy to enter some kind of college and easy to switch paths once they get there. In contrast, the European system is high in transparency but low in permeability. European adolescents know which path of education and training leads to which job, but once they choose a path—as they are required to do at the age of just 14 or 15—the system makes it difficult for them to change their minds.

Some critics of the American system have argued that we should move closer to the Europeans. For example, one pair of scholars argues that "adolescents need help in developing coherent life plans" (p. 109) while still in high school, so that by the time they leave high school they can "commit to a course of action to achieve specific goals" (p. 84).[27] But why urge them to make this commitment if they are not ready? Essentially, this is an argument for eliminating the kind of free identity exploration that is at the heart of emerging adulthood. But it is through these explorations that emerging adults have the opportunity to find the choices that will suit them best.

Most emerging adults have no intention of marrying and having children until at least their late twenties. Before they enter those obligations, most are responsible for no one but themselves. If it takes them several years of trying different college courses, and different college majors, going back and forth between work and school, before they find the direction that fits, well, why not? There is no good reason why they should rush to make a choice while still in their teens. It seems likely that by taking their time, exploring different possibilities, and waiting until they have a more fully formed identity, for most of them the choice they eventually make will be the basis of a more satisfying and productive adult work life than a hurried choice in their teens would have been. It is true, leaving college deeply in debt from student loans is a substantial burden, but that supports an argument for better financial aid to students and colleges rather than for ceasing to use emerging adulthood for educational explorations.

The College Experience

What kind of experiences do American emerging adults have in college? What kind of an education do they get? What sorts of things do they learn, and fail to learn, at college? How do they change during the course of their college years? These questions have been the target of considerable research and growing concern over the past 40 years.

At the outset, it should be noted that the college experience is many different things to many different people. The colleges emerging adults attend vary widely, from enormous research-oriented universities with tens of thousands of students, to small liberal arts colleges with a few hundred students, to community colleges whose students often work full-time as well as go to school. The nature of the college experience also depends on the goals and attitudes of the students themselves, as we will see in the next section.

Four Student Subcultures

One useful way of characterizing young people's college experience was developed in the early 1960s by sociologists Burton Clark and Martin Trow, who described four student "subcultures": the collegiate, the vocational, the academic, and the rebel.[28] The *collegiate* subculture centers around fraternities, sororities, dating, drinking, big sports events, and campus fun. Professors, courses, and grades are a secondary priority. Students in this subculture do enough schoolwork to get by, but they resist or ignore any encouragement from faculty to become seriously involved with ideas. Their main purpose during their college years is fellowship and partying. This subculture thrives especially at big universities.

Students in the *vocational* subculture have a practical view of their college education. To them, the purpose of college is to gain skills and a degree that will enable them to get a better job than they would have otherwise. Like collegiates, students in the vocational subculture resist professors' demands for engagement in ideas, beyond the requirements of the coursework. But vocationals have neither the time nor the money for the frivolous fun of the collegiate subculture. Typically they work 20–40 hours a week to support themselves and help pay their college tuition. Students who attend community colleges are mostly in this category.

The *academic* subculture is the one that identifies most strongly with the educational mission of college. Students in this subculture are drawn to the world of ideas and knowledge. They study hard, do their assignments, and get to know their professors. These are the students professors like best, because they are excited about and engaged with the materials their professors present.

Students in the *rebel* subculture are also deeply engaged with the ideas presented in their courses. However, unlike academics, rebels are aggressively nonconformist. Rather than liking and admiring their professors, they tend to be critically detached from them and skeptical of their expertise. Rebels enjoy learning when they feel the material is interesting and relevant to their lives, but they are selectively studious. If they like a course and respect the professor, they do the work required and often receive a top grade, but if they dislike a course and find it irrelevant to their personal interests, they may slack off and receive a low grade.

Clark and Trow described these student subcultures in the early 1960s, five decades ago. Do the same subcultures still apply to today's emerging adults attending college? Observers of higher education think so,[29] and from my long experience as a professor at various colleges and universities, I would agree that their description still rings true. All of these subcultures are likely to be familiar to anyone who teaches college students. But it may be best to see them as types of subcultures, not types of students. Most students are blends of the four subcultural types, to different degrees, although most identify with one subculture more than the others.

To put it another way, the four subcultural types represent different kinds of goals that emerging adults have for their college experience. As collegiates they pursue fun, as vocationals they pursue a degree, as academics they pursue knowledge, and as rebels they pursue an identity. Most students hope to make all of these things a part of their college years, even if they vary in which one they make their top priority. In a national study of college freshmen by the Higher Education Research Institute, 77% responded that it was "very important" for them during college "to learn more about the things that interest me" (an academic goal), and nearly as many, 75%, intended "to get training for a specific profession" (a vocational goal), but 52% also intended "to find my purpose in life" (a rebel goal).[30]

As for collegiate fun, 46% of students report binge drinking in the past two weeks, according to the latest annual survey of over 200,000 college students nationwide by the Core Institute of Southern Illinois University–Carbondale.[31] That is a higher rate than you would find in any older age group, but it is less than half of all students.[32] So, drinking is a common part of college life, but for most students it is within manageable boundaries.

Is College Worth It? What the Students Say

The college experience is romanticized in American society—the sunny quad filled with Frisbee-tossing students on a spring afternoon, the football stadium roaring on a crisp fall day, the inspiring professor teaching a life-changing course—but colleges and universities are also frequent targets of critiques and laments. Some have even advocated in recent years that emerging adults would be better off skipping the time and cost of a college education altogether, or assembling their own college curriculum for free via the Internet.[33]

So, is college worth it, or not? In terms of financial rewards, there is no doubt that the answer is a resounding yes. The economic benefits of a four-year degree are indisputable. College grads make about a million dollars more over the course of a career, compared to their peers who obtained no education beyond high school.[34] They are also more likely to be working. The unemployment rate is consistently at least twice as high for 25–29-year-olds with only a high school degree than it is for those who have a four-year college degree.

Most college grads are well aware of the benefits of having a degree. A 2011 survey by the Pew Research Center found that 84% of college grads said their degree had been a good investment; only 7% said it had not.[35] Some may be frustrated when they have trouble finding a good job in their field in the first year or two after graduating, but they recognize that a college education nearly always pays off over the course of a career.

Studies of current students also find that a large majority respond favorably to survey questions about the education they are receiving. In a national survey of over 9,000 students,[36] Arthur Levine and Diane Dean found that 79% indicated that they were "satisfied with the teaching at your college." Also, 76% indicated that there were faculty at their college who took a special interest in students' academic progress, and 78% had professors who had "greatly influenced" their academic career. More than half also had professors whom they felt they could turn to for advice on personal matters. In all respects, students' satisfaction with their academic experiences in college increased compared to earlier surveys Levine and colleagues conducted in previous decades.

Do the results of the survey by Levine and Dean mean that the critics are wrong, and that everything is fine with American higher education? Not exactly. Although students are generally satisfied with the education they receive, they tend to be more satisfied at small colleges with small classes than at large universities where the classes are often enormous. In the *Princeton Review*'s annual survey of students at 300 American colleges of various sizes,[37] small colleges consistently rank highest on almost all positive measures, such as "professors make themselves accessible," "professors bring material to life," and "best overall academic experience for undergraduates." In contrast, big research universities dominate the top rankings for all the negative items, such as "professors suck all life from material," "professors make themselves scarce," and "class discussion rare."

The responses of my students to questions about their satisfaction with their college experience show how students can be satisfied overall, even if they are dissatisfied with some aspects of the education they have received.[38] Most have had some professors they found impressive and inspiring, even if others were disappointing. Kayla complained about having professors who were "not challenging, engaging, or even remotely human," but also said she'd had "some wonderful, memorable, and influential professors." Some students have goals that are primarily vocational, so their satisfaction is based on the prospect of getting a degree. Timothy said, "I don't feel I have learned as much as I anticipated," but nevertheless he is pleased that "I am achieving a college degree, which is very satisfying," and he expects his degree to be "a great deal of help when I am looking for a job."

But the most common theme, when I have asked them to write about whether they are satisfied or dissatisfied overall with their college experience, is that their satisfaction is based mainly on what they have experienced in terms of *personal growth*.[39] This theme could be seen as a combination of the collegiates' search for fun and the rebels' search for identity, with an additional element of becoming more organized and responsible. Sherry said she had some classes where she "didn't learn much" and other classes where she had "extremely smart professors and have had a great experience with them." However, what makes her "very satisfied" with her college experience is that she has "learned a lot about myself and experienced many new things. I had to get myself up and get my own dinner, manage my money, and so on. These are all things I'd never done before." The requirements of her courses have "definitely taught me responsibility and dedication."

Ted said he was satisfied with his college experience, but his satisfaction "has nothing to do with school. I have experienced so many different things, become much more responsible for myself and have become more grounded in my views and beliefs." Juggling classes, homework, and a part-time job "has made me manage my time better and work harder." He also feels he has "become more reflective on my life as a result of having a certain amount of freedom and privacy in college." Linda feels that "most of my classes have been relatively enlightening and beneficial," but what she has learned in them has consisted mostly of "useless, easily forgotten knowledge." Far more important is that "college has forced me to think, to question, and sometimes just to accept. All of these qualities I either didn't possess prior to college or had very little control over." Her college experience has been "full of revela-tions and growth. Because of college, I am closer to possessing the knowledge I need to be who and what I want to be."

A large body of research supports these students' accounts that college has multiple benefits. Ernest Pascarella and Patrick Terenzini have studied this topic for over three decades.[40] They report a variety of intellectual benefits from attending college, in areas such as general verbal and quantitative skills, oral and written communication skills, and critical thinking. These benefits hold up even after taking into account factors such as age, gender, precollege abilities, and family social class background. Pascarella and Terenzini also find that in the course of the college years, students become less "vocational" in their college goals—that is, they place less emphasis on college as way to a better job—and more "academic"—that is, they place more emphasis on learning for its own sake and for the purpose of enhancing their intellectual and personal growth.

In addition to intellectual, academic benefits, Pascarella and Terenzini describe a long list of non-academic benefits. In the course of the college years, students develop clearer aesthetic and intellectual values. They gain a more distinct identity and become more confident socially. They became less dog-matic, less authoritarian, and less ethnocentric in their political and social views. Their self-concept and psychological well-being improve. As with the academic benefits, these non-academic benefits hold up even after taking into account characteristics such as age, gender, and family social class background.

The long-term benefits of going to college are also well established, according to research by Pascarella and Terenzini as well as many others.[41]

As noted earlier, emerging adults who attend college tend to have considerably higher earnings, occupational status, and career attainment over the long run, compared to those who do not attend college. They also have lower rates of substance abuse, physical and mental health problems, and divorce throughout adulthood, and higher life expectancy.

It seems clear, then, that going to college yields a variety of rewards for emerging adults, both personally and professionally. Is college too expensive? Yes. Is attending college at a big university often frustrating and alienating? Yes. Could the college experience offered to emerging adults be improved? Certainly. But despite these limitations, going to college pays off in multiple ways.

Waves of the Future? MOOCs and the Gap Year

The university is an ancient institution, going back at least a thousand years. In some ways, surprisingly little has changed over that millennium. Professors present information and ideas, based on texts believed to represent current knowledge. Students read the texts, and in classes, students ask questions and professors and students discuss and perhaps investigate key issues. Eventually, professors evaluate students on their grasp of the materials.

This is still, essentially, how colleges and universities educate students today. However, there are many ideas and proposals in the air for changing tertiary education in the United States so that it is better suited to the twenty-first century. Let's look at two possible changes, one that is already happening, the delivery of courses online, and one that I believe should happen, the "gap year."

Virtual Education: The Promise and Limitations of MOOCs

The Internet, which has changed so much in our lives in recent decades, seems poised to change tertiary education as well. If professors can tape their lectures so that students can watch them online and discuss the materials with each other and (perhaps) the professor, is it really necessary any more for students to live on or near a campus and go to a classroom to watch a professor do essentially the same thing and to have the same kinds of discussions with other students? Students would still have to be evaluated on their comprehension of the materials, but couldn't they be evaluated electronically, by taking an exam or writing a paper that an instructor (or a computer program) then grades?

Currently there is much excitement about the potential of the electronic university. It seems to offer the possibility of vastly reducing the costs of obtaining a college degree. For students who have little or no money, whether they are among the lower social classes in developed countries or live in developing countries where universities are few, the electronic university may open doors to knowledge that would otherwise be closed to them. Much of the excitement has concentrated on Massive Open Online Courses, known as MOOCs. Prominent universities and well-funded private corporations have already made available a wide range of courses taught by renowned professors, and millions of students worldwide have enrolled. And this is just the beginning. The idea is only a few years old and is sure to grow in the years to come.

So, is the excitement merited? Will MOOCs usher in a new era of tertiary education that is easy, inexpensive, and available to nearly everyone? It would be nice if it were so, but so far I am a skeptic. MOOCs are so new that there is little research yet on their effectiveness, but there are several reasons to think that students will not learn as well with MOOCs as they would in a traditional college classroom.

The main reason is that MOOCs require a great deal of personal initiative, focus, and self-discipline on the part of the students, to a degree that most people simply do not possess—and certainly not at the "college age" of the late teens and early twenties, when, as most of them acknowledge, they have not yet attained an adult level of maturity and responsibility. It is true that MOOCs offer an astonishing range of information, but so do encyclopedias, and without some kind of formal structure, students are no more likely to make a complete education out of MOOCs than they would be to make it past "aardvark" in the encyclopedia. It is estimated that over 90% of students who sign up for MOOCs fail to finish, and even among the less than 10% who do, it is not clear how many of them actually read and understood the materials.[42] MOOCs are moving toward having students evaluated in a more systematic way, for example by going to a testing site for a monitored exam, or having students monitored by a webcam as they take the exam on their computer. But cheating is a problem even in a classroom vigilantly monitored by a professor, so it will be a challenge to make these less direct methods effective.

I am also skeptical that MOOCs will be able to conjure the interpersonal magic of the classroom. Most professors who have taught for a while, and (I would hope) most students in the course of four-plus years of a college education, know the thrill of that magic, when the classroom discussion is sizzling and new perspectives are forming and insights emerge that no one had imagined before (yes, even the prof). MOOCs are never going to be able to simulate that electronically in any comparable way. And those are the moments that change lives, the moments that shape views of the world in an enduring way, the moments that students will carry with them years, decades, later.

Remember, too, that students say that the most important things they learn in the course of their college education are personal and interpersonal. Professors are more than simply founts of information, they are—at least some of them are, some of the time—figures of admiration and inspiration who can influence students in profound ways. Beyond the classroom, college teaches students how to work with others, how to organize their time, and how to carry out responsibilities. It also helps them clarify their identities and lays out an array of possibilities that allows students to find one that seems like a calling, something that fits just right with their abilities and interests, that offers the promise of the modern ideal of enjoyable, identity-based work. It is difficult to see MOOCs being able to accomplish the same goals.

I do not dismiss entirely the potential of MOOCs or other forms of online courses. There may be many topics can be taught effectively through these methods. No one needs the magic of the classroom to learn auto mechanics, or statistics, or photosynthesis (although personal instruction surely helps the learning process, in all cases). The majority of students taking MOOCs may not have the self-direction and self-discipline required to make the most of them, but some will. There is also a great deal of potential, MOOCs aside, in using electronic methods to make the traditional college classroom more interactive, for example by having students give immediate electronic feedback to the professor on material that has been presented. A great deal of educational research demonstrates that students learn far more through active learning than through passively listening to a lecture, and electronic methods can be developed to promote active learning.[43]

The potential of MOOCs may be greatest for ambitious, highly motivated emerging adults in developing countries, for whom MOOCs may prove to be a valuable—and their only—road to knowledge. But they are unlikely to replace or even undermine the college and university system.

What's the Hurry? The Promise of the "Gap Year"

Given that only 59% of American students who enter a four-year college or university have attained a degree six years later, and that students especially struggle during their first year, there is a lot of room for ideas on how to improve the success of the college experience. One idea I believe is worth considering is the "gap year," that is, taking a year or two after high school to mature and have other experiences before entering tertiary education.

Taking a gap year is rare in the United States. It is estimated that only 2% of American emerging adults deliberately wait a year or two after high school for other planned experiences, then enter college. However, it is far more common in the United Kingdom, Australia, Israel, and northern Europe.[44] Consequently, research on the gap year has taken place almost entirely in these populations, but it suggests the potential benefits of making the gap year more common in the United States.

Andrew Jones, an education researcher at the University of London, summarized the results of research in the United Kingdom, where taking a gap year has become increasingly common in recent decades.[45] British emerging adults have a variety of motivations for taking a gap year, including:

- Desire for a break from formal education;
- To gain a broader perspective on life;
- To develop personal skills;
- To earn money;
- To experience other people, places, and cultures; and
- To do some good in the world, either locally or abroad.

In the United Kingdom, "gappers" are diverse in the range of their gap year experiences. Many simply find a job. Others seek work overseas, for example as an au pair, an English instructor, or doing seasonal work. Some volunteer in service organizations, either in their community or internationally.

Taking a gap year has a variety of benefits, according to Jones's review. Gappers have higher motivation when they enter tertiary education afterward, compared to non-gappers. They report developing life skills, social values, and non-academic skills and qualifications during their gap year. They clarify their educational directions and career choices. Once they enter tertiary education, their educational performance is higher than non-gappers, and once they graduate, having a gap year enhances their employability and their career opportunities. There are drawbacks, too, for some. Unless some kind of formal activity is planned, there is the risk of a wasted year. As one gapper in Jones's report warned, "You've got to avoid the danger of lying in bed for a year doing nothing else than watching daytime TV." But for most emerging adults in the United Kingdom, taking a gap year turns out to be a rewarding choice.

I have found similar results in my research on emerging adults in Denmark.[46] Nearly all the young Danes I interviewed had experienced a gap year—or two, or three. For most, their motivation for taking a gap year was that they were not sure what they wanted to do next, and they were in no hurry to take on either more education or the enduring responsibilities of adult life. Typically, they worked for a while in a low-paying service job— bartender, child-care worker—and when they had saved up some money, they traveled until the money ran out, then worked again. One young man worked as a ski instructor in Switzerland during the winter. When ski season ended, he had saved enough money to travel and goof off until ski season came around again. By the time he had done this for three years, he was eager for the challenges of a university education.

So, why is taking a gap year so common in the United Kingdom, Australia, and northern Europe, and so rare in the United States? One reason may be that there is a long tradition of something like a gap year in the United Kingdom and Europe, going back to the nineteenth century.[47] Another reason is the difference in how the tertiary education systems are structured. As noted earlier in this chapter, in the United Kingdom and Europe, tertiary education is focused on one professional area. Whether your focus is on accounting, electrical engineering, or computer programming, you enter tertiary education to learn that topic, specifically. So, you need to have a fairly well-developed identity—a sense of your abilities and interests—in order to choose a course of tertiary education. In contrast the American university is structured so that the first two years are general education in a wide range of subjects. You are not required to have any idea, when you enter, of what your eventual focus will be. Consequently, British and European emerging adults wait until their identities are clarified, then make their choice.[48] Americans, in contrast, can allow themselves two years of identity development within the college context before they have to make a comparable choice.

The growing frenzy of the college application process in the United States may also have something to do with the reluctance of American emerging adults—and their parents—to make room for a gap year before college, at least among the upper middle class, where the frenzy is concentrated.[49] After all that labor and stress centered on getting into college, who would want to go through the whole thing again the next year? Some colleges now allow students to defer their enrollment for a year, but most do not. Americans are more likely to take a gap year, or at least a few gap months, once they graduate from college, before they enter a long-term job. Participants in programs such as Americorps, Teach for America, and the Peace Corps are mainly post-college emerging adults.[50]

Conclusion: College as a Safe Haven for Identity Explorations

Attending college has become a near-universal aspiration for young Americans, and a majority of them do attend college and experience college life, at least for a while. They take a wide variety of courses, especially their first two years, and gain a foundation of general education that most of them missed in their generally undemanding, uninspiring high schools. They try possible majors, looking for something that matches their abilities and interests, and most of them eventually make a choice they find satisfying.

But college is more than simply vocational training, for most emerging adults. They want to leave college with skills that enable them to find a good job, certainly, but that is not all they want from their college experience. They want to have their share of collegiate fun, too, and take part in the friendships, camaraderie, romances, partying, and communal *joie de vivre* that is naturally generated by having so many unattached young people together in one place. Most are also open to being inspired by new ideas, and most find at least some professors who provide that inspiration. Above all, college is a place for experiencing personal growth. The social experiences, the intellectual experiences, and the experience of being on your own and learning to take responsibility for your day-to-day life combine to transform the green emerging adults who entered as freshmen into graduating seniors who have taken great steps toward maturity, toward becoming an adult.

In many ways, the American college is the emerging adult environment *par excellence*. It is expressly designed for the identity explorations that are at the heart of American emerging adulthood. You have two years to try different courses before you commit yourself to a major. Even after you choose a major, you can switch to another major if you find something you like better. As you try out different courses and different majors, you explore a variety of different ideas that help you develop your worldview. Meanwhile, as you are exploring possible directions for your work future and possible ways of looking at the world, there are hundreds, probably thousands, of other people around you every day, having experiences similar to your own, few of them married, all of them with a considerable amount of unstructured time—the perfect setting for explorations in love. College is a social island set off from the rest of society, a temporary safe haven where emerging adults can explore identity possibilities in love, work, and worldviews with many of the responsibilities of adult life minimized, postponed, kept at bay.

Of course, it is not always so simple or idyllic as all this. A majority of students are employed part- or full-time in addition to their course work, which makes for a busy and sometimes stressful life. Students are often dissatisfied with some aspects of their college experience—large, alienating classes and indifferent professors who view undergraduates as a burden to be avoided—even as they are satisfied overall. Barely half the students who enter a four-year school have obtained a degree six years later. Even those who do obtain a degree are often left with a daunting burden of debt from their college tuition and expenses that will take years, if not decades, to pay off.

All of these are serious problems. Undergraduate education, especially at large universities, has substantial room for improvement. The fact that half of freshmen fail to graduate is deplorable, especially since minorities disproportionately drop out, often for financial reasons. Nevertheless, college persists as a widespread aspiration for emerging adults in the United States. For all its problems, the promise it offers in terms of career advantages, personal growth, and opportunities for exploration remains alluring.

Of course, not all emerging adults aspire to college, and not all are well-suited to the demands of college, as the near-50% failure rate attests. Some emerging adults, for reasons of personality, interests, or intellectual capacities, never liked school, couldn't wait to leave, and would never volunteer for more. They have not even the slightest interest in learning history, astronomy, or English literature; in fact, it feels like torture to them to be required to do so. What they want, and what they need, is to learn practical skills they can apply directly to a job: how to fix a heating system, pour concrete, or remove computer viruses. But in the service-oriented economies of developed countries, *everyone* needs to know *something* that most other people don't know, in order to be able to provide services that other people will be willing to pay for.

This is the crucial conclusion: *tertiary education must become a free, universal entitlement in the twenty-first century, as primary school did in the nineteenth century and high school in the twentieth century.* It should not be only in the form of a four-year college education. Many emerging adults will be happiest and best served if they receive practical instruction, lasting perhaps a year or two, that they can apply directly in the workplace. But in one form or another, all emerging adults need some kind of tertiary education in order to prepare themselves adequately for the modern economy. Their ability to obtain it should not hinge on the financial resources of their families. All of them need it; all of them should receive it; and it is in the interests of their society to provide it, in order for them to become productive contributing members, making the most of their abilities to the benefit of themselves and others.

Won't that be expensive? Sure, it will—just like providing primary education was in the nineteenth century and providing secondary education was in the twentieth century. None of us regrets those investments now; in fact, we could hardly imagine our societies without them. By the end of the twenty-first century, we will see tertiary education in precisely the same way. What would be intolerably expensive would be to squander the talents and energies of twenty-first–century emerging adults by failing to provide them with the education and training they need. Europe, Japan, and nearly all other developed countries already make tertiary education inexpensive or free. There is no excuse for the United States, the richest country the world has ever known, not to do the same.

Chapter 7

Work

More Than a Job

Some of the funniest and most biting parts of the novel *Generation X* involve work. To describe the jobs that many emerging adults take to pay the bills while they look for something better, Coupland coined the term "McJob," defined as "[a] low-paying, low-prestige, low-dignity, low-benefit, no-future job in the service sector. Frequently considered a satisfying career choice by people who have never held one." At one point Dag, one of the main characters, complains, "I mean, really: why *work?* Simply to buy more *stuff?* That's not enough." Another character, Claire, is "a garment buyer-daywear" at the beginning of the book, but says "I don't think it's making me a better person. . . . I'd like to go somewhere rocky, and just empty my brain, read books, and be with people who wanted to do the same thing."

Although Coupland's characters are extreme types—at the end of the novel, they all quit their McJobs and move to Mexico, where they plan to buy a cheap hotel—they personify some of the themes that show up in the work lives of many emerging adults. Emerging adults often hold a series of McJobs in their early twenties while they look for something that will be more satisfying. They have high expectations for work. They aspire to find a job that will be an expression of their identity. Merely being able to "buy more stuff" is not enough. Most want to find a job that will make them "a better person" and hopefully do some good for others as well. In the national Clark poll, 79% of 18–29-year-olds agreed that "[i]t is more important to enjoy my job than to make a lot of money," and 86% agreed that "[i]t is important to me to have a career that does some good in the world."[1]

Work follows a course similar to love from adolescence through emerging adulthood. In love, as we have seen, the first experiences begin in adolescence, but explorations become more serious and enduring in emerging adulthood. With work, too, emerging adulthood is a time when choices become more serious, the stakes riding on those choices become higher, and the foundation for adult life is being laid. And with work as with love, emerging adulthood is a time not only of exploration but of instability.

Work experiences begin in adolescence, for most people growing up in American society. Over 80% of high school seniors have held at least one part-time job by the time they leave high school.[2] However, for the great majority of adolescents, their part-time jobs have little to do with preparing them for a future occupation. Most of their jobs are in the low-wage service sector of the economy—restaurant server, cook, retail sales clerk, and so on.[3] They take these jobs not with the intention of gaining important skills that will form the basis for the work they will do as adults, but mainly for the purpose of financing their current consumption and leisure—clothes, digital devices, movie and concert tickets, fast food, vacation travel, car expenses.[4] They work to provide for the pleasures of the moment, not to lay a foundation for the future.

Work takes on a much larger significance in emerging adulthood. Now it is not enough to work for the moment without giving a thought to how the current job is leading to long-term prospects. Now emerging adults start to think seriously about what kind of work they want to do throughout their adult lives. Work becomes not simply a way of gaining extra cash to finance weekend and vacation fun, but a central part of life, the other pillar on which an adult life is built, along with love.

The rise of emerging adulthood has changed the nature of work for young people in their late teens and early twenties. Half a century ago, when the typical age of marriage and entry to parenthood was in the very early twenties, most young women worked for only a short time, until their first child was born, and few of them had career goals, focusing their energies instead on being wives and mothers.[5] Most young men, meanwhile, were under pressure at an early age to find a job that would enable them to support a wife and children. Rather than taking years to look around for a job that would be satisfying and enjoyable, they had to focus on finding a job that would provide enough income to support a family.

Now that the typical ages of entering marriage and parenthood are in the late twenties, today's emerging adults have their late teens and most of their twenties to try out various possibilities in school and work in the hopes of finding an occupational direction that fits well with their interests and abilities. Young women are now as likely as young men to plan to have a career, in addition to being a wife and a mother.[6] Both young men and young women recognize that the time to make career progress is now, before they commit to family roles. During the emerging adult years, both young men and young women can go to college, combine college and work, or move from job to job without the obligations that come with the roles of spouse and parent.

The other major difference between work for young people 50 years ago and work for today's emerging adults is that there has been a dramatic shift in the nature of the economy and the kinds of jobs available.[7] As described in Chapter 1, in the 1950s and 1960s the US economy had a vigorous and expanding manufacturing sector that provided abundant, well-paying jobs in sectors such as the automobile and steel industries. Young men with no more than a high school education (or even less) could get manufacturing jobs that provided relatively high wages, enough to support a wife and children. It was hard work, but it paid extremely well.

Since that time, however, most high-paying manufacturing jobs have disappeared, as companies used new technologies to reduce the number of workers needed and moved their manufacturing sites out of the United States to countries where they could pay lower wages to their remaining workers. Employment in the American economy has shifted from a manufacturing base to services. The best service jobs in the new economy require skills in using information and technology, and tertiary education credentials are widely taken as signifying these skills.

Consequently, as we have seen in Chapter 6, emerging adults who have tertiary education credentials have a huge advantage in employment and income compared to those who do not. In the past 25 years, new jobs available for persons with tertiary education have increased substantially, as shown in Figure 7.1, whereas jobs available to persons with a high school degree or less have fallen by 14%.[8] Similarly, from the early 1970s to the present, inflation-adjusted incomes rose substantially more for persons with tertiary education than for those without.[9] In fact, incomes declined steeply for workers with a high school degree or less over this period, and their unemployment rates were three times as high as for their peers with college degrees.[10] Consequently, in the early years of the twenty-first century, emerging adults face a workplace situation that is challenging and in some ways formidable, especially if they lack tertiary education credentials.

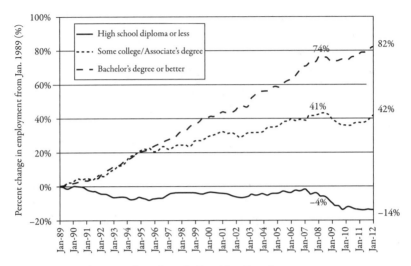

Figure 7.1 Employment Growth in the Past Two Decades.

Adapted from: Georgetown Center on Education and the Workforce, The College Advantage. Authors' estimate using Current Population Survey data (1989–2012). Employment includes all workers aged 18 and older. The monthly employment numbers are seasonally adjusted using the US Census Bureau X-12 procedure and are smoothed using four-month moving averages.

In this chapter the focus will be on how emerging adults go about searching for satisfying work. We will see that emerging adults are highly diverse both in the ways they search for satisfying work and in their success in finding it. I start out by emphasizing that the ideal for emerging adults is finding a job that clicks with their developing identity, and I describe emerging adults who look for this identity fit in a systematic way. Then I describe emerging adults whose search for work is less than systematic, who "fall into" various jobs either because they are unsure of their work identity or because they need to find a job in order to pay their bills. Next we look at variations in being ready to make a long-term decision about work, with a focus on differences between emerging adults in their early twenties, who often remain uncertain, and those in their late twenties, who typically have made a definite choice. This is followed by a section describing influences on job choice, especially the complex influences that parents can have, and a section describing the dreams that some emerging adults have for an alluring and sometimes elusive work ideal. The chapter ends with a section on unemployment and underemployment.

Finding the Right Job

Work in emerging adulthood focuses on identity questions: What do I really want to *do*? What am I best at? What do I enjoy the most? How do my abilities and interests fit in with the kinds of opportunities that are available to me? In asking themselves what kind of work they want to do, emerging adults are also asking themselves what kind of person they are. In the course of emerging adulthood, as they try out various jobs they begin to answer their identity questions—that is, they develop a better sense of who they are and what work suits them best.

Many young people have an idea, in high school, of what kind of career they want to go into.[11] Usually that idea dissolves in the course of emerging adulthood, as they develop a clearer identity and discover that their high school aspiration does not align with it. In place of their high school notions many find another career that does fit their identity, something they enjoy and really want to do. The ideal is *identity-based work,* a job that you believe makes the most of your talents and interests and that you look forward to doing each day.

For most emerging adults, the process of finding a long-term job takes several years, at least. Usually the road to a stable, long-term job is long, with many brief, low-paying, dreary jobs along the way. For the average college graduate, it takes four years to find a job that will last five years or more; for emerging adults who have a high school degree and maybe some college, it takes 10 years; and for those who never even graduated from high school it takes at least 15 years.[12] The average American holds eight different jobs between the ages of 18 and 29.[13]

There were many examples of this pattern of instability in my original study, when I asked emerging adults what jobs they had held since high school. Wilson is only 24, but already since high school "I've had about five different jobs. I worked as a DJ, I worked in a bakery, I worked at a grocery store, I worked for a cleaner, I worked at a plant that made air filtration products." Now he is working in the circulation department at a newspaper and studying to be a meteorologist. Terry's job history is similarly diverse. "I was a waitress for two years until I got burned out on it. And then I worked at a big warehouse, and through working there I got the job at a bookstore. Then after I graduated [from college] I quit and I went on a little vacation and came back and just took the first job I could find which was at a daycare, like, running a day camp. That was just for two weeks until I found a better job which was with a newspaper as a classified ad rep. I was only there for about

3 months, and then I got a job working for a man who was doing research on fish. I did that for about six months." Now she works in a job she enjoys, as a lab technician.

As these examples illustrate, not all of emerging adults' job-hopping is motivated by identity explorations. Often it is simply to pay the bills, to help them pay their way through college, or just to make it from one month to the next. Their eventual goal is to find a job that they love and that fits their interests and abilities, but virtually all of them have many jobs in their late teens and early twenties that have little or nothing to do with this goal.

Looking for Identity-Based Work

The career choices young people make as emerging adults often result from having a job experience that clicks with their identity and leads them to change directions from the career path they had been following. Kim was majoring in journalism at college when she took a part-time job at a preschool to help pay her college expenses. "They asked me to teach a three-year-old classroom, and I did it and I loved it and I thought 'You know, this is what I need to do.'" She changed her major to education and is looking forward to graduating soon and becoming a teacher. It is evident that she has found the right job to fit her identity. "I love teaching," she says. "I can't imagine doing anything else."

Leslie says that when she entered college she did not have any career direction in mind. "I had no idea. I had no clue. I went in undecided." Then, in her second year of college, she started working in an X-ray research lab in a hospital. Her experiences with that job led her to choose a career in medicine. "As I worked with my job and slowly got more exposure to patients and medicine in general, I got more and more interested in it."

Cliff majored in political science in college and then entered law school, but law did not seem to fit his identity. "I decided that wasn't really what I wanted to be doing." He went to graduate school in business for a while and got a job in corporate banking. A decent job, and it paid well, but he still felt he had not found the right fit. However, through his job at the bank he worked with builders, and in their lives he saw a vision for his own future. "They had a great life. They were doing what I wanted to be doing, and making good money at it. I talked to them and went to work for a while for a builder just to get a good idea of what I was getting myself into." After that apprenticeship he went off on his own, and now he builds homes in the town where he grew up.

Although most emerging adults go through a process of exploration before finding a line of work that fits their developing identity, some know what they want to do from an early age and stick with it all the way. This seems to be especially common for people with technical abilities. Raul said, "Ever since I was little I always liked messing with things. Radios at my house that were broken, I'd try to see if I could fix them." His love of "messing with things" has led him to become a computer technician. Craig has always been driven by "[t]he fascination of how things work; what makes them tick. Basically, I took everything apart I could. Anything that's mechanical or works, I want to figure out what makes it work; there's got to be a reason." By the time he was in 10th grade he had a job doing electrical wiring for new houses, and now he is a maintenance electrician, which involves repairing machines and working on "high-tech electrical problems." "I love it," he says. "That's what I've always wanted to be. I love problems. It's the challenge of can you fix it or not."

Of course, some people think they know at an early age what they want to do as their adult work, but find the door closed to them when they reach emerging adulthood. This is especially common for people who have aspirations in athletics, the arts, or entertainment, fields that are attractive to many but also extremely competitive, in which only the people at the very top are able to make a decent living. When he was growing up, Isaiah had hopes of playing professional basketball. By now, "I thought I was going to be in the NBA, to be honest with you." But "things didn't work out," and he had to give up his basketball dream. Instead he is a district manager for a food company, but he is dissatisfied, perhaps in part because his job is such a long way down from his dream. "It's really not what I want. It's stressful, underpaid."

Beth grew up with a grandfather who "almost worked for Disney. He was always creative. I watched him when I was a child." Soon she discovered that she also "liked to make things." She majored in art in college, with an emphasis in sculpture. After college, however, she discovered that her skill as a sculptor "has nothing to do with money, unfortunately." Now she works as a library clerk, but she still does sculpture on the side, hoping someday to "get discovered, where somebody actually buys your things."

There are also people who discover in emerging adulthood that the job they dreamed of in childhood is not all they imagined it would be. Clive said, "I've liked trucks all my life since I was a little kid. You know, trucks just fascinated me." However, when he began to look into truck driving seriously as a possible occupation, he discovered "I really didn't want to have anything to do with it. It's like, you just live in this big metal machine with wheels. Just sitting and staring at the road like a zombie all the time. And I want more for my life than that, you know." Instead, he does yard work, but he hopes eventually to design and build houses. Chalantra recalled, "I always knew I wanted to be a doctor. I liked kids." She planned to become a pediatrician, and was awarded a college scholarship as a pre-med major. However, she soon became disillusioned. "Pre-med took up too much time and I didn't have a life. And I figured that once I became a doctor I still wouldn't be able to spend time with my kids, and I want to have kids and be around them." Now she is working as a nurses' aide and thinking about studying to be a nurse.

Chalantra's remarks illustrate the kinds of work-family tensions that young women face today. Although they have much broader career opportunities than in the past, nearly all of them also plan to have children, and many of them want to be the primary caregiver when their children are very young.[14] While they are still emerging adults, years away from having their first child, young women often anticipate the crunch they are likely to face between their roles as worker, spouse, and mother. This realization affects their occupational choices, in that it sometimes makes them less likely to choose jobs that will be highly demanding and time-consuming, even if the job is high-paying and high-status and in an area they enjoy and in which they have talent.[15] Women who do enter demanding high-status professions are considerably less likely than their peers to have children.[16] Thus, for many women in emerging adulthood, choosing a career direction means not simply making a choice that clicks with their identity but making a choice that will allow them to balance their dual identities as workers and mothers.

Most young men today want to be involved dads, closer to their kids than they were to their own fathers, so they, too, face the challenge of balancing their work and family roles. In the national Clark poll, 60% of 18–29-year-olds agreed that "I expect to have to give up some of my career goals in order to have the family life I want," and this view was shared equally by young men and young women.[17] Most young men today anticipate taking an equal share of the household work and child-care duties when the time comes, although young women tend not to believe that this will actually happen.[18]

Do emerging adults ask too much out of work? The answer to that question is in the eye of the beholder, but certainly many parents and employers believe the answer is "yes."[19] Emerging adults aspire to work that is enjoyable, fulfilling, and makes the most of their unique abilities and interests.

But employers don't typically wake up in the morning and ask themselves, "Whom can I fulfill today?" Their goal is much more likely to be limited to how to find someone to do the work they need to have done, for as little money as possible. Emerging adults enter the labor force expecting a lot more, which sometimes leads to exasperation for employers, who find them presumptuous and spoiled, and parents, who may be thinking (and perhaps saying), "Why can't you just get a *job?* Work isn't supposed to be *fun.* That's why you get *paid* for it!" Just like their parents may have said to them when they were in their twenties.

One employer at a publicity firm reports the following story. After working for her for a few weeks, her new assistant, Laura, requested a conference with her. When they met, Laura explained that she was not finding the work very stimulating, and in order to stay she would have to have a raise or have fewer hours at the same salary. "I was really affronted!" remembers Jade, her boss. "You'd like more pay for fewer hours? Join the club!"

Rather than blowing up and firing her on the spot, Jade told her an instructive story, about how when she had her first job, she and the other lowest-level employees banded together to protest the low pay, long hours, and general abuse of their workplace. Their boss listened carefully, then walked to the door, opened it wide, and said, "There are a hundred people out there who can't wait to take your place." Cowed, they scuttled meekly back to their desks.

"There!" Jade thought to herself. "That would show my young charge how important work is and how grateful she should be for the job, right?" Quite the contrary. Laura smiled at Jade and said, without any hesitation, "I would never work at a place that treats employees like that." Not the answer Jade was expecting. "I was dumbstruck!" For the second time in 10 minutes Jade was tempted to fire her, but she held her tongue for a moment to think. In that moment she realized, she recalls now, that *Laura was right.* "Boomers like me, raised by the so-called Greatest Generation and their Depression-era ethos, let the workplace become the cold, harsh place it is," Jade says now. "I think perhaps this new generation will truly build a better place for themselves and everyone if they can hold fast to their confidence, optimism and fearless approach to accepting their gifts without guilt! Maybe they'll bend the world to a less driven state."

Now, I hasten to add, the employers have a legitimate interest here, too. Understandably, they want their employees to do the work that needs to be done, and understandably, they pay their young employees less because as a rule, the younger they are, the less experienced, less knowledgeable, and less productive they are. Nearly everyone in every job has to do things they really would prefer not to do, and would like to be paid more money. But I agree with Laura, and the converted Jade, that employees, especially young employees, should press to be rewarded fairly for what they do and to avoid exploitation. Emerging adults are often well positioned to do so, because they are not yet committed to a long-term career path, and because they do not yet have a spouse or children depending on them. If all else fails, and the employer does not bite her tongue as Jade did but fires them for their insolence, most have the option to return home to Mom and Dad for a while, an option that becomes less acceptable in the thirties and beyond.

"Falling Into" a Job

I have been using the word "exploration" to describe how emerging adults go about looking for a career path they wish to settle into for the long term, and for many of them that word applies. They think about what they want to do, they try a job or a college major in that area to see if the fit is right, and if it is not, they try another path until they find something they like better. But for many others, "exploration" is a bit too lofty a term to describe their work history during their late teens and early to mid-twenties. Often it is not nearly as systematic, organized, and focused as "exploration" implies.[20] "Meandering" might be a more accurate word, or maybe "drifting," or even "floundering." For many emerging adults, working simply means finding a job, often a McJob, that will pay the bills until something better comes along.

This is especially true for emerging adults who do not have a clear idea of where their interests and abilities lie. Katy has been working as an assistant manager in a music store for the past year and a half. She says it is a decent job, it pays the bills, but "I don't want to do it for too much longer." She does it now only because of the lack of a promising alternative. "I've always been real clear about what I don't want to do, but not coming up with what I actually do want to do." She has a bachelor's degree in psychology, but she does not know where that might lead, if anywhere. "I want to go back to school at some point and get a Ph.D., but I don't know exactly in what area. So I'm taking a little time off to try to figure that out." Until her interests become clearer, she will simply mark time in her job at the music store.

Many emerging adults express a sense that they did not really choose their current job, they just one day found themselves in it, like a ball that rolls randomly on a pocked surface until it lands in one of the holes. "I just fell into it" is a frequently used phrase among emerging adults to describe how they found their current job. That's how Patrick described how he got his job as an audio engineer for radio advertisements. "I kind of fell into it. I got this job through a friend. Like, I had some computer experience and I do sound work, so I got the job." He has mixed feelings about the job, but "[i]t's better than when I was working [as a server] in a café and not making any money." Bridget used similar language to describe how she got her current job as a supervisor at a temp agency. She was a temp herself while she looked around for something more enduring, and her supervisor for the temp jobs decided she had the right qualities and experience to be a supervisor, even though she was not looking for that job. "I kind of fell into this position...this just kind of fell in my lap."

For the most part, emerging adults who found their jobs in this random fashion are looking for something else. Falling into a job rarely results in the kind of identity fit that makes a job fully satisfying. Most emerging adults want to find that kind of fit, and any job that does not provide it is viewed as a way station on the road to it. "I didn't really choose it. It chose me," Wendy says of the job as a bank teller she has had for the past five years. She got the job through a job placement service, not because she aspired to be a bank teller. Now she is taking night classes to become a nurse, which is what she has finally decided she really wants to do. Tamara is a graduate of an Ivy League university, but she took a job as a legal assistant in a law firm only because "I needed the money. I was so broke! And they pay well." Still, the money is not enough. "I hate my job!" she said. "There's no opportunity for growth there." She is planning to go to graduate school to train herself to do something she likes better, but she is not sure what, maybe "the healthcare field or fashion industry."

It may be this instability and uncertainty in work that gives many emerging adults a sense of experiencing a "quarterlife crisis,"[21] as they bounce from one job to another without any sense of how to find their way. In part, this is simply an identity crisis. It is hard to choose a direction in work until you know yourself well enough to decide what you really want to do, and it takes many emerging adults until their mid-twenties to develop a clear identity. However, this crisis may be especially common in the United States, where there is little assistance in making the school-to-work transition, and there is no program or institution that provides emerging adults with information and guidance. Some scholars have argued that the American system results in a "tyranny of freedom" that leaves emerging adults with too many choices and too little direction in how to sort through them.[22]

As I mentioned in the previous chapter, there are distinct differences between the United States and European countries in this area, with the American system allowing for greater choice but providing less guidance and the European system providing greater structure but allowing for less freedom to change direction.[23] Perhaps the decades to come will see both extremes move toward a hybrid system: structure and assistance for emerging adults who would like to move directly into the kind of work they know they want, and freedom of exploration for emerging adults who want to take their time and try different options before committing themselves to one career.[24]

Deciding on a Long-Term Direction

Even for emerging adults who meander or drift through various jobs rather than exploring their options in a systematic way, the process of trying various jobs often serves the function of helping them sort out what kind of work they want to do. When you are in a dead-end job, at least you find out what you do *not* want to do, as Katy put it. You may also come to the realization that a job has to be more than a paycheck, that you are not willing to do something boring and pointless in the long run even if it pays the bills, so you are willing to keep looking and striving until you find something interesting and enjoyable. And there is also the possibility that as you drift through various jobs you may happen to fall into one you enjoy, one that unexpectedly clicks.

There is a definite difference by age in the extent to which emerging adults feel they have found a line of work they want to be in for the long run. People in their late twenties are more likely than those in their early twenties to have reached this point. In fact, this stability in work, marking an end to their work-related identity explorations, could be taken as an indication that they have left emerging adulthood and entered an established adulthood.

In my original study, this age difference was evident in responses to the question, "How do you see your life 10 years from now?" Most people gave a work-related response to this question, and those in their late twenties almost always had a definite answer. They had chosen their line of work, so they simply imagined how they would be likely to progress in it over the next 10 years. Russell, 28, who owns an electronics repair store, said that in 10 years he expects to be "doing what I'm doing now. I hope the business grows." Mason, 26, an attorney, said he expected to be "[s]till practicing law." Tina, 26, a nurse, saw her life in 10 years as "[c]ontinuing working in the nursing field at a higher level, whether with management or a higher clinical level of practice." Joyce, 28, who works in human resources for a large company, saw herself "[p]robably going up even farther in my job, or moved up to a higher position maybe."

In contrast, emerging adults in their early twenties often answered, "I don't know" in response to the question of what they would be doing in 10 years. Still in the process of exploring job options, or still drifting through a series of short-term jobs, they found it difficult to extrapolate from their current work situation to their future work. Still in the process of resolving identity issues about their true abilities and interests, they found it difficult to answer a question that required a clear work identity.

So they said they did not know or gave a vague response when asked to imagine what life would be like in 10 years. Leslie, 20, who had just changed her college major to nursing, said of her life in 10 years, "I have no idea. It's changed so much since I've started school, I can't even imagine." Amos, 20, said, "I don't know. I haven't thought that far ahead." His only work goal was the vague one of "hopefully have a high-paying job." Bridget, 23, said, "I look at what's happened in the last two years of my life and it's changed so much that I can't possibly see what's going to happen in 10 years. It'll be pretty exciting, I'm sure." Leah, 23, said, "I don't know. It's really hard for me. I'm really not sure. I'm not sure what will happen, and at this point in time, there's not anything specific that I really want to happen." Jerry, 24, said, "That's hard. I don't know. I can't really see that far. I don't like to make plans for next week, really." Ariel, 24, said, "I have no idea. I think one of the things that I've noticed in the last couple of years is that there's no telling what can happen between now and then. I think I've had a lot of things that have occurred that were unexpected, and I try to plan things out and a lot of times it just doesn't work out that way."

Ian, 22, was still trying to reconcile his ambitions in writing and music, or maybe combine them. "I don't know what I'm going to be doing, because I've got a lot of things I want to pursue and I don't know which ones will pan out and which ones won't. Probably have a pretty good journalism job, be in a local band hopefully, and hopefully by then I will have written a novel." Renee, 24, said, "I don't even know where I'm gonna live next year. I just really have no idea what my future is." She was optimistic that she would know in 10 years. "Hopefully by then I will be established, know what I want to do."

For the most part, emerging adults in their early twenties are unperturbed by not knowing what they will be doing in 10 years. They understand themselves to be at a period of life where they are still finding out what they want to do, and they are sanguine about finding the answer before too much longer. As the examples above illustrate, they use the word "hopefully" a lot to describe how they see their lives in 10 years, and that word fits; they are hopeful that eventually they will find the kind of work that is right for them. Although they may not yet have found what they want, few doors seem closed for good, and many options still seem possible.

Even in their late twenties, many people are still looking and still hopeful of finding a job that fits better than the one they have now. In the national Clark poll, 61% of 18–21-year-olds agreed that "I haven't been able to find the kind of job I really want," but so did 49% of the 26–29-year-olds.[25] However, the options often start to narrow once people reach their late twenties, as they leave emerging adulthood and take on the responsibilities of adult roles, especially marriage and parenthood. Being married means they have to coordinate their decisions about what job to pursue with a spouse. They can no longer simply leave their job and move somewhere else in hopes of finding something better. Maybe their spouse will support them in their desire to do something else, but maybe not.

Having children, even more than marriage, makes it difficult to change jobs or go back to school. Once you have a child, much of your life becomes structured around caring for and providing for that child, and that means your own options become limited. Harry is an auto mechanic who would like to retrain to be an electrician. But it would take three to four years, and that is time he does not have. "I've got a one-year-old son, so it's kind of hard right now. That makes it real tough." Patty would like to go back to school. "I wish I had a college degree, and I don't. Now that we have a mortgage and two kids, it's really hard to go back." In work as in other ways, having a child is the point of no return on the road to adulthood, the event that marks the definitive end to the relatively free explorations of emerging adulthood. We will discuss this more in Chapter 13.

Influences on Job Choice

Developing a work identity and making a long-term job choice is a mostly solitary process for most emerging adults. Finding the right career path is a matter of clarifying for themselves what they most want to do and then seeking out a job that fits, and no one else can answer the question of what they most want to do. However, some emerging adults describe how they were influenced by others in their search for work.

Sometimes this influence comes in the form of what sociologists call "social capital,"[26] meaning social ties that entail mutual assistance, including help in finding a job. An emerging adult may know somebody who knows of a job opening, and get a job that way. Although this rather random way of finding a job is unlikely to yield the kind of job that provides a satisfying identity fit, it may be welcomed by emerging adults who do not yet know themselves well enough to be able to decide what to look for. Alex works as a file clerk in a law office, a job he obtained through his college roommate's father, who is an attorney in the firm, but he views it as temporary. "I just figured I would do it for a little while, while I'm figuring out what else to do." Lonnie obtained an associate's degree in drafting but soon lost interest in it; now he works at his mother's dry cleaning store until he decides what to do next. "I'm kind of like taking it easy and not doing anything stressful and stuff like that."

Some emerging adults are willing to take a job that happens to come along through personal connections because they have set their sights low and are not very ambitious, but are happy with a job that pays decently and is reasonably pleasant. Kurt works as a clerk in a hospital, a job he learned about through his father, who is a security guard there. He does not get any particular satisfaction or fulfillment from the job, but it beats his previous one unloading trucks for a discount department store, which was "just hard work and very low pay for what you did."

However, it is rare for emerging adults to be satisfied with a job that is not identity-based. When emerging adults take such a job through friends or family, it is usually as a temporary way of supporting themselves while they continue to seek a job they really want. Gabriella helps her father manage his apartment building while she attends college in fashion merchandising. Tory has a part-time job with a package delivery service that he got when his mother, working at a job placement center, tipped him off to the opening, but he took it only to support himself while he pursues a degree in travel administration.

In addition to finding a job through social connections, another form the influence of others may take is that emerging adults may be inspired to pursue a particular work path by the example of someone they admire. Teachers are mentioned quite often as providing such inspiration. Monte is studying music education in college and is planning to be a music teacher.

He decided on this area from "just looking at my high school band director. I saw how he really enjoyed his job and he was really having fun. I enjoyed band, so I figured if I can get paid for doing that kind of stuff for the rest of my life I'll be pretty happy."

For some emerging adults, it is a parent who provides the inspiration. Trevor is working as a clerk in a hospital while he works on a degree in radiology, a field he chose because "both my father and my step mom are in the medical field, and I've always been kind of exposed to it that way." Vernon is a partner with his father in an insurance agency, and it is evident that his admiration and affection for his father led him into the business. "It's nice having him there in the office so I can learn from him and ask him questions. His dad was an agent before him, so I'm third generation." Vernon also sees his connection to his father as a boost to his own status. "You kind of feel like you have power when you go to the home office and you go 'That's my dad.' He gets automatic respect." Tina, a nurse, said her mom influenced her in a more general way, "just the fact that she did work all through my growing up probably influenced me to want to do that as well." Research indicates that adolescent girls whose mothers work have higher career aspirations than girls whose mothers do not work.[27]

Some emerging adults find that the kind of work their parents do happens to fit well with their own identity. Louis is in the construction business, as his father was, but he says this was "my own idea," not something his father influenced. It's just that, like his father, he enjoys the kind of work that means "just being outside all the time, working with your hands." Similarly, Gus is studying geography, and he denies that his father, owner of a lightning protection service, influenced his choice of occupations—but he adds that "the things that my dad does, he's got mechanical skills like drawing and engineering. I guess I got some of that, because I'm good at stuff like that."

However, parents are sources of work inspiration less often than one might expect. In response to the question, "Did your parents' occupations influence your own choice of occupation?" emerging adults in my original study were about twice as likely to answer "no" as "yes." Some of the "no" responses were adamant, from emerging adults who viewed their parents' jobs as the last thing they would want to do. This may have been because they saw how miserable and ungratifying their parents' work was. Leonard's mother "always either cooked or did custodial type things. That's why I'm like 'Oooh, get it away from me' because I don't want any of that. It's not that I'm above it. I'll do it if I have to, but this is what I'm trying to get away from. It stinks."

Rocky said that from watching his father in his job as a salesman "I realized I never wanted to be a salesman. That was one thing that I realized from my dad's job. I didn't want to have to go out and rub elbows and smile to people I absolutely didn't want to be around. He sucked up to so many people, I don't even want to talk about it. I just couldn't stomach that whatsoever."

Sometimes emerging adults start out following the work path blazed by their parents, but drop it when they come to realize it does not fit with their identity. Ken, whose father is a successful businessman, said, "I originally thought I might like to do something like what he does, but as I got into school, I found I didn't like business. I didn't have a mind for business." Barry, whose father is an accountant, said that because of his father's example, "[w]hen I was a kid I thought I wanted to be an accountant or a stock broker. I think when I was in 10th grade I took a business class, and I was just so turned off by it and I knew I didn't want to do that." Now he is a graduate student in English. Craig initially went into the family painting business, like his brothers, his father, and his grandfather, back "six or seven generations." But he eventually decided his heart was in electrical work, not painting. The decision was not easy to break to his family, but he eventually "kind of came out in the open and said 'I don't want to paint. I want to do this.' I felt I had to do it."

Even if parents have been highly successful in their work, emerging adults sometimes wish to avoid following in their footsteps if the costs of that success seem too high. Ian has a father who is a wealthy physician, but according to Ian, "[h]e has so much stress it's amazing." Ian has chosen to go into journalism, even though he knows "if I'm a journalist making $20,000 a year, my dad makes vastly more than that." More important than the money is to have a job he loves. "If I enjoy thoroughly doing what I'm doing in life, then I would be better off than my dad."

We can see again that what is most important to emerging adults in work is finding identity-based work, the right match between a job and their interests and abilities, so that they will "enjoy thoroughly" the work they do. Sometimes their parents provide them with opportunities to find a job with the right identity fit, but other times their parents provide them with a model of an anti-identity job to avoid.

Dreams, Pipe Dreams, and the Dreamless

Because emerging adulthood is a time of open possibilities, when little has been decided for certain, it is a time when dreams flourish. They may not yet have found a job they love, they may in fact be working at a lousy, stress-ful, low-paying job, but they can still hope and plan for bigger things, they can still imagine that the work they eventually settle into will be something wonderful. Just as they hope to find their "soul mate," they hope to find their dream job.[28]

A common dream among emerging adults is owning a small business. Perhaps this is a distinctly American dream, more common in a society that encourages free enterprise and individual initiative than it would be else-where. The reality of owning a small business is often harsh, in that many small businesses fail and the ones that succeed often require long hours and relentless responsibilities on the part of the owners. Nevertheless, for some emerging adults it is an attractive dream, seeming to hold the promise of independence and self-sufficiency, of being your own boss and being in con-trol of your fate. It also holds an identity allure, because they can choose as their business area something that is central to their identity.

Ned had tattoos of eagles, monsters, and women all over his arms and chest, and planned to get more. He was working as a truck driver, but his real dream was "to open up my own business. That's what we're thinking about now, you know, a tattoo business." He said the person who did his tattoos was "making well over $200,000 a year," and Ned did not see any reason why he could not be successful as well. "I think if you put into it what you can do, and don't do friends for free like a lot of people I know do, but do it as a busi-ness, then I think you'll make money."

Perhaps the most common small-business dream for emerging adults is owning a restaurant. Derek, currently working as a server in a restaurant, said that was his "long-term plan. Even in the last year, I've talked to some people, like the chef from the café I used to work at, who's planning on starting some-thing, and he said he wanted me to be with him when he started it, which wouldn't be bad." They knew of some potential investors. "There's customers that used to come into the old café that are willing to put money into it. So we're starting the wheels in motion for that, like actually making a legitimate plan. And people are legitimately interested."

Other common work dreams in emerging adulthood involve music or sports.[29] Charles, who was profiled in Chapter 2, was doing temp jobs to support himself while he focused on promoting his singing group, the House Cats. Brock was working as a bartender, but soon he was moving to Kentucky to play for a semi-pro soccer team. "It's been my dream to play professional soccer since I was five years old," he said. "I played all through youth leagues and all through high school and I played in college, and I was successful at every level I played." In fact, he was an All-American in college, which was also something he had dreamed of. Now he hopes to extend the fulfillment of his soccer dreams. "This is just the next step, hopefully, on the ladder that goes up a little further."

Of course, there are dreams, and then there are pipe dreams. That is, there are dreams that emerging adults like Charles and Brock are working toward, pouring their hearts into every day, and then there are dreams that are only the wistful wishes of emerging adults who enjoy imagining a glorious future but are doing little to make it happen. Albert works in an ice cream store, but he says, "what I really want to do is play professional baseball." However, he did not play baseball in high school, nor is he playing organized baseball now. How is he planning to make his way into playing professionally? "I don't know," he says. "I'll see what happens."

There are also emerging adults who are dreamless, who have already, at a relatively young age, nearly given up hope of finding fulfilling work that will be the basis of a satisfying life. For some, this unfortunate status is a consequence of being unable to develop a clear identity that could serve as a map through the maze of occupational choices. Carrie is working as a library assistant. It started out as an assignment from a temp agency, and she continued with it because "they hired me full-time and it's easy." But she says it is "not really what I'm interested in." What *is* she interested in? That's the problem. She doesn't know. "I'm totally floundering right now," she admits. "I don't know what I had hoped for, and I think that's part of the reason that I'm floundering, because I still don't know what I'm hoping for." She had once hoped to do something in international relations or politics, but that dream is "long gone." Now she has "no idea what I'm gonna do." She has more or less given up on finding satisfying work. "In my plans for my life what I'm probably gonna end up doing is like working at a yucky job like this for a year or so and like saving money, and then traveling."

In contrast to Carrie, Curtis, a 29-year-old African American, knew just what he wanted to do, but his problem was finding a good job doing it. He learned how to be a printer while in prison in his late teens, and by now "I've been operating presses for close to 10 years." It's work he enjoys. "I like doing things with my hands. I couldn't be an office person. I like working with machinery and that kind of stuff." However, he has been frustrated by the inconsistency of the work. "It's not really like solid, you know. You get in there, and then all of a sudden it gets slow and you probably have to lay off a couple of weeks." So he went to work for a Kinko's copy center. He liked that job, too. "It's more stable, and the benefits is excellent. And plus they got shares, you know, you can invest in this and get a little share of this. And they have a lot of good things going. So I wanted that. Plus, the opportunity to become something else, you know, like a manager."

But Kinko's let him go after 90 days because he made personal calls on company time and came in late "a couple of times." Now he has taken a job with a different copy company, for lower pay with fewer benefits, and he is starting to lose hope, as he feels himself sliding down in pay and status from his printing job to his Kinko's job to his current copying job. He can see his dreams fading. "I would like for myself to be established in my little house, you know, and everything is together. But I know it's not gonna be that way. It's too hard, you know, the way things is changin'. It ain't gettin' no better, you know. There's a lot of things that gets in the way at times, breaks you down. So I don't know. Ten years from now, hopefully I'll still be alive. That's all I have to say."

Curtis's story is a microcosm of the plight that many young men in urban areas have faced in recent decades.[30] As noted in Chapter 1 and in the introduction to this chapter, beginning in the 1960s high-paying manufacturing jobs became scarcer as technology was developed to require fewer workers and as factories moved overseas for cheaper labor or to suburban areas for cheaper land. That left young men like Curtis who "like to work with [their] hands" with limited job options. Increasingly, the better-paying jobs have required tertiary education. But as the economies of urban areas declined, so did the quality of the public schools, leaving children attending those schools ill-prepared for pursuing tertiary education. Thus in emerging adulthood many of them find themselves like Curtis, in a low-paying, unpromising job, struggling to keep their hopes up but sliding toward the despairing conclusion that "[i]t ain't gettin' no better."

Unemployment and Underemployment

Glum as Curtis is over his going-nowhere printing job, it could be worse. At least he has a job, which is more than many of his peers can say. The unemployment rate among 15–24-year-olds—known as the "youth unemployment rate"—is consistently at least twice as high as the rate for adults, across decades and all around the world, as Figure 7.2 illustrates.[31] So, even when times are good economically, and the overall unemployment rate is, say, 5%, it is likely to be at least 10% for 15–24-year-olds, which would be considered catastrophic if it were the overall rate. And when times are not good, emerging adults have it even worse than the rest of the adult population. In the second decade of the twenty-first century, in the aftermath of the worldwide financial crisis, unemployment rates in southern Europe reached around 25% overall, and the youth unemployment rate surpassed an appalling 50% in some countries, as you can see in Figure 7.2.[32]

Why is youth unemployment always considerably higher than the overall rate? After all, they are often cheaper to employ than older workers are. There are two kinds of reasons, one universal and one *structural,* that is, a consequence of the structure of the economic system.

The universal reason is that younger workers are almost always less experienced and less knowledgeable than older workers are, for the obvious reason that they have not been working for long. No matter how cheap it is to employ them, it will not be worth it if they cannot do anything useful, and nearly always it will be a while before they can be useful. Even if they have brought in excellent skills and knowledge gained from their education and training, it will take time for them to learn the specific skills required in a specific job. So, when an employer hires a young employee, it is both an investment and an act of faith. It will only pay off if the young employee stays around long enough to generate valuable work after mastering the skills required.

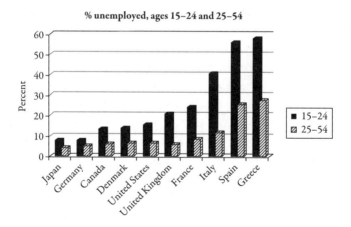

Figure 7.2 Unemployment Rates, Youth and Adults, Selected Developed Countries, 2013.

OECD (2014). OECD.statextracts. Short-term labor market statistics: Unemployment rates by age and gender. Retrieved from http://stats.oecd.org/index.aspx?queryid=36499

For this reason, entering the labor market is nearly always challenging and difficult for young workers. Because they are less productive than older workers, even though they come cheap, employers will usually take the somewhat older, more experienced workers when they can. The only exception is when an economy is booming and labor is scarce, so that employers are scrambling to find any qualified workers they can get. This is the case in many developing countries, where economies may be expanding at 10% per year, but it has not happened in many years in developed countries, where economic growth is generally 1%–3% per year, at best. So, in developed countries, the youth unemployment rate is likely to remain persistently twice as high as the overall rate through the twenty-first century as well.[33]

The structural reason for high youth unemployment is that in most developed countries, the economic system protects the job security of older workers at the expense of labor market entry for younger workers. In most of Europe, hiring a full-time employee is a long-term commitment. Unions are strong, and they negotiate labor agreements that make their members difficult to fire. Governments have additional rules restricting employers' ability to terminate jobs. For example, employers may have to give an employee a warning of a year or more that the job is ending, or may have to continue to pay ex-employees for months after they are no longer working for the company. Workers appreciate having this kind of job security, but not surprisingly, employers are reluctant to hire new workers under these conditions unless absolutely necessary, because they will not have the flexibility to let them go if they prove to be unproductive or if business conditions change for the worse.

Consequently, the winners in this system are those who already have jobs, who are mainly the older workers, and the losers are the ones who are trying to break into the labor market, who are mainly the younger workers. Some governments have responded to this problem by making a separate set of rules so that employers can hire emerging adults on temporary or part-time contracts.[34] This makes employers more willing to hire young workers, but it also gives the young workers less job security and usually lower pay as well.

The United States has fewer labor protections than any other developed country. Unions are weak and government regulations are relatively few, so employers can generally hire and fire as they wish and as business conditions change. That's bad for job security, but good for breaking into the labor market. The youth unemployment rate in the United States is generally lower than in most of Europe.[35] However, it varies widely, depending on how much education emerging adults have. As noted earlier in the chapter, the unemployment rate for emerging adults who have no education beyond high school is typically three times as high as for emerging adults who have obtained a college degree.[36] According to economic analyses, long-term unemployment in the twenties undermines earnings for decades afterward, a phenomenon known as "scarring."[37]

Part-time work and underemployment are also more common in emerging adulthood than afterward. Often their jobs in their twenties are part-time, because they are also going to school or because that is all they can find. Even for those who obtain a college degree, many of them are "underemployed" for years afterward, doing work that has no relation to what they learned in school and that may not even require a degree.[38] Into their mid-twenties many of them are still unsure what they want to do, which makes it difficult to search for identity-based work, and even if they know, they may not be able to find a job in that field.

Eventually, nearly all find their way to a stable career path. As noted earlier, by their late twenties most college grads have found a job they will hold for at least five years. For those who have less education, it may take until their early thirties, but most of them, too, find a stable job. However, most governments could do a lot more to develop effective policies to assist emerging adults in navigating the entry to the job market. The Scandinavian countries are widely regarded as being at the forefront in this area, providing individualized plans that offer training to emerging adults and link their training to the skills employers need. These countries, along with Germany and Switzerland, also have a long tradition of apprenticeships that remain effective in preparing new workers and linking them to employers.[39] But these programs cost money, and in the southern European countries— which need such programs most because of their astronomical youth unemployment rates—it is difficult to generate funding for a vast new government program, however valuable it might be for young people and for the country's future.

As for the United States, the sheer size of the population makes it difficult to construct such programs, but states could develop their own programs to a far greater degree than they have so far. Employers in the United States may expand their job-training programs if economic growth improves to the point where they have a shortage of qualified young workers. However, in times of economic stagnation or decline, they have little incentive to do so because there are so many young job-seekers available.[40]

Conclusion: High Hopes and Hard Realities

In this chapter, the emphasis has been on work as an identity quest. Emerging adults want more out of work than a decent wage and a steady paycheck. They want their work to be an expression of themselves, to fit well with their interests and abilities, to be something they find satisfying and enjoyable, and to do some good in the world. If necessary, they are willing to endure frequent job changes and a long series of relatively low-paying, short-term McJobs as they move closer to clarifying what kind of work suits their developing identity. Even amidst the instability and uncertainty of their work in emerging adulthood, most of them remain hopeful that their identity quest will end in success, and they will find identity-based work.

Arguably they have a better chance of finding such a job than people did in the past. When people married and had their first child in their early twenties, men quickly experienced pressure to find a job that would enable them to support a family, and women experienced pressure to leave the work force to devote themselves to caring for the children and running the household. Now, with the postponement of marriage and parenthood into the late twenties, young people can use their emerging adulthood years to seek out satisfying work without the pressure of family obligations. For young women, the range of possible occupations is suddenly vast, greater than it has been for any generation of women in human history.

However, there is a dark side to the work prospects of emerging adults. With such high expectations for what work will provide to them, with the expectation that their jobs will serve not only as a source of income but as a source of self-fulfillment and self-expression, some of them are likely to find that the actual job they end up in for the long term falls considerably short of this ideal. Also, the service economy of today requires a high level of education for the best jobs, and emerging adults who lack the abilities or opportunities to pursue tertiary education often find themselves excluded from competition for these jobs and left with only the lowest-paying and least-rewarding service jobs.

More than ever, education is a divider in adulthood. College-educated emerging adults generally have the happy prospect of a prosperous and comfortable middle class adult life. Some emerging adults who do not have a college education may prove to have an exceptional gift in music or sports or for running a small business. However, for most emerging adults without tertiary education, adulthood is likely to be a perpetual economic struggle, and they are likely to fall considerably short of the goal of finding satisfying, well-paying, identity-based work.

Even for emerging adults who have been fortunate enough to find something resembling identity-based work, this does not mean that identity issues have been resolved, never to return. As Erikson observed, "A sense of identity is never gained nor maintained once and for all.... It is constantly lost and regained."[41] For those emerging adults who find a kind of work they like, they may grow tired of it after some years, or their interests may change, or they may wish to find something they like even better, and their explorations will continue. Nevertheless, emerging adults who come to know themselves well, and who develop a clear idea of what their abilities are and what they want to do, have a good foundation for the career decisions they will make as adults.

Chapter 8

Digital Natives

Emerging Adults' Many Media Uses

Silence is golden? Perhaps it used to be, but for this generation of emerging adults, silence is nonexistent. Like no other generation before them, they are connected all day long to one form of media or another. Their "phones" accompany them constantly. Even when they are hanging out together, they will pause occasionally to look at a text message that has just popped up, and use their dexterous thumbs to tap out a rapid reply. And their "phones" are not just phones but digital devices, used not only for telephoning and texting but for listening to music, surfing the Internet, and taking pictures and videos. They make time, too, for the old-fashioned media forms like television, movies, and electronic games. Young men in their twenties are the group with the highest rates of playing electronic games, with some of them playing hours a day.[1]

For this generation of emerging adults, media have been a constant presence from infancy onward. They are the first generation of "digital natives," as writer and educator Marc Prensky terms them, in contrast to the "digital immigrants," their elders who have had to learn (or who refuse to learn) new media technologies in adulthood.[2] Like any immigrant to a new land, most of us who are digital immigrants will never have quite the same fluidity and ease with the language as the natives do.

For the most part in this book I have avoided generational terms, for two reasons. One is that, for the most part, terms like "Generation X" and "Millennials" are used in popular culture but not by scholars, and there is a lot of glib nonsense written about the supposedly distinctive generational characteristics of today's "Millennials" that has no research basis. The other reason is that I see emerging adulthood as a permanent life stage, not a passing generational phenomenon. The factors that led to the rise of emerging adulthood are not going to change in any forseeable future. The proportion of young people obtaining tertiary education is not going to fall, in an economy that is heading inexorably away from manufacturing and toward services. The median age of marriage is not going to decline, women are not going to go back to staying out of the workplace and having three to four children each, and premarital sex is not going to go back to being taboo. There will be changes over time (and across cultures) in how people experience emerging adulthood, but as a normative stage of the life course, emerging adulthood is here to stay.

However, there are certain characteristics of today's emerging adults that should be recognized as generationally distinctive, and electronic media use is foremost among them. Far more than any generation before them, emerging adults today are electronically connected, all day long.

Given the abundance of time they devote to their digital diversions, no account of the lives of emerging adults would be complete without attention to their media use.[3] This chapter begins with an elucidation of their rates of media use and how those rates compare to other age groups. Then we consider the role that media play in emerging adults' lives and in their development, particularly their identity development. At the end of the chapter, we will explore the contentious question of whether all this media use is a positive or negative force in their development.

The Ubiquity of Media in the Lives of Emerging Adults

To gain a sense of the media-intensive environment that today's digital natives have experienced, just consider all that has happened since this generation of emerging adults was born.[4] During their early years, in the 1990s, personal computer use was rapidly expanding in homes and schools, DVDs and MP3 players were introduced, Google, Amazon, and Ebay were founded, and the total number of websites worldwide sprang from a few thousand to tens of millions. As they passed through adolescence, Facebook, YouTube, Wikipedia, and Twitter were founded, and iPhones and tablet computers were introduced. By the time they reached emerging adulthood, "smart phones" were smarter than ever and were used for everything from texting to surfing the Internet to watching movies and even, on occasion, making a phone call.

Small wonder, then, that as emerging adults they feel like digital natives, entirely comfortable in an environment where technology is a constant presence. It is estimated that the typical American emerging adult is engaged with media of some kind for about 12 hours a day—for most of their waking hours, in other words.[5] They may wake to music, watch TV with breakfast, listen to music in the car on the way to school or work, use the Internet at school or work, listen to music on the way home, hear more music while socializing with friends or updating their Facebook page, and watch TV to close out the evening. And they take time for texting, of course, punctuating the course of each day, even each hour. Often they combine their activities in "media multitasking," listening to music while posting on Facebook, or texting while watching TV.[6]

Music is the media type that attracts the most time, about 3.5 hours a day.[7] Technology has made it easy to have a virtually infinite library of music available at all times, so the songs they love lift the spirits of emerging adults as they work, socialize, exercise, and do household chores. They rank listening to music first in importance among their leisure activities, above watching TV, electronic games, sports, books, and their favorite hobbies.[8] Music also helps them manage their moods, calming them down after a bruising experience at work or pumping them up as they look forward to going out with friends.

Rates of Internet use among emerging adults are comparable to rates of music listening, about 3.5 hours a day.[9] Internet use encompasses a wide variety of specific uses, from reading the latest news to researching information for school or work to watching pornography, but social media use is the largest category, about one hour of that 3.5 hours a day.[10] Rates of social media use show a consistent generational pattern: highest among the youngest, lowest among the oldest, as Figure 8.1 illustrates. A similar pattern applies across developed countries for overall Internet use. In a survey by the World Internet Project, the percentage of Internet use among 18–24-year-olds was 88% or above in all nine developed countries in the survey, but dropped substantially among 55–64-year-olds and further still among those 65 and older.[11]

Television may be old-fashioned compared to most of the other media technology that is part of the lives of emerging adults, but it remains remarkably popular. According to Nielsen ratings, American emerging adults ages 18–24 spend over 23 hours a week watching television.[12] Only about 10% of their TV watching is done on new technology such as smart phones or the

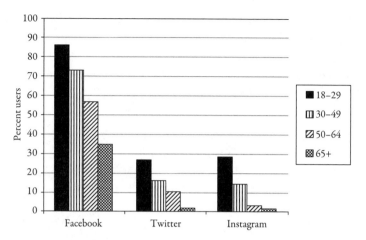

Figure 8.1 Social Media Use by Age.
Source: Duggan & Brenner (2013).

Internet. However, their 23 hours is less time per week than any other older age group devotes to TV. Time devoted to TV watching increases steadily with age, throughout adulthood. In the 65+ age group, Americans watch an average of over 49 hours a week, more than twice the amount watched by 18–24-year-olds.

Television is popular not just in the United States but all over the world. What is it that makes television so attractive as a leisure activity? Does it make people feel great? Does it bring them pleasure? Does it make them feel more fulfilled and engaged? Oddly, the answer to all these questions is a definite "no."[13] On the contrary, studies that assess the moods of adults during and after watching television find that TV makes viewers more passive and less alert.[14] Time diary studies show moods while watching TV to be about equal to moods while doing housework—low, that is, much lower than all other leisure activities, and lower than moods while working, too. One survey found that only 52% of college students said they "really enjoy" watching TV, compared to 70% who "really enjoy" recreational reading—yet they spend far more time on TV than on recreational reading.[15]

Why, then, do people devote so much of their leisure time to watching TV, when TV watching is often an unsatisfying experience? Simply put, watching television is attractive because it is easy and requires so little from us. As two researchers observe, "Much of television's attraction is that it is ubiquitous and undemanding. . . . It requires no advance planning, costs next to nothing, requires no physical effort, seldom shocks or surprises, and can be done in the comfort of one's own home."[16] Emerging adults, and their elders, too, watch TV as a way of tuning out the other stresses and demands of modern life.

Texting does not take up as much sheer time as music, Internet use, and TV—about 45 minutes a day, according to one estimate[17]—but in some ways it is the most important media form in the lives of emerging adults, because it keeps them constantly connected to the people most important to them. They keep their phones by their sides at all times, and most will stop whatever they are doing when the tone announcing a new message sounds, in order to reply or at least see who the message is from, even if this means interrupting a conversation with friends, a date, or a family meal. As shown in Figure 8.2, in a study by the Pew Research Center, four out of five emerging adults had texted in the past day, a far higher proportion than any older age group. Furthermore, of people who had texted in the past day, for 18–29-year-olds the median number of texts sent was 20, again far higher than other adults. The typical American emerging adult is sending a couple of text messages per hour (and receiving a couple as well, no doubt), all day long.

Why is use of texting, social media, and the Internet highest among the young, and why does it decline with age? The simplest answer would be that as digital natives they have grown up with these types of media use and consider them a normal part of life. Another part of the explanation may

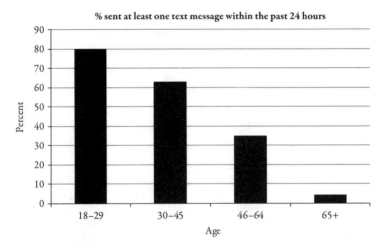

Figure 8.2 Texting by Age.

Source: Taylor & Keeter (2010).

be that emerging adults are at a stage of life when they are on their own a lot—the "self-focused" age, as I described it in Chapter 1. Almost all of them have periods in their twenties when they have moved away from their parents and siblings, have no current romantic partner, and do not have any friends because they have moved to a new place. Under these circumstances, texting and social media comfort them and allow them to keep connected to the people they love, even if those people are on the other side of the country or the world. In the national Clark poll, 51% of 18–29-year-olds agreed with the statement, "I rely a lot on the support I get from friends and family though email, texting, and social networking websites."[18]

Rates of electronic game use are more varied than other types of media use. Young men are far more avid players than young women are. In one study of college students on six campuses in different parts of the United States, 55% of young men reported playing electronic games at least one or two days a week, compared to just 7% of the women.[19] Furthermore, most of the electronic game playing of the young men was in (self-defined) "violent" games, compared to virtually none for the women. Among young male players, interest in electronic games varies from occasional fun to obsession, but fewer than 10% appear to be so involved with electronic games that their playing interferes with the rest of their lives.[20]

Emerging adulthood as the self-focused age also helps explain why young men in their twenties play electronic games at higher rates than people in any other age group. Being self-focused means having fewer daily social obligations, responsibilities, and restraints than people do at other stages of life. Unlike in childhood or adolescence, parents are not around in emerging adulthood to ask (or order) the young man to turn off the games and do homework, or come to dinner, or go to sleep, or... *something*. Once the commitments of adulthood come along, there will be a spouse or partner to tell him to turn off the games, and probably children who need a lot of care and attention that is incompatible with long hours in front of a screen. It is only during emerging adulthood that it is possible to spend hours a day playing electronic games without anyone else objecting.

Emerging Adults' Uses of Media

Clearly media use plays a large role in the daily lives of emerging adults, but what does this mean? How—if at all—does it shape their attitudes, their behavior, and their sense of themselves? Two ways of answering this kind of question have developed in media research. One is to look for direct effects. So, for example, a correlation might be found in young men between playing violent electronic games and having violent attitudes toward conflict resolution, and this would be interpreted as indicating that playing violent electronic games influences young men to have violent attitudes.

Another way of looking at the role of media in the lives of young people is to recognize that people make choices about media and use media for a variety of purposes. This is known as the "uses and gratifications" approach.[21] So, for example, a uses and gratifications approach to understanding young men and electronic games would recognize that only some of the young men choose to play violent electronic games. What is different about the ones who choose to play violent electronic games, compared to those who do not? Do they already have more violent attitudes toward conflict, irrespective of their game playing? What draws some men to play violent games, and what do they say about their reasons for playing and the effects of the games on their moods and behavior?

I regard the uses and gratifications approach to media use as a lot more valid than the direct effects approach. Especially once they reach emerging adulthood, people have a vast range of media content to choose from, and they make choices based on their preexisting characteristics. It may be that media have effects on some people's attitudes and behavior, but these conclusions should be made with care; certainly, researchers should avoid leaping to the conclusion that correlations imply causation. Even if using certain types of media is *correlated* with certain attitudes and behavior, this does not mean that using those types of media *causes* the attitudes and behavior.

Media researchers also need to avoid assuming that media content affect all people in similar, predictable ways. Part of the value of the uses and gratifications approach to media use is that it takes seriously media users' own reasons for choosing specific media content, by listening to what they say about the gratifications and rewards they obtain from it. I received a lesson in this early in my research career, when I did a small study on fans of heavy metal music.[22] It is violent music, and at the time (the early 1990s) it was widely feared that it might inspire its devotees to violence. I am no fan of the music myself, and I generally found it depressing and (at concerts) an assault on the senses. However, in the course of interviewing the "metalheads," I found that none of them reported being depressed by it. In fact, to my surprise, the most typical response was that they listened to it especially when they felt depressed or angry, and it had the subsequent effect of *calming them down* and making them feel less rather than more violent.

In research on adolescents' media use, a theory has been proposed by Jeanne Steele and Jane Brown that takes a uses and gratifications approach and recognizes the importance of identity issues in adolescents' media choices.[23] They call it the *Media Practice Model.* I think it can be usefully applied to emerging adults' media use as well, given that, as noted throughout this book, identity issues are even more prominent in emerging adulthood than in adolescence.

An illustration of the model is shown in Figure 8.3. It shows how *identity* is what originally motivates the *selection* of some kinds of media content rather than others. One study found that emerging adults regard their selection of music, in particular, as a way to construct and express their identity, more than other types of media use or other leisure.[24] They regard music as a way to explore possible identities and discover who they really are, because the range of their choices in music is so much greater than for other media.

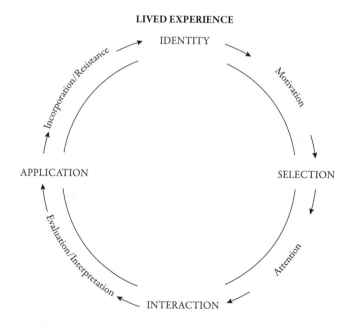

Figure 8.3 Media Practice Model.

There are literally millions of songs to choose from, in genres ranging from country to techno to hip hop and death metal, and each genre has distinctive themes and implicit ideologies.

Once media selection has taken place, *attention* is a crucial link to emerging adults' *interaction* with the media content. Television is a media form for which attention is minimal, and consequently interaction is minimal as well. As noted earlier, television induces a passive, "blah" state of mind and mood in most people. Emerging adults are often engaged with a more active media form while they have the TV on—texting or talking on the phone, reading or using the Internet. In contrast to TV, use of social networking websites like Facebook inherently requires attention and subsequent interaction. Several recent studies show that emerging adults interact with social networking sites in ways that make implicit identity statements about who they are and how they want to represent themselves to others.[25] Interacting with social networking sites often involves posting links, blog commentary, photos, and information as ways of trying on possible selves. As emerging adults' identities develop, these changes can be reflected through what they choose to post on their websites. In this way, social networking websites become a semi-public forum in which emerging adults explore identity issues and gradually move toward establishing and expressing the "real me."[26]

The next link in the Media Practice Model is *evaluation/interpretation*. As they interact with media content, emerging adults do not simply respond passively and predictably, as in the old direct effects model. On the contrary, they make judgments about the content and respond in a variety of ways that reflect their individual characteristics. So, for example, studies have found that adolescents and emerging adults interpret the lyrics of a given song in a wide variety of ways, with a corresponding diversity in the message that they believe the lyrics are intended to express.[27] Studies of electronic game playing report that boys evaluate the situations depicted in the games and recognize the distinction between the game world and real life.[28]

Last in the model comes the *application* of the media experience, either through *incorporation* or *resistance*. Sometimes emerging adults incorporate their media experiences into their identities. Being a fan of specific singer or actor or TV show, or being a "gamer" (devotee of electronic games), eventually becomes part of "who I am." Other times, they respond with resistance, actively critiquing media content, even media content they like, and rejecting it as part of their sense of themselves.

In 2013 there was a classic example of resistance that also provides an illustration of the speed of media technologies in the modern age. A student at Brown University, Clare Beyer, tweeted "idea for a single purpose Twitter: feminist Taylor Swift." A fan of the singer, Beyer nevertheless felt that Swift's lyrics often portrayed young women in a submissive, traditional way that merited resistance. Plus, she thought a parody would be funny. Urged on by friends, she followed through the next day and began to post her reworking of lyrics of Swift's most famous songs, from a feminist perspective. So, for example, "You were Romeo, you were throwing pebbles / And my daddy said 'Stay away from Juliet' / And I was standing on the staircase, begging you 'Please don't go'" became "You were Romeo, you were throwing pebbles / And my daddy said 'Stay away from Juliet' / But I'm a grown woman who can make her own decisions." Within a week, @feministtswift had more than 100,000 followers, showing that a substantial audience shared Beyer's resistance to the gender portrayals in the songs and appreciated her humorous take on them.

In sum, the Media Practice Model highlights the complexity of media use, and the diversity of people's uses of the same media content. Crucially, it shows how identity drives media use, and how media use is an active process. People are not simply passive, easily manipulated victims of media companies. For emerging adults, media are ubiquitous in their everyday lives, and most could scarcely imagine a world without media. But, among a vast universe of media content, they make choices that reflect their identities, they decide how much attention to devote to their media at any given time, and they evaluate and sometimes resist the content of the media they enjoy.

Are There Media Effects as Well as Uses?

Despite the promise of the Media Practice Model for providing a nuanced, complex understanding of media use, most studies on media use still take the old direct effects approach. This usually entails either (1) exposing college students to certain types of media under experimental conditions and then assessing their attitudes or behavior following exposure, or (2) finding a correlation between emerging adults' self-reported media use and their self-reported attitudes or behavior.

Both of these approaches are deeply flawed. The main problem with exposing college students (or anyone else) to media content under experimental conditions is that many of them would never have chosen that content outside the lab. So, for example, hundreds of experimental studies have shown that college students are more aggressive (both physically and interpersonally), have more aggressive thoughts, show less empathy, and are less likely to help those in need immediately after exposure to media violence in the laboratory.[29] Typically, participants in these studies are randomly divided into an *experimental group* that is exposed to media violence and a *control group* that is exposed to nonviolent media. This may look like a strength of the research design, but it is actually a weakness. There is no way of telling if the students who reported increased aggressiveness would have chosen that media content on their own, since they were divided randomly, not on the basis of their preferences for violent or nonviolent media content. Perhaps exposure to violent media leads to greater aggressiveness only among those who would have chosen the violent content; perhaps the opposite is true, but it is impossible to tell from this design. Furthermore, there is no evidence that the effects found in the experimental situations have any lasting influence.

The problem with finding a correlation between media preferences and certain attitudes or behavior is the usual problem with correlations: there is no way of telling whether or not causation is involved. So, to continue with the violent media example, finding a correlation between a preference for violent media and aggressive attitudes and behaviors in no way implies that using violent media caused the participants to become more aggressive. In fact, such correlations can be highly misleading, as I found in my research on metalheads. They were, in fact, more prone to aggressive behavior and attitudes than non-heavy-metal-fans their age,[30] yet none of them reported being inspired by the music to greater aggression, and many of them reported the opposite effect, a *cathartic effect* of feeling calmer and less aggressive after listening to metal.

In any case, concerns about the negative effects of media are much greater for children than for emerging adults or even for adolescents. Even most media researchers who claim media effects on children recognize that adolescents are more capable than younger children of understanding the distance between the media world and reality. Rowell Huesmann, one of the most prominent proponents of the claim that televised violence causes aggression in children, states that "we do not need to be as concerned about adults' or even teenagers' exposure to media violence as much as we do with children's exposure. Media violence may have short-term effects on adults, but the real long-term effects seem to occur only with children."[31]

The greatest and most definite danger to emerging adults from electronic media is not from media with violent content but from the seemingly innocuous practice of texting. Alarmingly, nearly two-thirds (64%) of 18–29-year-olds say they have texted while driving.[32] Given that automobile accidents are the number one cause of death in this age group, texting while driving should be a focus of public policy concern and action. Since 2007, 41 states have made texting while driving illegal, and another 6 ban the practice for novice drivers (usually defined as those under age 18).[33] However, the fact that two-thirds of 18–29-year-olds nevertheless state that they have texted while driving raises the question of how well these laws are being enforced.

Does Media Use Undermine Social Relations?

Although the caveats in the previous section should be kept in mind when interpreting media research, and most research claims of "effects" do not hold up well under scrutiny, there is a legitimate concern about how the ubiquity of new media might change social relations, not just for emerging adults but for all of us. If our digital devices are constantly present, summoning our attention every few minutes with a message from someone who is somewhere else, are we ever truly together with the people who are physically present with us, in the here and now? Are we reaching the point depicted in the *New Yorker* cartoon that shows a young person saying to her parents, "I'm inviting all my friends over tonight so we can stare at our phones"? Is the satirical point of the cartoon not just an amusing exaggeration but the way things really are? Are young people becoming more devoted to displaying their experiences to impress their Facebook "friends" than to spending time with actual friends?

Many emerging adults themselves share these concerns. In the national Clark poll, 50% of 18–29-year-olds agreed that "[s]ometimes I feel like I spend too much time on social-networking websites."[34] Many people feel concerned enough about the amount of time they spend on social media to cut back for a while. A 2013 report by the Pew Research Center found that 61% of Facebook users had taken a "Facebook break" at some point, that is, they had stopped using it for a period of several weeks or more.[35] Reasons for taking the break were diverse, but most often centered around the amount of time Facebook seemed to require of them. Another intriguing finding of this report was that 42% of 18–29-year-olds said the amount of time they spend on Facebook on a typical day has *decreased* in the past year, a higher percentage than adults in any older age group. Nevertheless, other research reports that the number of social media users continues to expand daily, worldwide, across age groups.[36]

Similar concerns exist around emerging adults' uses of their "phones." It may be too strong to call their use of these devices an "addiction," but there certainly are signs of a degree of dependence for many of them that may not be healthy. In the national Clark poll, 36% of 18–29-year-olds conceded, "I feel anxious if I have to go more than a couple of hours without checking for electronic messages."[37] The compulsion to check their devices constantly may be inspired in part by "fear of missing out," which is common enough to have inspired the popular acronym "FOMO." For emerging adults, FOMO is the anxiety that, no matter how much you might be enjoying what you are doing and the people you are with, there is a better party going on someplace else, and that nagging worry can cast a shadow on the experience a person is actually having.

Sherri Turkle, a media scholar, has sounded the alarm over where modern media technologies are taking us. Increasingly, she warns in the subtitle of her book *Alone Together*, we "expect more from technology and less from each other."[38] Turkle's critique is especially notable because she was one of the first scholars to focus on the potential effects of Internet use and was once a proponent of the Internet's positive potential for enhancing social connections. By now, however, she has concluded that new media have become too intrusive in our social lives, to the point of virtually taking over. The persistent distractions of our media technology draw us away from being entirely present with each other and make us "alone together."

I have heard examples of Turkle's point from my students at Clark. One student recounted, "My best friend and I have an agreement that when we're together we don't use our phones. I love spending time with him, but every time I hear my phone ringing when we're together, I feel distracted." Another student took a similar step, finding technology so disruptive to her friendships that she and her friends found it necessary to impose restrictions. "A couple of years ago my friends and I decided that technology was too present in our lives and that every time we were together our attention was divided. So we decided that every time we went out with each other we'd put our phones on the middle of the table and no one was allowed to touch them unless it was an emergency." It would be worth researching further how common it is for emerging adults to agree on these kinds of customs with their friends, in order to preserve the intimacy of their friendship.

Although the concerns about the effects of ubiquitous electronic media no doubt apply to many emerging adults, other research on the social effects of new media technologies is surprisingly positive. As noted earlier, in the national Clark poll, half of 18–29-year-olds agreed that "I rely a lot on the support I get from friends and family through e-mail, texting, and social networking websites."[39] Other research reports that users of social networking websites experience higher levels of social support than non-users do.[40] Research also indicates that the use of social networking sites complements rather than replaces offline relationships. For example, one study found that for each hour that college students' use of cell phones or social-networking sites increased, average face-to face social interaction increased about 10 to 15 minutes.[41] This suggests that students use new media technologies to plan face-to-face social activities with friends, as well as to meet new people and keep in touch with others.

There is no doubt that some devotees of new media technologies use them as a substitute for actual social contact, but this does not mean that the media technologies caused them to be socially isolated. As the Media Practice Model reminds us, media use begins with the person's identity. If people choose to spend large portions of time using media technologies, there is something about them, prior to their media use, that drove that selection.

Patty's account of her 19-year-old son Neil's media use provides a good illustration.[42] In contrast to Patty's other son, the gregarious Jake, Neil has only "a couple" of friends, and has "never had a date." He is "very much the loner" and "spends most of his time in his room." Yet his isolation is relieved by the connections he has made through playing games on his computer. He is "huge into gaming," and through the games he "talks to people all over the world." This example is consistent with research showing that players of Massive Multiplayer Online Role Playing Games (MMORPGs) see their games as highly sociable environments that provide a way to develop and maintain friendships over time.

Maybe, if there were no computers and no MMORPGs, Neil would be motivated to come out of his room and develop a social life within his own community. But maybe he wouldn't. Given his introversion and his social insecurities, maybe he would stay in his room anyway and have no relief from his social isolation.

Is it possible to specify a threshold at which media use in emerging adulthood becomes problematic? Douglas Gentile has attempted this for children and adolescents (ages 8–18) with respect to electronic games, and the attempt is instructive in its possibilities and its limitations. Following the guidelines for diagnoses of other mental health disorders, Gentile developed a 10-item scale of electronic game use and defined "pathological gaming" as any score of 5 or more affirmative responses.[43] A "diagnosis" of pathological gaming was correlated with a variety of other problems, including lower academic achievement and higher impulsivity, anxiety, aggression, and depression. However, a number of questions could be raised about this approach. Five of ten is an arbitrary threshold; there is no inherent reason why there should be the same threshold for "pathological gaming" as for other, quite different, mental health disorders. And there is, of course, the usual chicken-or-egg problem with correlations, making it difficult to state with confidence that gaming caused the other characteristics. Clearly in Neil's case his social anxieties preceded his electronic game use, and gaming provides him with a safe form of social interaction that relieves his isolation.

Are the cognitive effects of using new media technologies also worthy of concern? A striking feature of new media is that they are always present, and that they make it difficult to sustain an uninterrupted conversation or train of thought. Pew Internet Project researcher Linda Stone coined the phrase "continuous partial attention" to describe the media environment that young people today experience.[44] Stone and others fear that this state of perpetual media overstimulation makes it difficult to accomplish anything that requires more focused attention. Of course, to the digital natives, this is simply their normal environment. I have had many students tell me, when I express skepticism that they can adequately study for my exams while listening to music, watching TV, or texting—or all of the above—that, on the contrary, they cannot study if their media stimulation is shut down and they are left only with the eerie, unfamiliar silence. For example, Sophie claims that "I feel that I need to have multiple things going to stay on task. If I didn't have music on when I'm doing my homework, I wouldn't be able to concentrate." Yet research has shown consistently that for most people, cognitive performance is lower under conditions of divided attention.[45]

Another way to examine this issue would be to look at performance on national academic exams that have been conducted annually. If new media technologies interfere with learning and cognitive performance, it could be predicted that scores on the exams would have declined since the rise of these technologies over the past two decades. However, patterns on these scores do not support the view that academic performance has declined with the rise of new media technologies. The best and most representative of these national exams for the United States is the National Assessment of Education Progress (NAEP), which assesses the knowledge of high school students. Scores on the NAEP have gone up, not down, in recent decades, especially in math.[46]

So, learning is taking place after all among today's young people, despite the distractions of new media technologies.

Or perhaps it is happening *because* of those new technologies? There is more to the new media than texting, Facebook, and MMORPGs. There is also the astonishingly vast information universe available through the Internet, which allows young people—and the rest of us—access to information on virtually any imaginable topic. Perhaps the benefits of the new media technologies compensate for, or even outweigh, the cognitive costs, so far.

Conclusion: Toward a Balanced Interpretation of Emerging Adults' Media Use

It was 1904, and G. Stanley Hall, writing his magnum opus on adolescent development, was concerned about rising crime rates among American youth. He discerned a variety of causes, but one key source of the problem was the media. As Hall saw it, a young man may be induced to commit crimes in part because "his mind becomes inflamed with flash literature and 'penny dreadfuls'" [cheap magazines] that portray crime as glamorous and heroic" (p. 361).[47] This was not the only problem of youth that Hall attributed to media influences. Johann von Goethe's 1774 novel, *The Sorrows of Young Werther,* remained popular in Hall's time, with pernicious effects, according to Hall. "The reading of romance has great influence on the development of youthful passion. Werther has created a distinct psychosis known as Wertherism."[48]

Throughout the rest of the twentieth century and into the twenty-first, each new media form was greeted with enthusiasm by the general public but with fear and predictions of doom by many academics and social critics. Radio brought the Jazz Age into every household, which meant also bringing in short skirts and sexual licentiousness. Television brought us Elvis and rock-and-roll, which included more incitements to sexual licentiousness and boundary breaking of every kind. Violence on television grew with each passing decade, and it was feared that TV violence would make its watchers violent as well. TV was, in any case, a "vast wasteland" that was sure to make all of us dumber, more passive, and less sociable than before. Now it is the new media technologies that are supposed to herald our demise, as they deepen our social isolation and make it impossible for us to carry on a decent conversation or sustain a train of thought longer than a nanosecond.

Not all of these concerns were misplaced. Premarital sex really did increase during the Jazz Age, and further still with the advent of rock-and-roll.[49] Television really did weaken community involvement, as it made people more inclined to stay at home during the evenings rather than venturing out to the Rotary club or school committee meeting.[50] Nevertheless, the fears of the doomsayers were always overstated, and their predictions of doom consistently overblown. There is no question that media content has become more violent in the past two decades that have comprised the growing-up of today's emerging adults, in media from television to movies to music to electronic games, yet rates of violent crime have plunged by half over that time.[51] Sexual content is more explicit and available than ever before, yet rates of sexual risk behavior are declining rather than rising, as we saw in Chapter 6. Television may indeed be a vaster wasteland than ever, but median IQ scores have risen substantially since TVs became a standard item in every home.[52]

Our media technologies have changed us, undoubtedly, but in complex ways, with benefits as well as costs, in different ways for different people. For emerging adults, media are a major part of their daily environment, and most of them could not imagine life without their digital devices as constant companions. Some of them use media in ways that are extreme or unhealthy, but in most cases these emerging adults may have had problems whether those media were available or not. The identities and individual characteristics that motivated their pathological media use may have been expressed in some other way, had they been born in an earlier time. But as a group, today's emerging adults integrate their media use into their lives in ways that promote more than undermine their social connectedness and their enjoyment of life.

Chapter 9

Sources of Meaning

Religious Beliefs and Values

The third pillar of identity, along with love and work, involves developing an ideology, a worldview, a way of making sense of everything.[1] A worldview invariably includes religious beliefs, for example, beliefs about the ultimate origin of life, the nature of the soul, the existence of supernatural beings, and our destiny after death. Religious faith addresses questions about what theologian Paul Tillich called issues of "ultimate concern,"[2] that is, existential questions about what really matters and what our lives mean in light of our mortality. Because such questions are inherently part of being human, developing an answer to them is invariably part of developing an identity.

This does not mean that human beings are invariably religious, only that we invariably address religious questions as part of our lives. Even to conclude that there is no soul, that there are no supernatural beings, and that we have no destiny after death is to address religious questions and include the answers in a worldview. People in various cultures have created a marvelously diverse array of religious beliefs, but virtually every culture has religious beliefs of some kind.[3] Forming religious beliefs appears to be a universal part of identity development.

Another essential part of a worldview is a set of values, that is, a set of moral principles that guide decisions about the issues that come up in the course of daily life. Beliefs and values are often connected; religious beliefs often include a set of explicit moral principles that are meant to guide daily life, such as the Ten Commandments that are part of the Jewish and Christian faiths. But values can also be nonreligious. For example, individualism and collectivism are systems of values that do not necessarily have a religious basis.[4] Individualism means guiding moral decisions on the basis of what is believed to be best for promoting individual growth, freedom, and personal development. Collectivism means guiding moral decisions on the basis of the needs and interests of the group rather than the individual. Most cultures have an overall orientation that leans toward either individualism or collectivism, but each person also forms a moral orientation that includes some combination of individualism and collectivism to guide the moral decision-making of everyday life.[5]

Emerging adulthood is a crucial time for the development of a worldview, as it is for other aspects of identity development. The process takes place throughout childhood and intensifies in adolescence as we develop the capacity for the kind of abstract reasoning that can be applied to worldview questions about concepts such as God, death, and right and wrong. However, for most people the process of forming a worldview is not completed by the time they leave adolescence. It is during emerging adulthood that people address worldview questions most directly, and it is during emerging adulthood that most people reach at least an initial resolution to their worldview questions. Like identity development in love and work, forming a worldview becomes more intensive and serious in emerging adulthood. Few people enter emerging adulthood at age 18 with a well-established worldview, but few people leave their twenties without one, just as few people leave their twenties without a definite direction in love and work.

In this chapter we examine the religious beliefs and values that are part of the worldviews of American emerging adults. The section on religious beliefs examines both the diversity of emerging adults' beliefs and their common determination to think for themselves with regard to religious issues. We also examine the ways that emerging adults think about the possibility of an afterlife. In the section on values, the focus will be on emerging adults' responses to two questions concerning their values for their own lives and the values they wish to pass on to the next generation. Together, these two questions provide insights on the extent to which emerging adults' values reflect individualism and collectivism.

Religious Beliefs

In this section we will explore the striking diversity of emerging adults' religious beliefs, from atheism and agnosticism to devout traditional beliefs, and everything between. We will see how emerging adults' religious beliefs have only a limited connection to their religious training in childhood and adolescence, a reflection of their resolve to think for themselves and decide on their own beliefs. We will also see how ethnicity is related to religious beliefs in distinctive ways.

I will rely mainly on the findings from the National Study on Youth and Religion (NSYR), directed by Christian Smith.[6] This study began with a national sample of 13–17-year-olds in 2003, and has now followed them over a decade afterward, through their twenties. So far the published results examine how the religious beliefs and attitudes of the 13–17-year-old adolescents changed by the time they were 18–23 years old, but more findings will be released as the study continues. I will use interviews from my original study to illustrate the NSYR findings.

A Congregation of One: Individualized Religious Beliefs

Overall, the NSYR found a decline in religiosity from adolescence to emerging adulthood, both in behavior and in beliefs. Only about 30% of 18–23-year-olds attended religious services at least once a month; over half attended only a few times a year or less. Beliefs were stronger than behavior; 44% reported that religious faith is "very" or "extremely" important in their lives, and 75% reported believing in God. Nevertheless, these percentages were lower than they had been in adolescence.

Emerging adults' religious beliefs are highly diverse. The NSYR findings can be classified into these four categories, listed here from least to most religious.[7]

- Agnostics/Atheists (40%): This includes emerging adults who do not believe in God (atheists) or who believe it is not possible to know if there is a God or not (agnostics), along with emerging adults who say they have no opinion on religion or do not think about it. Some are strongly anti-religious, but to most young people in this category, religion is simply irrelevant to their lives.
- Deists (15%): Emerging adults in this category believe that there is "something out there," a God or spiritual force of some kind, but beyond this they are not sure what to believe.
- Liberal Believers (30%): When it comes to religion, these emerging adults take what they want and ignore the rest. That is, they believe only the parts of their denominational faith that appeal to them, and

they often add other elements from sources including other religions and popular culture.

- Conservative Believers (15%): These are emerging adults who hold to a traditional, conservative faith.

Let's look at how emerging adults in each of the four categories describe their beliefs.

Agnostics/Atheists

Emerging adults in this category explicitly reject any belief in God (atheists) or are unsure what to believe about religious questions (agnostics). For example, when asked about his current religious beliefs, Stuart exemplified the atheist view when he responded "I don't believe in a soul. I don't believe in a god. I don't believe in an afterlife." Wilson exemplified the agnostic view in responding, "I really don't know. I can't say for sure if I believe there is a supreme being out there or not. I just don't know."

Some emerging adults in this category are actively hostile to religion. Palmer said, "I think religion's probably one of the biggest problems this world has. I really do. Look at all the wars between people because they're one religion and somebody else is another. In India, you know, you've got cows walking across the damn street, and people starving to death. That just doesn't register with me at all." Some contrast religion with science and rationality, and choose the scientific worldview as superior. Denny said, "I kind of lean more towards science and stuff like that. I can see how evolution happened easier than I can believe in some spiritual super-being." Others are still exploring religious questions and hope to find answers eventually. Sandy said she was an agnostic, but added, "Someday I'll figure it out, but right now I just really am not sure. I'm just kind of waiting for a flash of lightning. You know, someday something will probably spark a belief in something."

Deists

These emerging adults declare a belief in God or a "higher power" or "spirituality," but only in a general sense, not in the context of any religious tradition. They do not call themselves "deists," but they fit the definition of a deist as someone who holds a general belief in God. For example, Amelia said, "I definitely believe in a greater being, but I don't think I could specify, you know, I'm Buddhist or I'm Presbyterian." Often, emerging adults in this category specify that their beliefs do not include participation in organized religion. As Don said, "I have my own unique relationship with God. I don't ascribe to any institutionalized religion right now, at all."

Many deists use the word "spiritual" in describing their beliefs, and contrast this with "religious," meaning part of organized religion. Rachel described her beliefs by saying, "I'm a very spiritual person. I don't consider myself a religious person because I don't claim one religion. I mean, I've experienced all sorts of different religions, and I've learned about a lot of different religions. But I basically consider myself a more spiritual person than religious." Although some reject all organized religion, others believe that each religion holds part, but only part, of the truth about religious questions. José said, "I kind of believe that if there's a God, I don't think that God is a Catholic. God is God and you can go through God whichever religion you want to go through."

Liberal Believers

Liberal believers share with deists a skepticism regarding organized religion and an acceptance of different faiths. What distinguishes liberal believers from deists is that liberal believers nevertheless describe themselves as members of a specific religious tradition (e.g., Catholic, Baptist, Jewish). For example, Christy sounded very much like a deist when she said, "Religion is a shoe that fits everyone differently, and there isn't one good or bad religion. In fact, if you look at it, everybody worships the same god, whether they call him 'Buddha' or whatever." However, she also described herself as a Catholic and said, "I'm drawn to the very basic beliefs that Catholics hold true."

Even though they consider themselves part of a specific religious tradition, most liberal believers do not see participation in religious services as essential to the expression to their faith. Juan said, "I believe in God, but I don't go to church every Sunday. You know, very little. The role of the church in my life has been just a Catholic baptism, first communion, confirmation, and that's it." Liberal believers often state that they do not accept all aspects of their religious tradition. Trey said, "I belong to the Lutheran Church. As far as religiously, I guess most of their teachings I go along with. There are certain ones that I question. Some people that belong to the church would say to me 'No, you can't question it. If you belong to the church, you've go to take it all or nothing'. But I don't think that's right."

Conservative Believers

Emerging adults who are conservative believers express a belief in traditional religious doctrine, such as, for Christians, the belief that Jesus is the son of God and the only way to heaven. For example, Kurt said, "I believe that through Christ is how you have your eternal salvation. I believe that he died on the cross for our sins, and that you have to repent of your sins and be baptized into Christ for the remission of your sins." Conservative Christians are highly conscious of issues of salvation and life after death, but they also use their faith as a guide to daily life. Manuela said, "Everything I try to do in life, I always try to see it how God is seeing it. You know, what I wear, the way I look, what I say, the way I ... you know, just everything." They tend to have an especially strong sense that their lives are guided by God. Clive said, "Since I gave my life to Christ, I've been like a whole new person. I have something to live for. I feel that this higher power is over me, guiding my life. It's like the more faith I put in Him, the better my life goes." Unlike deists and liberal believers, who hold that there are many different legitimate ways of believing in God, conservative believers regard their faith as the only true faith. As Shalanda bluntly stated, "I believe if you're saved, you're goin' to heaven. If you're not, you're goin' to bust hell wide open."

Do-It-Yourself Religions

These four categories portray great diversity in emerging adults' religious beliefs, but the diversity is actually even greater than this, because there is also diversity within the categories, especially the deists and the liberal believers, who together comprise about half of emerging adults. Atheists/agnostics are quite similar to each other, in rejecting religious beliefs (atheists) or in declaring that they do not know what to think about religious questions (agnostics). Conservative believers also sound highly similar to each other, because they all subscribe to a particular doctrine, and being conservative means, by definition, not deviating from that doctrine. But deists and liberal believers feel free to form their own individualized belief system, constructed from a variety of religious and nonreligious sources, including popular culture.[8]

For example, Leah's father was a minister in a Disciples of Christ church and she went to church every Sunday growing up, but by now her beliefs have become a singular pastiche of New Age, Eastern, and Christian ideas. "A lot of my beliefs border on what would be labeled as witchcraft," she said. "I believe that objects can capture energy and hold it...I do believe it's possible to communicate with people who have died...I do believe in reincarnation...I believe I've had past lives...I am what I would label a 'guardian angel,' and there are certain people that I'm supposed to help out."

Jared invoked ideas from the movie "Star Wars," which he combined with ideas from a variety of religions. "I've read the theory that all these religions, Mohammed and Buddha and Jesus, all the patterns there are very similar....And I believe that there's a spirit, an energy. Not necessarily a guy or something like that, but maybe just a power force. Like in Star Wars—the Force. The thing that makes it possible to live."[9]

One reason the beliefs of many emerging adults are highly individualized is that they value thinking for themselves with regard to religious questions and believe it is important to form a unique set of religious beliefs rather than accepting a ready-made dogma. For example, Nate described himself as a Christian, but he also said he believed that "[y]ou don't have to be one religion. Take a look at all of them, see if there is something in them you like— almost like an *a la carte* belief system. I think all religions have things that are good about them." Melissa said, "I was raised Catholic...and I guess if I had to consider myself anything I would consider myself Catholic," but she also said, "I don't have any really strong beliefs because I believe that whatever you feel, it's personal....Everybody has their own idea of God and what God is, and because you go to a church doesn't define it any better, because you still have your own personal beliefs of how you feel about it and what's acceptable for you and what's right for you personally." Emerging adults such as Melissa see it as their responsibility to develop a set of religious beliefs that is uniquely their own.

Unifying Principles: Moralistic Therapeutic Deism

Although American emerging adults' beliefs are highly diverse, there does seem to be a common underlying core of beliefs that most of them hold. This foundation is not any traditional set of beliefs from an established religion. Rather, according to Christian Smith, the director of the NSYR, it is a loose collection of sentiments about religious issues. He calls it "Moralistic Therapeutic Deism (MTD)," a belief system defined by these principles:[10]

- A God exists who created and orders the world and watches over human life on earth.
- God wants people to be good, nice, and fair to each other, as taught in the Bible and by most world religions.
- The central goal of life is to be happy and to feel good about oneself.
- God does not need to be particularly involved in one's life except when needed to resolve a problem.
- Good people go to heaven when they die.

So, Moralistic Therapeutic Deism is *moralistic* in the sense that it emphasizes being a good person; it is *therapeutic* in the sense that it emphasizes that God wants you to feel good about yourself; and it is *deism* in the sense that it is a general belief in God, not tied to any specific doctrine. It is only for a small segment of Conservative Believers that religion is still about traditional ideas of sin, grace, and redemption. For most emerging adults, if they adhere to religion at all, they see it as being about how to be a good person and feel happy.

Skepticism of Religious Institutions

As Melissa's comments suggest, the individualism valued by many emerging adults makes them skeptical of religious institutions and wary of being part of one. The NSYR results indicate that religious participation is much less important to emerging adults than their religious beliefs are. Only 26% of 18–23-year-olds stated that their religious beliefs were "not very" or "not at all" important to them, but 54% attend religious services either "never" or only "a few times a year."[11]

In part, their disinclination to take part in religious services is due to their lifestyle. Many of them work hard during the week, often combining work and school, and they see the weekend as the time to sleep late and relax. They often stay out late with friends on weekend nights, and large quantities of alcohol may be involved, which does not make the prospect of getting up for religious services any more appealing.

Consider, too, how low-tech and sleepy the typical religious service must seem to the digital natives of this generation of emerging adults, who have had electronic companionship almost constantly since childhood.[12] It's so unnaturally *quiet*. It may feel to them like walking into a set for a play about the olden days: nineteenth-century hymns; the cleric up front in ultra-formal garb, reading from a text centuries old; the silent collective prayer. Maybe it could be changed to suit the livelier preferences of the young, but the tranquility is exactly what many of the older folks like about the service, the way it provides a respite from the relentless technological barrage of modern life. This contrast helps explain why religious participation has declined steadily with each generation, as we will see in detail in the next section.

Even if the format changed, participating in religious services would have limited appeal to most emerging adults, precisely because it is, by definition, a collective rather than an individual expression of faith. Participation in a religious institution, even a liberal one, requires them to abide by a certain set of beliefs and rules, and therefore constitutes an intolerable compromise of their individuality.

For example, Charles grew up attending an Episcopal church with his parents, but stopped attending when "I realized that I was not being encouraged to think for myself. And that has been my fundamental problem with certain forms of organized religion. It is not a matter of, 'Take this service for what it is and integrate it into your own life for whatever it means to you.' It is, literally, 'This is black. This is white. Do this. Don't do that.' And I can't hang with that." Similarly, Burt said he believed in God, but "I'm just not real big on the church thing. I think that's a man-made thing. I don't need anyone telling me what's right or wrong. I know what's right and wrong." Dana grew up in a Jewish home and attended synagogue, but stopped attending as she reached emerging adulthood because "there was this pressure from the people at the synagogue to be, like, kosher, and I just didn't like having anyone telling me what my lifestyle should be."

Emerging adults tend to personalize their relationship with God in a way that makes participating in organized religion unnecessary or even an impediment to the expression of their beliefs. Jean, who was raised Catholic but rarely attends mass now, said, "I'm the kind of person that feels that you don't have to go to church just to be religious. I mean, it's not necessary to be in a certain place to be religious." Joseph said he experienced stronger spiritual feelings in the outdoors than in church. "Just being outside in the woods or fishing is more spiritual to me than going in and sitting in a church with a bunch of people and somebody preaching from the Bible. I kind of like to be independent and free to think on my own."

According to the NSYR, most emerging adults have "a lot of respect" for organized religion.[13] However, some emerging adults have had negative experiences that have led them to view such institutions as bastions of corruption and hypocrisy. Terry was disillusioned about organized religion because of "hypocritical things in Christians that I knew." She gave as an example her grandmother, who "only reads the Bible and has it in her lap every day," yet freely casts racist aspersions on Black people. Hayley described herself as "brought up Baptist" and said she "still believes in God," but she also said she rarely attends church. Based on her experience she has concluded that "I don't feel that going to church every Sunday makes you a good Christian. You can go to church every Sunday and be a hypocritical asshole, as far as I'm concerned."

Beth had unpleasant memories of her church experiences in childhood. "I remember going to church and being bored, and seeing everybody around me being bored." By emerging adulthood she had rejected the Catholicism of her youth because of "the guilt. I got so sick of feeling guilty all the time. And, oh God, 'lust is so awful.' I really feel like there are things that are natural to us, because I really believe that yes, we are human, but we also still have animal tendencies, and you can't guilt those out of people. And that's pretty much when I decided that yes, I did have an animal in me and I wasn't going to guilt my animal any more because it made me unhappy. So I gave up being Catholic." Disillusioning experiences such as Beth's are quite common among emerging adults, and have turned many of them away from religious institutions.

The Steady Generational Decline in Religious Beliefs

Emerging adults' skeptical views of religious institutions are reflected in some excellent recent studies on religious beliefs and practices in American life. All show the same unmistakable pattern: that younger people are less religious than older people in every way, and that religiosity has declined with each successive generation.

The Pew Research Center conducts frequent surveys on religion as part of the Pew Forum on Religion & Public Life. One of their most striking findings is the high proportion of 18–29-year-olds who are classified as "unaffiliated," meaning that they do not consider themselves to be a member of any religious denomination or organization. People in this category are also known to researchers on religion as "the Nones," because, when asked what religion they are, they respond with some version of "none"—atheist, agnostic, spiritual but not religious, or just not religious. As Figure 9.1 shows, one-third (32%) of the 18–29-year-olds in the Pew survey are Nones, a far higher proportion than among their parents or grandparents.

In fact, one-third is probably an underestimate, because interviewing emerging adults about their religious beliefs shows "affiliation" to be a misleading indicator of religiosity. When people respond to a survey question about their religion by stating "Catholic" or "Jewish" or "Methodist," it may not mean much about what they actually believe. Here, for example, is how one young man I interviewed responded to a question about what his current beliefs are: "I would say I'm Catholic. I believe there's something to be said for religion, I just don't know if any of them are right." If he had been asked in a survey what his religious beliefs are, no doubt he would have answered "Catholic," but he does not believe that it is any more likely to be "right" than any other religion is. And for good measure he added that he has not gone to mass even once in the past year. In the NSYR, among 18–23-year-olds who gave a religious affiliation classified as Catholic or Mainline Protestant, over one-third also stated that they *never* attend religious services.[14] How much sense does it make classify someone as having a religious affiliation if they *never* attend services of that affiliation?

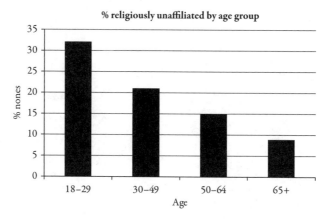

Figure 9.1 The Rise of the "Nones".

Source: Pew Research Center (2012).

Other surveys, using measures other than religious affiliation, report a similar pattern of generational decline in religiosity. The General Social Survey (GSS), a national survey that has been taking place annually since 1978, classifies respondents by generation, as follows:

- Millennials (born 1981 or later);
- Generation X (born 1965–1980);
- Boomers (born 1946–1964);
- Silent (born 1928–1945); and
- Greatest (born before 1928).

The GSS reports a steady decline in weekly religious attendance across generations, as shown in Figure 9.2.

Like the GSS, the Gallup organization takes a generational approach, and reports findings similar to Pew and the GSS. Today's emerging adults are far less likely than their parents or grandparents to say religion is "very important" in their lives (Figure 9.3). The decline is remarkably linear and steady, ever downward with each new generation.

Clearly, religion is less important to today's emerging adults than it was in the past, and less relevant to their lives. Still, nearly half of American emerging adults say that their religious faith is "very important" to them. At all ages, Americans are more religious in both beliefs and practices than Canadians,

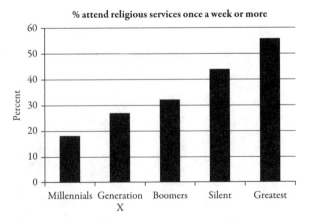

Figure 9.2 Religious Attendance by Age.

Source: Pew Research Center (2010).

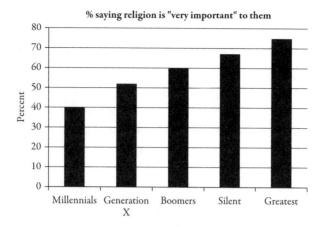

% saying religion is "very important" to them

Figure 9.3 Importance of Religion by Age.
Source: Pew Research Center (2010).

Australians, or Europeans are. In northern Europe, especially, young people rarely enter a church or synagogue except for weddings or funerals.[15]

The Missing Link? Childhood Religious Training and Current Beliefs

How do emerging adults develop their religious beliefs? The answer might seem to be obvious: from their parents. Most American parents provide some kind of religious training to their children. In my original study, about 60% of emerging adults were classified as having "high exposure" to religious training in childhood, meaning that their parents took them to religious services on a regular and frequent basis.[16] About 20% were classified as having "moderate exposure" (parents took them to religious services now and then, but without much involvement or commitment), and 20% "low exposure" (parents rarely or never took them to religious services). The NSYR seems to support the effectiveness of this training. About two-thirds of the 18–23-year-olds in the NSYR viewed their religious beliefs as "similar" to their parents' beliefs.

However, there is also a substantial amount of contrary evidence. As the generational patterns in the previous section show, today's emerging adults are considerably less religious than their parents and grandparents, which indicates that the religious training that parents provide may fail to take root in the next generation. In a longitudinal study focusing specifically on Catholics, little correlation was found between Catholic religious training in childhood and adolescence and the religious beliefs and practices of the same people in their thirties and forties.[17] Even the NSYR shows that between one-fourth and one-half of young people change their religious affiliation from age 13–17 to age 18–23, with some becoming more religious but most becoming less religious.[17] Similarly, a study by the Pew Foundation found that about one-fifth (18%) of 18–29-year-olds reported that they were raised in a religion but are now unaffiliated.[18] And this is just for religious affiliation, which, as we have seen, can make people seem to be more religious than they actually are.

In my original study, the lack of a connection between religious training and emerging adults' current beliefs was even more stark. There was no statistical relationship between exposure to religious training in childhood and *any aspect of their religious beliefs* as emerging adults—not to their current classification as Agnostic/Atheist, Deist, Liberal believer, or Conservative Believer; not to their current attendance at religious services; not to their views of the importance of attending religious services, or the importance of their religious beliefs, or the importance of religion in their daily lives; and not to their belief that God or a higher power guides their lives, or to the certainty of their religious beliefs in emerging adulthood.[19]

This is a different pattern from that found in adolescence. During adolescence there does tend to be a relationship between the religiosity of the parents and the religiosity of their children. For example, studies have found that adolescents are more likely to embrace the importance of religion when their parents talk about religious issues and participate in religious activities.[20] Evidently, however, something changes between adolescence and emerging adulthood that often dissolves the link between the religious beliefs of parents and the beliefs of their children.

Still, how could it be that childhood religious training so often makes little difference in the kinds of religious beliefs and practices that people have by the time they reach emerging adulthood? It does not seem to make sense. Parents take their children to religious services repeatedly over many years, have them baptized or confirmed or bar mitzvahed, and it all comes to naught in emerging adulthood?

Yet that seems to be a common pattern, surprising as it may be. Emerging adults' own accounts of the change are vivid and persuasive. Wilson said, "I was brought up as a Christian. I was baptized when I was seven years old, went to church every Wednesday, every Sunday, and Sunday night. I had to go for years and years in a row.... I'm surprised I'm not a complete saint right now, as much church as I was subjected to." Now, however, he says, "I'm not religious at all. Zero. I question the credibility of religion now. I can't say for sure if I believe there is a supreme being out there or not. I just don't know." Brady said that he "went to church every Sunday until I was 16." By now, however, he has decided "I'm an atheist...I look at the Bible as just being a myth. It doesn't make any sense. I don't see how there can be a God, with the condition of the world. Especially not an all-knowing, all-powerful God."

Keith was especially vehement in rejecting his childhood religious training. He was "raised Catholic," and he went to mass every Sunday and also went to Catholic schools. However, his current beliefs are far from Catholicism. "I don't believe in anything. I really don't, and it goes far beyond atheism for me. Organized religion, I mean, everybody's got a void to fill and that's just one way of filling it. I mean, we have to realize that these books that they're reading were written by men, you know, men just like you or I. And for somebody to take that literally and to call it a religion, to me that's just utterly ridiculous, completely ridiculous to take it as the only truth and totally close your mind to all other things. You make yourself stupid."

A typical pattern was attendance at religious services throughout childhood and early adolescence, but increasing resistance during adolescence, leading to a rejection of religious participation in late adolescence or emerging adulthood. This is consistent with the NSYR pattern of declining religiosity from adolescence to emerging adulthood. Sandy said, "I was pretty much dragged to church every Sunday until I was 18. Finally, at that point I said, 'I'm not going any more.' I just didn't want to. I was going out on Saturday night and getting drunk, and the last thing I wanted to do was get up at 7:00 in the morning and go to church." Craig said he was a "full-blown Catholic" as a child, but when he was 17 years old "I just flat told Mom I wasn't going to go any more. It was a waste of time. I didn't like it. I went because I was under Mom and Dad's rules. I did what they said to do, went to Sunday school and stuff like that. But I can go to church all you want, and I'm still going to believe what I believe. You're not going to change me."

Usually the change in late adolescence and emerging adulthood is away from religious beliefs and religious participation, but in some cases it is in the other direction, toward greater faith. The NSYR found one-quarter of 13–17-year-olds who were non-religious reported a Christian affiliation of some kind by ages 18–23.[21] Bridget said, "My parents were atheists. They didn't believe in God." Now, in emerging adulthood, she attends an evangelical church and says her own beliefs are "definitely that there's a God, and that he controls every part of your life, of everyone's life. I believe in the Bible." But this course is relatively unusual, both in the NSYR and in my original research. It is more common for emerging adults to have high exposure to religious training in childhood but fall away from religious beliefs and practices by emerging adulthood, thus leading to a decline in religiosity from one generation to the next.

Let's return now to the original question. Why does religious training in childhood and adolescence often have little influence on religious beliefs and practices in emerging adulthood? One reason is that in the course of growing up, people gradually become exposed to more and more influences and ideas outside the family. Going to college, especially, can challenge the beliefs that emerging adults learned in their earlier religious training. Joan said she had been brought up to be a "very strong Catholic." However, she said, "I stopped practicing the Catholic religion somewhere during college when I took a class in theology, and I'm going, 'Wait a minute. These Catholics have lied to me my whole life.'"

Yvonne gave a similar account. "I used to be a strong Catholic," she said. "During high school I was very dedicated in church, went every Sunday to mass with my family. But then after college I guess I became more open-minded about different beliefs, from learning about Buddhism and just different religions. And I guess I had doubts of what's really true and what's not." Now she is a deist, and no longer attends mass. "I know there is a being out there, God, you know, who has created this earth, but to actually go to church every Sunday and actually pray to him, I don't feel there's a need to."

Exposure to new ideas is part of the explanation for why religious beliefs often change by emerging adulthood, but probably even more important is the responsibility that emerging adults feel to decide for themselves what they believe about religious questions.[22] As mentioned in Chapter 1, "making independent decisions" is one of the Big Three criteria for adulthood, near the top of the criteria that emerging adults consider most important for becoming an adult. This includes decisions about religious beliefs. For most emerging adults, simply to accept what their parents have taught them about religion and carry on the same religious tradition would represent a kind of failure, an abdication of their responsibility to think for themselves, become independent from their parents, and decide on their own beliefs. Quite consciously and deliberately, they seek to form a set of beliefs about religious questions that will be distinctly their own.

Is the change in their beliefs temporary? Will they eventually resume participation in the religious institution of their childhood? There is evidence to suggest that this pattern will apply to at least some of them. The main years of emerging adulthood, ages 18–25, are the nadir of religious participation in American society, and religious participation rises somewhat in the late twenties and beyond after many young people marry and have children.[23] In my original study, too, some of those whose religious participation had waned after high school saw their nonparticipation as temporary, to be resumed after they had children. Perry was among those who viewed religion as something he had no interest in now but wanted his future children to be exposed to. "Growing up, we went to church every Sunday. I don't go to church every Sunday now, just because the weekends now, to me, are a time to relax and sleep late. But I will come around. I firmly believe that a religion should be a part of a kid's growing up."

The people in my original study who had become parents were more likely than nonparents to attend religious services, sometimes motivated by wanting to provide religious training for their child. For example, Leila and her husband recently had begun attending church with their four-year-old daughter because "we both decided that we better start going because we have a child now and we need to give her some type of feeling of church." So, some of the emerging adults who have rejected religious participation—but by no means all of them—may return to it later, spurred this time not by their parents but by their children.

Ethnic Differences

So far we have been talking about emerging adults' religious beliefs and practices in general terms, but it is also important to discuss the ethnic differences in this area. Emerging adults in each of the major American ethnic minorities—African Americans, Latinos, and Asian Americans—have accounts of their religious experiences that are distinctive to their group. Overall, they tend to be more religious than Whites are, and the trend toward lower religiosity described earlier in this chapter has taken place primarily among Whites.[24] We should be careful not to generalize too much about ethnic differences, because each ethnic group is diverse and every ethnic group has many emerging adults who sound like the ones we have been listening to so far in this chapter—the quotes were taken from emerging adults in all the ethnic groups—but our focus in this section will be on the characteristics that make the ethnic groups distinct.

African Americans have been widely observed to be highly religious, and the strength of their religious beliefs is evident among emerging adults. In the NSYR, they were the most likely of all ethnic groups to state that religion is important in their daily lives.[25] Similarly, on every measure of religiosity in my original study, they were more religious than other emerging adults. For example, 82% stated they believe that God or some higher power watches over them and guides their lives, compared to 44% Whites, 46% Latinos, and 63% Asian Americans. Forty-six percent reported attending religious services at least three or four times per month, compared to 14% Whites, 20% Latinos, and 35% Asian Americans. Fifty-four percent were "very certain" about their religious beliefs, compared to 26–34% in the other three groups. Not one of the African Americans we interviewed was an agnostic or atheist (compared to 29% of Whites).

When African American emerging adults talk about their religious beliefs, they often do so in a way that is frank and uninhibited, reflecting the acceptance of open religious expression in African American culture. "I want to be one of God's prayer warriors," said Monique, who credits her faith with helping her break an addiction to crack cocaine. "I walk out on the street and pray if I feel weak or something, or just talk to God." Ray said, "I still believe in God all the way. I travel with my Bible everywhere I go. I read it when things aren't going my way and when they are going my way." Conservative believers in other ethnic groups sometimes use similar language to describe their religious beliefs, but in other groups conservative believers are on the fringe, maybe 10%–15% of the group, whereas for African Americans conservative religious beliefs are the mainstream.

Like African Americans, Latinos are rarely agnostics or atheists, and in Latino culture, as in African American culture, the expression of religious beliefs is a common part of everyday life.[26] But Latino emerging adults talk less about their personal relationship with God and more about religious faith—usually the Catholic faith—as something that provides an organizing structure for their families and communities. Gloria was one of several Latinas who spoke glowingly of memories of their *quinceañera*, a kind of religious coming-out ceremony for girls when they turn 15. "Everyone always has a *quinceañera* when they're 15 and it's something that you get a big party and you have a mass and it's all about you. It's really special. It's kind of like a presentation to the community and to God."

Carlos viewed community service as the most important expression of his faith. "I'm in a [church] group that when people need things, maybe like they're elderly or they're handicapped or they just don't have the time or the money to clean their yard or paint their house, we go out there on Saturday and we paint their house for them, clean up their yard. It's like a community effort, a church effort. Give back to the community." Many Latino emerging adults expressed skepticism about or even rejected some of the teachings of the Catholic Church, but virtually all of them considered themselves part of a Catholic faith community.

For many Asian American emerging adults, their religious experience is a combination of two very different influences. On the one hand, many of them have been exposed to Buddhist beliefs through their parents, who brought those beliefs with them to the United States from their Asian homelands (the Asian Americans in my original study all had parents who were born outside the United States). On the other hand, many of them have been exposed to Catholic beliefs from years of attending Catholic schools. Their parents have often sent them to private Catholic schools in an effort to provide them with the best possible education.[27]

By the time they reach emerging adulthood, Asian Americans have responded in a variety of ways to these two influences. Many of them have become Catholics, which they acknowledge is the result of their Catholic school religious training. "My sisters and I all went to 12 years of Catholic school, so we're Catholic," as Cindy put it simply. Few consider themselves Buddhists, perhaps because Buddhism is so far out of the mainstream of American society. Nevertheless, many of them said they join their parents in Buddhist practices of praying to their ancestors and engaging in various rituals that show their ancestors honor and respect.

Most often, they end up in emerging adulthood neither Catholic nor Buddhist but as deists, with a blend of beliefs that emphasizes a common theme of honoring a higher power and trying to live a morally good life. "I don't know what I am basically," said Jane, whose parents immigrated from Japan. "I went to Catholic schools, I believe in God, I believe in Buddhism. I read everything, and for me, I came to the conclusion it really doesn't make a damn bit of difference as long as you're a good person. You can call it God, Buddha, Providence, Allah, whatever you want to call it."

From "Worm Food" to "Infinite Bliss": Views
of the Afterlife

Emerging adults are remarkably insightful and articulate on a wide range of topics, as this book and especially this chapter have shown. In my original study, no other topic brought out their everyday eloquence more than the topic of what happens when we die. Here as elsewhere, their beliefs were highly diverse:[28]

- 11% believed in no afterlife;
- 21% responded "don't know";
- 15% believed there was some kind of existence after death but were unclear as to the nature of it;
- 15% believed in heaven only;
- 25% believed in heaven and hell;
- 13% held other beliefs (such as reincarnation, energy forces).

Let's examine how beliefs were articulated in each of these categories.

No Afterlife: "When you die, you die"

Eleven percent of participants did not believe in any kind of afterlife. Often this observation was made with mordant humor. "I think we either turn into ashes when we're cremated or we become worm food," said Brendan. "We push up daisies," said Laurel. "I don't believe in reincarnation. I don't believe in heaven or hell at all, and I don't really think that a soul lives on, either." "I think we just become fertilizer," said Tracy.

Others had a more sober perspective. "I really think there is only one life and that's why you have to make the most of it," said Cindy. "If there is an afterlife, I'll find out then, but right now I don't believe there's an after-life. I really think that when you die, you die." Catharine wistfully imagined heaven but ended up coming down to earth: "I mean, the concept of a heaven is a beautiful concept, in that if you accept that, at some point you can get in touch with your family and other people and so on. I think that's a beautiful idea, and having a community who's just all for one, a truthful, honest community. That's a great concept, but I don't think I believe it. I mean, I do believe that you're just going to be fertilizer."

Catharine's comments are useful for drawing our attention to how the promise of something desirable after death exerts an extremely strong psychological pull, even for many people who believe in no afterlife. Although the existence of life after death is impossible to prove, it is also impossible to refute, leaving considerable space for the imagination to create something alluring out of our desires and our existential anxieties. Coming down definitely on the side of no afterlife is rare, as we will see in the sections that follow.

Don't Know: "No one has the right answer"

The "don't know" responses, 21% of the total, fell into two subtypes: confirmed agnostic, and avoidant/oblivious. The confirmed agnostics believed that an answer to the question of what happens after death was simply unknowable. For the living, there is no way of answering that question, in their view. "I'm one of those people that, you know, there's got to be some kind of proof," said Lonnie, "and if there's no proof, then you can't make a judgment." Amos had a similar view: "It's just too confusing to even dwell on it, because you'll never get an answer, right? I mean, you can speculate and speculate, and no one has the right answer." These emerging adults had considered the claims and the possibilities and concluded that none of them was valid.

Laurence reflected: "I think we're all going to die and what happens, nobody knows. I mean, does this electrochemical thing just quit and that's the end of it? Or does it actually go somewhere? Because that's all it is, is electricity. So what happens to it? Does it just stop? Is it like a battery? What happens? Nobody knows, because once you die, you can't come back and tell anybody. I mean, sure, you might see this white light and go towards it, and there might be power in that white light. But who knows?"

Sometimes their agnosticism about life after death was tinged with fear and anxiety. "It just scares me to think about death, like, where do we really go?" wondered Yvonne. "Do we reincarnate or is there a heaven? And then I think, if there is a heaven, how can it hold all of us? There are just so many beliefs that I don't know which one to believe in."

Some in this category were avoidant, that is, they found the question terrifying to contemplate and so tried to avoid thinking about it. "That's a terrible thing to think about now!" exclaimed Cheryl, when asked the question about what happens when we die. "I don't want to think of what happens when I die!" Jane also tried to avoid the topic. "I don't really think about it. It's too morbid for me. I'm too much of an optimist to think about it. I mean, I choose not to think about it." There were also some who were oblivious, dismissing the question as irrelevant to them in their youthful time of life. "I don't think about dying," said Jerry. "I'm 24. I don't think about that stuff."

In sum, there were a variety of different "don't know" responses from the emerging adults, but all of them had in common that they neither believed nor disbelieved in life after death.

Something, But Not Clear What: "I think that we kind of go on"

Fifteen percent of emerging adults believed in some kind of afterlife but were unclear what it might entail. The emerging adults in this category were similar to those in the "don't know" category in that they were uncertain about what lies after death and skeptical that anything could be known for certain. However, unlike those in the "don't know" category, they had at least tentatively decided that there is some kind of life after death, although they remained vague about the nature of it. "I believe that there's something there," said Ariel, "but I don't think we can know exactly what it is." "I don't know exactly," began Sharon, but she added, "I definitely don't think that it's just, like, the end. I think I believe in people's spirits like remaining somehow and maybe having a sort of impact on life, like, mortal life. I guess I don't want to believe that that's just it, and I don't. So something with like spirits being around. That's pretty much like the vague idea that I have about it."

Often the emerging adults in this category conceded that their belief in some kind of life after death was motivated by fear that there may be nothing and the wistful hope that there might be something after all. They found the prospect of personal extinction unpalatable, and the belief in some kind of continued existence more appealing, but their beliefs were tentative at best. "Selfishly, I think that we kind of go on and our spirit goes on," said Peggy, "just because it's kind of a depressing thought to think that it just ends there. But I don't know. I guess I've always just kind of believed that our spirit continues in some other place." Ryan admitted, "I mean, no one on earth has any concrete evidence, but I hope and what I believe is that there is something after. I'm not sure what it is, but I don't think it's that you just don't exist anymore."

Hopeful agnostics, one might call the emerging adults in this category. They were uncertain about what lies beyond death, and concerned that there might be nothing after all, but they persisted in the vague belief that there might be some kind of continued and pleasant existence.

Heaven Only: "Infinite bliss"

Fifteen percent of the emerging adults believed in heaven only. Some of them sounded close to those in the "something but unclear what" category, in that they seemed uncertain about what to believe, but they ultimately decided that there must be some form of heaven after death. "I don't know," answered Joanne at first when asked about life after death, but she continued, "The thing is you get to live life in heaven. That's my afterlife. That's what I would want. That's my perception. I would want to make it to heaven. You know, be a part of the riches and all that." "I believe your soul goes to heaven," said Brock. "I'm not quite sure where it is or what form it is or how it works, but I believe it's out there somewhere."

Others in this category were more confident that heaven awaits after death. "I think that we go to heaven," said Marian. "I think that we are united with God in infinite bliss." Some were confident that heaven awaits not only for themselves but for all. "I think everybody goes to heaven because everybody is God's children," said Kay. "And even those criminals who go around killing people are forgiven, because I think God forgives everybody. Sometimes it's hard to believe, but I really do think God forgives everybody for what they do and I think everybody deserves, in some way or another, to go to heaven."

However, some in this category had mixed feelings about believing that everyone would make it to heaven. They did not believe in hell, but they found the concept of heaven for all problematic in some ways. "That's something that I struggle with," said Bridget. "I'm not a 'fire and brimstone' Christian, but there are evil people in this world. I'd hate to think that I'd be walking around in heaven someday and run across Adolph Hitler and give him a high five, you know. It's a difficult question."

Bridget described herself as a Christian, and some of the emerging adults who believed in heaven for all mentioned aspects of Christianity, but more often the belief in heaven was not phrased in any particular theological language. It was simply a hopeful belief that death would be followed by something good—"infinite bliss," or at least something more pleasant than the struggle of life on earth.

Heaven and Hell: "People don't realize they're going to hell"

Unlike any other category of afterlife beliefs in this study, for the 25% of emerging adults who believed in heaven and hell this belief was drawn from a specific creed, the Christian faith. However, even here there were variations on the theme. Some stated standard Christian beliefs in heaven and hell, but others modified the standard beliefs in individualized ways.

Some of those who embraced the standard Christian beliefs in heaven and hell were blunt and direct. As Theresa put it, "I think of what's in heaven. They've got mansions in heaven and [you] don't die, don't get sick, don't be sad. [But if you're not a Christian] you're going to hell. You're going to burn forever. People don't realize they're going to hell and they're going to be tormented forever." For some of these emerging adults, the firmness of their beliefs in heaven and hell inspired an urgency to try to convert others to the faith. Wanda was a Christian, but her parents were not. "That means if we don't save them before they die, then they will end up going to hell, unfortunately. And that's a problem."

Others admitted their belief in heaven and hell more reluctantly and cautiously. They recognized that this belief may be offensive to non-Christians who are deemed to be going to hell. Kevin observed, "I believe you'll go to heaven if you're a Christian. If you're not, then you go to hell. But I don't tell that to people, you know, because that's just very unpleasant to hear. That's what Christianity is, though." Rob recounted an interaction with a Jewish friend. "He asked me one time, 'Well, according to what you're saying, if I died, I'd go to hell. Do you believe that?' And I had to answer 'Yes.' And it's tough; it really is, because you don't want to believe that, but according to what I've read in the Bible, that's the way I believe it's going to be."

Even for Christians, the destination of heaven or hell was not necessarily tied to faith but rather to whether or not a person had lived a good moral life. "I do believe that you're judged on what you do in your life," said Candace. "If you treated people badly, I think you're going to get paid back for it someday. I really do. I think that if you don't make the peace with Him, you're going downtown." Arthur, although Catholic himself, did not believe that being Catholic was an important criterion: "I think it has a lot to do with what you do with your life. You don't have to be a Catholic, you don't have to be x religion. There are different ways to get up to the mountain, and I think every faith is seeking to get to that metaphorical top of the mountain. There's different ways to go about it, but whether you get up there depends on how you live your life. *[What if you live a bad life?]* I don't think you get there. *[Where do you go?]* You take the down button! And you go to a bad place."

It is interesting to note that some emerging adults in this category used mordant humor, as Candace and Arthur did, with euphemisms such as "going downtown" and "take the down button." This is an element of similarity between them and the emerging adults who believed there is no afterlife. Perhaps in both cases the humor is used to conceal anxiety and discomfort, in the "no afterlife" emerging adults due to the prospect of extinction, and in the heaven/hell emerging adults due to admitting to a belief that many of those deemed to be going to hell may find offensive.

Other Beliefs: Reincarnation and Energy Forces

Thirteen percent of emerging adults stated afterlife beliefs that did not fall into any of the previous categories. About half of the responses in this category concerned reincarnation, and most of the rest concerned some idea about an energy force to which the soul returns.[29] When reincarnation was mentioned, it was not in the context of Buddhism or Hinduism, the two major religions that include reincarnation in their afterlife beliefs. Rather, it was a vague belief that we return to earth in some form. "I don't know, for some reason I sort of believe you come back again," said Osvaldo. "Because I have dreams where I see myself like being in a place, my first time there, like I've been there before. Like a deja vu sort of thing." Tory stated his belief in reincarnation only half-seriously: "I think it's more fun to believe in reincarnation. Like, you can come back as somebody at any point in time in history, or in a different world. Who knows? I think it's a lot more fun to believe in that one. I hate to think you just die and that's it."

Beliefs in returning to some kind of energy force framed the transition to the afterlife as an impersonal process based on natural laws. "I believe you just go back to the One," said Christy. "I think we are just fragments of the light and that at some point you go back to that." Similarly, Carl said he believes that "there's just this planetary aura, that everyone's thought and actions and feelings generate this energy. And when you die, the energy that you are, the non-physical part of you, is dispersed back into that aura and kind of gets recycled. It becomes part of a million other people that are being created at that time or a little bit later."

Values

As noted at the outset of the chapter, the worldview formed by emerging adults includes not only a set of responses to religious questions but also a set of values, that is, a set of moral principles that provides a guide for making life decisions, small and large. Your values come into play when you have a decision to make and you have to ask yourself, what is really most important to me? For example, if you had chosen someone to marry and your parents were opposed to the marriage, the decision you made about whether to marry that person anyway would be a reflection of your values, of what was of ultimate importance to you.

One useful way of thinking about values is in terms of individualism and collectivism.[30] Individualistic values center on the rights and needs of the each person. Examples of individualistic values would be freedom, independence, self-sufficiency, self-esteem, individual achievement, personal enjoyment, and self-expression. Collectivistic values prize most highly the person's obligations and duties to others. Examples of collectivistic values would be duty, loyalty, kindness, generosity, obedience, and self-sacrifice. Individualism and collectivism have been used most often to describe cultural differences in values. For example, the United States is often described as individualistic, whereas Japan, China, and other Asian cultures are often described as collectivistic.[31]

Most American emerging adults are moral individualists, according to Christian Smith, who explored their moral views in his book *Lost in Transition: The Dark Side of Emerging Adulthood*.[32] According to Smith, emerging adults believe that morality is a matter of personal choice, and it is best to avoid judging others about moral issues because they are entitled to their own opinions. Emerging adults place a high value on *tolerance*, believing that people should generally be allowed to do what they like as long as they do not harm others. Their moral individualism is rooted in moral relativism, according to Smith. They recognize that standards of right and wrong vary across cultures and across history, and conclude that morality is nothing more than the temporary consensus in a specific time and place. Yet they also believe that there are certain moral truths that are valid everywhere, such as the belief that it is wrong to do harm to others and that laws, rules, and regulations should generally be followed.

Smith sees the moral individualism of emerging adults as a sign that they are "morally adrift," and that "the adult world that has socialized these youth...has done an awful job when it comes to moral education."[33] However, this dire claim is difficult to square with other evidence about their lives. For example they volunteer in higher proportions than their parents did, and service organizations such as the Peace Corps, Americorps, and Teach for America are composed almost entirely of emerging adults. Furthermore, rates of several types of risk behaviors have gone down in recent decades, as we will see in detail in Chapter 11. These favorable patterns do not seem to reflect a generation that has no moral foundation.

Also, Smith's portrayal of their individualism is one-sided. Yes, they are individualistic, as we have seen, but that is not all they are. Most of them balance their individualism with a collectivistic concern for others in their moral thinking. In the terminology of Lene Jensen's cultural-developmental model of morality, they draw on not only an individualistic *Ethic of Autonomy* but also a collectivistic *Ethic of Community,* and some also are guided by a religion-based *Ethic of Divinity.*[34]

I have found similar evidence that their moral values balance individualism and collectivism. In my original study, I asked emerging adults two questions whose answers reflected their values:

1. When you get toward the end of your life, what would you like to be able to say about your life, looking back on it?
2. What values or beliefs do you think are the most important to pass on to the next generation?

Let's look at their responses to each of these questions to see what the answers reveal about the values they hold.

When You Get Toward the End of Your Life . . .?

Virtually all of the emerging adults in my original study had a ready response to the question, "When you get toward the end of your life, what would you like to be able to say about your life, looking back on it?" I think this reflects the fact that emerging adulthood is a time for forming life goals and a rough timetable for achieving them. I can't say for sure if adolescents would also have a ready response to the question because I only asked it of emerging adults, but I suspect that adolescents would find it more difficult to answer. Adolescents are usually very wrapped up in the here-and-now, the social whirl of peers and popularity, fleeting romances and would-be-romances. Emerging adulthood is a time for more serious self-reflection, for thinking about what kind of life you want to live and what your Plan should be for your life. Most emerging adults answered the "When you get to the end of your life. . .?" question as if they had already given it considerable thought.

Their answers sometimes reflected individualistic *Ethic of Autonomy* values, sometimes collectivistic *Ethic of Community* values, sometimes a combination of the two.[35] It is not surprising that their answers were often individualistic. They live in an individualistic society, and emerging adulthood is in many ways a self-focused time of life, a time when people focus on their self-development before they have committed themselves to a marriage partner and a child. So, even though the question asks them to think about the perspective they will have as they near the end of their lives, and even though nearly all of them expect to marry and have children eventually, in emerging adulthood their answer to this question is often phrased in terms of their individualistic pursuit of happiness.

For many emerging adults, pursuing individual happiness means obtaining a wide range of life experiences. Christy said that by the end of her life she hoped to say "that I lived it to the fullest. That I didn't just sit back and wait to die. There's too much out there to enjoy and experience. So I want to look back and say I traveled, I ate bizarre food, I met the neatest people. And I want to say I ran a marathon this year, I went kayaking this year, and I skydived . . . because I think all those experiences give some sort of a color and taste to your life." Nicole's comments were similar. "I'd like to say that I lived a good life and I didn't limit myself. If there's something that I wanted to do, I did it, and I didn't let anything hold me back. If somebody says, 'I've got a ticket for you to go to Brazil for two weeks. Do you want to go?,' if I felt like going, I did it, you know. Just live a sky's-the-limit life."

Some emerging adults spoke of individual accomplishments rather than experiences as their life goals. Dalton hoped to be able to say that he "started from the bottom and worked my way to the top and accomplished basically what I really set out to do." Larry had very specific material goals in mind. "I would hope that I have achieved all that I thought I could. I want that big house, four-car garage, 50 acres of land and be able to go on vacation for a month out of the year."

For other emerging adults, their life goals were described less in terms of specific experiences or accomplishments and more in terms of whatever would bring them the most enjoyment. For example, by the end of his life Jerry hoped to be able to say "that I had a good time, because if I'm having a good time, I'm happy, and that's pretty much what I've gathered that everybody wants to do is just live a happy life, you know. It's not going to be free from grief at all times, but I'd say just that I had fun. I'm a fun seeker." Likewise, Joan hoped to say "that I had fun. I want to be able to say 'If I wanted to do it, I did it.' I want to have tons of fun, and no regrets." That phrase, "no regrets," was used often by emerging adults to describe how they hoped not to let any opportunity for enjoyable and interesting experiences pass them by in the course of their lives.

It seems likely that for many of these "fun seekers," their life goals will change in the future. Once they marry and have children, their goals are likely to be focused less on their individualistic pursuit of happiness and more on their responsibilities to others, especially their spouses and children. But while they are in emerging adulthood, as long as their future spouses and children remain hypothetical, when they think of their life goals they often think mainly in terms of what they want for themselves.

It is understandable that emerging adults often have individualistic life goals. What is perhaps more interesting and more surprising is that many of them have life goals that reflect an Ethic of Community, emphasizing what they hope to do for others in the course of their lives. Robert Bellah and his colleagues argued that Americans have a "first language" of individualism, meaning that when they speak about moral issues, Americans most typically and most easily speak in terms of individualistic values.[36] But for many emerging adults, especially in ethnic minority groups, it is collectivism rather than individualism that seems to be their primary moral language.

Their collectivistic values are often reflected in what they hope to do for their families, both their current families (parents, siblings, etc.) and their families of the future (spouse, children). Amber, who is African American, hoped that by the end of her life she could say "that I was a good and loving family member, and that goes for my mother, my brothers, my husband, my children, grandchildren, on down the line." Raul, a Latino, said, "Things I want to say about my life when it comes to the end are that I've contributed to having a family, a better life for my children and taking care of my parents when they get older." Elaine, an Asian American, said, "I hope I have lots of nephews and nieces, and I hope that I've learned a lot of things in life by that time and I can share my knowledge and my experiences with the younger generations."

Many emerging adults also hope to help people outside their families. Benny's main life goal was "to say that I helped lots of people, physically, mentally, helped somebody stuck on the road and changed a tire, or somebody's all sad and you give them a shoulder to cry on." Gerard hoped to be able to say "that I had a lot of friends, that I had a lot of people that I cared about and that cared about me, and that I feel like maybe I helped some people."

Often, emerging adults plan to express collectivistic values of generosity and care for others through the work they choose. Sophie, studying to be a teacher, hoped to be able to say "that I was able to help the students that I'll be teaching through life and helping them if they had any trouble or problems or anything." Sylvia hoped to be able to say that "I've been able to help a lot of people in terms of being a nurse and caring for them when they're sick. That I was a good nurse, that I was able to do my job and comfort them." In the national Clark poll, 86% of 18–29-year-olds agreed that "[i]t is important to me to have a career that does some good in the world."[37]

There were emerging adults whose life goals reflected an Ethic of Autonomy and others whose life goals reflected an Ethic of Community, but there were also emerging adults whose life goals reflected both kinds of values. Individualism and collectivism are not necessarily in opposition to each other, but can both be part of the ideal that emerging adults have for their lives.[38] Rosa hoped to say "that I experienced as much as I possibly could, lived a full life" but also "that I spent as much time with my friends and my family as possible, and that people know how I feel about them. I tell my mom I love her every time I talk to her." Arthur said, "I'd like to say that I was really good at something. I'd like to say that I was happy and fulfilled," but he added that "I'd like to say that I made an impact on other people. I mean, I want to know that I have made other people's lives better in some way." Emerging adults may be individualistic, but their individualism is often leavened by collectivistic values of care and concern for others.

What Values and Beliefs . . . to Pass on to the Next Generation?

Like the question about life goals, the question "What values or beliefs do you think are the most important to pass on to the next generation?" typically evoked a thoughtful and articulate response from the emerging adults we interviewed in my original study. Perhaps this is because emerging adults are reaching the age when most of them will soon think about having children of their own, which has led them to think about what kinds of values they would want those children to learn. Also like the question about life goals, the question about the next generation evoked some individualistic Ethic of Autonomy responses, some collectivistic Ethic of Community responses, and some responses that combined the two types of values.[39]

Some emerging adults were distinctly individualistic. Catharine said, "I think it's important to teach them to be proud of themselves. I think personal self-confidence is very important.... Do what you want to do and be strong in what you want to do." Similarly, Jake said he wanted the next generation to learn the value of "having a sense of purpose in yourself. I think a lot of people view taking care of themselves as being selfish, or doing things for themselves as selfish. But I have a perspective that if you don't take care of yourself, you can't help anybody else and you can't take care of anybody else."

For those who wished to pass on collectivistic values to the next generation, those values were most often spoken of in terms of some version of "the Golden Rule." Laurie said, "as long as you treat people the way you want to be treated, that is the biggest thing to me." Ryan also wanted to pass on the value of "[d]o unto others as you would want them to do unto you. Just basically treat your neighbor kindly."

Some of the emerging adults who favored collectivistic values were actively hostile to individualism. They equated individualism with selfishness, and viewed individualistic values as a source of problems. Tammy was especially vehement. What she wants the next generation to learn is that "everything you do or say or believe or feel, every action, every thought, every movement you make affects everyone else. It's such a self kind of society. 'You're first. You're number one. You're the best. No one will take care of you if you don't take care of yourself.' It's all so self, self, self. And look what's happened. We're so into doing for ourselves that nobody is helping anybody else."

However, as with the "life goals" question, so with the "next generation" question many emerging adults reconciled individualistic and collectivistic values in their responses. Bob said, "I would hope that they could learn to balance loyalty to themselves, being true to themselves, with being good to the people around you. The bottom line for me is do whatever you want to do to make yourself happy, as long as it's contributing to other people's happiness, too."

Religious values also came up in response to the "next generation" question. I noted at the outset of the chapter that values are sometimes based on religious beliefs. For emerging adults for whom religious beliefs are especially important, there is a strong connection between their religious beliefs and the values they would like to pass on to the next generation. Shonitra said she would advise the next generation that "you've got to have God in your life. I feel like you have to have Him in your life in order to succeed. I know that the devil is here to really destroy us, and if you don't have that protection, then most people aren't going to make it." Deanna explicitly made a connection between values and religious beliefs. "Nothing else really does as much as the word of God, I believe. And that determines your values and how you live your life and how you treat your family and how hard you work at school. It's all shaped by your beliefs."

Conclusion: The Diversity of Beliefs and Values Among Emerging Adults

The freedom that American emerging adults have to choose how to live results in a striking diversity of beliefs and values. Emerging adults are atheists, religious conservatives, and everything between. Many of them have developed their own idiosyncratic beliefs from combining different religious traditions in unique ways and adding a dollop of popular culture. With regard to their values, some are avidly individualistic, some are collectivistic, and some combine the two ethics.

If there is a unifying theme in all this diversity, it is their insistence on making their own choices about what to believe and what to value. In their religious beliefs, there is a limited relation between what they have been exposed to by their parents in childhood and adolescence and what they believe now, as emerging adults. Even the 15% of emerging adults who are religious conservatives have come to those beliefs through their personal process of questioning and searching. Emerging adults' values, too, are self-chosen. Even for those who embrace collectivistic values, their values are the product of their own ruminations on their life experiences and observations, in addition to the teachings of their family and culture.

However, the emphasis on independent thinking that is so characteristic of emerging adults does not mean that they are selfish, or alienated from society, or that they wish to live an atomistic life unconnected to others. Over half of emerging adults attend religious services at least now and then, and more plan to attend once they grow a bit older and have children. For those who reject religious institutions, it is usually not because they are self-absorbed but because they doubt the morality of those institutions. In their values, most emerging adults are not extreme individualists, and many are either predominantly collectivistic or try to live by both ethics, wishing to live a personally fulfilling life while also doing some good for others. Although emerging adults are at a self-focused time of life, independent of their parents but not yet committed to new family ties, most of them nevertheless seek to find a balance between striving for the kind of life they want for themselves and treating others as they would wish to be treated.

Chapter 10

How Important Is Social Class?

Although the theory of emerging adulthood has been widely embraced since it was first proposed, it is not universally beloved. Like all theories, it has had its critics. In the view of these critics, mostly sociologists, a key problem with the theory is that it does not apply to a substantial proportion of young people in the age period from the late teens through the twenties.[1] Specifically, say these critics, it applies to the middle- and upper-middle-class young people who go to university and have enough financial support from parents to experience personal freedom and leisure during these years, but not to the working-class and lower-class young people who have far fewer options. It is young people in the middle class who are able to experience their late teens and early to mid-twenties as self-focused years of identity explorations and who look forward to a future of promising possibilities. In contrast, young people in the lower social classes have no such good fortune, and experience their late teens and twenties as a time of struggling to enter an unpromising and unwelcoming labor market. They look at work not as a form of self-expression and identity fulfillment but as a way to make a living, and seek only to get a stable job that pays a decent wage. When they look to the future, they see not a wide-open expanse of possibilities but only a succession of closed doors.

I have emphasized from the beginning the importance of taking education and social class background into account in research on emerging adults. My own research, including the research presented in this book, has consistently included people with a variety of educational levels, not just college students or college graduates. In the first article sketching the theory of emerging adulthood, I argued that one of the benefits of the theory is that it would draw greater research attention to the "forgotten half" of young people who do not attend college or university after secondary school.[2]

The forgotten half remains forgotten by scholars, in the sense that studies of young people who do not attend college in the years following high school remain rare.... Emerging adulthood is offered as a new paradigm, a new way of thinking about development from the late teens through the twenties, especially ages 18–25, partly in the hope that a definite conception of this period will lead to an increase in scholarly attention to it.

Throughout this book, especially in Chapter 6, on college, and Chapter 7, on work, I have emphasized that obtaining tertiary education—or not—marks a crucial turning point in the occupational and social class destiny of emerging adults. In an economy based mainly on information, technology, and services, tertiary education is more important than ever before in determining the course of a person's adult life. I have also noted the importance of social class background in likelihood of becoming a single mother and having a successful lifelong marriage. For all these reasons, it is not accurate to claim that the theory of emerging adulthood is based on middle-class college students and applies only to them.

Nevertheless, there is a serious point of difference here between me and my critics. Both sides acknowledge that educational levels and social class matter in this age period, but how much? Are the social class differences within the age period from the late teens through the twenties best understood as important variations within a group that still has enough similarities in common to be called "emerging adults"? Or, are the experiences of working-class young people in this age period so different from the experiences of those in the middle class that they cannot reasonably be said to belong to the same life stage?

In this chapter I take a step toward answering these questions. First, let us review research from the national Clark poll showing similarities and differences among 18–29-year-olds with respect to social class. Then, I will present four case studies of African Americans in their twenties who have various social class backgrounds. In my view, the Clark poll findings and these case studies show that even though there are clear and sometimes dramatic differences in life prospects depending on social class, there is enough similarity across social classes to merit the application of "emerging adulthood" to the age group as a whole.

Emerging Adulthood Across Social Classes: Similarities and Differences

What does the evidence say about the role of social class in emerging adulthood? Throughout this book we have seen how social class is related to a variety of aspects of emerging adults' lives, from the timing of marriage and parenthood to educational attainment to the length of time it takes to find a long-term job. Here, let's look specifically at the results of the national Clark poll, which provides information on social class similarities and differences across a wide range of areas.[3]

The analysis of the Clark poll data used mother's educational attainment to represent social class, as is typical in social science research.[4] Mother's education was divided into three categories: low (high school diploma or less, 29% of the sample), medium (some college or vocational school, 34%), and high (four-year college degree or more, 37%). In the tables that present the data by social class, the statistical analyses referred to in the right column are chi-square tests; p means probability, and "ns" means that the differences between the three social class groups were not statistically significant.

The Five Features and Views of Adulthood

As noted in Chapter 1, the five features of emerging adulthood that I proposed in 2004 have now received research support from a variety of studies, most notably from the national Clark poll. But does this support hold across social classes? Apparently yes, as Table 10.1 shows. For all items pertaining to the five features proposed in the theory, the differences between the three social class groups are minimal and are not statistically significant.

With regard to views of adulthood, as shown in Table 10.2, there were no differences across social classes in preferring never to become an adult or in believing that adulthood would be boring. There was a slight difference in beliefs that adulthood would be more enjoyable than life is now. However, emerging adults from the lowest social class category were *more likely* to believe that their future lives would be more enjoyable than their lives are now. This is in contradiction to the claim that emerging adults from lower social classes feel hopeless, excluded, and defeated.[5] On the contrary, they remain hopeful and optimistic despite entering adulthood without much support in the way of family resources.

Table 10.1 The Five Features by Social Class

	% Agree by Social Class			
	Low	Medium	High	Significant?
Identity Explorations				
This is a time of my life for finding out who I really am.	77	73	79	ns
Instability				
This time of my life is full of changes.	83	81	84	ns
This time of my life is full of uncertainty.	65	62	64	ns
Self-focus				
This is a time of my life for focusing on myself.	67	71	71	ns
Feeling In-between				
Do you feel that you have reached adulthood? (no or yes/no)	50	48	51	ns
Possibilities				
At this time of my life, it still seems like anything is possible.	85	81	81	ns
I am confident that eventually I will get what I want out of life.	92	87	93	ns

Emotional Lives

How does it feel to be an emerging adult? Good, and not so good. It is an emotionally complex life stage, in which exhilaration and anxiety are both common, as we saw in Chapter 1.

These complexities apply across social classes, as Table 10.3 shows. A strong majority of 18–29-year-olds agrees that this time of their lives is characterized by freedom and is fun and exciting. They are satisfied, overall, with how their lives are going. However, a majority also agrees that this time of life is stressful, and they frequently experience anxiety.

Table 10.2 Views of Adulthood by Social Class

	% Agree by Social Class			
	Low	Medium	High	Significant?
If I could have my way, I would never become an adult.	35	31	26	ns
I think adulthood will be boring.	23	22	16	ns
I think adulthood will be more enjoyable than my life is now.	61	55	57	p <.05

Table 10.3 Emotional Lives by Social Class

	% Agree by Social Class			
	Low	Medium	High	Significant?
At this time of my life, I feel I have a great deal of freedom.	71	72	78	ns
This time of my life is fun and exciting.	80	80	90	p <.001
This time of my life is stressful.	71	68	74	ns
Overall, I am satisfied with my life.	77	80	86	p <.05
I often feel depressed.	38	35	25	p <.01
I often feel anxious.	54	56	54	ns
I often feel that my life is not going well.	37	30	24	p <.01

There are also significant differences by social class, and these differences are consistent in revealing emerging adults from lower social classes as experiencing their emotional lives less positively and more negatively than their higher social class peers. Specifically, those from the lowest social class category are less likely to regard their lives as satisfying, fun, and exciting, and more likely to report feeling depressed and to be concerned that their lives are not going well. Nevertheless, emerging adulthood is experienced positively across social classes, despite these differences. For example, 80% of emerging adults from lower social classes view their lives as fun and exciting— lower than the 90% among the highest social class, but still a strong majority. Similarly, 38% of emerging adults from the lowest social class category say they often feel depressed, significantly higher than the 25% proportion in the highest social class, but well short of a majority.

It is easy to understand why emerging adults from lower social classes might feel less positive about their lives than emerging adults from higher classes. Those from lower classes are less likely to be employed, and as we will see shortly, they are more likely to lack the family financial resources to allow them to get the education that is so crucial to the good life in today's economy. What is more surprising is that, despite their disadvantages, most of them remain remarkably positive about their lives and feel a sense of freedom, fun, and excitement, despite their formidable obstacles.

Relations with Parents

There is little connection between social class background and relations with parents (Table 10.4). Most emerging adults agree that their relationships with parents have improved since adolescence, across social classes. Nor are there

Table 10.4 Relations with Parents by Social Class

	% Agree by Social Class			
	Low	Medium	High	Significant?
I get along a lot better with my parents now than I did during my mid-teens	78	75	76	ns
My parents are more involved in my life than I really want them to be	32	31	27	ns
I would prefer to live independently of my parents even if it means living on a tight budget	74	72	76	ns
I believe that, overall, my life will be better than my parents' lives have been	80	72	74	$p < .001$

social class differences in feeling like parents are too involved in their lives, or in their desire to live independently of parents.

The one item for which social class is significant in this area is in emerging adults' beliefs that their lives will be better than their parents' lives have been. However, in contrast to the sociological claim that emerging adults from lower social classes see nothing but doom and gloom in their futures, these emerging adults are *more,* not less, likely to believe their lives will be better than their parents' lives have been. Their parents may have struggled throughout their adult lives from lack of money and limited opportunities, but most emerging adults from a low social class background see their own future adulthood in a much brighter light. Like other emerging adults, they see their current life stage as an age of possibilities.

School and Work

School and work are areas in which we might most expect to find social class differences among emerging adults. After all, social class background is defined by mother's educational attainment, and it strongly predicts emerging adults' own educational attainment.[6] In turn, educational attainment predicts the kinds of work opportunities that people have throughout adulthood.[7]

However, the data from the national Clark poll show few social class differences among emerging adults in their views of school and work (Table 10.5). Regardless of social class, they see a college education as key to success in life, yet they believe that it is possible to find a good job without one. Regardless of social class, it is more important to emerging adults to find enjoyable work than to make a lot of money. Over half of emerging adults have been unable to find the kind of job they really want, across social classes, and about one-third are in no hurry to find a long-term job. Emerging adults from the lowest social class category are as likely as emerging adults from the highest social class category to agree that it is important to them to find a job that does some good in the world—a strong majority, across social classes.

Despite these similarities, the one notable social class difference in views of school and work is crucial. As noted in Chapter 6, emerging adults in the lowest social class are substantially more likely than emerging adults in the highest social class to state that they have not been able to find sufficient financial support to obtain the education they believe they need (45% to 28%). The fact that nearly half of emerging adults from the poorest

Table 10.5 School and Work by Social Class

	% Agree by Social Class			
	Low	Medium	High	Significant?
One of the most important keys to success in life is a college education.	76	73	83	ns
It's possible to get a good job even if you don't have a college education.	72	62	65	ns
I have not been able to find enough financial support to get the education I need.	45	34	28	$p < .001$
I am in no hurry to get a job that I will have for many years to come.	33	37	37	ns
It is important to me to have a career that does some good in the world.	89	78	89	$p < .001$
It is more important to me to enjoy my job than to make a lot of money.	77	85	83	ns
I haven't been able to find the kind of job I really want.	64	59	54	ns

backgrounds have not had access to the kind of education they need represents an enormous waste of human potential. Even among the emerging adults from the highest social class category, over a quarter have found they do not have the financial resources to obtain sufficient education. This unfortunate state reflects the rise in higher education costs in recent decades, as discussed in Chapter 6.

It also represents a misguided stinginess on the part of their society. As the economy shifts increasingly from manufacturing to services requiring knowledge of information and technology, there is more and more of a need for people with the kinds of skills that tertiary education provides. Societies that fail to make tertiary education broadly available to anyone who wishes to obtain it are likely to find—as they are already finding—that they lack sufficient workers with the skills to participate successfully in the new economy. They will also find—and are already finding—that they have a surplus of young workers who do not have the skills to obtain a job that will pay enough to support themselves, and consequently must be supported by the government. Thus the funding that was not spent on tertiary education must eventually be spent instead, much less fruitfully, on unemployment benefits.

Love, Sex, and Marriage

In the area of love, sex, and marriage, emerging adults across social classes combine traditional values with the modern ideal of a striking a balance between work and family roles (Table 10.6). Most believe that it is wrong for two people to have sex if they are not emotionally involved, and that couples should be married before they have a child. They expect to find their soul mate and have a lifelong marriage. The modern twist is that they expect to have to sacrifice some of their career goals in order to reach their family goals.

Table 10.6 Love, Sex, and Marriage by Social Class

| | % Agree by Social Class | | | |
	Low	Medium	High	Significant?
It's OK for two people to have sex even if they are not emotionally involved with each other.	40	38	48	ns
Couples should be married before they have a child.	68	67	73	ns
I expect to have a marriage that lasts a lifetime.	87	83	89	ns
I expect to have to give up some of my career goals in order to have the family life I want.	61	57	62	ns

As noted in Chapter 7, young men are as likely as young women to anticipate making this trade-off.

The finding that there is no social class difference in the belief that couples should be married before having a child is notable. As described in Chapter 5, statistically, emerging adults from the lowest social class category are considerably more likely to have a child outside marriage. The fact that they are no less likely than emerging adults from higher social classes to believe that this is unwise is more evidence calling into question the sociological claim that young low-SES women often decide to have a child because they see no hope for their educational or occupational prospects and no reason to wait for marriage to a potentially unreliable and impecunious man.[8] Instead, the lack of social class differences on this item is more in line with the *Fog Zone* findings (also presented in Chapter 5) that single motherhood in the twenties usually takes place not as a planful choice but as a consequence of insufficient knowledge of reproductive biology and inconsistent use of reliable contraception.[9]

The finding that there is no social class difference in the expectation of having a lifelong marriage is poignant, in light of the reality that emerging adults from low-SES families are much more likely to divorce than higher-SES emerging adults (see Chapter 5). Despite this hard fact, nearly all emerging adults believe their love will prevail and endure, across social classes.

Conclusions from the Clark Poll: More Similarities Than Differences

The findings of the national Clark poll clearly point to the conclusion that across social classes, there are more similarities than differences among 18–29-year-olds. There were no differences in their responses regarding the five features proposed in the theory of emerging adulthood, and no differences in their expectations of what adulthood would be like—except that emerging adults from the lowest social class category were more likely to expect adulthood to be more enjoyable than their current lives, a refutation, not a confirmation, of the claims of emerging adulthood's critics. In their emotional lives, across social classes emerging adults are similar in regarding their lives as free, fun, and exciting, although most also experience stress and anxiety. Across social classes, most get along well with their parents, with the one social class difference that emerging adults from the lowest category are more, not less, likely than their higher-class peers to believe their lives will be better than their parents' lives have been—another refutation of claims of working-class despondency. In school and work, emerging adults across social classes recognize the importance of a college education, and are idealistic in their aspirations for work that is enjoyable and does some good in the world. Regarding love, sex, and marriage, most hold to traditional values, but both men and women expect to make career sacrifices for the sake of family goals, regardless of their social class background.

The social class differences in the national Clark poll, though few, are important. Emerging adults from the lowest social class category are more likely to report that they lack the financial resources to get the kind of education they believe they need. Perhaps for this reason, they are more likely to report that they often feel depressed. This is understandable, given how important education is to adult success in the modern economy. Yet their optimism shines through in multiple ways, despite formidable odds against them.

Overall, the national Clark poll provides strong support for common experiences of emerging adulthood in American society. Across social classes, the five features proposed in the theory of emerging adulthood are consistently endorsed by most emerging adults. In many other ways, too, emerging adults are similar across social classes. Their social class differences are important, undoubtedly, and need to be taken seriously in public policy, especially with regard to providing more opportunities for lower-class emerging adults to obtain tertiary education. But they are far more similar than different, and there is enough similarity among them to regard them as belonging to a common life stage.

Social Class and Emerging Adulthood: Four Profiles

So far in this chapter, we have examined the quantitative results of the national Clark poll with regard to social class. These results provide a valuable overview of how social class is related to various aspects of emerging adults' lives. However, as always, a deeper understanding of human development requires something more than survey results. In the remainder of this chapter, I present four profiles of emerging adults from my original study, with the goal of generating ideas and insights about what some of the most important similarities and differences might be among emerging adults of higher and lower social classes.[10] These profiles will show that social class is more complex and unstable than a simple classification into low, medium, and high might imply.

All four of the persons profiled here are African Americans. I chose African Americans because in the United States, social class issues are displayed most vividly in this ethnic group. In recent decades there has been a pronounced growth in the size of the African American middle class. Nearly one-third of African American families have incomes above the median for White families, and so could be considered middle class.[11] Yet the poverty rate among African American families is also high. In 2011, the poverty rate for African American families was 37%, compared to 34% for Latinos and just 11% for White families.[12] Consequently, if there are pronounced social class differences in the nature—or existence—of emerging adulthood, they are likely to be evident in the lives of African Americans.

We begin with two profiles of young men, then consider profiles of two young women.

Carl: "I'd Like to Be the Best Human Being That I Possibly Could Be"

Carl is 23 years old and lives with his parents in San Francisco. His background is working class. His father has worked for the city electric company for 30 years as a lineman, repairing damaged or defective electrical lines, and his mother is a physician's assistant. Currently, Carl is working as a sales person in a retail computer store, a job he calls "not the most thrilling career." However, he is also working toward a college degree in computer science and expects to obtain it within the next year.

He likes computers and wants to pursue a career in that area, but he is still in the process of forming a more specific work identity. When asked how he saw his life 10 years from now, he first responded, "I haven't the foggiest notion to be honest with you." After we talked about it a bit more, it turned out he did have a vision for his work future. "By then, I will hopefully have started, actually, my own consulting company" in database programming.

In love, too, his identity formation was clearly still in progress. When asked about his love life, he stated emphatically that he is single, but otherwise he was reticent on the topic. "There's people I go to, you know, from time to time, and that's the best I can do for you."

The instability found in many emerging adults' lives is evident in Carl's life, too. He left home at age 18 to attend the University of Mississippi, but dropped out after two years because he decided that San Francisco is "the place to be" for someone like him who is interested in computers. Now he has moved back home and changed universities, and his life will change again when he graduates and seeks a new job with his newly minted college degree.

Although neither of Carl's parents was educated beyond high school, they strongly advocated higher education for Carl and his siblings. "My father said you should go to college, and he really, really stressed that." Even though his parents did not have much money to spare, they "actually some way or another found some cash somewhere" to allow him to pursue a college degree.

Carl had the sense that living in an area with so much high-tech economic activity would allow him access to *social capital*, the personal connections crucial to finding employment. "I found that as far as career-wise, it would be better for me to be around here because I can meet a whole lot of people here that can get me jobs down the road." He had a similarly practical view of his education. The credential of a college degree would be valuable, even if the knowledge obtained from it was not really necessary. "There are excellent opportunities in the computer industry for people that have a high school education, because it's really based more on results, on what you can do. But I think that in the corporate world the first thing they look at is your degree."

Carl is a classic emerging adult in terms of feeling in-between. Like many emerging adults, he defined adulthood in terms of "being able to take responsibility for your decisions," and he admitted that "I'm not willing to take responsibility for all the things in my life, even though I know I should." He does not mind feeling in-between and is in no particular hurry to reach adulthood. He is making the most of his self-focused freedom, even if he feels a little guilty about it sometimes. "I've done things like just got up one morning and said, you know, 'I'm going to Mexico,' and just get up and go. And I should have been doing other things."

Carl sees the future as presenting a wide range of possibilities, and his optimism was evident in his forecast that he would be running his own database consulting firm in 10 years. His goal for life was to fulfill his potential: "I'd like to be the best human being that I possibly could be."

Carl has no sense of being excluded from opportunities because of his parents' working-class status. He has already obtained more education than they did and seems headed toward a higher social class destination. However, in his view, as a Black man he will always be a target of discrimination, no matter what his economic status. As a computer salesperson, he was reminded on a daily basis of how White people view him. "I get the impression that most White people think I don't know shit." He recounted a story of a time when he had been running home from a girlfriend's house in the small hours of the morning when he was picked up by the police as a suspect in a crime. He did not resist, because "most Black folks know that late at night, you don't argue with the cops." Although they let him go after a few hours, the experience left him feeling humiliated and angry. Asked if he felt Africans Americans have equal opportunity in American society, he said "No. Well, if that was so true, you could come down to my neighborhood and go tell all the guys on the corner they have equal opportunity." For Carl, it was race rather than social class that loomed as an obstacle to future success.

Gary: "Crab in a Bucket"

Gary's life started promisingly enough, with a father who was in the Navy and a mother who worked as a nurse, along with a brother and sister he loved (and still loves). However, his family life soon went awry, with his mother suffering a "nervous breakdown" when he was a baby that has incapacitated her ever since, and his father becoming an alcoholic and leaving the family. The family slipped from the middle class into poverty, and Gary grew up in shoddy public housing and rough neighborhoods.

Now, at age 29, his life is unstable bordering on chaotic. He has no set residence. Instead, he circulates among the households of his mother, brother, and grandmother. Where he ends up on a given night is unpredictable. "I just go ahead and crash out, wake up in the morning...I really don't have no real set place, as far as my own place, but I'm trying to work on that."

Although he is 29, Gary shows no signs of entering the stable adult roles in love and work that usually characterize the transition from emerging adulthood to a more established adulthood in the late twenties. He does not have a girlfriend, and in fact has never had one. "I've never been a relationship-type of person." Still, he seems to have a good idea of what he is looking for. "It all starts out with just trust and love. And basically, as I look at it, the foundation is a friendship, you know, open lines of communication where you're comfortable and can speak whatever's on your mind. And once you get to that point, everything else falls into place. So that's all I been lookin' for—somebody I can really just share my thoughts and feelings with and then won't feel like I'm getting negative input."

He works as a "repo assistant," copying documents, an unfulfilling job to say the least. "It's just a real tedious job. It's the same thing over and over again." He acknowledges that the job is nothing to celebrate. "It's more of a first time out of high school type of thing. You goin' to school, it's a nice little job to have, but as far as making a career out of it, it's not a good job to have." Still, it serves the important function of giving him something to do and helping him avoid trouble. "It's just somethin' to keep some money in my pocket, have somewhere to go during the day time and not put myself in an environment to actually do bad for myself."

Gary has learned from hard experience what can happen as a consequence of being in "an environment to actually do bad for myself." As a teenage boy, he was part of a group of boys involved in a wide variety of crimes, from the relatively innocuous (stealing bags of potato chips from the back of a delivery truck) to the serious (stealing automobiles). "One of my cousins had a chop shop, and we'd steal cars and bring them to him. He was givin' us $500 a car." Several times he was caught for one infraction or another, and each time put on probation, until finally he was picked up in a drug bust and sent to prison.

Looking back now, Gary sees his prison sentence as a key turning point in his life—for the better. "I was really bad off, 'cause I was doin' a lot of drugs, smokin' marijuana, cocaine, cigarettes, puttin' cocaine in the marijuana and smokin' it, put cocaine in tobacco, roll it up in a zigzag, smokin' it, and I drank a lot of alcohol and all that....When I finally sat down in jail and looked at my life to that point in time, I thought to myself, I really didn't get arrested, I got rescued."

Once his mind cleared and he was able to consider his life from a distance, he concluded that he had been led down a wrong path by a corrupt environment. "You're not really fucked up, you're just in a bad situation. If you get yourself out of that situation, you can do better. You're just caught up in an environment where they keep on pullin' you down. It's like a crab in a bucket. It's like somebody always grabbin' your last leg and pullin' you back in, and never want to see you get out. So I looked at it from a positive standpoint to try and change myself to be better."

However, getting out of that bucket has proven to be difficult. When he left prison in his early twenties, he had little education, few skills, and the stigma of a prison record. Finding a good job with little education or training is difficult; add a felony conviction and prison time, and the obstacles look insurmountable. "See, the scary thing about it is when you go to apply for a job, you put down that felony, most people would not even consider your application." Every time he applies for a job, he faces a dilemma when he reaches the question "Have you ever been convicted of a felony?" He can lie and respond "no," and be disqualified if they check his record. Or, he can respond "yes" and be rejected immediately. Given these unpalatable choices, he chooses neither and leaves the question blank.

Gary admits that his life at age 29 is not what he wanted it to be. "I thought I'd be a lot better off, honestly. I thought I'd be doin' somethin' more productive with myself as far as havin' more money, more stable, more financially secure, a career-oriented job by the time I was 30, lookin' to start havin' kids when I hit 30." Nevertheless, he has not lost hope, and sees at least the possibility of a brighter future ahead. "I'm tryin' to change. And the only thing I can do is just think about the things that I'm doin' on that day and do the things that I need to do.... I feel if I can just put a little bit more effort into my financial situation and just try to stay out of jail, try to get a good job, by the time I hit 40 I should be a whole person, as far as knowin' more."

In its outline, Gary's story is all too familiar: a young Black man who grew up in a poor family headed by a single mother, got involved in crime with his friends, served time in jail, and now finds himself 29 years old and with grim prospects. However, in terms of social class, his background is more difficult to classify. His origins are middle class, with a father in the Navy and a mother who worked as a nurse, but the family was downwardly mobile from the time Gary was a baby, and he grew up poor. Nevertheless, his sister and brother made it back into the middle class. Both have college degrees. His sister works for a corporation and is happily married. His brother became involved in crime in adolescence, as Gary did, but was given the alternative of entering the military or going to prison. He chose the military, where he learned computer skills that he has parlayed into a lucrative post-military career. Gary's struggles in emerging adulthood, then, are attributable not only to his social class origins but to the lack of happy accidents that favored his sister and brother, the contingencies of an individual life.

Erica: "I Was Spoiled"

You could say Erica grew up middle class, but the truth is considerably more complicated. Her mother and father divorced when she was a baby, and she never knew him. Soon her mother remarried, to a White man, and this is the man she calls her father, although he is technically her stepfather. He is an attorney, and the family lived a comfortable life through Erica's childhood. However, when Erica was in her second year of college, her parents went bankrupt. "He didn't invest well," Erica explains, "and she was overspending." Suddenly they could provide no more money for her education. For the next three years she worked and struggled to put herself through college, finally graduating two months ago.

Surprisingly, Erica sees this jarring decline in her family's financial fortunes as positive for her. "It was the best thing for me," she says, "because I was spoiled. I took advantage of things." Being abruptly cut off from her parents' finances required her to draw upon her own resources of hard work and determination. "I really had to learn a lot more about myself."

Now, at age 23, she is a college graduate, but is struggling anew in the work world. "I hate my job!" she exclaims when asked about work. "It's very repetitious. It's not stimulating at all. There's no opportunity for growth there." She works as a legal assistant in a law firm, a job she got through a temporary employment agency (not through her stepfather the attorney). She answers phones, makes copies, does errands, whatever the attorneys need. Her college degree is in public policy and social welfare, but when she looked into jobs in social service agencies she was dismayed to find that "a lot of them are nonprofit, and they pay less than what I'm making. They don't pay very well at all."

Because she is dissatisfied with her current work and her apparent options, she is thinking of going to graduate school. However, she admits that "I don't even know if I want to go back to school. And I want to make more money." What might she study in graduate school? She mentions art school, the healthcare field, and the fashion industry. "But, you know, I really need to determine between now and then what I want to do, 'cause I will not succeed if I just go back to do something that I don't like." Clearly her work identity is still unformed.

A more definite goal, 10 years from now, is to be "married with kids. I want tons of children, like five. And I would not mind, like, being a home-maker. I mean, I want my husband to be a professional. And I'm willing to work outside the home, too, or go back to work after my kids are five or six or something. But, I mean, family's really important to me. And if we can afford a lot of kids, then I would have a lot of kids."

One moment, she sounds like she is in no immediate hurry to embark on her plan to focus on family life. "I mean, that's 10 years, though. I'm not saying right now that's for me, you know. Between now and then, I want to experience as much as I can. I mean, I want to experience other things. I want to be well rounded." However, a few moments later she says, "I want a boyfriend. It takes too much energy to be dating all these people. It's tiring. I really want to get married. I mean, I have wedding books at home."

She is confident her life will be better than her parents' lives have been. "I'm gonna marry a man I really, really love," she says, a contrast with her mother, whom she sees as having married mainly for money. She also expects to avoid her parents' financial calamities. "I'm gonna handle my financial things better, 'cause that added way too much stress in their life."

Erica's life has great promise, with a college degree in hand and her personal qualities of optimism and determination. However, her current life is one of classic emerging adult instability, to say the least. In both love and work, she is unsettled and her future is unclear. She has a sense of being partly adult but definitely not all the way there. "I feel like I'm an adult in many ways, like the responsibilities I may take on. But there's so many other ways that I'm so naive, so childish." Her identity is a work in progress, most recently represented in an impulsive decision to change her hairstyle. "I cut all my hair off this weekend, I mean, 'cause I was freaking out. I woke up on Sunday thinking, 'I need a change.' Chop, chop, chop."

Like many emerging adults, Erica is ambivalent about this stage of her life, embracing the freedom of it even as she finds the instability of it aggravating. "This stuff drives me crazy. Like, now is the worst stage. The best, in terms of there's a lot of room for me to do whatever, and the responsibility is to myself. But, on the other hand, it's driving me crazy."

Monique: "A Car, a House, a Little Dog"

The key event in Monique's life took place at age seven, when her family broke up and she moved with her mother and brother into the housing projects in Oakland for low-income families. Previously, her family had lived in a decent lower-middle-class area of suburban Los Angeles, where her father worked as a butcher. However, as Monique describes it, "My father used to sell weed and stuff, and it was like the Black Mafia had wanted him to join, and he didn't want to get into that. And so we had to run." He left the family soon after the move to Oakland, and her parents divorced.

Living in the projects placed Monique in an environment with many snares and risks, and sent her life on a downward spiral from which she is now trying to escape, at age 27. With her father's income gone, the family slid into poverty and lived on social welfare payments throughout the rest of her childhood. Her mother had health problems, so Monique had most of the

262 • EMERGING ADULTHOOD

responsibility for caring for her younger brother, making it more difficult for her to attend to her own education. Her early responsibilities made her reach adulthood at a younger age than usual. "I think that's what an adult is, how to be responsible. I was always responsible for my brother, so I grew up real fast."

When she was 15, she became involved with a 29-year-old man. "I guess I looked up to him as a father figure 'cause my father had left us," she says now. Before long she was pregnant, and she gave birth to her first child at age 16. The pregnancy was not unexpected, and in some ways she welcomed it. "It was fun. I had a lot of help. My mom helped me a lot." Still, Monique recognizes that having a child at a young age impeded her education. She dropped out of high school when she became pregnant, then "I went to a computer learning center for a while, but I was pregnant with my son so I dropped out of there. And then I tried accounting for a minute, but my child care wasn't right. I was supposed to go to college, but then I got pregnant again."

Now that her children are 11 and 7 years old, she is determined to make her way into the workforce. However, this goal is impeded not only by her lack of education, her lack of work experience, and her responsibilities for two children, but by another legacy of the older boyfriend she had as a teenager: an addiction to crack cocaine. "He started me out and it just went on." She has found the addiction extremely difficult to break, but now—after 11 years—she feels she has finally begun to shake it through participation in a religiously based program. "They got me into prayer, more prayer. And I think that helped a lot." Still, she has no illusions that the temptation is gone and she is in the clear. "It doesn't happen overnight. People just stop for years and fall back. It's something you have to fight all your life."

Her dream for her adult life is a simple one, but given her history, daunting and elusive. Right now her children live with her mother and she lives with her father, so that she can try to get a stable job without the responsibilities of caring for her children on a daily basis. She would like to reunite with her children and her partner (who is also the father of her second child) in a household of their own. "I want to move from the city and get into a quiet, nice little place," far from the perils of American lower-class life. She hopes someday to have "a car, a house, a little dog. Typical dream, I guess."

Is Monique an emerging adult despite having her first child at 16, or not? There is no easy answer to this question. She shows some of the features I have described as common among American emerging adults, such as instability and maintaining high hopes (despite many setbacks). However, in many ways, having a child is the point of no return for entering adulthood, at least for young people who keep the child and care for it. In Monique's case, her social class background put her on a path to early parenthood, and early parenthood not only shut off her emerging adulthood but curtailed her adolescence, as she quit high school and focused on raising her child. She never had the period between the end of adolescence and the taking on of adult responsibilities that defines emerging adulthood. However, she is trying to get it back now, in some form, by leaving her children with her mother while she attempts to make her way into the workforce.

Conclusion: The Complexities of Social Class

Social class is unquestionably an important element in the lives of emerging adults, as it is in the lives of people of other ages. Specifically, the pursuit of tertiary education structures the lives of some emerging adults but not others, and this difference has repercussions for their lives in emerging adulthood and beyond. For those who pursue tertiary education, their lives are structured around going to classes and doing coursework. Many of them work at least part-time as well, to support themselves and to pay educational expenses, which can make for a very busy life. Those who are not in school but working or seeking a job face the formidable challenge of finding a well-paying, enjoyable job without educational credentials, at a time when such jobs are increasingly elusive. Furthermore, future prospects vary greatly for these two groups, with those pursuing tertiary education having a higher likely social class destination than those who do not, in terms of income and occupational status.

The case studies presented here illustrate the substantial influence of social class background in how emerging adulthood is experienced, and also how social class is not as simple or stable a variable as one might assume. Carl and Erika came from backgrounds of relative advantage. Carl's parents received no tertiary education, yet they stressed education and were able to support him financially as he pursued his college degree. Erika's parents were well-off and she grew up in conditions of material comfort, although their bankruptcy while she was in college pulled the financial rug out from under her and made her struggle to support herself so that she could finish her college education.

Gary and Monique grew up in a lower social class than Carl or Erika, and the effects of this on their lives by their twenties are painfully evident. Gary slid down the path unfortunately common among young African American men in urban areas, becoming involved with friends in crime and drugs, culminating in prison time. Monique fell into the life unfortunately common among young African American women in urban areas, becoming a single mother at a young age and becoming addicted to drugs, making it difficult to build a life of her own in her twenties. She lost her opportunity to experience emerging adulthood fully and will never get it back.

Both Gary and Monique fell into problems that were very clearly the consequence of their bleak social class conditions. Put Gary into Carl's childhood environment, and Monique into Erika's, and it is impossible to believe that by their late twenties he would have ended up a drug addict and convicted felon and she would have ended up a drug addict and single mother. For Gary and Monique, their human potentials have been stunted and twisted by a grim set of social class conditions. Both still strive to rise above their environments—the optimism of emerging adulthood shines through even for them, although barely—but by now it is difficult to be optimistic on their behalf. Drug addiction, felony conviction, single motherhood, poor education—these are weights that can drag even the most determined crab back into the bucket.

Although social class is crucial to how the years from the late teens through the twenties are experienced, people in this age range can be considered to be emerging adults across social classes. At its core, the rise of emerging adulthood over the past half century is a demographic phenomenon, arising from the substantial increase in median ages of marriage and parenthood in every developed country. A half century ago most people entered these roles at ages 20–22, placing them in "young adulthood" right after adolescence, with adult responsibilities of coordinating work and family life, including maintaining a marriage, running a household, paying the bills, and caring for children. Now that the median ages of entering marriage and parenthood have moved into the late twenties or even the early thirties, a stage of emerging adulthood has opened up between adolescence and young adulthood, during which people are more independent of their parents than they were as adolescents but have not yet entered the roles that structure adult life for most people. Young people in lower social classes may enter these roles earlier than their peers in the middle and upper classes,[13] but for most, that still leaves a period of several years between the end of secondary school and the entrance to adult roles, certainly long enough to be called a distinct life stage.

My original research, as well as the national Clark poll and many studies by other researchers, has indicated other similarities among American emerging adults across social classes, beyond the demographic similarities. For both the lower/working class and the middle/upper-middle class, the years from the late teens through the twenties are a time of trying out different possibilities in love and work, and gradually making their way toward more stable commitments. For both groups, instability is common during these years, as frequent changes are made in love and work. For both groups, their hopes for the future are high, even though the real prospects for those with relatively low education are not as promising. However, other features of the age period may be found to vary, between social classes within the same country, as well as between cultures and countries. Emerging adulthood is growing as a worldwide phenomenon, in demographic terms, and there is sure to be a great deal of variation world-wide in how it is experienced.[14]

A useful analogy can be made here to the life stage of adolescence. Cross-cultural studies, most notably Schlegel and Barry's study of 186 cultures worldwide, have found that adolescence exists in nearly all human cultures, as a period between the time puberty begins and the time adult roles are taken on.[15] However, the length of adolescence and the nature of adolescents' experiences vary vastly among cultures. Some adolescents attend secondary school, and some drop out or never go. Most live in the same household as their parents, but some become "street children" and live among other adolescents in urban areas. Some marry by their mid-teens, especially girls in rural areas of developing countries, whereas others will not marry until after adolescence and a long emerging adulthood. Consequently, it makes sense to speak not of one adolescent experience but of *adolescences* worldwide.[16] Yet we still recognize adolescence as a life stage that exists in nearly all cultures, in some form.

In the same way, we can state that there are likely to be many emerging adulthoods—many forms the experience of this life stage can take—depending on social class, culture, and perhaps other characteristics such as gender and religious group.[17] Some emerging adults obtain tertiary education, and some do not. Some live with their parents, and some do not. Some experience a series of love relationships, whereas others live in cultures where virginity at marriage is prized and love relationships before marriage are discouraged. Yet emerging adulthood can be considered to exist wherever there is a period of at least several years between the end of adolescence—meaning the attainment of physical and sexual maturity and the completion of secondary school—and the entry into stable adult roles in love and work.

Chapter 11

Wrong Turns and Dead Ends

In the classic rock song "Glory Days," Bruce Springsteen glowingly remembers the magic and exuberance of youth. Adult life pales in comparison. All your life, sings the Boss, you will be remembering those days fondly, "Just sittin' back, trying to recapture / A little of the gloria." In general, emerging adults, too, believe they are living their glory days. In the national Clark poll, 83% of 18–29-year-olds agreed that "[t]his time of my life is fun and exciting."[1] However, it is certainly not all exuberant play for emerging adults. In fact, a wide variety of behavioral problems and psychological disorders reach their peak during the emerging adult years. No other stage of life has such high rates of so many different problems. The exuberance and the problems coexist, making emerging adulthood an exceptionally complex life stage, psychologically. As a more contemporary songwriter, Taylor Swift, puts it in "22," "We're happy, free, confused, and lonely at the same time / It's miserable and magical."

Researchers typically distinguish between *externalizing problems* and *internalizing problems*. Externalizing problems (such as crime and substance abuse) are viewed as the projection of psychological conflicts into the outer world, in behavior and relationships.[2] Internalizing problems (such as depression and anxiety disorders) are viewed as a consequence of turning psychological distress inward, toward the self.[3] Externalizing problems are generally more common among males, and internalizing problems are generally more common among females. Both kinds of problems appear to be more prevalent in emerging adulthood than in any subsequent adult life stage. In this chapter, first we examine rates and sources of externalizing and internalizing problems. Then we look at the recent trends in rates of some externalizing problems and possible reasons for those trends.

Externalizing Problems: Automobile Driving, Crime, and Substance Use

Three of the most common externalizing problems among emerging adults are risky automobile driving, crime, and substance use.

Automobile Driving

The number one threat to life and health in emerging adulthood is automobile crashes.[4] Nothing else is even close. In nearly all developed countries, automobile crashes are the leading cause of death in the twenties and thirties,[5] but rates are highest in the United States. This is due to partly to the relatively low cost of automobiles in the United States (other developed countries tax cars and gasoline more heavily). It is also due to the relative lack of mass transportation options (trains, busses, subways) in the United States, outside major urban areas. Most other developed countries are more densely populated than the United States is, making mass transportation a more desirable investment for their societies. However, the United States also has a greater romance with the automobile. Cars have long held the promise of youth and freedom for Americans, in a way they do not for most Europeans or Asians. Consequently, Americans drive more and are more resistant to taxes on automobiles and gasoline that could be used to fund a more extensive mass transportation network. They are also more resistant to strict laws punishing reckless and drunk driving.

Whatever the rewards of the American romance with the automobile, the costs are substantial, especially for emerging adults. Figure 11.1 shows the relationship between age and fatalities from automobile crashes in the United States. There is a sharp peak at ages 21–24, followed by a steady decline.

The peak of automobile crashes, injuries, and fatalities in emerging adulthood can be explained partly by inexperience.[6] Young drivers make more mistakes than older drivers do, because they are less likely to be able to anticipate potential problems before a crash occurs. Rates of crashes are highest in the first year after a driver's license is obtained, when young drivers are confronting many driving situations for the first time. However, inexperience is not the entire explanation. Crash rates remain high even several years after a driver's license has been obtained. In fact, as Figure 11.1 shows, for young men rates of fatalities from crashes are higher at ages 21–24 than at ages 16–20. Young drivers take more risks than older drivers do, such as driving at

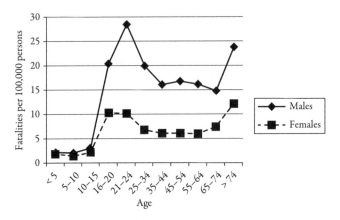

Figure 11.1 Rates of Automobile Fatalities by Age.

Source: National Highway Traffic Safety Administration (2012).

high speeds and driving while intoxicated.[7] Rates of fatalities involving drunk driving peak in the early twenties.[8]

Another characteristic that helps explain risky driving, as well as other types of externalizing behavior, is sensation seeking. Sensation seeking is a personality trait characterized by the degree to which a person seeks out *novelty* and *intensity* of experience.[9] Driving at high speeds and other driving risks are sometimes motivated by the pursuit of sensation-seeking thrills. Many other types of risk behavior, too, provide novelty and intensity of experience—for example, substance use leads to novel mental states, and breaking the law in delinquent and criminal acts is often described in terms of the intensity of the experience. For this reason, young people who are high in sensation seeking are more likely to engage in a variety of risk behaviors, including substance use, risky driving, delinquency, and risky sexual behavior. Sensation seeking rises at puberty and tends to be higher in the teens and early twenties than in adulthood, which helps explain why externalizing behavior is most common among the young.

Crime

Crime follows a similar age-related pattern, as shown in Figure 11.2. Like automobile crashes, injuries, and fatalities, arrest rates rise sharply in the late teens and then remain high in the early twenties before declining steeply in the late twenties, the thirties, and beyond. The relation between age and crime has been remarkably stable, across societies, in statistics

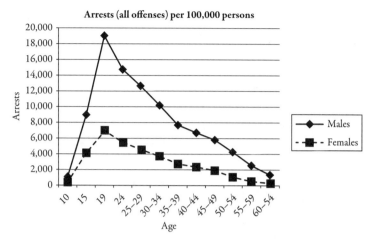

Figure 11.2 Crime Rates by Age.

Source: Bureau of Justice Statistics (2013).

going back more than 150 years.[10] Crime was one of the first areas for which systematic statistics were tallied, and the age-crime graph for 1842 in the United Kingdom looks essentially the same as for any recent year in the United States.[11]

Most externalizing problems are higher among males than among females, but crime is an area for which gender differences are especially skewed. Crime rates are always much higher for males than for females, in all places and in all historical times, and this is especially true for violent crime.

A vast literature has accumulated over more than a century to explain the relation between age, maleness, and crime. Some of the main reasons identified are:[12]

- *Biological tendency for aggressiveness.* Boys are more physically aggressive than girls are, from infancy onward. The gender difference in physical aggressiveness widens during puberty, when levels of testosterone, a sex hormone related to aggressiveness, rise far more for boys than for girls. Testosterone levels decrease after the twenties, which helps explain the corresponding decline in crime.
- *Other biological and cognitive factors.* Several other biological and cognitive differences between males and females contribute to the greater male tendency for criminal behavior, including sensation seeking, impulsiveness, learning disabilities, and attention deficits.

- *Male gender role valuing toughness and risk-taking.* In many cultures, the male gender role exalts toughness and the willingness to take risks, which may be demonstrated through criminal behavior.
- *Peer orientation.* The teens are the time when the desire to be part of a cohesive peer group is highest, as is responsiveness to the opinions of peers within that group. Some male peer groups demonstrate and reinforce their cohesiveness through criminal behavior. Unlike adult crime, nearly all youth crime is committed in groups.
- *Low social control.* The late teens and early twenties are the nadir of what criminologists call *social control,* meaning the roles, duties, relationships, and daily obligations that promote socially responsible behavior and discourage violations of social norms. Low social control allows for the expression of the other tendencies that inspire crime among young males, such as aggressiveness and impulsiveness. Crime tends to decline once young males take on stable social roles such as marriage, parenthood, and stable employment.

There has also been a strong emphasis on the role of poverty in crime.[13] Criminal behavior is highest among people from lower socioeconomic groups, and this has been interpreted as due to the lack of opportunities that people in these groups have for succeeding economically through socially acceptable channels. However, low SES does not explain young males' predominant participation in criminal activities. Females and adults are no less likely to be poor than young males are, yet it is mainly young males who are involved in crime.

Other factors promoting crime are harsh and punitive parenting, family conflict, poor schools, and disorganized neighborhoods.[14] As with low SES, these factors do not explain why young males would be so much more likely to be involved in crime than young females are.

Substance Use and Abuse

Substance use and abuse follows the same age-related pattern as risky automobile driving and crime: a steep rise in late adolescence and emerging adulthood, followed by a decline from the late twenties onward. Figures 11.3 and 11.4 show the patterns for binge drinking and marijuana use. Like other externalizing problems, substance use is higher among males than among females.

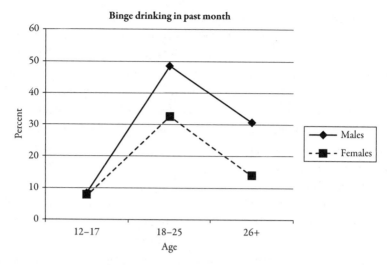

Figure 11.3 Binge Drinking by Age.

Source: Substance Abuse and Mental Health Services Administration (SAMHSA) (2011).

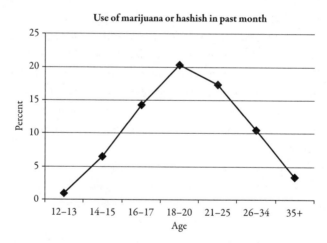

Figure 11.4 Marijuana Use by Age.

Source: Substance Abuse and Mental Health Services Administration (SAMHSA) (2011).

Substance use and abuse can be a way of ameliorating unpleasant emotional states. A high proportion of emerging adults report that they frequently experience stress, depression, and anxiety, as we will see in the next section. Substance use is sometimes a method of *self-medication* to relieve the distress of these emotional states.[15]

This kind of explanation for substance use and other types of risk behavior is known as a *deficit model,* which means explaining people's behavior on the basis of something they lack, such as parental warmth. However, not all substance use in emerging adulthood can be explained by a deficit model. Drinking alcohol and smoking marijuana are a typical part of the social activities of emerging adults in many cultural contexts, including in most developed countries. Much of this substance use is motivated not by personal distress but by sociability and the desire for sensation-seeking fun.[16]

Binge drinking is higher among college students than among emerging adults who do not attend college,[17] which should not be surprising. The college environment is well suited to social drinking in many ways. First and foremost, there are always many potential drinking partners around. For students who suddenly feel like going out drinking on a Thursday night, if there are dozens of other available people their age within shouting distance, it is likely they can find a few of them who like the idea of heading out to drink. The desire to fit in and find a comfortable social place in college also contributes. Even if students might not feel like drinking, and have that physics test in the morning, if a dormmate asks them to join a drinking expedition it is not easy to say no; if they do, maybe next time they won't be asked. Then there's the desire for romance—and sex. Potential partners are pretty much everywhere, and one of alcohol's attractions is that it is *disinhibiting.* Becoming intoxicated make students feel less fearful about getting their egos stomped if they muster the courage to talk to someone who looks good from afar.

So how much do college students drink? The Core Institute of Southern Illinois University–Carbondale surveys over 200,000 students yearly on their drinking attitudes and behavior.[18] Here are their latest findings:

84% of students consumed alcohol in the past year.
71% of students consumed alcohol in the past 30 days.
46% of students reported binge drinking in the past two weeks.
The national average per week for college students is 5.2 drinks.

So, almost half of students have been drunk—that is essentially what "binge drinking" means—within the past two weeks. On the other hand, the other half have not been drunk in the past two weeks, and almost 30% of students have not had any alcohol at all in the past 30 days.

Other items from the Core Institute survey provide a broader sense of the place that drinking holds in the college social environment:

82% of students see drinking as "central in the social life of college students."
76% had heard someone else brag about alcohol use.
75% said drinking enhances social activity.
63% said drinking allows people to have more fun.
53% said drinking facilitates sexual opportunity.
42% said drinking makes it easier to deal with stress.

These results indicate that most students approve of drinking and see it as having many useful and enjoyable purposes. On the other hand, most students do not exaggerate the benefits of drinking, and they see a downside to excess drinking:

Only 27% said drinking makes women sexier.
Only18% said drinking makes men sexier.
Only 18% said drinking makes "me" sexier.
54% said their friends would *disapprove* if they had five or more drinks at one sitting.

Overall, the Core Institute survey results provide a balanced portrait of college students' alcohol use. Drinking is a big part of the college environment, clearly, but most students have a pretty mature attitude toward drinking. They see it as having many benefits, but most of their parents, too, would agree that drinking enhances social activity, adds to the fun of many social events, and helps relieve stress. Relatively few students believe drinking makes them or others sexier, and a majority disapproves of binge drinking.

One of the challenges of understanding substance use in emerging adulthood is distinguishing between use and abuse. Many emerging adults binge drink occasionally, and many occasionally use marijuana, but how many of them can be said to have a substance abuse problem? At what point does a lively social life and a love of "partying" become a diagnosable disorder? According to a national epidemiological study, 30% of Americans ages 18–24 have fit the criteria for a substance use disorder (mostly involving alcohol) within the past 12 months[19]—a startlingly high figure, but what exactly does it mean?

For the purposes of this discussion, let's consider a substance use disorder "substance abuse" and all other substance use "substance use." Let's also focus on alcohol, as it is by far the most used and abused substance.

In the diagnosis of substance use disorder, a key criterion for distinguishing between use and abuse is that serious disruptions occur in other areas of functioning.[20] So, unlike substance use, substance abuse results in losing a job or in failure to perform a job adequately. The substance abuser may come late to work repeatedly due to difficulty getting up in the morning because of intoxication the previous night, or have a high proportion of "sick" days (i.e., too hung over to work), or miss a key meeting in the afternoon due to having too many drinks at lunch. Relationships, too, are affected. Unlike substance use, substance abuse results in damage to family relationships, friendships, and romantic partnerships. Substance abuse may result in becoming obnoxiously intoxicated at a family gathering, or failing to meet a friend when promised, or it may smooth the way to an impulsive episode of infidelity. The same disinhibition that is sought because it makes for more comfortable conversations and social relations can also make people more likely to say harsh things later regretted, or to hit a child or a spouse.

The distinction between substance use and abuse is important and useful, but it is harder to apply during emerging adulthood than at later life stages. A 50-year-old who becomes intoxicated so frequently that he misses work the next day and is fired from the job has a serious problem, no doubt. But what about a 21-year-old who experiences the same behavior and consequences? Maybe he, too, has a problem, but it is more difficult to tell. At 21, emerging adults are changing jobs frequently anyway—remember that there is an average of eight job changes from age 18 to 29—so losing a job at age 21 is not unusual. The consequences, too, are not as severe. The 50-year-old loses a job and suddenly the income to the family is lost. Perhaps, now, the mortgage cannot be paid and the house may be lost; perhaps the emerging adult child of the 50-year-old will have to drop out of school because the parents can no longer help pay tuition. But for the 21-year-old, there was no mortgage and no children to be provided for. The job probably did not pay very well anyway, and another job like it may be found soon. The 50-year-old, meanwhile, will have a harder time re-entering the job market.

With relationships, too, a similar comparison can be made. When a 50-year-old drinks to intoxication two or three times a week, the effects are sure to be evident in his relationships. His partner is likely to become frustrated and angry—unless the partner is also a substance abuser and each reinforces the other in a downward spiral. Friends are likely to drift away (unless, again, the friends are also substance abusers). Neighbors are likely to notice and may shun the drinker. Children are likely to be appalled and ashamed.

For the 21-year-old, the consequences are nowhere near as serious. Drinking to intoxication two or three times a week is unusual for a 21-year-old, but not nearly as unusual as it is for a 50-year-old. Because binge drinking is so common among 21-year-olds, it can still be framed, by the drinker as well as others, as a partying lifestyle rather than substance abuse. The 21-year-old may or may not have a romantic partner, but if he does, he is unlikely to be living with the partner. Consequently, the partner may not even be aware of how often he gets drunk. Friends may regard his partying with tolerance or even amusement, and they may well be joining in, although perhaps not to the same extreme or with the same frequency. Even if some of the drinker's relationships may be negatively affected by frequent binge drinking, the results are likely to be unpleasant but not catastrophic. Perhaps the girlfriend breaks up with him because he drinks too much, but a breakup is not nearly as wrenching as a divorce. Perhaps some friends drift away, but other friends who tolerate the drinking or join in will soon replace them. No children are around to witness and be disappointed.

In sum, the effects of substance abuse for the 21-year-old are serious and cause disruptions in love and work, but because emerging adulthood is in any case a stage where instability is common, the threshold between substance use and abuse may be more difficult to identify. Terri Moffitt makes a useful distinction, with regard to delinquency, between *adolescence-limited* delinquents (ALDs) and *life-course persistent* delinquents (LCPDs).[21] ALDs participate in delinquency briefly in their teens, as part of peer-group recreation, but leave it behind once they leave adolescence. LCPDs, in contrast, show signs of problems from early childhood on, and their delinquency in adolescence is not a brief phase but a harbinger of a life of crime and trouble. But during adolescence, ALDs and LCPDs are engaging in many of the same behaviors and are difficult to distinguish.

The same distinction can be usefully made with regard to emerging adulthood and substance use and abuse, particularly with regard to binge drinking. Emerging adulthood is the life stage when binge drinking is most common. Some emerging adults have a drinking problem serious enough to be classified as a substance abuse disorder. They will continue to binge drink beyond their twenties and may have a lifelong problem with alcoholism. Others will binge drink during emerging adulthood, once, twice, or three times a week, but after their twenties they will leave their excessive substance use behind and may rarely or never binge drink again. But during emerging adulthood—and this is the key point—it is difficult to distinguish between the *emerging adulthood–limited* binge drinkers and the *life-course persistent* alcoholics.

Internalizing Problems: Forms of Personal Distress

Three types of internalizing problems that are especially common during emerging adulthood are depression, anxiety disorders, and eating disorders.

Depression

Emerging adulthood is a time of high hopes, but it is also a time of struggle for most people. It can be exciting to be grappling with big identity questions about who you are and what you want to do with your life, but it can be confusing and overwhelming, too, especially if you have trouble coming up with any answers. It can be fun and fulfilling to try out a wide range of experiences—different educational paths, jobs, places to live, and love partners—but it can also be exhausting. Often the freedom of emerging adulthood is exhilarating—no one can tell you what to do and when to do it—but along with that freedom can come a sense of isolation, the chill of realizing you are on your own and have to swim constantly in order not to sink.

The result of these contradictory forces is this paradox of mental health during the emerging adult years: overall, self-esteem and life satisfaction are high, but rates of depression and anxiety are high, too. Out on their own, working their way toward building the structure of an adult life, most young people thrive on the freedom and independence, but many struggle to stay afloat.

The most severe form of depression is *major depressive disorder (MDD)*. This includes not only persistent sad moods but a wide range of other symptoms such as insomnia, significant weight gain or loss, and feelings of worthlessness. About 6% of Americans ages 18–25 have had symptoms that fit a diagnosis of major depression within the past 12 months, and this rate is about the same in emerging adulthood as in the rest of adulthood, until age 65.[22] Across countries, women are about twice as likely as men to have major depressive disorder. Major depression can be triggered by life events such as divorce or losing a job, but it is well established that people with major depression often have a biologically based susceptibility as well.[23]

More common than MDD is depressed mood, without the other symptoms of MDD. In the national Clark poll, 32% of 18–29-year-olds agreed that "I often feel depressed."[24] There was a substantial gender difference, with rates of 37% for females and 27% for males. Feeling depressed was also more common among younger emerging adults (36% at ages 18–21, declining to 27% for 26–29-year-olds). Emerging adults from lower SES families were more likely to feel depressed (38% if mother's educational attainment was high school or less, but only 25% if mother's educational attainment was four-year college degree or more). This difference may be due to the more limited job prospects for emerging adults from low-income families.

For parents of emerging adults, 28% reported often feeling depressed in the 2013 Clark Poll of Parents of Emerging Adults, similar to the 32% for emerging adults, which is consistent with other studies showing little change in rates of depression from emerging through middle adulthood.[25] So what is distinctive, if anything, about feeling depressed in emerging adulthood? Are the sources and consequences of depressed mood different at this life stage than at other life stages? This is an important research question that has not yet been adequately addressed, but I will offer some ideas later in the chapter.

Anxiety Disorders

Anxiety disorders take a variety of forms, such as agoraphobia (fear of being in public places), obsessive-compulsive disorder (repetitive intrusive thoughts and repetitive behaviors such as washing hands), panic disorder (sudden intense waves of fear), and specific phobias (for example, to heights, closed spaces, or certain animals or insects). According to a national epidemiological study in the United States, 12% of 18–24 year-olds have had symptoms in the past 12 months that merit a diagnosis of anxiety disorder.[26] Like MDD, rates of anxiety disorder are about the same in emerging adulthood as they are in the rest of adulthood. However, more general feelings of anxiety are strikingly high in emerging adulthood. In the national Clark poll of 18–29-year-olds, 56% agreed that "I often feel anxious."[27] For their middle-aged parents, in the Clark Poll of Parents of Emerging Adults, the proportion was considerably lower, 41%.[28] Among emerging adults, the proportion was slightly higher among women (58%) than among men (53%), but, unlike for depression, for anxiety there was no difference by social class.

What is it that emerging adults feel so anxious about? No research has yet asked them, but there are a variety of developmental challenges in emerging adulthood that might be expected to provoke anxiety in some people. As described throughout this book, emerging adults are often struggling with big identity questions about who they are and how they fit into the world. Their lives are in flux as they try to make their way toward building a foundation for adulthood. They leave their parents' home to live on their own or with friends or roommates, and certainly many anxieties are associated with learning to live independently for the first time and facing all the stresses of adult life. How do I wash my clothes, now that Mom isn't here to do it? Why hasn't this month's heating bill been paid? Aaarrghh, I burned the lasagna! Bounced a check! Forgot to pick up groceries! The challenges of love and work involve many anxieties: for love, initiating and breaking up relationships, and the many anxieties surrounding sex; for work, looking for a job, going to job interviews, and starting a new job with a new boss and coworkers, as well as failure to find a job, or getting fired.

There is also the anxiety of feeling pressure to make progress toward adulthood and worrying that the process is going too slow, that you are falling behind where you think you should be and the pace others are setting. The instability of emerging adulthood may provoke anxiety, as well. In the national Clark poll, 64% of 18–29-year-olds agreed that "[t]his time of my life is full of uncertainty" and 83% agreed that "[t]his time of my life is full of changes." For both these items, agreement was significantly correlated with anxiety.[29]

The fact that so many emerging adults often feel anxious or depressed should not lead to the conclusion that they are unhappy with their lives or that they regard their current stage of life as a miserable one. Their feelings of anxiety and depression manage to coexist with other, more positive feelings. According to data from the national Clark poll, although a majority of 18–29-year-olds often feels anxious, and about one-third often feel depressed, an even higher proportion agrees that "I am satisfied with my life" (81%) and that "[t]his time of my life is fun and exciting" (83%). This means that many of those who report feeling anxious and/or depressed are satisfied with their lives and also see their current lives as fun and exciting.[30] Emerging adulthood is an emotionally complicated life stage, a time of intense ambivalence, a swirl of both positive and negative feelings.

Eating Disorders

Another type of internalizing problem that is prominent during emerging adulthood is eating disorders. The two most common eating disorders are

anorexia nervosa (intentional self-starvation) and *bulimia* (binge eating combined with purging [intentional vomiting]). Eating disorders occur mostly
(but not entirely) among young females; the female-to-male ratio is 10:1.[31]
The age of onset of eating disorders is typically during late adolescence or
emerging adulthood. The age pattern is especially strong for anorexia nervosa.
A national study in the United States found that the age of onset for anorexia
among women was restricted entirely to 15–25 year-olds. No new cases of
anorexia were found before age 15 or beyond age 25.[32] Similar findings have
been reported in European studies.[33]

For a diagnosis of anorexia nervosa, food intake is reduced so much
that the person loses at least 15% of body weight. As weight loss continues,
it eventually results in *amenorrhea*, which means that menstruation ceases.
Hair becomes brittle and may begin to fall out, and the skin develops an
unhealthy, yellowish pallor. As anorexics become increasingly thin, they frequently develop physical problems that are symptoms of their self-starvation,
such as constipation, high sensitivity to cold, and low blood pressure.

One of the most striking symptoms of anorexia is the cognitive distor-
tion of body image.[34] The reduction in food intake is accompanied by an
intense fear of gaining weight, a fear that persists even when the person has
lost so much weight as to be in danger of literally starving to death. Young
women with anorexia sincerely believe themselves to be too fat, even when
they have become so thin that their lives are threatened. Standing in front
of a mirror with them and pointing out how emaciated they look does no
good—the anorexic looks in the mirror and sees a fat person, no matter how
thin she is.

Like anorexics, bulimics have strong fears that their bodies will become
big and fat.[35] Bulimia engage in binge eating, which means eating a large
amount of food in a short time. Then they purge themselves; that is, they
use laxatives or induce vomiting to get rid of the food they have just eaten
during a binge episode. Bulimics often suffer damage to their teeth from
repeated vomiting. Unlike anorexics, bulimics typically maintain a normal
weight because they have more or less normal eating patterns between their
episodes of binging and purging. Another difference from anorexics is that
bulimics do not regard their eating patterns as normal. Bulimics view themselves as having a problem and often hate themselves in the aftermath of their
binge episodes.

Studies of anorexia and bulimia provide evidence that these eating disorders have cultural roots.[36] First, eating disorders are more common in

cultures that emphasize slimness as part of the female physical ideal, especially Western countries. Second, eating disorders are most common among females who are part of the middle to upper socioeconomic classes, which place more emphasis on female slimness than lower classes do. Third, nearly all eating disorders occur among females in their teens and early twenties, which is arguably when cultural pressures to comply with a slim female physical ideal are at their strongest. Fourth, girls who read magazines that contain numerous ads and articles featuring thin models are especially likely to strive to be thin themselves and to engage in eating disordered behavior.

Although many girls in cultures that emphasize a thin female ideal strive for thinness themselves, only a small percentage actually have an eating disorder. What factors lead some young women but not others to develop an eating disorder? In general, the same factors are involved for both anorexia and bulimia.[37] One factor appears to be a general susceptibility to internalizing disorders. Females who have an eating disorder are also more likely to have other internalizing disorders, such as depression and anxiety disorders. Eating disordered behavior is also related to substance use, especially cigarette smoking, binge drinking, and use of inhalants.

For information on the treatment of internalizing disorders, see the website of the National Alliance on Mental Illness, www.nami.org.

Developmental Sources of Emerging Adults' Problems

In sum, diverse problems are more common during emerging adulthood than during other life stages. But why? What is it about being an emerging adult that makes for a greater risk of these problems? What is occurring, developmentally, that contributes to this vulnerability? Let us address these questions by examining the five features proposed in the theory of emerging adulthood in relation to the problems discussed in this chapter. Hypotheses will be proposed that extend from each of the five features.

Identity explorations. The process of exploring various possible selves and trying out possible future paths in love and work may contribute especially to internalizing problems. Wrestling with the question of "who am I" can be perplexing and confusing, and can evoke feelings of anxiety. In the national Clark poll, there was a correlation between agreement with "[t]his is a time of my life for finding out who I really am" and "I often feel anxious."[38] Feelings of anxiety and depression may also be triggered by breaking up with romantic partners and by losing or failing to find a satisfying job.

The relation between identity explorations and externalizing problems is not as direct, but trying out a range of experiences could be seen as part of identity explorations, including experiences that violate social norms, such as driving in risky ways, engaging in criminal behavior, and trying illicit drugs.[39] Substance use and abuse may also be a method of self-medication for depression and anxiety, for some emerging adults.

Hypothesis: As identity development progresses during emerging adulthood, externalizing and internalizing problems will become less likely. At any given age, there will be a correlation between identify confusion and both externalizing and internalizing problems.

Instability. Changing jobs, love partners, and places of residence is a typical part of emerging adulthood. These changes may be exciting, but they are likely to be stressful as well. Internalizing problems such as depression and anxiety may result, and substance use and abuse may be sought as self-medication for the stress as well as for the depression and anxiety. As noted earlier, in the national Clark poll, agreement that their current lives are "uncertain" and "full of changes" was associated with often feeling anxious among 18–29-year-olds.

Hypothesis: The more instability emerging adults experience, the higher their risk will be for depression, anxiety, and substance use and abuse. Declines in instability during and after emerging adulthood will predict declines in these problems.

Self-focus. This is perhaps the most important feature of emerging adulthood as a source of both externalizing and internalizing problems. With regard to externalizing problems, what makes emerging adulthood the self-focused age is that it is the time of life when people have the weakest network of daily obligations and commitments to others. This allows them an expanded range of individual freedom to make their own decisions about what to do and when to do it, in matters large and small. However, it also means that emerging adulthood is the nadir of social control. As noted earlier in the chapter, social control has long been recognized by criminologists as the strongest brake on tendencies for criminal behavior. What stops us from violating laws and other social norms is, in part, the daily obligations that we have to others, and the expectations of others that we will fulfill those obligations, as they fulfill their obligations to us. Because those daily obligations keep us busy, and because we wish to avoid damaging our social relations with those to whom we have daily obligations, most of us abide by social norms most of the time. Because social control is lowest in emerging adulthood, externalizing behavior is highest. When more exacting social roles are taken on—involving a spouse, children, a long-term employer, neighbors—externalizing behavior declines.[40]

With regard to internalizing behavior, the social relations that constitute social control not only keep us from violating social norms, they also provide us with support and with consolation in difficult times. So, weak social control makes emotions of depression and anxiety more likely and more intense. It also makes substance use and abuse more likely as self-medication for these emotions. Over a century ago, the great French sociologist Emile Durkheim described how variations in rates of suicide across Europe could be explained by examining patterns of social control.[41] The less social control, the more suicide. This principle has been verified many times since, not only for suicide but for depression and for various externalizing problems.[42]

Hypothesis: During emerging adulthood, those for whom social control is weakest will have higher rates of both externalizing and internalizing problems, with males especially at risk for externalizing problems and females especially at risk for internalizing problems. Declines in both externalizing and internalizing problems will be predicted by taking on the social roles that represent social control.[43]

Feeling in-between. Among the criteria that most emerging adults believe are important markers of adulthood are avoiding externalizing behaviors such as criminal activity, driving at high speeds or while intoxicated, and using illegal substances.[44] This implies that many emerging adults may believe that taking part in externalizing behaviors is more acceptable in their current stage of life, when they are not yet fully adult, than such behaviors will be later in life. With respect to internalizing problems, feeling in-between may elicit feelings of depression and anxiety in some emerging adults, especially those who believe they should be more adult at their current age than they actually are. In the national Clark poll of 18–29-year-olds, in responses to the question, "Do you feel that you have reached adulthood?" there was a significant relation between a "no" or "in some ways yes, in some ways no" response and reports of feelings of anxiety and depression.[45]

Hypothesis: At any given age within emerging adulthood, answering "no" or "in some ways yes, in some ways no," in response to the question, "Do you feel that you have reached adulthood?" will be more likely to be related to externalizing and internalizing problems than an answer of "yes." In the course of the twenties, increased likelihood of answering "yes" will predict declining rates of externalizing and internalizing problems.

Possibilities. The sense of having a wide range of possibilities for the future, accompanied by optimism about achieving the hoped-for life, is a widespread feature of emerging adulthood. This feeling of confidence in the attainment of a desirable adulthood may also contribute to what health researchers call the *optimistic bias,* which is the belief that the likelihood of negative consequences from engaging in a given behavior are lower for one's self than for others.[46] Because nearly all emerging adults believe the future will be bright, few of them may believe that their road to that future could be derailed by negative consequences that may result from externalizing behaviors such as risky driving, risky sexual behavior, crime, or substance use. With respect to internalizing behaviors, the small proportion of emerging adults who do *not* hold a strong confidence that their lives will turn out well in adulthood may be at especially high risk for depression and anxiety. In the national Clark poll, among 18–29-year-olds there was a negative correlation between agreement with "I often feel depressed" and "[a]t this time of my life, it still feels like anything is possible."[47]

Hypothesis: Among emerging adults, those with the strongest confidence in a favorable personal future will also have a relatively strong optimistic bias with respect to the consequences of externalizing behaviors and be relatively likely to participate in externalizing behaviors. Emerging adults will be higher in optimistic bias than older adults are, for a range of externalizing behaviors, which will help explain why rates of these behaviors are higher in emerging adulthood. Emerging adults who are not confident that they will reach their future goals for adult life will have higher rates of depression and anxiety.

Getting Better? Trends in EA Problems

Many types of problems are more prevalent during emerging adulthood than at other life stages, but are the problems worse than ever? It would be easy to believe this is true if you follow the popular narrative on emerging adults in American society, which is predominantly negative. Today's emerging adults have been accused of being selfish, even "narcissistic," and of never wanting to grow up, not just by journalists but by some academic researchers.[48] Young men, in particular, have been portrayed as increasingly dangerous brutes whom we should all fear.[49]

Actually, however, most data show positive rather than negative trends in the behavior of emerging adults over the past 20 years. Let's look first at positive trends, then at some negative and mixed trends. Then we will consider reasons for the trends.

Positive Trends

One of the most definite positive trends among emerging adults in the past 20 years is also the most important: declining rates of automobile fatalities. As noted earlier in the chapter, auto accidents are by far the number one cause of death during the emerging adult years. However, rates of fatalities in the late teens and early twenties have declined by almost half in the past 20 years, as Figure 11.5 shows.

Explanations for this trend have focused on improved safety designs for automobiles and better training for young drivers.[50] Passenger cars are now engineered so that they absorb the energy of frontal crashes better than before, making it less likely that injuries or fatalities will result. Enhanced seatbelt laws have led to increased seatbelt use.

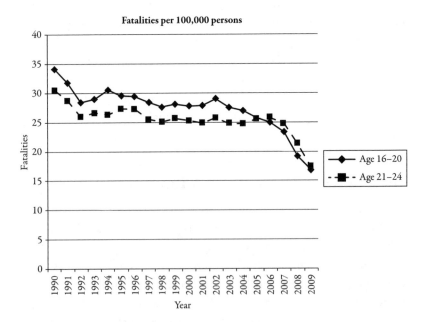

Figure 11.5 Trends in Automobile Fatalities, Ages 16–24.

Source: National Highway Traffic Safety Administration (2012).

These safety improvements apply to all drivers, and auto fatalities have declined across all age groups, but the decline has been steeper among emerging adults than among other adult age groups, probably due mainly to the growing prevalence of *graduated driver licensing programs.*[51] Graduated driver licensing programs restrict young people's driving privileges when they first learn to drive, for example, prohibiting driving at night or with same-age passengers, and expand privileges gradually, contingent on safe driving practices. Typically, the programs also require many hours of driving with a parent before the new driver is allowed to go solo. These programs have been shown to be highly effective at reducing auto accidents and fatalities, and have expanded over the past 20 years to nearly all American states.

Another area of striking improvement is crime rates.[52] Rates of a wide range of crimes have declined dramatically over the past 20 years among 18–24 year-olds, as Figure 11.6 shows. Juvenile crime (10–17-year-olds) has also declined sharply, but the patterns for adult crime are mixed. Crime rates have decreased among 25–39-year-olds and persons age 60 and over, but have increased for 40–59-year-olds.[53]

For the decline in youthful crime, there has been a wide variety of explanations.[54] More police were hired in the early 1990s in American urban areas, under national legislation promoted by President Bill Clinton. Police tactics

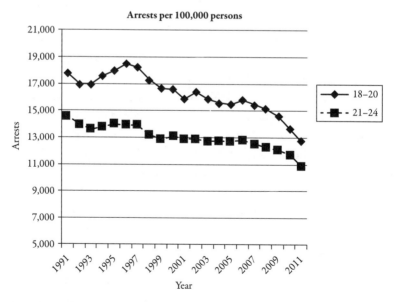

Figure 11.6 Trends in Crime Rates.

Source: Bureau of Justice Statistics (2013).

changed, focusing more on high-crime areas and targeting not just major crimes but nuisance crimes such as graffiti, littering, and panhandling, under the "Broken Windows" theory that establishing an orderly environment would drive down crimes of all types. The crack cocaine epidemic of the late 1980s ebbed in the course of the 1990s, and the crimes fueled by the epidemic waned as well. One theory proposed that crime has declined because abortion was legalized in 1973 by the *Roe v. Wade* Supreme Court decision, and subsequently fewer poor mothers gave birth to unwanted children who would be at high risk for criminal activity.[55] However, this theory has not been supported; the first post-*Roe* children had higher, not lower, crime rates when they came of age in the late 1980s, and the young women most likely to have abortions are not those most at risk for having children who grow up to engage in crime but those who get better grades, are most likely to finish school, and are less likely to be on welfare.[56]

Another crucial area of positive trends is cigarette smoking. Automobile fatalities are the top source of mortality during ages 18–29, but smoking addiction kills far more in the long run, an estimated 400,000 adults per year in the United States alone.[57] Furthermore, the median age of smoking initiation is 14, and virtually no one begins smoking beyond age 30. Consequently, if smoking rates drop in the teens and twenties, mortality from smoking is sure to drop in future decades. Over the past 20 years, and especially in the past 10 years, smoking rates have fallen dramatically among emerging adults, as Figure 11.7 shows. Similar trends have occurred among American adolescents in middle school and high school. Declines in smoking have occurred for other adults as well in the past decade, but have been greater for adolescents and emerging adults.[58] Unlike other types of substance use, rates of smoking are now lower for emerging adults than for adults ages 30–64.[59]

The decline in youth cigarette smoking is typically attributed to the wave of litigation in the late 1990s that caused the tobacco companies to accept restrictions on advertising and marketing to youth.[60] Many states instituted smoking prevention programs for adolescents in the past two decades, and these programs have often been effective. Also, the expenses resulting from the litigation, as well as increases in state taxes, drove up the price of cigarettes beyond what many young people could afford.

Overall, the declines in automobile fatalities, crime, and cigarette use can be seen as a triumph of public policy. The laws, programs, and restrictions put into place during the 1990s were effective: Graduated licensing reduced

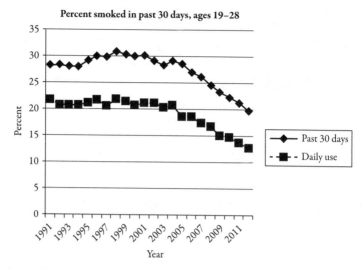

Figure 11.7 Trends in Smoking Rates.
Source: Johnston et al. (2012).

automobile fatalities, new policing methods helped reduce crime, and litigation and anti-smoking programs reduced smoking rates. However, not all the trends are good, as we will see in the next section.

Negative and Mixed Trends

Although most trends in problems during emerging adulthood are positive, some problems are becoming worse or have remained unchanged over the past 20 years. With regard to substance use, although rates of smoking are down, rates of both binge drinking and marijuana use are up, as shown in Figures 11.8 and 11.9. This indirectly demonstrates the importance of public policies, as the effective strategies used to lower rates of smoking have not been similarly applied to binge drinking or marijuana use. In fact, penalties for marijuana use have been weakened in recent years, and there is a growing movement toward legalizing marijuana use for medicinal purposes and decriminalizing recreational use. This movement is questionable from a public health standpoint. Although research indicates that smoking marijuana can help reduce the side effects of certain types of medical treatments, frequent marijuana use causes damage to cognitive, physiological, and reproductive functioning.[61]

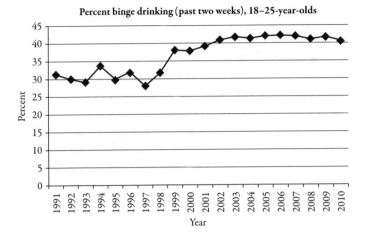

Figure 11.8 Trends in Binge Drinking.

Source: Substance Abuse and Mental Health Services Administration (SAMHSA) (2011).

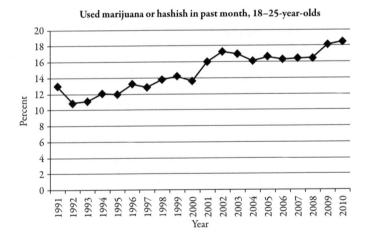

Figure 11.9 Trends in Marijuana Use.

Source: Substance Abuse and Mental Health Services Administration (SAMHSA) (2011).

For internalizing problems, trends are more difficult to discern. There is not the same kind of excellent decades-long data record for internalizing problems as there is for externalizing problems. A variety of studies seem to indicate a rise in rates of depression over the course of the twentieth century, although all the studies have flaws. Several studies indicate a rise in major depression from the early twentieth century to the late twentieth century, across Western countries, not just among young people but among all adults.[62] However, these studies mostly rely on retrospective memories of depressive symptoms over a lifetime, an obviously flawed method. A meta-analysis of studies of college students from the 1930s to the early twenty-first century found a rise in depression over that period, as measured by the Minnesota Multiphasic Personality Inventory (MMPI), a commonly used measure of personality traits.[63] However, college students do not represent most emerging adults, and these are not just college students but mostly college students in introductory psychology courses at large research universities, an even more dubious sample. This meta-analysis also found a rise in depression among high school students, but another meta-analysis showed no increase in depression among children or adolescents over a 30-year period in the late twentieth century.[64]

All studies on this topic must be interpreted in light of the fact that it became more socially acceptable in the late twentieth century to report symptoms of depression, as psychotherapy and mental health treatment became more widespread and less stigmatized.[65] This change may have made more recent cohorts more willing to report symptoms of mental health problems than previous cohorts were. Nevertheless, it can be concluded that there is tentative evidence for a rise in depression over the past half century, among emerging adults and other adults, if not in children and adolescents.

Anxiety also appears to have risen over the past half century.[66] However, as with depression, the rise in rates of anxiety disorders has taken place across the adult stages, not just in emerging adulthood. Also, as with depression, the reported rise in anxiety may simply reflect a rise in willingness to report psychological symptoms in recent decades, rather than an actual rise in anxiety problems.

Eating disorders, too, seem to have risen in the late twentieth century. One analysis found a steady rise in incidence of anorexia nervosa from 1935 through 1999.[67] Another found increases in bulimia nervosa and binge eating disorder in the late twentieth century.[68] Here again, however, is the problem of distinguishing a rise in rates from a rise in willingness to report symptoms.

Making Sense of Divergent Trends

Overall, the trends in the lives of emerging adults are positive in many ways. There have been declines in the most important and serious externalizing problems, including automobile fatalities, crime, and cigarette smoking. In addition, as we have seen in previous chapters, volunteering has risen substantially, and emerging adults are notably more tolerant than their elders of differences in ethnicity, sexual orientation, and religion. However, rates of depression and anxiety appear to have risen, although increases in these areas appear to have occurred not just among emerging adults but in other adults as well.

One way of explaining these trends is that individualism has increased in American society. As many scholars have observed, individualism rose dramatically in the 1960s and 1970s. Robert Bellah and his colleagues described the rise of "expressive individualism" during this period, as self-restraint became viewed less as a virtue and more as an impediment to psychological health, whereas "letting it all hang out" changed from socially stigmatized to socially valued.[69] Similarly, Robert Putnam identified the many ways that participation in civic activities and organizations declined after the 1960s and 1970s, as people turned toward more individualized leisure at home.[70]

For today's emerging adults, such individualism is no longer radical or revolutionary; they grew up with it. So, they are tolerant and accepting of variations in ethnicity, sexual orientation, and religion because they believe that all people have a right to believe and behave as they wish, as long as they do not harm others. But individualism has costs, too. As Durkheim already observed in late nineteenth-century Europe, the more individualistic a society becomes, and the less people feel they have meaningful roles in a stable social system, the more they find themselves "unable to escape the exasperating and agonizing question: to what purpose?"[71] Consequently, incidence of depression and anxiety increases, as has been seen in the United States and other Western countries in recent decades.

Yet this explanation seems difficult to square with the other trends among emerging adults. Greater individualism means lowered self-restraint and impulse control, which should result in wider prevalence of risky driving behavior and crime—but these problems have declined dramatically in the past two decades. One would think volunteerism would be inconsistent with rising individualism as well, as it involves work on behalf of others. Yes, the volunteer may also gain personal rewards, in the satisfaction of helping others, but community service nevertheless entails a sacrifice of personal time and a priority on helping others.

For now, then, the puzzle remains as to why there should be these strikingly divergent trends in the lives of emerging adults. This presents a tantalizing challenge for EA researchers, and raises the intriguing question of where these trends may be headed in the decades to come.

Chapter 12

Sometimes Goodbye Is a
Second Chance

Resilience in Emerging Adulthood

Is emerging adulthood only for the privileged? As we have seen in Chapter 10, there are those who believe so. Being an emerging adult in the United States often means exploring different possibilities in love and work before settling on long-term choices, and it is true, coming from a family with substantial resources might make it easier in some ways to extend your period of exploration. With regard to work, certainly, if your parents can give you financial support through college and maybe even graduate school, you have more of an opportunity to explore possible careers than someone who feels compelled to go to work full-time after high school just to pay the bills, instead of going to college.

But this is only part of the story. In another sense, reaching emerging adulthood offers even more opportunity for someone from a difficult background than for someone from a privileged background. Children and adolescents are at the mercy of their parents, for better or worse. If their parents are well-off financially, happily married, and loving toward their children, the children benefit from those advantages. But if their parents live in a poor and violent neighborhood, or fight often, or are physically abusive, or go through a bitter divorce, or are addicted to alcohol or other drugs, or are mentally or physically ill—just a few of the problems exhibited by the parents of the emerging adults we interviewed in my original study—then the children inevitably suffer from the kind of family environment that the parents' problems create. They cannot escape; there is nowhere else for them to go.

In emerging adulthood, however, this changes. Now they are capable of leaving home and living on their own. Their parents' problems need no longer be their problems, too. When they reach emerging adulthood, they have a chance to transform their lives and set out on a different path from their parents. Unlike children, emerging adults *can* leave, and when they do, sometimes a whole new, healthier life opens up before them. Sometimes goodbye is a second chance.[1]

This is one of the most important qualities of emerging adulthood, that it represents an opportunity for people from difficult backgrounds to transform their lives. Emerging adulthood is arguably the period of the life span when the possibility for dramatic change is greatest. Children and adolescents are too limited in what they can do on their own to have much opportunity for changing the direction of their lives. After emerging adulthood, once people make enduring choices in love and work and take on long-term obligations, especially the obligation of caring for a child, it becomes more difficult to change course. Emerging adulthood is the freest, most independent period of life for most people. For people who are unhappy, who feel their lives are headed in the wrong direction, who desire to make a dramatic change for the better, emerging adulthood is the time to do it.

But isn't it too late by then? If a person grows up in an unhealthy family environment, isn't that the environment that is unfortunately but indelibly stamped on their personalities, for the rest of their lives? This is the view that has long been dominant in Western thought. "The child is father to the man," the poet William Wordsworth famously declared some two centuries ago. At the dawn of psychology over a century ago, Freud proposed that the personality, and therefore one's fate in life, is more or less fixed by age six. Even today, there is far more research on infancy and early childhood than on the rest of the life course combined, indicating that the belief still reigns that it is in the early years of life that our fate is determined once and for all.

Clearly, many people believe this, scholars and non-scholars alike. But maybe this claim is exaggerated. Even if it is generally true, even if there is a correlation between childhood experiences and later development, there may be many people for whom this does not apply. And the proportion of people for whom it does not apply may grow sharply in emerging adulthood, as people gain greater freedom to run their own lives.

In this chapter we look at four emerging adults whose lives defy the assumption that our early years permanently decide the path we will follow in the future. All of them experienced terrible events or circumstances in childhood, all of them had lives that were in disarray by adolescence, and all of them transformed themselves in emerging adulthood and turned their lives in a dramatically different direction, toward health and happiness. Their lives suggest that whatever may have happened from infancy through adolescence, emerging adulthood represents a second chance—maybe a last chance—to turn one's life around.

First, let us review briefly the research on resilience in emerging adulthood.

Research on Resilience

Resilience is defined as "good outcomes in spite of serious threats to adaptation and development."[2] Sometimes "good outcomes" are measured as reaching notable milestones (such as graduating from college or holding a stable job), sometimes as internal conditions (such as good mental health), and sometimes as the absence of notable problems (such as early pregnancy, homelessness, substance abuse, or criminal behavior). Young people who are resilient are not necessarily high achievers who have some kind of extraordinary ability. More often they display what resilience researcher Ann Masten calls the "ordinary magic" of being able to function reasonably well despite being faced with unusually difficult circumstances.[3]

A number of longitudinal studies examining resilience have begun in childhood or adolescence and continued through emerging adulthood and beyond.[4] One classic study of resilience is known as the Kauai (*kow' ee*) study, after the Hawaiian island where it took place.[5] The Kauai study focused on a high-risk group of children who had four or more risk factors by age two, such as problems in physical development, parents' marital conflict, parental drug abuse, low maternal education, and poverty. Out of this group, there was a resilient subgroup that showed good social and academic functioning and few behavior problems by ages 10–18. Compared with their less resilient peers, adolescents in the resilient group were found to benefit from several *protective factors,* including one well-functioning parent, higher intelligence, and higher physical attractiveness.

In the Kauai study, a surprise finding was that many of the participants who had been placed in the nonresilient category in adolescence turned out to be resilient after all in emerging adulthood.[6] The experiences that helped them change their lives for the better included participation in higher education, learning new occupational skills through military service, marriage to a psychologically healthy partner, and involvement in a religious faith that provided a community of support. They also managed to separate themselves from their most dysfunctional family relationships, while maintaining relations with some family members. Reaching emerging adulthood allowed them to leave an unhealthy family environment.

Several other longitudinal studies have reported similar findings.[7] Overall, these studies highlight two protective factors that seem to be most important in promoting resilience in emerging adulthood. One is cognitive abilities, including general intelligence, planfulness, and self-control. Having these abilities allows people to make the best use of the freedom of emerging adulthood to reflect on their problems, understand how the problems developed, and make conscious choices about how to change their lives for the better. The second crucial protective factor is at least one healthy relationship with someone who cares. It could be to any of a wide range of people—a parent, stepparent, sibling, extended family member, neighbor, friend, teacher, coach, youth director, or romantic partner. Having that one person to provide support, encouragement, information, and guidance helps give emerging adults the strength and resources to rebuild their lives after years of hard times.

But most important of all may be simply the freedom of emerging adulthood, as we will see in the following four profiles.

Resilience in Emerging Adulthood: Four Profiles

All kinds of emerging adults are resilient. They may be working class or middle class, male or female, of any ethnic group. For all of them, reaching emerging adulthood presents an opportunity for them to remake their lives. The independence of emerging adulthood, along with the advances in cognitive development that allow them greater understanding of how they got where they are and what they need to change, may open a door to a new life.

Jeremy: "I'm Equipped to Make Better Judgments"

Jeremy, 25, was an imposing physical presence, six feet tall with a muscular build and a thick, strong neck. He had light reddish-blonde-brown hair and a beard to match, about one week's growth, neatly trimmed. We met at his sparsely furnished apartment near my university office on a weekend afternoon, and he was dressed for leisure: black jeans and a T-shirt with a map of Australia on it. His warm smile made the big man seem gentle despite his size.

Hearing about his childhood, it was surprising that he smiled at all by now. From infancy through adolescence, his life was tumultuous and painful. His parents had divorced, remarried each other, then divorced again by the time he was three. Shortly after they divorced the second time, his mother remarried, a different man this time. While she was at work, his stepfather "threw me in the closet as soon as she'd leave for the day."

That marriage lasted only a year, and then he and his mother were on their own for a few years. He remembers that period as "probably the happiest time of my life," even though his mother "had to leave me alone a lot because she couldn't afford baby sitters." What made it happy was that they "always got along. My mom was always more like my big sister than my mom."

However, by the time he was eight his mother had remarried again, and his second stepfather was even more abusive than the first. "He'd come in and beat on me while she was in the bathtub or when she left. He'd hide it from her." His mother and stepfather quarreled often, and the worst beatings took place when he tried to intervene to protect his mother. "They were fighting all the time, and I couldn't handle it. I couldn't help my mom and I felt frustrated and helpless there. I'd go in and yell at him and I'd get sent to my room. And then she'd leave and he'd come beat the hell out of me for interrupting."

This was the beginning of "the whole cycle, where I went from one abuse to the next." At age 11 he moved to Arizona to live with his father and stepmother, but there he fought constantly with his stepmother. He "hung out with a bad crowd" of kids who "kind of accepted me when my parents didn't." The younger boys in the gang went "back and forth with backpacks full of drugs" for the older boys, who paid them in pizza and video games. He got in fights, and "got beat up real bad once." He had altercations with the police, and spent time in a juvenile jail.

Jeremy's father and stepmother got fed up and sent him back to his mother and stepfather, but they did not want him either, and he went to live with his grandparents for a while. They were Jehovah's Witnesses, and they set about "trying to take control of me and make me a Jehovah's Witness, which I didn't want to do." Suspicious of outsiders, they would not let him have friends over, and he spent a lot of time alone. "It was hard enough to make friends, moving here from Arizona, but not being able to ever have anybody over made it harder."

He tried moving in with his mother and stepfather again, but the old pattern of conflict soon re-emerged. Finally, all his other options exhausted, he moved out on his own. He was 15 years old.

How could Jeremy live on his own at age 15? His mother and stepfather were willing to pay the rent on his apartment to get rid of him, and he got a job to supply himself with food and other necessities. Not surprisingly, his schoolwork "kind of took a back burner" to his job and the responsibilities of daily life on his own. With no parents around to keep an eye on him, throughout high school he got drunk often, smoked pot daily, "just a lot of wild things." He lived for the moment and gave little thought to the future. "When I was in high school, I didn't really think I'd make it to this age. I didn't really think about where I wanted to go or what I was going to do."

To look at Jeremy's life as he entered emerging adulthood, you would have thought he was damaged beyond repair. In fact, as he puts it, "Everybody says I should be some kind of a mass murderer or something after all the things I've gone through." The physical abuse, the bitter divorce of his parents, the hostility from his stepparents, the experience of being "bounced around" from one household to the next, the substance abuse, the school problems, the gang involvement—any one of these experiences might have predicted a troubled future, and in combination you would think his fate was sealed.

Yet here he is at age 25, engaged to be married, attending college full-time while working 20–30 hours a week, no longer a substance abuser, seemingly at peace with himself and the world, an all-around good guy. What was it about his experiences in emerging adulthood that enabled him to overcome the influences of his childhood?

Meeting his fiancee three years ago was a big turning point. Their relationship "pushed me in a totally different direction than where I was headed." He calls her "my best friend," and says "she meets every requirement I could ever have in a friend. I feel like I can trust her. We just click and get along." As noted earlier, research on resilience has indicated that a healthy love relationship is one of the strongest promoters of resilience. Love gives people something to live for, a compelling reason to plan for the future and stay out of trouble, and structures daily life in a way that makes opportunities for deviance less likely.

But the change in Jeremy's life is perhaps due even more to simply reaching emerging adulthood, because it meant gaining a new cognitive maturity in his understanding of his life. To Jeremy, becoming an adult entailed learning how to manage whatever life throws at him, without becoming overwhelmed. "There's a lot of things that people say makes you an adult that I don't agree with, because I was doing those things when I was 16 or 17, and I was definitely not an adult then. Once you know how to handle most things that come your way and nothing really throws you for a loop and you don't get upset every time something goes wrong, I think that's one of the first steps toward being an adult."

This new maturity in his thinking has enabled him to see the potential benefits of his past trials. "Hopefully with what I've got behind me and the experiences I've had, I'm equipped to make better judgments to push my life in a better direction." He believes that coming through such difficult times has made him stronger and more resilient. "There's a lot of bad things that have happened in my life, and I just kind of feel like, anymore, they kind of roll off."

It is not only that he has become better equipped to handle what others might do to him. He also takes a share of responsibility for the troubles he has had in the past, and he has tried to change how he treats others. "I take a lot more care to think about other people and think about how my actions are going to affect them, where before I was more interested in what I could get for myself. I've just become a lot less self-centered."

As a consequence of these changes in himself, the changes in Jeremy's life have been profound. For several years out of high school, he worked in semi-skilled manual labor for a company that did flood and fire restoration. At the time he was happy enough to earn some money and did not think much about making a long-term plan. But by his early twenties he started thinking of what his life would be like 10, 20, 30 years down the road, and he realized he wanted to do something other than manual labor. So he entered college at age 23 to pursue a business degree, and he has stuck with it and maintained "a straight B average," something that he does not think he would have been capable of doing when he was younger. Note the change in his ability to plan. "Before, it was difficult for me to put any energy in anything that I didn't get a paycheck out of. If I didn't get something immediately back for it, I didn't want to put the effort into it. I couldn't look far enough ahead. I wanted instant gratification." Now, however, "I just kind of feel that I can see a goal. I'm much more prepared."

A profound change has also taken place in his relationships with his parents and stepparents. "I get along fairly well with my stepmother and my stepfather now. Let bygones be bygones, you know, and I've let them go. And I've really grown to like my mom and dad. Moving out helped. And time's helped. Time's helped a lot of things. Everybody's grown up."

Nicole: "I Needed to Experience Freedom"

Nicole, 25, met me for our interview at an outdoor café in Berkeley, California. She came straight from her job as a receptionist and medical assistant at a dermatology center, and she was dressed very professionally: a nice lavender dress, and a silver necklace with matching earrings. An African American woman, her skin was very dark, and she had long, straight black hair. She was a small woman, but she had a large, expressive mouth.

To look at her, so polished and professional, and to listen to her, so thoughtful, articulate, and ambitious, you would never have guessed that she grew up in dreadful circumstances in what she called "the ghetto," the housing projects of Oakland, with no father and a poor, mentally ill, entirely incompetent mother. Nicole was just six years old when her mother had "her nervous breakdown." The functioning of the household was already shaky, but after her mother's collapse it totally disintegrated. Nicole remembers "days, sometimes even weeks" when the only meal she got was the free lunch for poor kids at school.

It was Nicole, her mother's oldest of four children by three fathers, who took over and pulled the household together—*at age six*. Already at that age she exhibited unusual ability for what psychologists call *planful competence*.[8] "I became the mother. I had to be the strong one. It was never something that was put upon me. It was just I saw it had to be done." She made sure her brothers and sister got washed, dressed, and fed each day. She cleaned the house and kept it in order. By the age of eight, she was working in order to make money that would enable her to buy food and other essentials for the household. "I swept stores, I baby-sat. I did whatever I could, because otherwise we went without. At like eight years old, I had neighbors who were like, 'Oh, Nicole, can you watch my kid?' Everybody thought, 'Well, she's older than her age. She can handle this.' And I could. I made a couple bucks and helped my mother out, helped my family out."

Still, the help she gave to her family came at a personal cost to her. Because she was so consumed with family responsibilities, she rarely had time or energy left over for schoolwork, and through high school her grades were low. She graduated from high school, but she was never regarded as a promising student, the kind who might go on to college or even get a graduate degree.

It was only when she reached emerging adulthood that she was able to turn her attention to her personal goals. She got a full-time job, found an apartment, and moved out on her own. Soon, she started taking college courses in the evening. Despite having a full-time job in addition to taking courses, she got excellent grades. Removing herself from the chaos of her family household was the key. "I needed to experience freedom. I needed to experience living out of my mother's home in order to study. I couldn't really get my studying skills down pat until I moved out, and when I moved I'm like, gosh, I always knew I could excel in school. In order for me to go to school and function properly I need to be on my own."

Because she works full-time and can only take evening courses, her progress toward a degree has been slow, but she is undaunted. "I'm going to get my degree, however long it takes." She is within one course of an associate's degree, but that is just the beginning of her educational ambitions. She plans to get a bachelor's degree next, and eventually a Ph.D. in psychology. Talking about getting a Ph.D. sent her into rapture. "Ooooh, I love the word. I want to have it in 10 years, by 35. That's feasible."

Still, she tries not to look too far ahead. "I'm just trying to get through the day-to-day. If I focus so long term, I'll like get crazy. I'm so hard on myself. I really set unrealistic goals at times. So now I'm just like, okay, take it one step at a time. Look ahead, but just for five seconds. You know, 'your future's still there.' It's like, 'I'm just checking on you, Future.' And then move on."

Her goal of getting a Ph.D. and becoming a clinical psychologist is inspired partly by her childhood experiences and partly by her distress in witnessing her mother's decline. Because of her own experiences, she plans to work with "so-called dysfunctional children and kids from broken homes." She hopes to help children avoid the problems that plague her mother. "As a young child, I remember my mother working and just this beautiful woman. Then she had a nervous breakdown, and she went kind of crazy. She stopped working, she got on welfare. So that's something very important to me, to be constantly building a person's self-esteem and getting in touch with themselves and just accepting life, you know, no matter what happens to you. Just deal with it and move to the next level." She talks about working with girls, in particular. "I'd like to have like a consultation agency, kind of like a wellness group—bring young girls in, talk to them about self-esteem and problems they were having at home."

Nicole is so focused on work and school that love has been moved to the back burner for now. "Right now, I'm not really focusing too much on guys," she said. "I don't have time. Most of the guys I meet, they're like time wasters or time thieves. So I'm just not into the whole dating scene right now." She realizes her reluctance to get involved with a man makes her different from most of the women she grew up with. "I see my friends, and they're like, 'Well, don't you want to get married? Don't you want children?' I mean, by this time, 25, I'm an old maid to them, I'm over the hill. I might as well be 50. You know, by this time I should have two kids by two daddies. But I'm not ready right now. I can wait."

She prefers to focus on her own goals and her own identity at this point in her life. Like many emerging adults, she feels that only after she has a fully formed identity and has learned to stand on her own will she be ready to commit herself to someone else.[9] She believes that she needs to be self-focused during this time in order to succeed. "I'm just trying to focus on me and get my life together. Right now, I guess this is kind of like a selfish time for me. I'm just really trying to get into myself so that when I come out of that, I can deal with someone else. Right now, I just gotta keep the tunnel vision."

After so many years of being devoted to the needs of her mother and her siblings, she relishes the opportunity for her identity explorations and regards them as an exciting adventure. "Every day that I wake up, I learn something new about myself. Learning about yourself is a really emotional thing because it's like you wake up one day and you think you're living the way you want to live, and then the next day you get up and it's like, 'Wait a minute, I'm doing everything wrong. I don't know who I am.' And you have to be willing to take that step forward and say, okay, I'm going to get to know myself no matter if it's painful or if it's going to make me happy. I have to dig deep within myself and figure out who I am. And this is a learning process every day."

Nicole's optimism in the face of difficulties, her ability to see the potential benefits of even the most dire circumstances, is perhaps the most striking feature of her personality, and it is this ability that is at the heart of her resilience.[10] She calls her childhood of growing up with a deficit of resources and an overload of responsibility "a big learning experience. I don't think I regret it because had I not gone through it, I wouldn't be the person I am today." She believes the deprivations of her childhood have made her more appreciative of the things she has now. "It's like a blessing. If I see somebody on the street who's dirty and smelly, I think, gosh, at least I have some place to sleep. I mean, it always could be worse. Had I not experienced that maybe I wouldn't think that way."

Similarly, she sees no reason to regret her delay in going to college and the slow progress she has made so far. "I don't think everyone is set to go to college as soon as they get out of high school. Some people have life experiences that they need to get, and that's something I needed to do." She sees her current job in the same optimistic light. Although she does not find much satisfaction in the work she does as a receptionist and medical assistant, seeing it as a step on the way to something better makes it less onerous now. "I just look at it all as temporary because I know what I want to do in the future."

Although Nicole is enjoying her emerging adulthood as a long-awaited chance to focus on her own goals and her own life, she still has a strong sense of duty and obligation to her family. I asked her if she had thought about working fewer hours in order to take more college courses. "The only thing is I would worry about my family because right now I think of them," she said. "That's one thing I still battle daily is like if I should just waitress or do something part-time and go to school full-time and just worry less about my family, supporting them. I just feel like I gotta take care of them."

Her ambitions are driven in part by the dream of taking her mother's worries away so that she could finally recover from her psychological problems. "That's why it's so important for me to be really successful and make a lot of money, so I can buy my mother a house and put her in a situation where she doesn't have to worry about the bills, she doesn't have to worry about her clothes, she doesn't have to worry about having food. It will all be there. It's like, 'Now you've got everything—move on.'"

If only she could bestow on her mother some of her own planful competence, her own steely determination. "I just wish I could give her that strength to say, 'I'm gonna take care of me. I'm gonna make a choice. I'm gonna do something with my life.' It's never too late." As for Nicole, in spite of a childhood full of adversity, in emerging adulthood her hopes are high, her optimism undiminished. "It's like, the more you come at me, the stronger I'm going to be."

Bridget: "Now I Answer to Myself"

Bridget, 23, arrived at my research office one evening directly from her job as a supervisor at a temporary employment agency. She was sharply dressed in a green turtleneck, green plaid jacket, and blue skirt, and her shoulder-length blonde hair was nicely groomed.

The story of her past was a sharp contrast to her polished appearance in the present. "It wasn't a terribly happy childhood," she said of her first

18 years, and as she described her family life that seemed like an understatement. Physical abuse, emotional abuse, alcoholism, bitter conflict, estrangement—"my family is the role model for the dysfunctional family," she said. Her mother claims "I caused her 18 years of unhappiness" just for being born, because the pregnancy forced her parents into a loveless marriage. Throughout her childhood her mother told her "I would never have married him if it hadn't been for you." Needless to say, her parents' marriage was no garden of delights. "They fought like crazy," Bridget recalls. "It was very physically abusive. He hit her a lot. She has an alcohol problem. And he would come home from work sometimes and just beat the holy living crap out of her. He had the anger problem and she had the alcohol problem."

When her parents were not abusing each other, they abused Bridget and her younger sister. "Mom was good at verbal abuse, and Dad was good at the physical. Of course, the verbal was worse." Bridget's mind still resonates with all the nasty things her mother told her as she was growing up. "You're ugly. You're fat. You'll never have any friends. You're stupid."

It is true she rarely had any friends as a child, mainly because her mother was so hostile to any kids who came around. "I never really had neighborhood friends because my mom would always find fault with their families or find fault with them. She made it very difficult for me to have friends as a child. Very difficult. Because she didn't get along with the parents. She was jealous of everyone. Anyone who was thinner than her, prettier than her, had hair that was nicer than hers, had a car that was nicer than hers."

How did Bridget emerge from this nightmare to become the happy, healthy young woman she is today? One key was the development of her religious faith, which has been found to be an important protective factor in studies of resilience.[11] She had little exposure to religious training as a child. "My parents were atheists. They didn't believe in God." However, when she reached high school she became involved in a religious organization almost accidentally, and something about it resonated with her.

"I started going to church when I was a sophomore in high school, because I dated a boy that I had a really big crush on, and when he broke up with me I was devastated and I was like 'I'll just go to his church, and that way we'll have something in common.' So I started going and I thought 'My gosh, I like this. I like these people.' And so by a year later, I was saved. Definitely, that was something that influenced my life."

Her church was a refuge during her otherwise painful high school years. "I wonder now what my life would have been like had I not had this positive influence. All throughout high school, because of that church group I was always around happy people, people that had fun with their lives, people that really enjoyed living. And out of all this gloom that I had in my home life, I could always escape to my friends, and I'll always be grateful for that." She continues to attend the same church, and she remains close to many of the people there, and grateful to them. "I am so close to some families at church that just really helped me out. They give this unconditional love. That's something I still don't understand, how people that barely knew me could give me unconditional love because of Jesus, so much more than my own parents. That just didn't make sense, and it still doesn't and it never will."

Bridget's faith kept her afloat during high school, but the real turning point in her life came in emerging adulthood. Becoming an emerging adult made it possible for her to remove herself from her toxic family household. "It's always been bad, and now it's just not there, which I guess is good. I feel more peaceful. I don't have to deal with it on a daily basis. I don't have to worry about whether they would yell at me about something. Now I answer to myself." Once she had moved out, it was easier to avoid their destructive influence. "I tried not to be around them a lot, not spending a lot of time at home, going away to college, getting away for a complete year in Sweden, where I had to do it or die."

Her college year in Sweden was a watershed, "a huge turn of events," Bridget says. It was there that she realized that she no longer needed to rely on her family, that she could stand alone as a self-sufficient person—that, really, she had no other choice. "I got to Sweden and I called to try to talk to them and they wouldn't accept my calls. So, I think that when I was thousands of miles away from home in a strange country, not knowing what I'm going to do when I get back, I knew that kind of thrust me into adulthood, whether I wanted to or not." It was then that she accepted responsibility for her life. It was then that she realized "that I had to be accountable for my actions, and that I am my own person and that what I do is going to directly affect my entire life."

In emerging adulthood, not only has Bridget separated herself from destructive family influences, but she has also reinterpreted her past family experiences, so that she sees her suffering as something that has built her up rather than tearing her down. "There's been a lot of pain and a lot of hurt, but I've really grown from it," she says. She sees her experiences, even the bad ones, as an essential part of her identity development. "It's made me the person who I am today," she says. "It all happens for a reason."

Coming back from Sweden she knew she faced a challenge, being entirely on her own, but she accepted it with relish. "I could have, when I came back, worked at Wal-Mart for the rest of my life because, you know, I'd had the hard breaks or whatever." Instead, she finished her college degree, all paid for with her own hard work, and laid the foundation for a promising future. "I'm very proud of what I've done and how I got there," she says. "I've worked my ass off to get where I am."

One of Bridget's definite dreams is to have a husband and children. Witnessing her parents' awful relationship has made her cautious about marriage, but not cynical. "I love the idea of falling in love and being with one person, and having someone to share your life with. I think I'd be ready for that if I found the right person. But I'm not going to rush it. I'm not going to settle for anything less than I deserve." She envisions providing her own children with a family environment much different from her own. "A real loving household. Open communication. No violence. I will never strike a child." Her resilience despite horrendous family conditions makes her optimistic about how her own children might fare in the world. "Something that I've noticed around people my age is that they're very cynical about 'Well, I'm not going to have kids because I don't want to bring them up in a world like this.' I don't really have that view because I look at myself growing up in a very bigoted household—prejudiced, backwards, any other negative term you could use—and I got out of it. So I have hope."

She also has career ambitions, although they are not clearly defined at this point. "I do want a career in something like human relations," she says, but shortly after she adds, "I would really like to teach high school. I think I would be a good teacher." She also remains open to new possibilities. "Tonight if someone called and said 'You have an opportunity to go to Eastern Europe to teach English as a second language, would you do it?' I'd say 'Yeah, when does my flight leave?'"

Although Bridget's life right now is uncertain, one thing she is certain about is that the future is bright. "I look at what's happened in the last two years of my life, and it's changed so much that I can't possibly see what's going to happen in 10 years. It'll be pretty exciting, I'm sure."

Derek: "I Feel I've Been Very Fortunate"

Derek was 28 years old, but he had the look of someone in no hurry to reach adulthood. He was African American but he had dyed his hair blonde, which made for a striking contrast to his coffee-colored skin. He had silver studs in his chin and his tongue. His tan felt beret was on backward, and he wore a striped T-shirt and light pants. In short, he looked much more like he was in the role of his part-time job, as a DJ in a San Francisco nightclub, than of his full-time job, as a server in a restaurant.

His family history was so chaotic and tragic that if it were fiction it would be rejected as unbelievable. He was given up for adoption at birth, and after five months in a foster home he was adopted by a White, affluent New England family. But his adoptive father was an alcoholic, and when Derek was three years old his parents divorced, an event he calls "a catastrophe." Then, when he was five years old, his mother died in a car accident, along with a sister and an aunt. Derek was in the car, too, and he remembers that the accident seemed to happen in "slow motion, and it was basically loud and confusing."

Derek and his remaining two sisters and brother went to live with his father, but his father's alcoholism had worsened since the divorce and he was in the midst of a downward spiral, in no condition to raise four children. "He started drinking more and spending his money and getting really extravagant," Derek recalled. He was soon forced to sell his share of the advertising agency that had made his fortune, and the downward spiral continued as "he gambled, sold his cars, hit rock bottom." Derek and his siblings were dispersed to other family members, and Derek was passed to an aunt and uncle, then his grandparents, then to a boarding school for three years (from age 11 to 14), then to "a 60-acre organic commune" for half a year, then to another aunt and uncle through high school. His father did eventually stop drinking, when Derek was in 5th grade, but "the rest of his life was spent trying to recover, physically and financially," and Derek never lived with him again. He died the year after Derek graduated from high school, from years of too much alcohol and cigarettes.

As an African American growing up in "90% White" areas of New England, Derek had substantial experience with what he calls "the brutality of childhood." During recess at school, the other kids played a game they called "Chase the Nigger," starring Derek. After school he ran all the way home, trying to avoid kids who were hoping to beat him up and sometimes did.

By high school, Derek was chronically anxious. "I was in a constant panic. I was depressed a lot. I didn't think about the future." His anxieties were projected outward in the form of fear of nuclear war. "I had a very nihilistic attitude toward the world, and I thought it was going to end from a nuclear war. I was mortified and petrified by the whole prospect of nuclear war. If I looked up in the sky and I saw a trail from a jet, I was worried that it was a missile. Any incident that was reported in the news would panic me, like war or terrorism—anything would stimulate that fear." In Derek's case this seems like a projection of his personal anxieties rather than a politically informed concern, because he was not politically involved or interested in world affairs except for this one issue. Also, he was extremely anxious about sexual issues as well. "I was a virgin until I was 20, and I was scared of women because, like, the only thing worse than nuclear war would be losing my virginity."

How did he change from an adolescent wracked with anxieties to an emerging adult who is happy, confident, content with himself and his life, and hopeful about the future? The key was that once he became an emerging adult, he was more in control of his life. He was no longer simply moved around from one place to another by other people. Perhaps for this reason, his anxieties about nuclear war eased soon after high school. "It just finally came to the point where I just had to let go of fearing war," he recalls. It also helped ease his anxieties when, early in emerging adulthood, he had an intimate relationship with a woman for the first time, and sex no longer seemed more terrible than a nuclear holocaust. "My first girlfriend, I went out with her for two years, and we lived together and it was fun. The timing was right."

For Derek, it has been important to have emerging adulthood as a self-focused time to recover from the upheavals of his childhood and get his psychological house in order. "In the last year or two, I've focused more on myself for the first time, where before, as a child, I was afraid to be alone. I was afraid to be with people, but I was scared to be alone. Then I started to communicate with people, but I was still completely petrified of being alone. Now, I'm comfortable being alone and being with people, and I don't have to be with as many people as I used to."

Although he is 28 years old, an age when most others have left emerging adulthood for the long-term commitments of young adulthood, Derek remains unsettled at this point in both love and work. He does have many female friends. "I have a strong base of female intimate friends that I've known for 5 to 10 years," he says. And he now feels ready to find a life partner. "Lately I've had ideas of marriage and engagement and long-term relationships. And I've recently met a woman who just broke off an engagement with somebody, so there's the potential for a relationship right there." As for work, he realizes that his jobs as a server and a DJ do not hold much potential as long-term careers. But his experience in his last restaurant job involved him in all aspects of the business, and he thinks of owning and running a restaurant or café as something he might want to do. Still, these dreams are amorphous right now, and he realizes that he is reaching a point in his life where it is time to focus his efforts. "I'm starting to feel like it's really time to explore my potentials."

Derek's success in prevailing over his difficult childhood and adolescence are reflected not so much in definite accomplishments in love and work as in the kind of person he is. Despite being subjected to frequent upheavals as he was growing up, in emerging adulthood he has developed a strong sense of himself. "As I get older, I have learned not to sell myself so short. That's one thing about growing older, take more pride in who you are and don't feel that you're not valuable. That crosses over into relationships. That crosses into living situations." Despite being subjected to prejudice, he holds no grudges toward people of other ethnic groups. "My friends are so many different ethnicities and races and creeds that I forget what they are, as well as what I am. They're just my friends with a capital F. There are no hyphen-friends in my life." Despite suffering more chaos and tragedy by age 28 than most people suffer in a lifetime, he sees the good that has come out of his past experiences. "I've had a good life. I don't feel that a lot of people have wronged me. For every like 50% tragedy, there's been like 150% support. I feel I've been very fortunate."

Conclusion: Distinctive Features of Resilience in Emerging Adulthood

What is it that makes it possible for a person to transcend adverse family circumstances in childhood and adolescence, and nevertheless become healthy and hopeful in emerging adulthood? Research on resilience has identified a number of protective factors that are echoed in the lives of the four emerging adults profiled in this chapter.[12] It helps to be intelligent, and a fierce intelligence is evident in Nicole and Bridget, who have succeeded academically in spite of numerous obstacles. It helps to have at least one loving relationship with a parent, as Jeremy did with his mother, or with an adult outside the family, as Bridget had. Religious faith can be a source of strength and hope, as it was for Bridget. Personality characteristics such as persistence, determination, and optimism can be invaluable, and those qualities are evident in all four emerging adults described here.

But in addition to these characteristics, which have been known for some time to be related to resilience among children and adolescents, there is something about reaching emerging adulthood that opens up new possibilities for transformation for people who have had more than their share of adversity during their early years. Let us look now at three aspects of resilience that are *developmentally distinctive* to emerging adulthood: leaving home, reaching a new level of cognitive understanding, and transforming the meaning of a negative past into a positive identity.

Perhaps most important, reaching emerging adulthood makes it possible to leave a pathological family situation. This is not an option available to children and adolescents. They do not have the skills and resources to leave a destructive home and go off on their own. Those who try often move from the frying pan into the fire, as the case of Jeremy illustrates.

In contrast, for emerging adults leaving home is normal and expected in American society, and most of them are quite capable of living on their own. For emerging adults whose family lives have been damaging them and undermining them for years, simply leaving that environment represents a great liberation, a chance to wipe the slate clean and start anew. Now, instead of being subjected daily to the pain and fear of an unhappy family life, their lives become their own.

In addition to the effect of moving out on their own, there is another change that is more subtle but may be equally important in making it possible for emerging adults to transform their lives. It is their growing cognitive ability for self-knowledge and self-understanding. Gene Bockneck calls this their *sens de pouvoir,* meaning a sense of one's own capabilities, of what *can be,* experienced as a feeling of inner power.[13] As they move away from the noise and confusion of adolescence, they become more capable of appreciating the ability they have to change what they do not like about their lives. It is this that enables emerging adults to step back and assess their lives, and decide, "This is why it is not working, and this is what I need to do to make it better."

The third developmentally distinctive aspect of resilience in emerging adulthood is the ability to incorporate negative past experiences into a healthy new identity. As noted often in this book, identity development is a central part of emerging adulthood. During the emerging adult years, young people reflect on their past experiences, their abilities, and the opportunities available to them in their society, and draw important conclusions about who they are as a person and what their likely future will be. This can be problematic if their past experiences are characterized by pain, unhealthy relationships, and even physical and psychological abuse.

But many emerging adults have the ability to perform a cognitive transformation on their past suffering. Instead of a burden to be borne for life, it becomes redeemed as a challenge they have overcome, the essential spice in the stew of their self-image.[14]

It is striking how the emerging adults profiled in this chapter were able to interpret terrible experiences in a positive way. No matter what they suffered, they managed to see their experiences favorably as what "made me the person who I am today," as Bridget put it. They have managed to construct a healthy identity, and they embrace even their worst experiences as necessary to making them into what they have become.

Even when emerging adults' lives change for the better, this does not mean that none of the effect of the previous 18 years of their lives will remain with them, and it does not mean that the transformation of their lives once they move out will be easy and immediate. In fact, for all the emerging adults described in this chapter, it has taken them years in emerging adulthood to gain a solid footing after being buffeted around so much in their youth. But once they reach emerging adulthood, it is possible for people with a difficult past to begin to take hold of their lives and make choices that will gradually enable them to build the kind of life they want.

Of course, it could be that some people's lives take a turn for the worse in emerging adulthood. Reaching emerging adulthood means making more of your own choices, but some people may make choices that are unwise or unlucky. Others may suffer troubles in emerging adulthood that send a life once seemingly headed toward a bright future suddenly careening off the road—anything from an unintended pregnancy to a terrible automobile accident to abuse of alcohol or other substances. No one in my original study seemed to have taken this path, but that could be because such people are too preoccupied with their current problems to be willing to take part in a study like this. I would predict that for emerging adults in general, the correlation between parents' characteristics and their own characteristics declines considerably from what it was in childhood and adolescence, as they make more of their own decisions and become responsible for constructing their own lives, sometimes for better, sometimes for worse.

Nevertheless, there is evidence that in emerging adulthood life is more likely to take a turn for the better than for the worse. National surveys, including the national Clark poll, show that emerging adulthood is a time of rising optimism and well-being for most people,[15] whether they go to college or not, whether they have a stable job or not, whether they were doing well back in high school or not. Emerging adulthood is time of looking forward and imagining what adult life will be like, and what emerging adults imagine is generally bright and promising: a loving, happy marriage, and satisfying, well-paying work. Whatever the future may actually hold, during emerging adulthood hope prevails.

Chapter 13

Beyond Emerging Adulthood

What Does It Mean to Become an Adult?

The end of adolescence and the beginning of emerging adulthood is fairly easy to define in American society. Adolescence ends at about age 18, because that is the age at which most Americans finish high school and move out of their parents' household. Nearly all adolescents have in common that they attend high school, they live with their parents, they are minors under the law, and they are experiencing the physical changes of puberty. None of these remain typical after age 18, so it does not make sense to call them adolescents any more. After age 18 come the freedom, exploration, and instability that distinguish emerging adulthood.

But when does emerging adulthood end and a more established young adulthood begin? This is a much trickier question. I have described emerging adulthood as lasting from about age 18 to age 25, but always with the caveat that the upper age boundary is flexible.[1] Twenty-five is an estimated age that does not apply to everybody. For some people the end of emerging adulthood comes earlier, and for many it comes later, which is why I often use age 29 as the upper age boundary. Part of the theory of emerging adulthood is that it is a period of being in-between adolescence and young adulthood, on the way to adulthood but not there yet. But how do you know when you have arrived? It all depends on how you define adulthood.

In this chapter we look first at how adulthood has been defined in traditional cultures and in the past in American history, then at how emerging adults today define adulthood and assess their own progress toward adult status. Next they reflect on their mixed feelings about leaving adolescence; from the perspective of emerging adulthood, it seems like an easier time. Then they describe their mixed feelings about becoming adults; from the perspective of emerging adulthood, reaching adulthood promises stability but inspires fears of stagnation. Finally, we examine their views of the future, and how they foresee a happy and successful life for themselves even as they believe the world in general is fraught with peril.

Making the Transition to Adulthood

Let's begin by looking at beliefs about adulthood in traditional cultures and in the American past, then at how young Americans see the transition to adulthood today.

Traditional and Historical Conceptions of Becoming an Adult

In other places and times, the crossing of the threshold to adulthood has been relatively clear, with the focus on a single event: marriage. According to anthropologists, cultures all over the world have shared a common belief that marriage marks not only the joining together of two persons in a life-long partnership but also the attainment of full adult status.[2] After marriage a young man is welcomed into the men's social group, no longer kept with the boys. A young woman who marries is elevated to equal status with other women. Historians of American society have come to a similar conclusion.[3] Through most of American history, until late in the twentieth century, getting married meant reaching full adulthood.

Marriage no longer has this meaning in American society. It is meaningful in other important ways, of course, but its significance as a marker of adult status has passed. In the many studies that I and others have conducted on what people of various ages believe defines the transition to adulthood, marriage consistently ranks near rock-bottom out of 40 or so possible markers of adulthood.[4] This is true not only in the United States, but in a wide range of other developed countries, from Austria to Israel, from Argentina to the Czech Republic. In interviews, when people are given a chance to state their views about what is important to them personally as a marker of their progress toward adulthood, marriage is almost never mentioned—even by people who are married!

What explains the demise of marriage as a marker of adulthood in developed countries? Perhaps most important is that marriage is a much less dramatic transition than it used to be. Think for a moment of what marriage meant to your grandparents and great-grand parents. Their wedding night probably marked their first-ever experience of sexual relations. Upon marriage many also moved out of their parents' household for the first time. For many, especially young women, it would have been their first experience of living with anyone outside their immediate family. The transition to marriage was usually more abrupt for women than men, because young men were more likely to have left home for war or work or adventure, but even for many young men, marriage marked this kind of dramatic transition.[5]

In contrast, for the majority of today's emerging adults, by the time they marry each has had years of independent living. They have already known each other for several years, had a regular sexual relationship, and may even have lived in the same household. Being married may feel different to them psychologically than cohabiting did, as we discussed in Chapter 5, but in fact not much changes in their daily lives. For example, Pam married four months ago but says it had nothing to do with making her feel more like an adult. "We had been together for four years and I just felt like it was a continuation of our relationship. I mean, we lived together anyway, so I don't think it's changed much." Compare this to the historical pattern—when getting married usually involved leaving your parents' household for the first time, having a sexual relationship for the first time, and living for the first time with someone outside your immediate family—and it is easy to see why marriage would have had greater significance as a transition to adulthood in the past than it does now.

Adulthood Here and Now: Learning to Stand Alone

But if it is not marriage that marks adulthood, what is it? What do emerging adults today believe makes a person an adult? I have researched this question now for 20 years, in many different parts of the United States, with people from a variety of different ethnic groups and social classes, and I have found that there is a remarkably strong American consensus across all these groups. Becoming an adult today means becoming *self-sufficient*, learning to stand alone as an independent person.[6]

As described in Chapter 1, three criteria are at the heart of emerging adults' views of the self-sufficiency required for adulthood: *taking responsibility for yourself, making independent decisions,* and *becoming financially independent.* Table 13.1, summarizing a variety of studies on this topic, shows that the Big Three are favored by an overwhelming percentage of

Table 13.1 The Big Three Criteria for Adulthood, Across Countries

	% Important		
	Accept responsibility for one's self	Make independent decisions	Become financially independent
US Whites	91	82	71
US African Americans	89	80	72
US Latinos	85	72	79
US Asian Americans	93	82	75
Argentina	99	93	92
Israel	99	90	87
Austria	98	89	67
Greece	95	93	83
China (students)	97	89	93

Sources: US Whites, African Americans, Latinos, and Asian Americans: Arnett (2003); Argentina: Facio & Micocci (2003); Israel: Mayseless & Scharf (2003); Austria: Sirsch et al. (2009); Greece: Petrogiannis (2011); China (students): Nelson et al. (2004).

emerging adults on a questionnaire containing about 40 possible criteria for adulthood.[7]

Responsibility is a word that comes up over and over again in interviews when emerging adults respond to the question of what it means to be an adult, and usually it means responsibility for yourself, not others. Tammy has begun to feel like an adult recently because "I finally realized that I'm responsible for everything I do and say and believe, and no one else is, just me. That's all, so I'm an adult." Ray said that becoming an adult means "[t]aking care of your own responsibilities and not having to lean on people for everything. If you can take care of your every need without relying on other people, then I really believe you should be pretty much an adult."

In part, taking responsibility for yourself means accepting responsibility for the consequences of your actions rather than looking for someone else to blame if things go wrong. "A boy doesn't necessarily take responsibility for his own actions," said Cliff. "It can be someone else's fault that he acts up. It's the parents' fault or it's society's fault. But a man is responsible for whatever he does and his choices are his and he succeeds and fails on his own." Hoyt gave a specific example. "I bought a truck one time for $500. It was a junker. Put a new engine in it, put a new transmission in it, did all the work myself and spent some money on it, and it was still a junker when I got done with it. It's one of those things where you realize 'Well, I really screwed this one up. I'm going to have to take the responsibility for it. I can't put it off on anybody else this time. I'm an adult and I made the decision to buy the heap of junk. This is a learning experience.'"

Making independent decisions is the second most important marker of adulthood. Emerging adults believe that to be considered an adult, a person has to use independent judgment in making the decisions, small and large, that come up in the course of daily life. To Arthur, becoming an adult means "having the freedom to make decisions about your own life, I think, as opposed to having someone else dictate them to you." Likewise for Vicky, reaching adulthood involves "actually making your own decisions. Not having someone always tell you what to do, but saying 'This is what I want to do, and this is how I'm going to go do it.'" Wendy feels she has reached adulthood because "all the decisions I make are my own. I discuss them with other people for input, but they don't make the final decision for me."

The scope of independent decision-making includes not only questions such as where to live and what career to pursue, but also the less tangible area of what your beliefs and values should be. For Mindy, this area was crucial to her sense of reaching adulthood. "I was from a very religious background—Southern Baptist—and I had to learn to believe what I believe and not let my parents or anyone else tell me what to believe. And I think once you can establish your own beliefs and control your own life, then you're an adult."

For some emerging adults, there was one especially important decision that marked their transition to adulthood because they made it themselves. Chalantra, now 20, married young; she was just 18. Too young, as it turned out, because they divorced a year later. "When I decided to get divorced, I made that decision on my own," she says now. "And I feel like that makes you an adult, when you can sit down and weigh out things and realize that something is for you or isn't for you." For Laurie, choosing to have sex for the first time was the crucial decision. "I don't think that I really considered myself a woman until my first sexual experience. I grew up in a really strict home and always believed you should wait until you're married. And basically when I did it, that was a big turning point for me because it was my own decision. I didn't look to somebody else for answers." Notice that it was not the sexual experience itself but the independent decision that made her feel she had reached adulthood.

Financial independence is the third pillar of adult status for emerging adults. They believe they need to make enough money to "pay the bills" on their own before they can be considered fully adult. Sylvia feels she has not yet entirely reached adulthood because "I kind of feel that being adult should mean that you're financially independent, which I'm not. I'm very dependent on my parents in that way." In contrast, Melanie does feel adult because "I'm paying for everything. I'm paying for school, I'm paying for my car, and I'm paying for my credit card bills that were my fault a long time ago." In Tory's view, "I think financial independence has a lot to do with it. Paying your own bills, not going to Mom and Dad and saying 'Can I have $300 to go to Florida with the guys for spring break?'"

As noted in Chapter 3, for all of the Big Three criteria for adulthood, becoming an adult is defined in terms of independence *from parents*. According to Shaneequa, "A woman is someone who can take care of herself. She doesn't need her parents to take care of her." Korena said she has not yet reached adulthood because "I'm still pretty dependent. I know that whenever I need help, I can just tell my parents and they will help me. Even though I'm 22, I still think that I'm sort of a child because of the way I depend on my family." In contrast, Joan said her passage to adulthood took place "when my parents finally stopped taking care of me. When they wouldn't pick up my bounced checks anymore, when they finally said no and put their foot down."

Establishing independence from parents is a gradual process that begins well before emerging adulthood, but a major thrust toward adulthood comes with moving out of the parents' household. Ariel said that for her, becoming an adult "started with just moving out of the house. I don't think that was the end of it, but I think that started me to build my own belief system and to question life in general, and figure out who I was and what I wanted and everything." Yvonne still lives at home, but she anticipates that she will enter adulthood "when I move out of the house. When I'm like finally in an apartment by myself, taking care of the bills, taking care of everything, depending on nobody but myself."

For many emerging adults, moving out is part of going off to college after high school. In Tom's view, his passage to adulthood "started when I went to college. I had to be on my own. It was the first time I'd ever really been away from my parents, and I had been real close to my parents. So, having to be on my own then made me think that I was grown up." Hazel recalled that "moving off to college really made me feel adult just because of being able to be autonomous, being able to make all my decisions on my own and survive without the help of my parents except for the financial aspect."

As Hazel's comments suggest, it is not just moving out itself that is important as a marker of adulthood, but the way that moving out requires emerging adults to take on new responsibilities, make independent decisions, and become more independent financially. Casey says he felt he was on his way to adulthood at 21, "when I first moved into the house I'm renting now. To pay my own rent, pay my utility bills, pay for my own car insurance. Being responsible for having to clean my own house, do my own laundry, do my own ironing, keep my own schedule, everything. When you're doing it all by yourself and you're generating all the money that makes it possible, and you're making all the decisions— I think that's when I started really feeling like an adult." Dale, in contrast, feels that his progress toward adulthood is inhibited by living with his parents, because it allows him to avoid taking responsibility for himself. "I'm totally dependent on my parents. Even if they gave me all the money I needed, I would still have trouble living on my own. I mean, sometimes I'd really like to not be living in their house with them. I'm ready in a way, but there's just so much stuff I don't know how to do because my mom has always done it. Not just paying the bills. I mean laundry, food, everything."

Because it is not so much moving out that matters but rather taking on the Big Three transitions (of responsibilities, making independent decisions, and financial independence) that moving out often requires, emerging adults can feel they have reached adulthood even if they have returned home or never left. Trey lived with his parents through college and for two years afterward, but he says, "I really considered myself an adult even living at home and being with my parents. I don't think that's a requirement to be considered an adult." I asked him what made him feel he was an adult while he was still living at home. "Making independent decisions," he said. "I mean, I used my parents as support, but I was able to say 'This is what I want to do,' or 'This is what direction I want to go.'" Palmer was able to consider himself as an adult while living at home because he was capable of being financially independent if necessary. "I could afford rent, that wouldn't be a big deal. I couldn't buy some of the things I buy, but I don't really use my parents' home for anything except for a place to sleep. Other than that, I pay for everything."

Learning Consideration for Others

With their view of what it means to be an adult defined so much by learning to stand alone as a self-sufficient person, independent of parents or anyone else, emerging adults give the strong impression of measuring their progress toward adulthood strictly in terms of themselves and their personal development. I have noted that emerging adulthood is a self-focused age, and this self-focus is evident in their conceptions of adulthood. They live in an individualistic society and are at an individualistic time of life, and the combination makes their self-focus strikingly high. Eventually they do want to commit themselves to others through marriage and parenthood, but first they want to demonstrate to themselves and others that they can fend for themselves in the world.

Still, even during emerging adulthood they do not lose sight of the needs and concerns of others. On the contrary, the individualism of their view of what it means to be an adult is tempered by an emphasis on consideration for others. Being self-focused does not mean being selfish, and becoming self-sufficient does not entail becoming self-absorbed. Becoming an adult means learning to stand alone, but it also means becoming less self-oriented and more considerate of others.[8]

Some emerging adults place consideration for others at the heart of their conception of adulthood. Gerard said that in his view of what it means to be an adult, "I'd say not being selfish is a big part of it. Being able to look out for other people's interest and not just think of your own." Similarly, Peggy holds the view that in order to be an adult "I think you have to take into consideration how your actions will affect other people. You know, like drunk driving. I don't have problems with people drinking, but when you drink and then you get in a car and drive and hurt someone else, that's not taking into consideration other people that you might harm through your actions."

However, emerging adults who place concern for others at the center of their conception of adulthood are relatively rare. More often, they view self-sufficiency as the most important part of becoming an adult, but they temper this focus with concern for others. The word "responsibility" comes up often again here. Responsibility has an elastic meaning, the way emerging adults use it. It can refer to taking responsibility for yourself—and that is how they use it most often—but it can also be used to refer to responsibility toward others.

According to Mindy, reaching adulthood means "being responsible and knowing what your priorities are. Not looking out just for yourself, but when you have the well-being of others in mind and knowing that you are not just responsible for yourself but for other people around you, and not harming them." Corey said becoming an adult involves "learning to take responsibility for yourself, and maybe also feeling somewhat responsible for the others around you instead of just being irresponsible and not worrying about anything but personal gratification."

It is another paradox of emerging adulthood that becoming more self-sufficient can also mean becoming less self-centered, that learning to stand alone can be combined with learning to be more considerate of others. We have seen, in Chapter 3, how the same kind of change takes place in their relationships with their parents. As they move away from their parents, they also become closer to them. In the same way, as emerging adults take more responsibility for themselves, they often become more aware of the responsibilities they have toward others.

What Matters for Some: The Complex Meanings of Parenthood

Along with marriage, the other traditional marker of reaching adulthood is becoming a parent. Has parenthood suffered the same decline in significance as marriage over the past half century?

Yes and no. Across studies, on a questionnaire of possible criteria for adulthood, parenthood ranks near the bottom in the responses of emerging adults, right down there with marriage.[9] In interviews, emerging adults sometimes preface their statements about what is important for adulthood by stating emphatically that having a child does *not* make you an adult. When I asked Cecilia what it means to be an adult, she said, "Certainly not having kids," then went on to talk about what did matter for her. Charles, too, began his response by saying "You have to have a child? I don't think so."

This might make it seem that becoming a parent is not an important part of reaching adulthood, but the meaning of parenthood in relation to adult status is more complex than that. Although few nonparents view having a child as a significant marker of adulthood, and few parents would say that parenthood is a *requirement* for adulthood, for themselves personally, those in their twenties who are parents usually regard it as the most important event in their passage to adulthood.[10]

This is especially true if they have become parents relatively early, in their teens or early twenties. At these ages pregnancies are often unexpected and unintentional, as we saw in Chapter 5. Those who become parents early do not have the luxury of moving gradually toward adulthood according to their personal assessment of their progress toward self-sufficiency. Instead, parenthood thrusts them into adulthood immediately and abruptly, as they are suddenly required to change their lives to care for their newborn child.

Leanne, 23 and the mother of three children, had her first child at 18 and says, "That has a tendency to make you grow up real fast. Even when I was pregnant, it was like 'I've got to plan for this baby's future. Things have got to be different now. I've got somebody else that depends on me.' And that tended to make me grow up a lot, just in my thinking." Celine, 22, had her first child at 20 and now has a four-month-old as well. Asked if she felt she had reached adulthood, she replied, "With kids, definitely! Adulthood overnight, you know! The focus is on them and not on you. You think of that other person before you think of yourself." Larry, 26, became a father at 23 and says, "if you want to grow up fast, that's a sink or swim. I went from happy-go-lucky to 'You've got a baby to take care of. You've got to put a roof over its head. You've got to do this and this and this.' It's not 'Well, you can if you want,' it's 'This is what has to be done, period.' It seemed like it just happened overnight."

We can see, then, that parenthood requires people to take on weighty new responsibilities whether they would have chosen to or not, whether they feel ready or not. It "has to be done," as Larry said. Unlike most emerging adults, who take on the responsibilities of adulthood gradually, at their own pace, as they feel ready for them, young parents must take on all at once the tremendous responsibility for the life of a tiny, vulnerable child. They become adults because of what their new role as parent requires of them, *right now*, not because their long personal journey toward self-sufficiency is at last complete.

Does this mean that 40 or 50 years ago, when most people became parents by their early twenties, they had a sense of reaching adulthood at a much earlier age than most emerging adults do today? I think this is likely. We can only speculate, because there is limited evidence going back that far, but it seems like a reasonable speculation.[11] Back then, the *majority* of young people were in a situation like the young people just described, of being thrust into adulthood at a young age with the birth of their first child, rather than reaching adulthood gradually, at their own pace. Of course, it is also possible that they had their first child earlier because they already felt they had reached adulthood earlier and so they felt ready for parenthood. But either way, it is very likely that they felt like adults at an earlier age than emerging adults do today.

Ambiguity and Ambivalence

Because it takes longer to become an adult than in the past, there is now a period of years where young people feel they are adults in some ways but not others. In fact, this is what originally inspired the term *emerging adulthood,* the way so many of the 18–29-year-olds I interviewed in my original study described themselves as on the way to adulthood but not there yet.

Feeling In-Between

Although becoming a parent often has the effect of catapulting emerging adults into adulthood overnight, those who become parents in their late teens or early twenties today are the exception. Because parenthood does not come for most people until the late twenties or beyond, by the time they become parents they already feel they have reached adulthood through other markers. Most emerging adults deliberately wait to marry and have children until they have first established their self-sufficiency and feel they have a definite sense of their identity as individuals.

Because for most people today the journey to adulthood is long and winding, emerging adulthood tends to be experienced as a period of being in-between adolescence and adulthood. As 20-year-old Leslie put it, "There's not a break and then you become an adult. It's just a long, gradual process. I'm more of an adult than I was when I was 15 or 17, but in five years I'll probably be more of an adult than I am now." As Figure 1.5 in Chapter 1 showed, based on data from the national Clark poll, for most emerging adults it takes at least until their mid-twenties until they feel they have made it all the way to adulthood, and sometimes later.

Often, the sense of being in-between occurs when emerging adults continue to rely on their parents in some ways, so that their attainment of self-sufficiency is incomplete. For example, Malinda, 21, says she feels she has "somewhat" reached adulthood. On the one hand, she takes responsibility for herself. "I think I behave responsibly. Now it's only me that I account to. No one's checking up on me and anything I do has got to be up to me." But on the other hand, she does not yet make her decisions independently. "My parents are nearby and I still depend on them for some things. I don't have them do things for me, but I ask for their advice." Holly feels like an adult in most ways, but her lack of financial independence holds her back from completely reaching adulthood. "When I have my mom pay half the rent, that makes me feel like a kid again, but otherwise I feel like an adult." Similarly, Dan said he had reached adulthood in "all but the financial part of it. I mean, I live my own life. I act like an adult and I think of myself as an adult, but I guess I haven't crossed the line as far as money goes."

For other emerging adults, they have become entirely self-sufficient to all appearances, yet there is still some part of them that just doesn't feel adult. Terrell gives a definite impression of adult maturity. He has a promising career with a computer software company, he is entirely independent from his parents, and he seems to have a clear idea of who he is and what he wants out of life. Yet when I asked him if he had reached adulthood, he replied, "Not absolutely, because I still sometimes get up in the morning and say, 'Good Lord! I'm actually a grown up!' 'Cause I still feel like a kid." Shelly, a college junior, feels she has come a long way toward adulthood since she left home for college three years ago, but also feels she has a long way to go. "I feel like I'm much further than I was when I started college. I've made this huge jump, I think, in just being more comfortable with myself and just being more settled with myself. But then there are a lot of areas where I still haven't figured all this stuff out, and there's still so much more to figure out. Like, when people call me 'ma'am,' I'm like 'Whoa!' So, not really totally yet."

The proportion of emerging adults who move from feeling in-between to feeling fully adult increases steadily in the course of the twenties, and by age 29, according to the national Clark poll, 80% feel they have reached adulthood and are no longer in-between.[12] However, during the twenties, age is only a very rough marker of whether or not a person feels like an adult. There are 21-year-olds who say they have definitely reached adulthood, and 28-year-olds who say they still feel in-between.

Some emerging adults feel adult earlier than their peers because they have a relatively conservative personality. They are not interested in having an extended period of trying out different love partners and occupational paths before making enduring decisions. Instead, they learned early who they are and what they want out of life, and were happy to settle into a stable adult life in their early twenties.

For others, feeling adult early is due to growing up in difficult circumstances that required them to take on adult responsibilities at a young age. Nicole, who was profiled in the previous chapter, exemplifies this pattern, as she was already taking care of three younger siblings and her psychologically disabled mother when she was still in primary school. "At a young age, I saw that things weren't being taken care of," she recalled. "And so I just took responsibility. If the house wasn't clean enough, I was there to clean it up. If the food wasn't ready, I was there to make it." Taking on these early responsibilities made her grow up faster.[13]

Adulthood: A Dubious Honor?

In most societies, reaching adulthood is a valued achievement. Becoming an adult means having new authority, commanding respect, and being allowed to participate in activities forbidden to children and adolescents. In American society, too, entering adulthood is something most emerging adults regard as an achievement. They take pride in being able to fulfill the responsibilities necessary for independent adult life: holding a job, paying their bills, running a household. They enjoy being able to run their own lives and make their own decisions, and they believe their lives will become even better as they become more adult. In the national Clark poll, 59% of 18–29-year-olds agreed that "I think adulthood will be more enjoyable than my life is now."[14] The majority see adulthood as promising a relief from the stress and instability of their current lives.

However, many emerging adults are ambivalent about reaching adulthood. Yes, it is nice to have the freedom to run your own life, and it is satisfying to be able to handle adult responsibilities competently. But mixed with their pride in reaching adulthood is dread and reluctance. In the national Clark poll, 35% of 18–29-year-olds agreed with the statement, "If I could have my way I would never become an adult"—not a majority but nevertheless a substantial proportion.[15]

In part, this ambivalence results from a realization that adult responsibilities can be burdensome and annoying. Laurie said she has reached adulthood "for the most part," but adds that her adult responsibilities seem "overwhelming sometimes. There are times when I really wish that I was being taken care of by my mom and dad." Amber thought of a specific example. "I was just looking at this thing for my life insurance and naming beneficiaries. And I was thinking, you know, this is the kind of thing I want my parents to do for me. I don't want to be faced with these grim decisions myself."

The other source of their ambivalence about entering adulthood, for some emerging adults, is that they associate becoming an adult with stagnation. Gerard said that, at 27, "I feel like I'm kind of teetering on the brink of adulthood, you know. I guess in some ways I feel like it and other ways I don't. I associate being an adult with being really boring, and I just don't feel quite that boring yet."[16] Dylan also had a bleak view of adulthood. "I think in some respects I feel like I'm an adult, and in some respects I kind of hope I never become an adult. Maybe I associate adultness with being overly constrained or something. Losing your fresh approach."

In this view, reaching adulthood means the end of fun, of spontaneity, of personal growth. Cindy said "I don't think I'll ever feel that I've fully reached adulthood, because I think every day is going to be a quest for me. Every day you're going to learn new things in life. Once you accept that you're an adult and there's nothing else to learn, then your life becomes stagnant." Martin put it this way: "I don't know if I've reached adulthood yet because I don't know if I ever want to. How do you define an adult? Do you want an adult to never be childlike? Because I always like to play and I don't know if I ever want to quit playing, if that's what that means." Emerging adults like these idealize childhood, and adulthood looks pale in comparison. Trey said, "I always think it's best to have somewhat of a child in you, otherwise you get too set in things and you're not able to look at things in certain ways. So I don't think it's always good to say 'I'm 100% adult.' I'm probably somewhere around 50% most of the time."

Emerging adults also realize—wisely—that once they enter adulthood there will be no going back. Rob said, "I'd have to say that maybe I'm not 100% an adult. And maybe I don't want to be. What's the hurry? I have my whole life to be an adult, you know." Renée, 24, realizes she is not as mature as her parents were at her age, "obviously because they were married and having me." But she adds that at this point in her life, "it's not that I want to be that mature, you know. I guess I'm an adult as much as I want to be an adult."

Looking Back to High School: Those Were the Days?

The ambivalence that many American emerging adults feel about reaching adulthood also appears when they reflect on how their lives have changed since high school. In my original study we asked them, "Would you say your high school years were *less* stressful and difficult than your life now, or *more?*" I expected that most emerging adults would say their high school years were worse, because adolescence is well known to be stressful and difficult for many people.[17] By emerging adulthood, I expected most people would say they were happier and they were glad to have left the upheavals of adolescence behind. This would fit with other research indicating that life satisfaction and overall well-being rise substantially from adolescence through emerging adulthood.[18]

However, their actual responses were more complicated. To my surprise, most of them (58%) said their high school years were *less* stressful and difficult; only 24% said high school was *more* stressful and difficult (with the rest responding "about the same").

Some remember their high school years as simple, happy, and carefree. Like Heather, who recalled, "In high school I had no concerns. I just hung out with my friends all the time, school wasn't real tough, financially my parents took care of me. It was just fun." And Sean, who said, "I didn't have the demands on my time then that I do now. I mean, in high school, you went to school for 6 or 7 hours a day, and my parents didn't ask me to work, so basically I had all the time in the world on my hands to go to school and have fun, and that was basically it. Whereas now, that's not the case." Some, like Tom, appreciated the structure and security of daily life in high school. "It was just 'you get up, you go to school; you're going to go to school until May, and you're going to go to this class and this class.' I mean, every day was just like a routine. And in the summer, I'd play baseball. It was a pattern, and I knew that I'd come home and the food was there, Mom would fix dinner. There weren't that many decisions and choices I had to make."

More often, however, emerging adults say that high school seemed highly stressful and unpleasant *at the time.* It is just that, from the perspective of emerging adulthood, the trials of high school seem trivial. The high school years may have seemed stressful, said Lillian, "but they were that silly kind of stressful. Peer pressure stuff. You know, you worry about who's saying what about you, or are you going to have a date to this event or that event. That was all pretty stupid." Rocky finds it all mystifying now. "I look back and I'm like, why in the hell did I even care about that shit? Why did I care if I was having a good hair day or a bad hair day? It was no big deal! I could care less now. But it was something back then where the slightest things would stress you out."[19]

Many emerging adults recall the pressure cooker of their peers' judgments as the most stressful thing about high school.[20] Tammy remembers high school as being all about thinking "I'm just not okay and everybody else is and I look funny and I smell funny and I act funny and I dress funny. You think you're sticking out like a sore thumb, and that's pretty stressful. I hated it!" For Kim, too, high school involved "too much worrying about what other people thought. When you get older you don't have to worry about all that stuff. You can do what you want." On the questionnaire in my original study, three-fourths of emerging adults responded that they worry less now about what their peers or friends think of them, compared to high school.

If only they had appreciated back then how good they had it! "When I was in high school, I thought what I was dealing with was stressful, but that was nothing," said Larry. "And now it's like 'God, I wish I was a teenager, when everything seemed so carefree and there was some order to things.'" Mandy had similar regrets. "Looking back at my teenage years, I think 'Man, I've got a lot of responsibility. I should have enjoyed that freedom while I had it, you know, instead of trying to grow up.'" "No car payments or house payments," recalled Candace wistfully. "I had it made."

In contrast, the stresses of emerging adulthood are more serious and seem more legitimate. As Rita put it, "the problems that I have now are a lot more real than they were in high school. I mean, in high school your problem is, you know, what you look like, what your hair turned out like, and whether or not to tuck your shirt in because it might make you look too fat, stuff like that. It's just a lot bigger problems now, problems that matter." Wendy made a similar contrast. "Back then stress to me would have been 'What am I going to wear?' Now, it's like 'How am I going to pay this bill?' and 'Where am I going in life?' It may be more stressful because the things that are stressful to you are major, more difficult to think about, harder decisions to make." Rita's and Wendy's observations are consistent with the national Clark poll, in which 72% of 18–29-year-olds agreed that "This time of my life is stressful."[21]

College students remark on how much tougher their college courses are, compared to high school. "High school was just a cake walk," scoffed Martin. "It was easy. If you played the game in high school that the teachers wanted you to play, you could make A's. In high school it was rote memorization and now it's more independent thinking." High school was easier, said Ian, "because there were no all-nighters or three finals in a week. Teachers pampered you. I think college is just a blast, but the workload is immense."

More than anything else, emerging adults say their financial responsibilities are what make their lives stressful now compared to high school. Benny said high school was "less stressful because I didn't have the worries of paying the bills. You know, I did work but that money was mine. Now when I'm making my money it goes to the electric bill, the water bill and all that."

Denny also thought high school was easier because of fewer money worries. "You were at home and didn't have too many worries, just go to school and that was it. You didn't have all these bills. Now you've got to work and pay your bills."

Although moving toward adulthood means greater stress in some ways, it also means having greater abilities to deal with stress.[22] "The demands get harder but you're a little more prepared to deal with them," said Malinda. Emerging adults often take pride in being able to handle the stresses of their new responsibilities. Heather described the change like this: "In high school I had no concerns. I just hung out with my friends all the time, school wasn't real tough, financially my parents took care of me. It was just fun. And now, I'm 24, I work all the time, I'm financially on my own, I take care of myself. It's scary, but it's nice, too. You feel a lot of satisfaction out of it."

Emerging adults also realize that new stresses are a cost of their new freedoms. Leslie says her life now is more stressful "because of just the extra pressures of things like money and stuff like that," but she knows that these are stresses she has freely chosen. "I kind of brought it on myself, too. I like the financial independence. And living away from home has relieved so much stress that it kind of balances out." Mike summed up well the emerging adult paradox of greater stress and greater freedom:

"I would say high school was less stressful and difficult, but I'm having a hell of a lot more fun now than I was then. It was less stressful then obviously because you don't have bills to pay. Really, if you get up in the morning and somehow find your way to school and can flop a warm body in a chair, you've covered all your responsibilities for the day. Now, you're expected to perform, and the bank wants their money on the first of every month and all that good stuff. So from that standpoint I'd say yeah, it's a little more stressful. But driving nice cars is fun and going to Cancun is fun without having to say 'Mom and Dad are going to Cancun. I think I'm going to tag along with them this year,' you know. You can jump on a plane and go to Vegas if you want to. That's why it's more fun, you're not living under someone else's rules."

High Hopes in a Grim World

Despite the stresses of emerging adulthood, it is for most people a time of big dreams. When emerging adults look toward the future, they see the fulfillment of their hopes, in love and work: a lifelong, happy marriage, loving, thriving children, and satisfying and lucrative work.[23] This is, in part, because their dreams have not yet been tested by real life. In their twenties, it is still possible for emerging adults to believe that everything will work out as they have planned, because even if things are going badly now, no doors are firmly closed, and few decisions are irrevocable. Even if life is a struggle right now, their dreams may yet prevail. What Aristotle observed about the youth of his time over two millennia ago is still true: "Their lives are lived principally in hope.... They have high aspirations; for they have never yet been humiliated by the experience of life, but are unacquainted with the limiting force of circumstances."[24]

Their high hopes are evident in the national Clark poll, in which nearly 9 out of 10 of the 18–29-year-olds—89%—agreed with the statement, "I am confident that eventually I will get what I want out of life."[25] Also, despite many claims that today's young people will have a worse life than their parents have had, few emerging adults believe it. In the national Clark poll, 77% of 18–29-year-olds agreed that "I believe that, overall, my life will be better than my parents' lives have been." In my original study, the results were similar for separate questions about financial well-being, career achievements, and personal relationships.[26]

Their optimism is consistent across ethnic groups and social classes. In fact, in the national Clark poll as well as in my original study, emerging adults from lower social class backgrounds (measured by mother's education attainment) were *more* rather than less likely than their higher-SES peers to believe they would have better lives than their parents.[27]

When I asked this question in the interviews in my original study, about whether they expected that their lives would be better or worse than their parents' lives, their responses indicated that an important reason for their optimism about the future was that they expected to receive more education than their parents did. They believed their extended education would lead in turn to a better life, occupationally and financially. I have noted several times in this book the expansion in recent decades in emerging adults' participation in higher education, and in Chapter 7 I discussed the strong relation that exists between education and future income as well as occupational success. Emerging adults may not know the statistics, but they have a strong sense of the relation between education and future success. Gary, who is working on a degree in business advertising, said, "My father, the only thing he had was a high school education. He never went to college. And he worked his way up from the bottom. I mean, completely got his hands dirty and worked his way all the way up—took him 30 years to do it. Me, I don't see myself being where he's at in 30 years. I'm going to do a lot better than my parents, 'cause I'm only going upwards." Lance, who was about to complete a degree in history and government, said he expected his life would be "definitely better" than his parents' lives had been, because "my dad only graduated from 8th grade." Due to Lance's college degree, he anticipated that his life would be "much better educationally and financially, both."

The rise in participation in higher education has been especially striking for young women, and many of them are aware of how their opportunities in the wake of the Women's Movement are much greater compared to women of the past. Becky, who is working on a graduate degree in biology, said her life would be better than her parents' lives because "attitudes have changed. Women are given much more respect and are given more opportunities as far as having a career." Amelia, a marine scientist, reflected, "I think for me, being a woman, I've definitely grown up with a lot more opportunities than my mom ever did."

Educational attainment is higher among Asian Americans than in any other ethnic group in American society,[28] a reflection of the high value placed on education in Asian cultures.[29] In my original study, many Asian American emerging adults spoke of how their parents had been motivated to immigrate to the United States primarily because of the educational opportunities that would be available to their children. Consequently, Asian American emerging adults were especially aware of the importance of education as the foundation for happiness and success in adulthood.[30] Sylvia, a Chinese American who had just finished her degree in nursing, said her life would be better than her parents "because we were able to have a really good education here. In Hong Kong there's only one college, and you have to be really smart and really rich to enter." Vanessa, working on a master's degree in teaching English as a second language, said that for her parents "it was very, very difficult for them to get education" in Taiwan, their home country. For her, however, "I've got a chance to receive more education than my mom and my dad did, which is very important. Now I'll have more chances to reach a higher level later on in my life—my job, my career, my family—everything."

Korena spoke of her Chinese father, who "started working when he was 10. He never had a chance to go to school, even though he likes to go to school and he likes to learn a lot." In contrast to his experience, "I have my chance, and I've got my bachelor's degree and I have every possible criteria to pursue my Ph.D. So of course my life will be better than theirs." Korena and other emerging adults have an intuitive sense that is supported by a vast body of research, that having more education makes a "good life" more likely in a wide variety of ways, not just future income but everything from lower divorce rates to lower rates of substance abuse to higher life expectancy.[31]

In addition to anticipating more education and higher incomes than their parents, emerging adults also expect their personal relationships to be better. None of those whose parents divorced expects to repeat that debacle themselves. For example, Mason, in talking about how he expects his life to be better than his parents' lives, said, "I don't think about it so much financially, I think about it more from a personal standpoint. The fact that they got divorced, I consider that as not being successful and therefore I obviously hope that does not happen to me. So in that respect, I expect it to be better." Even those whose parents have stayed married often expect to exceed their parents' personal happiness because they expect the quality of their marriage relationship to be higher. Mindy said her life would be better because "I think definitely that my relationship with my husband is a lot closer than my mom and dad's and I think we have something stronger in that we're friends. My mom and dad, they're starting to be friends, but I don't think they were before. We have higher expectations of what we want out of marriage."

Even many emerging adults with parents who have had considerable financial and career success believe their lives will be better because they will have better personal relationships. Bruce was a singer in a struggling rock band and his father was a prominent biology professor at a major university, but Bruce thought his life would be better because "[t]he things that I'm looking for in life aren't going to come with a bunch of money and a big house. I don't think I'll make as much money as him, but I don't need as much either." Bruce's observation is a useful warning that it is mistake to define a "better" life strictly in terms of economic success, as studies on this topic often do.

Many emerging adults believe their lives will be better because they will strike a better balance between work and family. Cliff said, "I'm going to make time in the future to spend with family and coach Little League and that type of thing that my parents didn't do, and if that means I'm financially less set for life, then I'll drive a truck rather than a BMW. Fine. So what? I'll make that trade." Barry said, "I'm not sure I'll make that much more money than they will, but I'm not going to have to work the grueling job day in and day out like they had to." These comments suggest that surveys indicating that emerging adults place a high value on making money may be misleading.[32] Yes, they would like to make a lot of money, but many of them are unwilling to sacrifice happiness in their personal lives in order to do so.

Some of them mentioned their parents' early entry into marriage and parenthood as a disadvantage they will not have. Rita said she expected to be "better off financially, because they had like four kids in their twenties and neither one of them had great jobs. They were always struggling." Ariel said, "I think mine will be better, just because they got married right out of college, they had kids. I guess the way I think it will be better is just because I will hope to have done the things that I want to do, and they didn't have the opportunity because they got married and had kids." Sam thought his life would be better because "Dad and Mom got a real early start. My mom was 16 when she had my sister, and they went through hell for a real long period."

Even many emerging adults whose current lives seem unpromising believe that things will work out well for them in the long run. Bob has no current love partner and says "I hate my job!" yet he expects that his life will surpass his parents' lives. "Better economically. Better personally. I just think by the time my parents reached my age, they'd already run into some barricades that prevented them from getting what they wanted, personally and family-wise. And so far, I've avoided those things, and I don't really see those things in my life. I don't like my job. I'm frustrated about the lack of relationships with females. But in general, I think I'm headed in the right direction."

Although emerging adults believe their personal futures hold great promise, they are much less sanguine about the prospects for the world more generally. On the contrary, they believe the world is full of perils and the future of their country and their generation is grim.[33] Their concerns are various, but the most common issues they mention pertain to crime, the environment, and the economy. Ariel said, "It seems like the world just isn't as safe a place anymore. There's more violence on TV, and everywhere you go, it's there. People are more on guard much of the time."[34] In Millie's view, "There's so many things going on in the world that are so horrible now that haven't always been going on, from the ozone layer, to overcrowding, to AIDS and hunger and poverty, all those things."

For the most part, however, emerging adults believe in the promise of their personal future even as they are pessimistic about the future of the rest of the world. Jared, considering the state of the world, concludes that "[i]t's a big mess." But for himself personally, "I just try to deal with my little circle right in town here, and I'm having the time of my life, to tell you the truth, as far as the people, the friends I have and stuff, and I just love it." Even amid the world's problems, emerging adults persist in believing they will be able to carve out some measure of happiness for themselves and those they love.

Conclusion: Adulthood at Last, Ready or Not

We have seen in this chapter that the feeling of being in-between is a common part of being an emerging adult. Entering adulthood is no longer as definite and clear-cut as getting married. On the contrary, the road to young adulthood is circuitous, and the end of it usually does not come until the late twenties. Young people reach adulthood not because of a single event, but as a consequence of the gradual process of becoming self-sufficient and learning to stand alone. As they gradually take responsibility for themselves, make independent decisions, and pay their own way through life, the feeling grows in them that they have become adults.

However, they view this achievement with mixed emotions. The independence of emerging adulthood is welcome, and they take pride in being able to take care of themselves without relying on their parents' assistance. Nevertheless, the responsibilities of adulthood can be onerous and stressful, and emerging adults sometimes look back with nostalgia on a childhood and adolescence that seem easier in some ways than their lives now. Claims that most emerging adults experience a "quarterlife crisis"[35] in their twenties may be exaggerated; life satisfaction and well-being go up from adolescence to emerging adulthood, for most people. But even if it is not exactly a "crisis," emerging adulthood is experienced as a time of new and not always welcome responsibilities, a time of not just exhilarating independence and exploration but stress and anxiety as well.

Despite the difficulties that come along with managing their own lives, most emerging adults look forward to a future they believe is filled with promise. Whether their lives now are moving along nicely or appear to be going nowhere, they almost unanimously believe that eventually they will be able to create for themselves the kind of life they want. They will find their soul mate, or at least a loving and compatible marriage partner. They will find that dream job, or at least a job that will be enjoyable and meaningful.

Eventually this happy vision of the future will be tested against reality, and for many of them the result will be a jarring collision that will force them to readjust their expectations. But during emerging adulthood everything still seems possible. Nearly everyone still believes their dreams will prevail, whatever perils the world may hold for others.

Are they too optimistic? Oh yes, at least from the perspective of their elders, who know all too well the likely fate of youthful dreams. Yet is important to understand their optimism as a source of strength, as a psychological resource they will need to draw upon during a stage of life that is often difficult. Given their high expectations for life, they are almost certain to fall short, but it is their self-belief that allows them to get up again after they have been knocked down, even multiple times. They may be optimistic, but the belief that they will ultimately succeed in their pursuit of happiness gives them the confidence and energy to make it through the stresses and uncertainty of the emerging adult years.

NOTES

Preface to the Second Edition

1. Arnett (2000a).
2. Arnett (2000a), p. 477.
3. Arnett & Tanner (2006).
4. Arnett (2011).
5. Arnett, Kloep, Hendry, & Tanner (2011).
6. E.g., Arnett (2013); Arnett, Trzesniewski, & Donnellan (2013).
7. Most of the data from my research in Denmark and Italy remains unpublished, but I have begun to develop papers from the Danish research.
8. Arnett & Fishel (2014).
9. I addressed this explicitly in Arnett (2000a), in a section entitled "Why the Forgotten Half Remains Forgotten."

Chapter 1

1. US Decennial Census 1890–2012 (summarized in Stritof & Stritof, 2014). By 2013, the median marriage ages had risen still further, to 26.6 for women and 29.0 for men.
2. As Chapter 5 will show in detail, the median age of first birth for women is now lower than their median marriage age, because so many births take place outside marriage.
3. McGill & Bell (2013).
4. This figure is adapted from McGill & Bell (2013). I estimated their data from their figure for manufacturing, and for the services part of the figure I summed the following estimates from their figure: financial, real estate, professional and business, education, health, food and lodging, and information. Some estimates of the service proportion of the current economy are even higher (*Economist*, 2013). It depends on what is classified as "service." However, all estimates agree that manufacturing

employment has slid steadily since 1950 and that services have grown to dominate the economy.

5. This figure combines data from Arnett & Taber (1994) and National Center for Education Statistics (2013). The data pre- and post-1975 are not strictly comparable; before 1975, the data indicate the percentage of 18–21-year-olds attending college during the year indicated (from Arnett & Taber, 1994), whereas the data after 1975 indicate the percentage of high school graduates enrolling in college in the year following high school (from NCES, 2013). However, the figure provides an overall portrait of the historical trend over the past century.

6. Regnerus & Uecker (2009).

7. Modell (1989); Silva (2013).

8. National Center for Education Statistics (2013).

9. Modell (1989). There are no statistical data to confirm this, but this is the conclusion Modell draws on the basis of his insightful historical analysis.

10. Arnett (2011).

11. Kett (1977). In 1890, when the first US Decennial Census took place, the median marriage age was 26.1 for men and 22.0 for women. Then it declined steadily over the next 70 years, before turning upward in 1960 and ever since.

12. Silva (2013).

13. There are some scholars who argue that life stages can only be universal and biologically-based, but I disagree. For a full discussion of this issue, see Arnett et al. (2011).

14. See Arnett (2011) for a full analysis of the cultural basis of emerging adulthood, including variations in cultural patterns.

15. Erikson (1950).

16. Erikson (1968, p. 150).

17. Schwartz et al. (2015).

18. Furman et al. (1999).

19. Shulman & Connolly (2013).

20. Staff et al. (2009).

21. Ravert (2009).

22. The idea about Plan with a capital "P" is based on an essay by Elizabeth Greenspan (2000).

23. Goldscheider & Goldscheider (1999). This book is a bit dated by now, but it remains the best, most detailed work on when and why young Americans leave home.

24. Arnett & Schwab (2013); Goldscheider & Goldscheider (1999).

25. Martin et al. (2013); Stritof & Stritof (2014); US Bureau of the Census (2014).

26. Yates (2005).

27. There has been a remarkable consistency in studies on criteria for adulthood, across countries, including Argentina (Facio & Micocci, 2003), Czech Republic

(Macek et al., 2007), Romania (Nelson, 2009), Austria (Sirsch et al., 2009), the United Kingdom (Horowitz and Bromnick, 2007), Israel (Mayseless & Scharf, 2003), China (Nelson et al., 2004), and several cultures within the United States (Arnett, 2003; Nelson, 2003). See Nelson & Luster (2014) for a summary.

28. Reifman, Colwell, & Arnett (2007). I was a co-author on the paper that first presented the IDEA, but it was mainly Reifman's work.

29. E.g., Allem et al. (2013); Luyckx et al. (2011); Sirsch et al. (2009).

30. Arnett & Walker (2014); Arnett & Schwab (2012).

31. Arnett & Walker (2014).

32. Arnett & Walker (2014).

33. Bynner (2005); Silva (2013).

34. Arnett, Tanner, Kloep, & Hendry (2011).

35. Arnett & Walker (2014). SES was assessed by mother's educational attainment, the typical proxy for SES in social science studies.

36. Arnett & Schwab (2014). Agreement was higher among the adults aged 30–65 than I expected it to be. How can adults at those ages believe that "anything is possible," for example, when most of them are married, have kids, and have stable long-term jobs? This is certainly worth exploring further in interview studies.

37. Zhong & Arnett (2014).

38. Douglass (2007).

39. Most of the limitations of "young adulthood" also apply to "early adulthood," which is also sometimes used.

40. E.g., Hogan & Astone (1986); Shanahan et al. (2005).

41. The use of "youth" for the post-adolescent life stage is perhaps most closely associated with the scholarship of Kenneth Keniston (1971). Keniston is worth reading, but there are a number of problems with his conception of "youth." First, he wrote at a time when American society and some Western European societies were convulsed with highly visible "youth movements" protesting US involvement in the Vietnam War (among other things). His description of youth as a time of "tension between self and society" and "refusal of socialization" reflects that historical moment rather than any enduring characteristics of the period. Although Keniston's observations contain many insights into the young people of his time, his choice of the ambiguous and confusing term "youth" may explain in part why the idea of the late teens and twenties as a separate period of life never became widely accepted by scholars after his articulation of it.

42. See Arnett (2011) for an extensive discussion of the cultural context of emerging adulthood.

43. See Arnett (2002) for a discussion of globalization in relation to emerging adulthood.

44. Nelson (2003).

45. For perspectives on the darker side of emerging adulthood, including the limitations imposed by social class, see Silva (2013) and Smith (2011).

46. Arnett (2011).

47. Arnett (2002, 2011).

48. In the total sample there were 157 Whites, 56 African Americans, 48 Asian Americans, and 43 Latinos. I also drew upon my college students (mostly ages 18–23) at the University of Missouri, where I taught from 1992 to 1998, and the University of Maryland, where I was a visiting professor from 1998 to 2005.

49. Arnett & Schwab (2012, 2013, 2014). For more information on the Clark polls, see http://www.clarku.edu/clark-poll-emerging-adults/

50. All names have been changed to protect the anonymity of the participants.

Chapter 3

1. Arnett & Schwab (2012). In the Clark parents poll, an identical 55% of parents reported contact with their 18–29-year-old kids every day or almost every day (Arnett & Schwab, 2013).

2. Arnett & Fishel (2013). Karen Fingerman and her colleagues examined data from the American Changing Lives survey of adults in the United States that asked about contact with grown children, in person, by phone, or by mail in 1986, 1989, and in 1994 (Fingerman, Cheng, Tighe, et al., 2012). When they compared these rates of contact to data collected in 2008, they found a linear increase in contact among emerging adults ages 18–25 and their parents from the mid-1980s to the twenty-first century.

3. Prensky (2010).

4. Arnett & Schwab (2013).

5. The emerging adults' preferences here are based on parents' reports.

6. Arnett & Schwab (2012).

7. Arnett & Schwab (2013).

8. Arnett & Schwab (2013).

9. Arnett & Schwab (2012).

10. Goldscheider & Goldscheider (1999). Their book is a bit dated by now, but it remains the most thorough and extensive examination of when and why young Americans leave home.

11. Arnett & Schwab (2012).

12. Unpublished data; I conducted this analysis for the book.

13. Dubas & Petersen (1996).

14. Unpublished data, analyzed for this book. Seventy-eight percent of parents whose 18–29-year-old son or daughter lived outside the home described their relationship as "mostly positive," but it should be noted that even when kids were at home, most parents described the relationship as "mostly positive" (71%). Parents

with emerging adults (EAs) at home were also more likely to report that a change since the child was age 15 was that there was "more conflict" now (21% to 12%) and less likely to report that a change since age 15 was that "we enjoy our time together more" (82% to 69%). Again, relations tend to be positive whether the EA is living at home or not, but they tend to be *more* positive if the EA has moved out.

15. For an excellent account of both current and historical patterns of leaving home, see Goldscheider & Goldscheider (1999). Most of the information in this section is from this source.

16. Goldscheider & Goldscheider (1999).

17. Arnett & Schwab (2013).

18. All this information is from the Clark parents poll (Arnett & Schwab, 2013). Asnot Dor (2013) reported a similar blend of Israeli parents' reactions to their emerging adults living at home, mostly positive but in some ways negative.

19. Goldscheider & Goldscheider (1999).

20. Recent statistics on moving back home are difficult to find. Goldscheider & Goldscheider (1999) reported a figure of 40% in the late 1990s. Since then, data have usually been reported as the percent of young people living with their parents, which includes those who moved back home as well as those who never left. According to national data reported by the Pew Research Center, 56% of 18–24-year-olds lived with their parents in 2012; by age 25–31, the proportion fell to just 16% (Fry, 2013). That Pew report also shows a modest rise in the percent of 18–24-year-olds living at home in recent years, from 51% in 2007 to 56% in 2012. So, it can be estimated that the percent who have moved back home has risen since the Goldscheiders reported 40% in the late 1990s to "just over 40%," as I state here, but this should be understood to be a rough estimate.

21. Goldscheider & Goldscheider (1999).

22. Arnett & Schwab (2013). The rest described it as "equally positive and negative."

23. Arnett & Fishel (2013).

24. Age 23 for men and age 21 for women; Silbereisen, Meschke, & Schwarz (1996). See Fingerman & Yahirun (2015) for a summary of European variations in the timing of leaving home.

25. Chisholm & Hurrelmann (1995).

26. Goldscheider & Goldscheider (1999).

27. Côté (2000).

28. See the excellent ethnographic volume edited by Carrie Douglass (2005) on emerging adults in Europe, especially her own fine work on Spanish EAs.

29. Like the statistic for moving back home, a recent statistic for staying home is difficult to find, because this statistic tends to be reported as the percent of young people living at home, which includes both those who stayed at home and those who moved back home after a period outside the household (Fry, 2013; Payne, 2012).

Keep in mind, too, that the percent living at home usually includes 18-year-olds, many of whom have not even graduated from high school.

30. Payne (2012).

31. Parker (2012); Payne (2012).

32. Britton (2013); Goldscheider & Goldscheider (1999).

33. Many studies have shown higher interdependence and collectivistic values among American minority cultures, e.g., Fuligni & Tseng (1999); Xia, Ko, & Xie (2013).

34. Goldscheider & Goldscheider (1999).

35. Goldscheider & Goldscheider (1999).

36. Collins & Laursen (2006); Van Doorn et al. (2011).

37. Larson & Richards (1994); Richards et al. (2002).

38. Arnett & Fishel (2013).

39. Taylor & Keeter (2010).

40. Taylor & Keeter (2010).

41. Arnett & Schwab (2013).

42. Segrin et al. (2012).

43. Lipka (2007).

44. Fingerman & Yahirun (2015).

45. Fingerman et al. (2012).

46. Arnett & Schwab (2013). Parker (2012) reported similar findings.

47. Arnett & Schwab (2013).

48. Arnett & Fishel (2013).

49. Arnett & Fishel (2013). Fingerman & Yahirun (2015) summarize numerous other studies showing that parents' financial support of their grown children has risen in recent decades.

50. Arnett & Schwab (2013).

51. Arnett & Schwab (2013).

52. Amato (2007).

53. For an example of how vehement scholars can be on opposite sides of this issue, see the exchange between David Demo (1993) and Paul Amato (1993). One especially valuable approach is an original and insightful attempt to reconcile the opposing sides of the debate. Laumann-Billings and Emery (2000) noted that research on divorce typically focuses on disorders of behavior—how divorce affects functioning in school or work, for example—whereas clinical case studies typically focus on the distress that results from divorce—how divorce feels to those affected by it. In two studies of emerging adults, one with college students and one with a low-income community sample, they found that emerging adults often reported painful feelings, beliefs, and memories concerning the divorce, even if in their behavior they seemed to have recovered from it. So, it may be that both sides are right—children usually recover from divorce in most respects by the time

they become emerging adults, but the pain associated with divorce endures through emerging adulthood.

54. Lasch (1979).

55. Larson & Richards (1994, p. 164).

56. Hetherington & Kelly (2002).

57. Amato & Dorius (2010).

58. See Wallerstein, Lewis, & Blakeslee (2000) for qualitative descriptions of the anger and anguish that often result from divorce.

59. Amato & Dorius (2010). The effects are stronger for fathers, but relationships with mothers are affected as well. For example, O'Connor and colleagues (1996) found that emerging adults whose parents have divorced have less positive relationships with both mothers and fathers, with regard to closeness and frequency of contact.

60. Schwartz & Mare (2012). Men are somewhat more likely than women to remarry.

61. Jeynes (2007).

62. Jeynes (2007). For example, Hetherington and Kelly (2002) report that only 20% of emerging adults feel close to their stepmothers.

63. Moore & Cartwright (2005).

Chapter 4

1. Bailey (1989).

2. Brumberg (1997).

3. Bailey (1989).

4. Arnett & Taber (1994).

5. Dreyer (1982).

6. Hatfield & Rapson (2006).

7. See Chapter 1, Figure 1.1.

8. Popenoe & Whitehead (2001) reported that in their focus group interviews of 20–29-year-olds "all the women and almost all the men expected to marry and stay in their first marriages" (p. 9). According to Regnerus & Uecker (2009), across studies, 93%–96% of unmarried young Americans say they want to get married eventually.

9. Popenoe & Whitehead (2002).

10. Popenoe & Whitehead (2002).

11. Rosenfeld & Thomas (2012).

12. See Finkel et al. (2012) for an excellent summary of research on this topic.

13. In the focus group interviews with young men conducted by Popenoe & Whitehead (2002), among those who had tried Internet dating services "several commented that deception and misrepresentation were commonplace" (p. 9). In the

comprehensive review of research on Internet dating sites by Finkel et al. (2012), the authors concluded that there is no evidence that these sites increase the prospects for success in romantic partnerships, despite the sites' over-hyped claims of their "scientific" matching principles. The only value these companies can legitimately claim is that they connect people with potential partners they would not meet otherwise.

14. In a 35-year review of the literature, Eaton and Rose (2011) concluded that the dominant "dating script" still requires men to be the initiators, but women initiate more now than in the past.

15. Eaton & Rose (2011). On the basis of focus group interviews with young men ages 25–33, Popenoe & Whitehead (2002) reported that most believe it is best to become friends with a potential romantic partner and get to know each other by hanging out together before dating.

16. Berscheid (2006).

17. Furman & Simon (2008); Laursen & Jensen-Campbell (1999).

18. Michael et al. (1995). It is notable that, according to national survey data, most young people ages 20–29 do *not* see similarities as the key to lasting love; most believe similarities in areas such as religious beliefs are unimportant (Popenoe & Whitehead, 2001; Whitehead & Popenoe, 2002). Instead, they believe that lasting love is based on an intangible personality match with a "soul mate." Nevertheless, they tend to choose partners who are similar to themselves.

19. *Homophily* is another term for this, commonly used in the literature (e.g., Furman & Simon, 2008), but I think *consensual validation* is a better descriptor of what happens when people choose partners who are similar to themselves.

20. The information in this paragraph is from the 2012 report by the Pew Research Center (Wang, 2012).

21. Wang (2012).

22. The quote by John Updike is from Michael et al. (1995, p. 57).

23. Regnerus & Uecker (2009); Whitehead & Popenoe (2002).

24. A lot of the information in this section is from *Premarital Sex in America* by Mark Regnerus and Jeremy Uecker (2009), which I strongly recommend.

25. Regnerus & Uecker (2009).

26. Michael et al. (1995); Willoughby (2009).

27. Regnerus & Uecker (2009). These statistics, and a lot of other information in *Premarital Sex in America,* are from the Add Health study, which followed a large national sample of Americans from grade 7–12 through ages 24–32. So far, most of the published findings on these data, including in the Regnerus & Uecker (2009) book, go only through the 18–23-year-old period.

28. Halpern-Meekin et al. (2013)

29. Regnerus & Uecker (2009).

30. Claxton & van Dulmen (2014).

31. Bisson & Levine (2009).

32. Popenoe & Whitehead (2001).

33. Arnett & Schwab (2012).

34. Regnerus & Uecker (2009).

35. Centers for Disease Control and Prevention (CDC) (2013a). This is not a perfect statistic, as it includes 15–44-year-old men and women (there was no gender difference). It would be better to ask 25–29-year-olds, because few of them would be virgins but they would all be part of the same cohort. In contrast, for 15–44-year-olds, the 30–44-year-olds really grew up in a different cohort than the 15–29-year-olds.

36. Michael et al. (1995).

37. Zimmer-Gembeck & Helfand (2008).

38. Regnerus (2007).

39. Regnerus (2007).

40. Schlegel & Barry (1991).

41. Regnerus & Uecker (2009).

42. Kaye et al. (2009); Regnerus & Uecker (2009).

43. McKay & Barrett (2010); UNdata (2014). Rates of nonmarital births are also relatively high in Scandinavian countries, but these births usually take place in the context of a long-term cohabiting relationship. Increasingly, this is the case in the United States as well, as will be described in detail in the next chapter. As we will also see in the next chapter, whether nonmarital births are "unintended" is not a simple issue. Abortion rates are a better indicator of unintended pregnancies. The gap between the United States and other developed countries is not as large as it was 20 years ago, as US rates have declined steadily during that period.

44. Hatfield & Rapson (2006).

45. Regnerus (2007).

46. As noted previously, Regnerus & Uecker (2009) reported that 55% of American adults believe that sex is OK between two 18-year-olds, whereas only 15% give the OK to sex between 16-year-olds.

47. Regnerus & Uecker (2009). Also see Lefkowitz and Gillen (2006) for an insightful summary of how emerging adults view sex in their relationships.

48. Abma, Martinez, & Copen (2010). Unfortunately, good pre-HIV contraceptive use data are not available for emerging adults. The focus of most research on contraceptive use and nonuse has long been on 15–19-year-olds, even though women in their twenties now have much higher rates of single motherhood.

49. Lewis, Miquez-Burban, & Malow (2009) provide a recent review, and find little change in college students' HIV risk behavior since their previous review in 1997.

50. Civic (1999); Lefkowitz & Gillen (2006); Regnerus & Uecker (2009).

51. Centers for Disease Control and Prevention (CDC) (2013b).

52. Centers for Disease Control and Prevention (CDC) (2013b).

53. Eisenberg et al. (2011).

54. Centers for Disease Control and Prevention (CDC) (2013c).

55. Most public health authorities now recommend that girls receive the HPV vaccine when they are 11–12 years old. However, it is not clear that people who receive the vaccine at age 11 or 12 would still be protected by their early 20s, when they are most likely to be sexually active with a series of partners. The value of the vaccine is much clearer for women in developing countries, who are unlikely to receive Pap tests that could detect and treat precancerous cells that may otherwise develop into cervical cancer.

56. Miracle, Miracle, & Baumeister (2003).

57. Carroll & Wolpe (1996).

58. Michael et al. (1995).

59. Carroll et al. (2008).

60. Regnerus & Uecker (2009).

61. Centers for Disease Control (CDC) (2013d).

62. Regnerus & Uecker (2009).

63. Döring (2009).

64. Regnerus & Uecker (2009).

65. Pinker (2011).

66. Kosciw et al. (2012).

67. Washington Post (2013).

68. Heatherington & Lavner (2008)

69. Regnerus & Uecker (2009). The proportion who identified as bisexual was 5% for women and 2% for men.

70. Savin-Williams (2006).

71. Heatherington & Lavner (2008).

72. Goldberg (2010).

Chapter 5

1. Cohn et al. (2011). The 80% married by age 40 is lower than the 90% figure that applied though the twentieth century, but another 5%–10% are in long-term cohabiting relationships, so the total who have experienced a long-term union remains close to 90%.

2. Shulman & Connolly (2013).

3. Gonzaga et al. (2010).

4. Putnam (2001).

5. In a national survey (Popenoe & Whitehead, 2001), only 42% of 20–29-year-olds responded that it is important to them to find a spouse who shares their religion. But this is a little misleading. Those who are among that 42% are no

doubt the ones for whom their religious faith is most important. So, another way to put it would be to say that virtually everyone for whom religious faith is of high importance looks for a spouse who shares their beliefs.

6. Popenoe & Whitehead (2001).

7. Popenoe & Whitehead (2001).

8. Cherlin (2009, p. 71).

9. Bernice Neugarten and her colleagues examined the view of the "best age" for a variety of life transitions, including marriage, in the early 1960s (Neugarten, Moore, & Lowe, 1965) and again in the late 1970s (Neugarten & Datan, 1982). In the early 1960s a strong majority viewed the early twenties as the "best age" to marry, but by the late 1970s there was no consensus—less than half viewed any particular age period as a "best age." This study has not been conducted more recently, but I would predict that Americans would be even less likely now to endorse a "best age" for marriage than they were in the late 1970s.

10. Popenoe & Whitehead (2001); Whitehead & Popenoe (2002).

11. Erikson (1950; 1968).

12. Cohn et al. (2011).

13. Hymowitz et al. (2013); Regnerus & Uecker (2009).

14. According to a 2012 survey of college women, 85% want to be married by age 30 (Hussar, 2012). Of course, college women do not represent all female emerging adults, and the survey did not include men, but this finding accords with what I have found in my original interviews with a broader sample.

15. Xia et al. (2013).

16. Regnerus & Uecker (2009).

17. Popenoe & Whitehead (2002).

18. Figure 5.1 is based on Michael et al. (1995), Manning & Cohen (2011), and Hymowitz et al. (2013).

19. National Marriage Project (2012).

20. Hymowitz et al. (2013).

21. Cherlin (2009).

22. National Marriage Project (2012).

23. The distinction between premarital and uncommitted cohabitation (by various terms) has been made frequently in research on cohabitation (e.g., Manning & Cohen, 2011), but committed cohabitation is rarely discussed by American researchers because it is rare in the United States.

24. Popenoe & Whitehead (2001).

25. Popenoe & Whitehead (2001).

26. Manning & Cohen (2011).

27. Hymowitz et al. (2013).

28. Perelli-Harris et al. (2010).

29. Kiernan (2002).

30. Hymowitz et al. (2013); Waite & Gallagher (2000). However, for an excellent critique of the claim that marriage confers a wide range of benefits, see DePaulo (2006). I find DePaulo's critique convincing, but I think there is substantial evidence that marriage results in positive changes, although the benefits may not be as large as the proponents claim.

31. Arnett & Schwab (2012).

32. For an insightful qualitative investigation of gender differences in views of cohabitation, see Huang et al. (2011).

33. Huang et al. (2011). Whitehead & Popenoe (2002), in their focus group interviews with single 20–29-year-olds, also found parental disapproval of cohabitation.

34. This statistic, and much of the other material in this section, is drawn from an excellent report by the National Marriage Project, *Knot Yet: The Benefits and Costs of Delayed Marriage* (Hymowitz et al., 2013).

35. Hymowitz et al. (2013, p. 11).

36. Hymowitz et al. (2013).

37. Hymowitz et al. (2013).

38. Kaye, Suellentrop, & Sloup (2009).

39. Hymowitz et al. (2013).

40. E.g., Edin & Kefalas (2005).

41. Kaye et al. (2009).

42. Douglass (2005). Europe is diverse, however. Premarital sex is much more accepted in the north than in the south, and least accepted of all in Ireland.

43. Regnerus (2007).

44. Kirby (2008); Kirby & Laris (2009).

45. Kaye et al. (2009).

46. Hymowitz et al. (2013).

47. Hymowitz et al. (2013).

48. Edin & Kefalas (2005).

49. Cherlin (2009).

50. Cherlin (2009).

51. As noted, emerging adults justify cohabitation as a strategy for preventing divorce.

52. Hymowitz et al. (2013).

53. Hymowitz et al. (2013). Cherlin (2009) notes that sociologist Barbara Defoe Whitehead observes that Americans believe not only in the ideal of marriage but in what she calls the "expressive divorce," that is, they believe that two people should not stay married if they are not making each other happy.

Chapter 6

1. See Pascarella & Terenzini (2005) for a comprehensive review and analysis. Most research has taken place on students at four-year schools, but the limited research on community colleges shows similar results (Belfield & Bailey, 2011).

2. Arnett & Schwab (2012).

3. Schneider & Stevenson (1999).

4. National Center for Education Statistics (NCES) (2013).

5. NCES (2013). Most of the material in this chapter applies better to students in four-year colleges, whom I know better and on whom there is more research.

6. NCES (2014).

7. Arnett (2013); UNESCO (2013).

8. NCES (2013).

9. Shernoff & Csikszentmihalyi (2009).

10. UNESCO (2013).

11. In some countries, "college" is a term reserved for two-year schools, whereas "university" means four-year schools. Here I follow the American usage, in which "college" and "university" are used interchangeably.

12. NCES (2013).

13. According to Csikszentmihalyi & Schneider (2000), most students entering college have a narrow range of professions in mind—doctor, lawyer, engineer, maybe athlete or musician if they are especially fortunate. But these vague dreams bear little relation to the jobs that most of them will end up having.

14. NCES (2013).

15. Belfield & Bailey (2011).

16. Sperber (2000).

17. Johnston et al. (2012).

18. This is actually a complicated issue, far more so than the "College Costs Rise Again" headlines would suggest. Yes, college costs have risen faster than inflation in recent decades, and states have generally cut their funding for public universities. However, federal support and colleges' own aid programs have compensated substantially for the rising tuition costs, and students (and their families) rarely pay the advertised "sticker price." Also, costs vary enormously depending on whether the school is a private or public university and whether it is a two-year or four-year school. Two-year community colleges remain remarkably inexpensive. For an excellent analysis, see the annual summary by the College Board (2012).

19. Arnett & Schwab (2012).

20. According to the most recent figures, about 60% of full-time students take out student loans, and of those who take out loans, the average student has accumulated about $27,000 in college debt by graduation (College Board, 2012).

21. Hoxby & Turner (2013). In response to these studies, the College Board has launched a new initiative to reach these students and inform them and their families of opportunities for college scholarships (Leonhardt, 2013).

22. NCES (2013).

23. NCES (2013).

24. Levine & Cureton (1998). This is over a decade old by now, but it seems likely that, if anything, these proportions have gone up since 1998, given the steadily increasing rewards for obtaining tertiary education.

25. NCES (2013). This is not a perfect statistic, because the population of the United States has also increased substantially since 1970. Nevertheless, the increase is impressive, especially for females.

26. Hamilton (1994).

27. Schneider & Stevenson (1999).

28. Clark & Trow (1966).

29. Sperber (2000).

30. Higher Education Research Institute (2011).

31. Core Institute (2013).

32. Pryor et al. (2007); Pryor et al. (2008).

33. For example, Peter Thiel, a billionaire businessman, founded the Thiel Fellowship program to pay students under 20 years old to skip college and pursue their own entrepreneurial ventures. Thiel has claimed that students have been "conned" into thinking they need a college degree and that going to college makes them "worse off" because they graduate with large amounts of debt. But this only shows how ignorant a billionaire can be, as the next section of this chapter demonstrates.

34. Estimates vary from about half a million to a million and a half dollars over a lifetime. There are differences among majors, too, with engineering, computer science, and mathematics majors earning the most and liberal arts, communications, and journalism majors making the least. For more information, see the website of the Georgetown University Center on Education and the Workforce, especially the 2011 report by Carnevale, Jayasundera, & Cheah (2011).

35. Pew Research Center (2011).

36. Levine & Dean (2012). Levine and Cureton (1998) did previous surveys in 1969, 1976, and 1998, and the results over time show a study rise in student satisfaction.

37. Sperber (2000).

38. The responses here are from my students at the University of Maryland during 1999–2004. They are not representative of all American students, obviously, but I

quote them here because their responses fit remarkably well with the research findings I describe next.

39. See Marcia Baxter Magolda (2009) on the college experience as promoting *self-authorship*.

40. Pascarella & Terenzini (2005).

41. Pascarella and Terenzini summarize a massive amount of other research in their 2005 book.

42. Dennis (2012).

43. Bean (2011).

44. Precise rates on gap year prevalence are hard to come by, in any country. One Australian report estimates a 20% rate (Curtis et al., 2012).

45. Jones (2004).

46. I interviewed Danish emerging adults in 2005–2006. The data on their gap year experiences are unpublished.

47. In the nineteenth century there was an ideal, especially in Germany, of young men having a *wanderschaft* (also sometimes called a *wanderjahre* or *wandervogel*), that is, a period in their late teens or early twenties that would be devoted to travel and self-exploration before settling into adult commitments. Similarly, in Britain many upper-class young men had a "continental tour" or "grand tour" of Europe before entering long-term adult roles. These ideas are similar in some ways to today's gap year, but they were only for the elite, and never for young women.

48. King (2011) and others emphasize that a great deal of "identity work" goes on during the gap year, that is, gappers emphasize that taking a year before tertiary education helps them gain a better understanding of themselves and a clearer idea of what they would like to do professionally.

49. For an account of the college application process that is both enlightening and hilarious, see Ferguson (2011).

50. AmeriCorps (2012); Peace Corps (2012).

Chapter 7

1. Arnett & Schwab (2012).

2. Staff et al. (2009).

3. Staff et al. (2009).

4. Bachman & Schulenberg (1993). This finding is a couple of decades old by now, but there is the only one I know that addresses the question of where adolescents' income goes.

5. Modell (1989).

6. Gerson (2010).

7. McGill & Bell (2013); Wilson (1996).

8. Carnevale et al. (2013).

9. US Bureau of the Census (2013).

10. Lauff & Ingels (2013).

11. Schneider & Stevenson (1999).

12. Yates (2005).

13. US Department of Labor (2012). Actually, 8.5.

14. Goldberg et al. (2012).

15. Goldberg et al. (2012). Even before marriage, although they hope to find a husband who will share household work equally, young women generally expect that they will end up doing more housework and child care than their husbands do (Askari et al., 2010). Once married, young women also spend about twice as much time on household work as their husbands do—37 hours/week, compared to 18 hours/week for men (Smock & Gupta, 2000), even if both work full-time. This is what sociologist Arlie Hochschild (1990) calls "the second shift" faced by working women. However, it may be that the rising generation of emerging adult men will contribute more household work than their fathers did. They generally say they plan to be equal contributors, so we will have to see if that turns out to be true.

16. Of course, men are affected by this conflict as well, if not as widely. In Hewlett's (2002) study of highly successful business people, 42% of the women were childless, but so were 25% of the men. In the general population, the proportion is less than 10% (Marks et al., 2004).

17. Arnett & Schwab (2012).

18. Askari et al. (2010).

19. Some parents, but maybe not as many as widely believed. In the 2013 Clark Poll of Parents of Emerging Adults (Arnett & Schwab, 2013), only 16% of parents of 18–29-year-olds agreed that "expects too much out of work" was one of the "main worries or concerns" they have about their emerging adult.

20. Hamilton & Hamilton (2006). See Krahn et al. (2012) for a thoughtful comparison of "exploring" and "floundering." Using data from their 14-year longitudinal study of Canadian emerging adults, they concluded that changes of educational directions in the twenties usually signify productive exploring, whereas especially frequent job changes indicate floundering.

21. Robbins & Wilner (2000). In *Generation X*, Coupland (1991) anticipated this term, in his usual sardonic fashion, with what he called the "Mid-Twenties Breakdown" (p. 27) which he defined as "[a] period of mental collapse occurring in one's twenties, often caused by an inability to function outside of school or structured environments coupled with a realization of one's essential aloneness in the world. Often marks induction into the ritual of pharmaceutical usage." Elsewhere he calls it a "mid-twenties crisis" (p. 73).

22. Schwartz (2000).

23. Hamilton (1994); Marshall & Butler (2015).

24. It seems more likely that the Europeans will move toward the American system than vice versa. Already most European countries have added more flexibility to their system and have made it easier to change tracks, perhaps a tacit acknowledgement of emerging adults' desire to be able to explore their options and change if they wish. The US system urgently needs to provide better information and guidance to emerging adults entering the labor market, but there is no notable movement to do so.

25. Arnett & Schwab (2012).

26. Côté (2000, 2006) also proposes the compelling idea of "identity capital," meaning the self-direction and flexibility needed to succeed in a society that changes rapidly and provides little institutional guidance for finding a job.

27. Crouter & McHale (2005).

28. Daniel Levinson and his colleagues (1978), in their theory of adult development, proposed that the main developmental task of the twenties is to develop "The Dream," meaning an ideal for one's occupational future.

29. According to Csikszentmihalyi & Schneider (2000), dreams of musical or athletic stardom are also common in high school. Although I am not aware of any data comparing adolescents to emerging adults on this issue, I would predict that fewer emerging adults have such dreams, as they are more likely to have begun to find out just how difficult success in these fields can be.

30. Wilson (1996).

31. OECD (2010).

32. OECD (2010). Spain surpassed 50% youth unemployment and has been very slow to recover.

33. As populations age in developed countries, the demand for young workers may increase, as older workers leave the job market and fewer young workers are available to replace them. Japan and most European countries are expected to decline in population over the twenty-first century, due to low birth rates, so we will soon find out.

34. OECD (2010). Youth unemployment rates vary widely across Europe, depending on each country's employment policies. Denmark has become widely known for the effectiveness of its policy of "flexicurity," in which workers are relatively easy to hire and fire, but when they lose their jobs, government agencies help them find a new one and learn new skills if necessary.

35. OECD (2010).

36. Lauff & Ingels (2013).

37. OECD (2010).

38. A 2013 survey by Accenture reported that 40% of young Americans who had graduated in the past two years were underemployed, defined as working in a job that did not require their specific college degree (although it may have required a bachelor's degree of some kind). (Seehttp://www.accenture.com/us-en/

Pages/insight-2013-accenture-college-graduate-employment-survey.aspx.) Other estimates are similar. This sounds dire, and maybe it is, but keep in mind that it includes many emerging adults who are not looking for a long-term job right after college, either because they plan to obtain further education or because they are still not sure about what they want to do. In the long run, persons with a college degree are likely to do well; the concern of public policy should be focused on those who receive no tertiary education, because without it they face a lifelong struggle.

39. Hamilton & Hamilton (2006); Vazsonyi & Snider (2008).

40. Part of the problem with youth unemployment is that, even when employers need new workers, the young people who are looking for work may not have the necessary skills. One would think this would lead employers to expand their training programs, and sometimes they do, but this represents a greater investment in a young worker, and given how often they change jobs it may not pay off.

41. Erikson (1959, p. 118).

Chapter 8

1. Brown (2006); Coyne et al. (2015).

2. Prensky (2010).

3. This chapter was added for the new edition. I have written about media uses for 20 years, but did not include a chapter on media uses in the first edition of this book, mainly because I did not have good interview material on the topic in my original study. By the time I was writing this edition, it was clear to me that this topic could not be left out, as it had become so important in the lives of emerging adults.

4. Coyne et al. (2015).

5. Alloy Median & Marketing (2013).

6. Coyne et al. (2015).

7. Lonsdale & North (2011).

8. Lonsdale & North (2011).

9. Jacobsen & Forste (2011).

10. Duggan & Brenner (2013).

11. World Internet Project (2012). "Internet use" was defined broadly in this study, as *any* Internet use.

12. Marketing Charts Staff (2013). An addition 2.5 hours per week is devoted to watching TV shows or movies on the Internet or digital devices.

13. Putnam (2001).

14. Greenwood & Long (2009).

15. Mokhtari et al. (2009).

16. Robinson & Godbey (1997, p. 149).

17. Jacobsen & Forste (2011).

18. Arnett & Schwab (2012).

19. Padilla-Walker et al. (2010).

20. Gentile (2009).

21. Haridakis (2013).

22. Arnett (1996).

23. Brown (2006); Steele & Brown (1995).

24. Lonsdale & North (2011).

25. See Coyne et al. (2015) for a summary.

26. Tosun (2012).

27. Arnett & Amadeo (2002).

28. Olson et al. (2008). This was a study of adolescent boys, but we could expect emerging adults to understand this distinction even better, given their greater cognitive and personal maturity.

29. See Coyne et al. (2015) for a summary.

30. Arnett (1992).

31. Huesmann, Moise-Titus, Podolski, & Eron (2003, p. 219).

32. Taylor & Keeter (2010).

33. Governors Highway Safety Association (2014).

34. Arnett & Schwab (2012).

35. Rainie et al. (2013).

36. Associated Press (2013). By 2013, Facebook had over a billion users.

37. Arnett & Schwab (2012).

38. Turkle (2011).

39. Arnett & Schwab (2012).

40. Manago et al. (2012).

41. Jacobsen & Forste (2011).

42. This is a previously unpublished interview from the research I conducted for the book "When Will My Grown Up Kid Grow Up?" (with Elizabeth Fishel; Arnett & Fishel, 2013).

43. Gentile (2009).

44. See her website for details: http://lindastone.net/qa/continuous-partial-attention/

45. Spataro et al. (2011). However, one study found that watching TV interfered with adolescents' homework performance but listening to music did not (Pool, Koolstra, & van der Voort, 2003), so it may depend on the type of media.

46. NCES (2013).

47. Hall (1904, vol. 1, p. 361).

48. Hall (1904, vol. 1, p. 387).

49. Bailey (1989).

50. Putnam (2001).
51. Pinker (2011).
52. Flynn (2012).

Chapter 9

1. Erikson (1968) used the term "ideology," but he conceded that this term has pejorative connotations that he did not intend. "Worldview" has come into use more recently, and I think it is preferable.

2. Tillich (2001).

3. Bellah (2011).

4. Tamis-LeMonda et al. (2008).

5. See Killen & Wainryb (2000) for a discussion of individual differences in individualism and collectivism.

6. Smith (2011); Smith & Denton (2005); Smith & Snell (2010). Except where indicated, data from the NSYR in this chapter are drawn from Smith & Snell (2010).

7. The NSYR actually had six categories, with the following labels:

- Committed Traditionalists (15%);
- Selective Adherents (30%);
- Spiritually Open (15%);
- Religiously Indifferent (25%);
- Religiously Disconnected (5%);
- Irreligious (10%)

I combined the last three categories, Religiously Indifferent, Religiously Disconnected, and Irreligious, into one category of Agnostics/Atheists, because I do not think the finer distinctions that Smith & Snell make among these three categories are persuasive or helpful. I relabeled Committed Traditionalists as Conservative Believers, Selective Adherents as Liberal Believers, and Spiritually Open as Deists, because I think my categories are clearer, simpler, and make more sense.

8. As Smith & Denton (2005) observe, most emerging adults believe that "[p]eople should take and use what is helpful in [religion], what makes sense to them, what fits their experience—and they can leave the rest. [They] pick and choose what works" (p. 157).

9. Their references to the Force probably reflect the popularity of the Star Wars films at the time I was doing my original research, in the late 1990s, but it remains an interesting example of using popular culture for religious purposes.

10. Smith first identified MTD in the NSYR study of 13–17-year-olds (Smith & Denton, 2005), but has found that it applies just as well to emerging adults (Smith & Snell, 2010).

11. Smith & Snell (2010), Table 4.5, p. 112.

12. As noted in Chapter 8, Prensky (2010) is the one who created the useful distinction between *digital immigrants* and *digital natives*.

13. Smith & Snell (2010) report that a large majority (79%) of 18–23-year-olds have "a lot of respect for organized religion," whereas only a minority of emerging adults (29%) say that organized religion is "a big turn-off" for them.

14. Smith & Snell (2010). Similarly, in the Pew report on the Nones (Pew Research Center, 2012), 60% of those who reported a religious affiliation also said they "seldom" or "never" attend religious services.

15. For example, in Belgium only 8% of 18-year-olds attend religious services at least once a month (Goossens & Lucykx, 2007).

16. Responses to this question were coded by me and two colleagues. Rate of agreement was over 80%. Discrepancies were involved through discussion.

17. Hoge, Johnson, & Luidens (1993).

18. Pew Research Center (2012).

19. For details of this analysis, see Arnett & Jensen (2002).

20. Smith & Denton (2005).

21. Smith & Snell (2010).

22. As Smith and Snell (2010) observe, "The main job of emerging adults is to learn to stand on their own two feet, to become independent. The religion in which emerging adults were raised is connected with an earlier phase in their lives when they were dependent on their parents... [L]earning to stand on one's own two feet means, among other things, getting some distance from one's family's faith and religious congregation" (p.150).

23. Pew Research Center (2010).

24. Pew Research Center (2012).

25. Smith & Snell (2010).

26. Suarez-Orozco & Suarez-Orozco (1996).

27. Attending Catholic schools was common among the Asian Americans in my San Francisco sample, but I am not aware of any statistics indicating how common it is for Asian Americans nationally. I mention it here as in intriguing possibility for further study.

28. Most of the material in this section was previously presented in Arnett (2008).

29. Sixteen percent of the 18–23-year-olds in the NSYR said they believe in reincarnation (Smith & Snell, 2010, p. 123). This is higher than the percentage who mentioned it in my original study, because the NSYR mentioned it directly, whereas I recorded it only if they mentioned it at their own initiative.

30. Triandis (1995).

31. Triandis (1995). Scholars increasingly recognize that every culture is diverse, and most cultures are not "pure types" of either individualism or collectivism but have a combination of the two types of values in various proportions. Also, even a culture that is individualistic overall is likely to have some people who are more

collectivistic than individualistic, due to differences in personality, age, and other factors. For a discussion of these issues, see Killen & Wainryb (2000).

32. Smith (2011).

33. Smith (2011, p. 60).

34. Jensen (2008).

35. In my initial Missouri sample of 140, on this question 46% were coded as Autonomy alone, 19% as Community alone, and 30% combined the Ethic of Autonomy and the Ethic of Community. Small proportions (less than 10%) were coded as Divinity or as Divinity combined with other Ethics. For a detailed analysis, see Arnett, Ramos, & Jensen (2001).

36. Bellah et al. (1985); also see Jensen (1995).

37. Arnett & Schwab (2012).

38. The prevailing view among researchers on individualism and collectivism currently is that these are independent rather than opposing value systems (e.g., Tamis-Lemonda et al., 2008).

39. In my initial Missouri sample of 140, on this question 29% were coded as Autonomy alone, 28% as Community alone, and 20% combined the Ethic of Autonomy and the Ethic of Community. Small proportions (less than 10%) were coded as Divinity or as Divinity combined with other Ethics. For a detailed analysis, see Arnett, Ramos, & Jensen (2001).

Chapter 10

1. E.g., Bynner (2005); Côté & Bynner (2008); Heinz (2009). For a book-length debate on this topic, see Arnett et al. (2011).

2. Arnett (2000, pp. 476–477).

3. Information on the method and design of this survey can be found in Arnett & Schwab (2012).

4. Mother's educational attainment is a better representation of emerging adults' social class status than their own educational attainment or income, because many of them are still in the process of obtaining their education and have little or no income during these years.

5. E.g., Côté (2000); Silva (2013).

6. Hamilton & Hamilton (2006).

7. Hamilton & Hamilton (2006); Wilson (1996).

8. Edin & Kefalas (2005).

9. Kaye et al. (2009).

10. These case studies also appeared in Arnett et al. (2011).

11. Schaefer (2012).

12. ASPE Human Services Staff (2012).

13. Arnett et al. (2011).

14. Arnett (2011).

15. Schlegel & Barry (1991).

16. Larson, Wilson, & Rickman (2010).

17. Arnett (2011).

Chapter 11

1. Arnett & Schwab (2012).

2. Frick & Kimonis (2008).

3. Ollendick et al. (2008).

4. Graham & Gootman (2008).

5. Twisk & Stacey (2007).

6. Ferguson (2003).

7. Ferguson (2003).

8. Hingson & White (2010).

9. Zuckerman (2007).

10. Craig & Piquero (2015).

11. Craig & Piquero (2015).

12. Moffitt (2007); Wilson & Herrnstein (1985).

13. Pinker (2011).

14. Granic & Patterson (2006).

15. Robinson et al. (2011).

16. Arnett (2005); Zuckerman (2007).

17. Johnston et al. (2012).

18. For more results from the Core Institute, see http://www.core.siuc.edu.

19. Blanco et al. (2008).

20. Martin & Chung (2009). For example, one symptom is "Role impairment," defined as "Frequent intoxication leading to failure to fulfill major role obligations."

21. Moffitt (2007).

22. Hasin et al. (2005).

23. Oltmanns & Emery (2013).

24. Arnett & Schwab (2012).

25. Arnett & Schwab (2013).

26. Blanco et al. (2008).

27. Arnett & Schwab (2012).

28. Arnett & Schwab (2013).

29. Arnett & Schwab (2012). The correlations with anxiety were .28 for uncertainty and .13 for changes, both $p < .01$.

30. Arnett & Schwab (2012). It should be noted that there were negative correlations between anxiety and satisfaction (–.12) and between anxiety and "fun and exciting"

(–.09). There were also negative correlations between depression and satisfaction (–.27) and between depression and "fun and exciting" (–.47). All these correlations were *p* <.01.

31. Lask & Frampton (2011).

32. Hudson et al. (2007).

33. Smink et al. (2012).

34. Striegel-Moore & Franko (2006).

35. Striegel-Moore & Franko (2006).

36. Walcott et al. (2003).

37. Striegel-Moore & Franko (2006).

38. Arnett & Schwab (2012). The correlation was .14, *p* <.01.

39. Ravert (2009).

40. Andrews & Westling (2014).

41. Durkheim, E. (1897/1951).

42. Wilson & Herrnstein (1985). Various objections have been raised to the specific predictions of Durkheim's theory (e.g., Berk, 2006), but the main insight, that social control and social cohesion promote lower rates of suicide and antisocial behavior, has held up well.

43. This is, in fact, already well established: Johnston et al. (2012); Wilson & Herrnstein (1985).

44. Nelson & Luster (2014).

45. Arnett & Schwab (2012). For anxiety, chi-square (6,1022) = 20.77, *p* < 01; for depression, chi-square (6,1022) = 33.94, *p* <.01.

46. Harris et al. (2008).

47. The correlation was –.16, *p* < 01.

48. Twenge (2013).

49. Kimmel (2008).

50. NHTSA (2013).

51. Lyon et al. (2012).

52. Pinker (2011).

53. Bureau of Justice Statistics (2013).

54. Pinker (2011).

55. Donohue & Levitt (2001).

56. Pinker (2011).

57. Centers for Disease Control and Prevention ([CDC] 2013e).

58. Centers for Disease Control and Prevention ([CDC] 2011).

59. Centers for Disease Control and Prevention ([CDC] 2011).

60. Johnston et al. (2012).

61. Fischer et al. (2011).

62. Putnam (2001).

63. Twenge et al. (2010).

64. Costello et al. (2006).

65. Bellah et al. (1985); Silva (2013).

66. Kessler et al. (2010); Olfson et al. (2004).

67. Hoek (2006).

68. Hudson et al. (2007).

69. Bellah et al. (1985).

70. Putnam (2001).

71. Durkheim, E. (1897/1951, p. 212).

Chapter 12

1. This chapter title is borrowed from a brilliant song by Shinedown. See the music video at: http://www.bing.com/videos/search?q=Shinedown+YouTube&FORM=VIRE 6#view=detail&mid=621F2BD5912619C7249B621F2BD5912619C7249B

2. Masten (2001, p. 228).

3. Masten (2001, p. 227).

4. See Burt & Paysnick (2012) for a review.

5. Werner & Smith (1982, 2001).

6. Werner & Smith (2001).

7. Burt & Paysnick (2012); Masten, Obradovic, & Burt (2006).

8. Clausen (1991).

9. This pattern is in accordance with Erikson's (1950) theory: first identity, then intimacy.

10. See Seligman (2002) for more on optimism as a characteristic of resilience.

11. There is by now a substantial literature on the relation between religious faith and a variety of positive outcomes. For information on this issue related to adolescents and emerging adults, see Smith & Denton (2005) and Smith & Snell (2010).

12. Burt & Paysnick (2012); Masten (2001), Masten et al. (2006).

13. Bockneck (1986). Bockneck's book, a comprehensive look at the age period that I call emerging adulthood, is a neglected gem, full of insights and information, and I highly recommend it.

14. Erikson grasped this long ago. He made this statement regarding normal development, but I believe it applies even more to emerging adults with a difficult past:

> "To be [an] adult means among other things to see one's own life in continuous perspective, both in *retrospect and prospect*. By accepting some definition as to who he is, usually on the basis of a function in an economy, a place in the sequence of generations, and a status in the structure of society, the adult is able *to selectively reconstruct his past in such a way that, step for step, it seems to have planned him, or better he seems to have planned it.* In this sense, psychologically we do choose our parents, our family history, and

the history of our kings, heroes, and gods. By making them our own, *we maneuver ourselves into the inner position of proprietors, of creators*" (Erikson, 1958, pp. 111–112, *italics* added).

15. Arnett & Schwab (2012); Schulenberg & Zarrett (2006).

Chapter 13

1. E.g., Arnett (2000a, 2006a, 2006b, 2007, 2011).
2. Schlegel & Barry (1991).
3. Kett (1977); Modell (1989); Rotundo (1993).
4. E.g., Arnett (1997, 1998, 2001, 2003); Facio & Micocci (2003); Macek et al. (2007); Mayseless & Scharf (2003); Nelson (2003, 2009); Nelson et al. (2004); Sirsch et al. (2009). For a comprehensive summary, see Nelson & Luster (2014). Other traditional markers, such as obtaining a full-time job or finishing education, also rank consistently near the bottom in studies of the most important criteria for adulthood.
5. Kett (1977); Modell (1989).
6. For an analysis of the historical and cultural roots of the importance of self-sufficiency in the transition to adulthood, see Arnett (1998). For results comparing American ethnic groups, see Arnett (2003). The differences among ethnic groups on criteria for adulthood are few. However, African Americans, and to a lesser extent Latinos, often feel they have reached adulthood earlier than emerging adults in other ethnic groups, evidently because they often take on family responsibilities at an early age, due to family poverty or to having a child at an early age.
7. The early studies on this question used a yes/no format, asking participants to "indicate whether or not you believe each of the following must be achieved in order for a person to be considered an adult." The more recent studies have used a four-point scale from "not at all important" to "very important," asking participants to "indicate your opinion of the importance of each of the following in determining whether or not a person has reached adulthood." The numbers in the table indicate the percent who indicated "yes" in the early studies or "somewhat" or "very" important in the more recent studies. For a rare exception to the pattern in this table, see Zhong & Arnett (2014). This study, a dissertation project by my student Juan Zhong, surveyed Chinese women factory workers ages 18–29, and found that the most favored criteria for adulthood were "Learn to care for parents" (88%), "If a man, become capable of supporting a family financially (75%), "Settled into a long-term career" (74%), and "If a woman, become capable of caring for children" (72%). In contrast, the Big Three elsewhere were not big in this sample: "Accept

responsibility for the consequences of your actions" (54%), "Make independent decisions" (29%), and "Become financially independent" (23%).

8. Once I put an item for "Becoming less self-centered . . ." on the questionnaire, after my first several studies, it immediately became among the top two or three most widely endorsed items, below "responsibility" but above "financially independent" and right up there with "independent decisions" (e.g., Arnett, 2003). However, it has not come up in interviews as often as "independent decisions" and "financially independent" have (Arnett, 1998), so I continue to think the Big Three are biggest. I think this area, of how emerging adults change in their social understanding (compared to adolescents), is one of the most fascinating and promising for future research. See Bockneck (1986) for a rich theoretical discussion of this area.

9. See all the studies in Note 4 for this chapter, above.

10. Arnett (1998).

11. In a study of young White working-class men and women in the early 1970s, Rubin (1976) concluded that getting married was "a major route to independent adult status and the privileges that accompany it" (p. 56). Otherwise, however, evidence is scarce.

12. Arnett & Schwab (2012).

13. There was evidence that working-class emerging adults feel adult earlier, in the interviews in my original study and in a local multi-ethnic survey study I conducted (Arnett, 2003). However, in the national Clark poll, there were no social class differences in feeling adult (Arnett & Schwab, 2012). So, this remains an open question.

14. Arnett & Schwab (2012).

15. Arnett & Schwab (2012).

16. This view is worth mentioning, but it is not held by the majority of emerging adults. In the national Clark poll, only 24% agreed with the statement, "I think adulthood will be boring" (Arnett & Schwab, 2012).

17. For a discussion of the "storm and stress" of adolescence, see Arnett (1999). Some scholars on adolescence deny that it is stormy or stressful, but I have argued that in fact there is evidence that adolescence is more difficult than childhood or emerging adulthood, especially in terms of emotional upheaval and conflict with parents. Also see Larson & Richards (1994), who show that in the transition from childhood to adolescence there is an emotional "fall from grace" as happiness declines and anxiety and unhappiness increase.

18. E.g., Helson & Kwan (2000); Roberts, Caspi, & Moffitt (2001); Schulenberg & Zarrett (2006).

19. Larson and Richards (1994), using the Experience Sampling Method where people are beeped at random times during the day and then fill out a questionnaire about their moods and experiences at that moment, have found that adolescents have more emotional upheavals than either pre-adolescents or adults, partly because they

experience more frequent stressful events but partly because of how they respond to events. I would love to see an ESM study of emerging adults, but to my knowledge this has not been done.

20. This observation is confirmed by research on adolescents, e.g., Larson & Ham (1993); Larson & Richards (1994).

21. Arnett & Schwab (2012).

22. Bockneck (1986).

23. Arnett (2000b).

24. Quoted in G. S. Hall (1904, vol. 1, pp. 522–523).

25. Arnett & Schwab (2012).

26. Arnett (2000b).

27. Arnett (2000b); Arnett & Schwab (2012).

28. National Center for Education Statistics (2013).

29. Asakawa & Csikszentmihalyi (1999); Lee & Larson (2000).

30. For similar findings see Fuligni & Tseng (1999).

31. Pascarella & Terenzini (2005).

32. Twenge (2013).

33. Arnett (2000b).

34. My original study was conducted in the 1990s, and crime rates have gone down considerably since then (Pinker, 2011), so it could be that crime is a less prominent social concern among emerging adults today.

35. Robbins & Wilner (2000).

REFERENCES

Abma, J. C., Martinez, G. M., & Copen, C. E. (2010). Teenagers in the United States: Sexual activity, contraceptive use, and childbearing, National Survey of Family Growth, 2006–08. Washington, DC: National Center for Health Statistics.

Allem, J., Lisha, N. E., Soto, D., Baezconde-Grarganti, L., & Unger, J. B. (2013). Emerging adulthood themes, role transitions, and substance use among Hispanics in Southern California. *Addictive Behaviors, 38,* 2797–2800.

Alloy Media & Marketing (2009). 9th annual College Explorer Survey. Retrieved May 16, 2012, from http://www.marketingcharts.com/television/college-students-spend-12-hoursday-with-media-gadgets-11195/.

Amato, P. R. (1993). Family structure, family process, and family ideology. *Journal of Marriage & the Family, 55,* 50–54.

Amato, P. R. (2007). Life-span adjustment of children to their parents' divorce. In S. J. Ferguson (Ed.), *Shifting the center: Understanding contemporary families* (3rd ed., pp. 567–588). New York, NY: McGraw-Hill.

Amato, P. R., & Dorius, C. (2010). Fathers, children, and divorce. In M. E. Lamb (Ed.), *The role of the father in child development* (5th ed., pp. 177–200). Hoboken, NJ: John Wiley & Sons.

AmeriCorps. (2012). About Americorps. Retrieved from http://www.americorps.gov/about/overview/index.asp.

Andrews, J. A., & Westling, E. (2014). Substance use in emerging adulthood. In J. J. Arnett (Ed.), *Oxford Handbook of Emerging Adulthood.* New York, NY: Oxford University Press.

Arnett, J. (1992). The soundtrack of recklessness: Musical preferences and reckless behavior among adolescents. *Journal of Adolescent Research, 7,* 313–331.

Arnett, J. J. (1996). *Metalheads: Heavy metal music and adolescent alienation.* Boulder, CO: Westview.

Arnett, J. J. (1997). Young people's conceptions of the transition to adulthood. *Youth & Society, 29,* 1–23.

Arnett, J. J. (1998). Learning to stand alone: The contemporary American transition to adulthood in cultural and historical context. *Human Development, 41,* 295–315.

Arnett, J. J. (1999). Adolescent storm and stress, reconsidered. *American Psychologist, 54,* 317–326.

Arnett, J. J. (2000a). Emerging adulthood: A theory of development from the late teens through the twenties. *American Psychologist, 55,* 469–480.

Arnett, J. J. (2000b). High hopes in a grim world: Emerging adults' views of their futures and of "Generation X." *Youth & Society, 31,* 267–286.

Arnett, J. J. (2001). Conceptions of the transition to adulthood: Perspectives from adolescence to midlife. *Journal of Adult Development, 8,* 133–143.

Arnett, J. J. (2002). The psychology of globalization. *American Psychologist, 57,* 774–783.

Arnett, J. J. (2003). Conceptions of the transition to adulthood among emerging adults in American ethnic groups. *New Directions in Child and Adolescent Development, 100,* 63–75.

Arnett, J. J. (2005). The developmental context of substance use in emerging adulthood. *Journal of Drug Issues, 35,* 235–253.

Arnett, J. J. (2006a). Emerging adulthood: Understanding the new way of coming of age. In J. J. Arnett & J. L. Tanner (Eds.), *Emerging adults in America: Coming of age in the 21st century* (pp. 3–19). Washington, DC: APA Books.

Arnett, J. J. (2006b). The psychology of emerging adulthood: What is known, and what remains to be known? In J. J. Arnett & J. L. Tanner (Eds.), *Emerging adults in America: Coming of age in the 21st century* (pp. 303–330). Washington, DC: APA Books.

Arnett, J. J. (2007). Emerging adulthood, a 21st century theory: A rejoinder to Hendry and Kloep. *Child Development Perspectives, 1,* 80–82.

Arnett, J. J. (2008). From "worm food" to "infinite bliss": Emerging adults' afterlife beliefs. In R. Roeser, R. M. Lerner, & E. Phelps (Eds.), *Spirituality and positive youth development* (pp. 231-243). New York: Templeton Foundation Press.

Arnett, J. J. (2011). Emerging adulthood(s): The cultural psychology of a new life stage. In L. A. Jensen (Ed.), *Bridging cultural and developmental psychology: New syntheses in theory, research, and policy* (pp. 255–275). New York, NY: Oxford University Press.

Arnett, J. J. (2013). The evidence for Generation We and against Generation Me. *Emerging Adulthood, 1,* 5–10.

Arnett, J. J. (2014). Identity development from adolescence to emerging adulthood: What we know and (especially) don't know. In K. C. McLean and M. Syed (Eds.), *Oxford handbook of identity development.* New York, NY: Oxford University Press.

Arnett, J. J., & Amadeo, J. M. (2002). The sounds of sex: Sex in teens' music and music videos. In J. D. Brown, J. Steele, K. Walsh-Childers (Eds.), *Sexual teens, sexual media* (pp. 253–264). Mahwah, NJ: Erlbaum.

Arnett, J. J., & Fishel, E. (2014). *Getting to 30: A parent's guide to the twenty something years*. New York, NY: Workman.

Arnett, J. J., & Jensen, L. A. (2002). A congregation of one: Individualized religious beliefs among emerging adults. *Journal of Adolescent Research, 17*, 451–467.

Arnett, J. J., Kloep, M., Hendry, L. A., & Tanner, J. L. (2011). *Debating emerging adulthood: Stage or process?* New York, NY: Oxford University Press.

Arnett, J. J., Ramos, K. D., & Jensen, L. A. (2001). Ideologies in emerging adulthood: Balancing the ethics of autonomy and community. *Journal of Adult Development, 8*, 69–79.

Arnett, J. J., & Schwab, J. (2012). *The Clark University Poll of Emerging Adults: Thriving, struggling, and hopeful*. Worcester, MA: Clark University. Retrieved from http://www.clarku.edu/clark-poll-emerging-adults/.

Arnett, J. J., & Schwab, J. (2013). *Parents and their grown kids: Harmony, support, and (occasional) conflict*. Worcester, MA: Clark University. Retrieved from http://www.clarku.edu/clark-poll-emerging-adults/.

Arnett, J. J., & Schwab, J. (2014). *Beyond emerging adulthood: The Clark University Poll of Established Adults*. Worcester, MA: Clark University. Retrieved from http://www.clarku.edu/clark-poll-emerging-adults/.

Arnett, J. & Taber, S. (1994). Adolescence terminable and interminable: When does adolescence end? *Journal of Youth & Adolescence, 23*, 517–537.

Arnett, J. J., & Tanner, J. L. (Eds.) (2006). *Emerging adults in America: Coming of age in the 21st century*. Washington, DC: American Psychological Association.

Arnett, J. J., Trzesniewski, K., & Donnellan, B. (2013). The dangers of generational myth-making: Rejoinder to Twenge. *Emerging Adulthood, 1*, 17–20.

Arnett, J. J., & Walker, L. (2014). The five features of emerging adulthood: National patterns. Manuscript submitted for publication.

Asakawa, K., & Csikszentmihalyi, M. (1999). The quality of experience of Asian American adolescents in activities related to future goals. *Journal of Youth & Adolescence, 27*, 141–163.

Askari, S. F., Liss, M., Erchull, M. J., Staebell, S. E., & Axelson, S. J. (2010). Men want equality, but women don't expect it: Young adults' expectations for participation in household and child care chores. *Psychology of Women Quarterly, 34*, 243–252.

ASPE Human Services Staff (2012). Information on poverty and income statistics: Summary of 2012 Current Population Survey. US Department of Health and Human Services. Retrieved from http://aspe.hhs.gov/hsp/12/povertyandincomeest/ib.shtml.

Associated Press (2013). Number of active users at Facebook over the years. Retrieved from http://news.yahoo.com/number-active-users-facebook-over-230449748.html.

Bachman, J. G., & Schulenberg, J. (1993). How part-time work intensity relates to drug use, problem behavior, time use, and satisfaction among high school seniors: Are these consequences or just correlates? *Developmental Psychology, 29,* 220–235.

Bailey, B. L. (1989). *From front porch to back seat: Courtship in twentieth-century America*. Baltimore, MD: Johns Hopkins University Press.

Bean, J. (2011). *Engaging ideas: The professor's guide to integrating writing, critical thinking, and active learning in the classroom*. New York, NY: Wiley.

Belfield, C. R., & Bailey, T. (2011). The benefits of attending community college: A review of the evidence. *Community College Review, 39,* 46–68.

Bellah, R. N. (2011). *Religion in human evolution: From the Paleolithic to the Axial Age*. Cambridge, MA: Harvard University Press.

Bellah, R. N., Madsen, R., Sullivan, W. M., Swidler, A., & Tipton, S. M. (1985). *Habits of the heart: Individualism and commitment in American life*. New York, NY: Harper & Row.

Berk, B. B. (2006). Macro-micro relationships in Durkheim's analysis of egoistic suicide. *Sociological Theory, 24,* 58–60.

Berscheid, E. (2006). Searching for the meaning of "love." In R. S. Sternberg (Ed.), *The new psychology of love* (pp. 171–183). New Haven, CT: Yale University Press.

Bisson, M. A., & Levine, T. R. (2009). Negotiating a friends with benefits relationship. *Archives of Sexual Behavior, 38,* 66–73.

Blanco, M., Ozuda, M., Wright, C., Hasin, D. S., et al. (2008). Mental health of college students and their non-college-attending peers. *Archives of General Psychiatry, 65,* 1429–1437.

Bockneck, G. (1986). *The young adult: Development after adolescence*. New York, NY: Gardner Press.

Britton, M. L. (2013). Race/Ethnicity, attitudes, and living with parents during young adulthood. *Journal of Marriage and Family, 75*(4), 995–1013. doi:10.1111/jomf.12042.

Brown, J. D. (2006). Emerging adults in a media-saturated world. In J. J. Arnett and J. Tanner (Eds.), *Coming of age in the 21st century: The lives and contexts of emerging adults* (pp. 279–299). Washington, DC: American Psychological Association.

Brumberg, J. J. (1997). *The body project: An intimate history of American girls*. New York, NY: Random House.

Bureau of Justice Statistics (2013). *Arrest data analysis tool. National estimates*. Retrieved from http://www.bjs.gov/index.cfm?ty=datool&surl=/arrests/index.cfm#.

Burt, K. B., & Paysnick, A. A. (2012). Resilience in the transition to adulthood. *Development and Psychopathology, 24,* 493–505.

Bynner, J. (2005). Rethinking the youth phase of the life course: The case for emerging adulthood? *Journal of Youth Studies, 8,* 367–384.

Carnevale, A. P., Jayasundera, T., & Cheah, B. (2011). *The college advantage: Weathering the economic storm.* Washington, DC: Georgetown University Center on Education and the Work Force. Retrieved from http://www9.george town.edu/grad/gppi/hpi/cew/pdfs/CollegeAdvantage.FullReport.081512.pdf.

Carnevale, A. P., Smith, N., & Strohl, J. (2013). *Recovery: Job growth and education requirements through 2020.* Washington, DC: Georgetown University Center on Education and the Work Force.

Carroll, J. L., & Wolpe, P. R. (1996). *Sexuality and gender in society.* New York, NY: Harper Collins.

Carroll, J. S., Padilla-Walker, L. M., Nelson, L. J., Olson, C. D., Barry, C. M., & Madsen, S. D. (2008). Generation XXX: Pornography acceptance and use among emerging adults. *Journal of Adolescent Research, 23* (1), 6–30.

Centers for Disease Control and Prevention (CDC) (2011). Vital signs: Current cigarette smoking among adults aged >18 years—United States, 2005–2010. *Mortality and Morbidity Weekly Report, 60,* 1207–1212.

Centers for Disease Control and Prevention (CDC) (2013a). *Key statistics from the National Survey of Family Growth.* Retrieved from http://www.cdc.gov/nchs/ nsfg/abc_list_s.htm.

Centers for Disease Control and Prevention (CDC) (2013b). *HIV surveillance report, 2011.* Retrieved from http://www.cdc.gov/hiv/surveillance/resources/ reports/2011report/pdf/2011_HIV_Surveillance_Report_vol_23.pdf#Page=17.

Centers for Disease Control and Prevention (CDC) (2013c). Incidence, prevalence, and cost of sexually-transmitted infections in the United States. Retrieved from http://www.cdc.gov/std/hpv/.

Centers for Disease Control and Prevention (CDC) (2013d). National marriage and divorce rate trends. Retrieved from http://www.cdc.gov/nchs/nvss/marriage_ divorce_tables.htm.

Centers for Disease Control (CDC) (2013e). Tobacco fact sheet. Retrieved from http:// www.cdc.gov/tobacco/data_statistics/fact_sheets/adult_data/cig_smoking/.

Cherlin, A. J. (2009). *The marriage-go-round: The stage of marriage and the family in America today.* New York, NY: Knopf.

Chisholm, L., & Hurrelmann, K. (1995). Adolescence in modern Europe: Pluralized transition patterns and their implications for personal and social risks. *Journal of Adolescence, 18,* 129–158.

Civic, D. (1999). The association between characteristics of dating relationships and condom use among heterosexual young adults. *AIDS Education and Prevention, 11,* 343–352.

Clark, B., & Trow, M. (1966). The organizational context. In T. M. Newcomb & E. K. Wilson (Eds.), *College peer groups: Problems and prospects for research* (pp. 17–70). Chicago, IL: University of Chicago Press.

Clausen, J. S. (1991). Adolescent competence and the shaping of the life course. *American Journal of Sociology, 96* (4), 805–842.

Claxton, S. E., & van Dulmen, M. H. (2014). Casual sexual relationships and experiences. In J. J. Arnett (Ed.), *Oxford handbook of emerging adulthood*. New York, NY: Oxford University Press.

Cohn, D., Passel, J. S., Wang, W., & Livingston, G. (2011). *Barely half of U.S. adults are married—a record low*. Washington, DC: Pew Research Center.

College Board (2012). *Trends in college pricing*. New York, NY: Author.

Collins, W. A., & Laursen, B. (2006). Parent-adolescent relationships. In P. Noller & J. A. Feeney (Eds.), *Close relationships: Functions, forms and processes* (pp. 111–125). Hove, England: Psychology Press/Taylor & Francis.

Core Institute (2013). Executive summary, Core Alcohol and Drug Survey-Long Form. Retrieved from http://core.siu.edu/_common/documents/report0911.pdf.

Costello, E. J., Erkanli, A., & Angold, A. (2006). Is there an epidemic of child or adolescent depression? *Journal of Child Psychology and Psychiatry, 47,* 1263–1271.

Côté, J. (2000). *Arrested adulthood: The changing nature of maturity and identity in the late modern world*. New York, NY: New York University Press.

Côté, J. (2006). Emerging adulthood as an institutionalized moratorium: Risks and benefits to identity formation. In J. J. Arnett and J. L. Tanner (Eds.), *Emerging adults in America: Coming of age in the 21st century* (pp. 85–116). Washington, DC: American Psychological Association Press.

Côté, J. E., & Bynner, J. (2008). Changes in the transition to adulthood in the UK and Canada: The role of structure and agency in emerging adulthood. *Journal of Youth Studies, 11,* 251–268.

Coupland, D. (1991). *Generation X*. New York: St. Martin's Press.

Coyne, S. M., Padilla-Walker, L. M., & Howard, E. (2015). Media uses in emerging adulthood. In J. J. Arnett (Ed.), *Oxford handbook of emerging adulthood*. New York, NY: Oxford University Press.

Craig, J. M., & Piquero, A. R. (2015). Crime and punishment in emerging adulthood. In J. J. Arnett (Ed.), *Oxford handbook of emerging adulthood*. New York, NY: Oxford University Press.

Crouter, A. C., & McHale, S. M. (2005). The long arm of the job revisited: Parenting in dual-earner families. In T. Luster & L. Okagaki (Eds.). *Parenting: An ecological perspective* (2nd ed., pp. 275–296). *Monographs in parenting*. Mahwah, NJ: Lawrence Erlbaum.

Csikszentmihalyi, M., & Schneider, B. (2000). *Becoming adult: How teenagers prepare for the world of work*. New York, NY: Basic Books.

Curtis, D. D., Mlotkowski, P., & Lumsden, M. (2012). *Bridging the gap year: Who takes a gap year and why? Longitudinal studies of Australian youth.* Adelaide, Australia: National Center for Vocational Research.

Demo, D. H. (1993). The relentless search for effects of divorce: Forging new trails or stumbling down the beaten path? *Journal of Marriage & the Family, 55,* 42–45.

Dennis, M. (2012). The impact of MOOCs on higher education. *College and University, 88,* 24–30.

DePaulo, B. (2006). *Singled out: How singles are stereotyped, stigmatized, and ignored, and still live happily ever after.* New York, NY: St. Martin's.

Donohue, J., & Levitt, S. D. (2001). The impact of legalized abortion on crime. *Quarterly Journal of Economics, 116,* 379–420.

Dor, A. (2013). Don't stay out late! Mom, I'm 28: Emerging adults and their parents under one roof. *International Journal of Social Science Studies, 1,* 37–46.

Döring, N. (2009). The Internet's impact on sexuality: A critical review of 15 years of research. *Computers in Human Behavior, 25,* 1089–1101.

Douglass, C. B. (2005). *Barren states: The population "implosion" in Europe.* New York, NY: Berg.

Douglass, C. B. (2007). From duty to desire: Emerging adulthood in Europe and its consequences. *Child Development Perspectives, 1,* 101–108.

Dreyer, P. (1982). Sexuality during adolescence. In B. Wolman (Ed.), *Handbook of developmental psychology.* Englewood Cliffs, NJ: Prentice Hall.

Dubas, J. S., & Petersen, A. C. (1996). Geographical distance from parents and adjustment during adolescence and young adulthood. *New Directions for Child Development, 71,* 3–19.

Duggan, M., & Brenner, J. (2013). *The demographics of social media users, 2012.* Washington, DC: Pew Research Center.

Durkheim, E. (1897/1951). *Suicide.* New York: Free Press.

Eaton, A. A., & Rose, S. (2011). Has dating become more egalitarian? A 35-year review using *Sex Roles. Sex Roles, 64,* 843–862.

Economist (2013). The onrushing wave. January 18, pp. 24–27.

Edin, K., & Kefalas, M. (2005). *Promises I can keep: Why poor women put motherhood before marriage.* Berkeley: University of California Press.

Eisenberg, A., Bauermeister, J. A., Pingel, E., Johns, M. M., & Santana, M. L. (2011). Achieving safety: Safer sex, communication, and desire among young gay men. *Journal of Adolescent Research, 26,* 645–669.

Erikson, E. H. (1950). *Childhood and society.* New York, NY: Norton.

Erikson, E. H. (1958). *Young man Luther.* New York, NY: Norton.

Erikson, E. H. (1959). Identity and the life cycle. *Psychological Issues, 1,* 1–171.

Erikson, E. H. (1968). *Identity: Youth and crisis.* New York, NY: Norton.

Facio, A., & Micocci, F. (2003). Emerging adulthood in Argentina. In J. J. Arnett & N. Galambos (Eds.), *New directions in child and adolescent development*, 100, 21–31.

Ferguson, A. (2011). *Crazy U: One dad's crash course on getting his kid into college.* New York, NY: Simon & Schuster.

Ferguson, S. A. (2003). Other high-risk factors for young drivers—how graduated licensing does, doesn't, or could address them. *Journal of Safety Research*, 34, 71–77.

Fingerman, K. L., Cheng, Y. P., Tighe, L., Birditt, K. S., & Zarit, S. (2012). Relationships between young adults and their parents. In A. Booth, S. L. Brown, N. Landale, W. Manning, & S. M. McHale (Eds.), *Early adulthood in a family context* (pp. 59–85). New York, NY: Springer Publishers.

Fingerman, K. L., Cheng, Y. P., Wesselmann, E. D., Zarit, S., Furstenberg, F., & Birditt, K. S. (2012). Helicopter parents and landing pad kids: Intense parental support of grown children. *Journal of Marriage and Family*, 74(4), 880–896. doi:10.1111/j.1741-3737.2012.00987.x.

Fingerman, K. L., & Yahirun, J. J. (2015). Emerging adulthood in the context of the family. In J. J. Arnett (Ed.), *Oxford handbook of emerging adulthood*. New York, NY: Oxford University Press.

Finkel, E. J., Eastwick, P. W., Karney, B. R., Reis, H. T., & Sprecher, S. (2012). Online dating: A critical analysis from the perspective of psychological science. *Psychological Science in the Public Interest*, 13, 3–66.

Fischer, B., Jeffries, V., Hall, W., Room, R., & Goldner, E. (2011). Lower risk cannabis use guidelines for Canada: A narrative review of evidence and recommendations. *Canadian Journal of Public Health*, 102, 324–327.

Flynn, J. R. (2012). *Are we getting smarter? Rising IQ in the 21st century.* New York, NY: Cambridge University Press.

Frick, P. J., & Kimonis, E. R. (2008). Externalizing disorders of childhood. In J. E. Maddux & B. A. Winstead (Eds.), *Psychopathology: Foundations for a contemporary understanding* (2nd ed., pp. 349–374). New York, NY: Routledge/ Taylor & Francis Group.

Fry, R. (2013, August 1). *A rising share or young adults live in their parents' home.* Washington, DC: Pew Research Center.

Fuligni, A. J., & Tseng, V. (1999). Family obligations and the academic motivation of adolescents from immigrant and American-born families. *Advances in Motivation and Achievement*, 11, 159–183.

Furman, W., Brown, B. B., & Feiring, C. (1999). *The development of romantic relationships in adolescence.* New York, NY: Cambridge University Press.

Furman, W., & Simon, V. A. (2008). Homophily in adolescent romantic relationships. In M. J. Prinstein & K. A. Dodge (Eds.), *Understanding peer influence in children and adolescents. Duke series in child development and public policy* (pp. 203–224). New York, NY: Guilford Press.

Gentile, D. A. (2009). Pathological video game use among youth 8 to 18: A national study. *Psychological Science, 20,* 594–602.

Gerson, K. (2010). *The unfinished revolution: How a new generation is reshaping family, work, and gender in America.* New York, NY: Oxford University Press.

Goldberg, A. E. (2010). *Lesbian and gay parents and their children: Research on the family life cycle.* Washington, DC: APA Books.

Goldberg, W. A., Kelly, E., Matthews, N. L., Kang, H., Li, W., & Sumaroka, M. (2012). The more things change, the more they stay the same: Gender, culture, and college students' views about work and family. *Journal of Social Issues, 68,* 814–837.

Goldscheider, F., & Goldscheider, C. (1999). *The changing transition to adulthood: Leaving and returning home.* Thousand Oaks, CA: Sage.

Gonzaga, G. C., Carter, C., & Buckwalter, J. G. (2010). Assortative mating, convergence, and satisfaction among married couples. *Personal Relationships, 17,* 634–644.

Goossens, L., & Luyckx, K. (2007). Belgium. In J. J. Arnett, U. Gielen, R. Ahmed, B. Nsamenang, T. S. Saraswathi, & R. Silbereisen (Eds.), *International encyclopedia of adolescence* (pp. 64–76). New York, NY: Routledge.

Governors Highway Safety Association (2014). Distracted driving laws. Retrieved from http://www.ghsa.org/html/stateinfo/laws/cellphone_laws.html.

Graham, R., & Gootman, J. A. (2008). Preventing teen motor crashes: Contributions from the behavioral and social sciences and summary of the report of the national research council and institute of medicine. *American Journal of Preventive Medicine, 35* (3, Suppl. 1), S253–S257.

Granic, I., & Patterson, G. R. (2006). Toward a comprehensive model of antisocial development: A dynamic systems approach. *Psychological Review, 113* (1), 101–131.

Greenspan, E. (September 3, 2000). I had a Plan. It just fell apart. *Washington Post,* p. B4.

Greenwood, D. N., & Long, C. R. (2009). Mood specific media use and emotional regulation: Patterns and individual differences. *Personality and Individual Differences, 46,* 616–621.

Hall, G. S. (1904). *Adolescence: Its psychology and its relation to physiology, anthropology, sociology, sex, crime, religion, and education* (Vols. 1 & 2). Englewood Cliffs, NJ: Prentice-Hall.

Halpern-Meekin, S., Manning, W. D., Giordano, P. C., & Longmore, M. A. (2013). Relationship churning in emerging adulthood: On/off relationships and sex with an ex. *Journal of Adolescent Research, 28,* 166–188.

Hamilton, S. F. (1994). Employment prospects as motivation for school achievement: Links and gaps between school and work in seven countries. In R. K. Silbereisen & E. Todt (Eds.), *Adolescence in context: The interplay of family, school, peers, and work in adjustment* (pp. 267–283). New York, NY: Springer-Verlag.

Hamilton, S., & Hamilton, M. A. (2006). School, work, and emerging adulthood. In J. J. Arnett & J. L. Tanner (Eds.), *Coming of age in the 21st century: The lives and contexts of emerging adults* (pp. 257–277). Washington, DC: American Psychological Association.

Haridakis, P. (2013). Uses and gratifications approach. In A. N. Valdivia (Ed.), *International encyclopedia of media studies*. New York, NY: Wiley.

Harris, P. R., Griffin, D. W., & Murray, S. (2008). Testing the limits of optimistic bias: Event and person moderators in a multilevel framework. *Journal of Personality and Social Psychology, 95* (5), 1225–1237.

Hasin, D. S., Goodwin, R. D., Stinson, F. S., & Grant, B. F. (2005). Epidemiology of major depressive disorder: Results from the National Epidemiologic Survey on alcoholism and related conditions. *Archives of General Psychiatry, 62*, 1097–1106.

Hatfield, E., & Rapson, R. L. (2006). *Love and sex: Cross-cultural perspectives* (2nd ed.). Boston: Allyn & Bacon.

Heatherington, L., & Lavner, J. A. (2008). Coming to terms with coming out: Review and recommendations for family systems-focused research. *Journal of Family Psychology, 22* (3), 329–343.

Heinz, W. R. (2009). Youth transitions in an age of uncertainty. In A. Furlong (Ed.), *Handbook of youth and young adulthood* (pp. 3–13). New York, NY: Routledge.

Helson, R., & Kwan, V. S. Y. (2000). Personality development in adulthood: The broad picture and processes in one longitudinal sample. In S. Hampton (Ed.), *Advances in personality psychology* (Vol. 1, pp. 77–106). London: Routledge.

Hetherington, E. M., & Kelly, J. (2002). *For better or worse: Divorce reconsidered.* New York, NY: Norton.

Hewlett, S. A. (2002). *Creating a life: Professional women and the quest for children.* New York, NY: Miramax.

Higher Education Research Institute (2011). *The American freshman: Thirty-five year trends.* Los Angeles, CA: Author.

Hingson, R. W., & White, A. M. (2010). Magnitude and prevention of college alcohol and drug misuse: US college students aged 18–24. In J. Kay, V. Schwartz (Eds.), *Mental health care in the college community* (pp. 289–324). Hoboken, NJ: Wiley-Blackwell. doi:10.1002/9780470686836.ch15.

Hochschild, A. R. (1990). *The second shift.* New York, NY: William Morrow.

Hoek, H. W. (2006). Incidence, prevalence, and mortality of anorexia nervosa and other eating disorders. *Current Opinion in Psychiatry, 19*, 389–394.

Hogan, D. P., & Astone, N. M. (1986). The transition to adulthood. *Annual Review of Sociology, 12,* 109–130.

Hoge, D., Johnson, B., & Luidens, D. A. (1993). Determinants of church involvement of young adults who grew up in Presbyterian churches. *Journal of the Scientific Study of Religion, 32,* 242–255.

Horowitz, A. D., & Bromnick, R. D. (2007). 'Contestable adulthood': Variability and disparity in markers for negotiating the transition to adulthood. *Youth & Society, 39,* 209–231.

Hoxby, C., & Turner, S. (2013). *Expanding opportunities for high-achieving, low-income students.* Stanford University, SIEPR Discussion Paper 12-014. Retrieved from http://siepr.stanford.edu/publicationsprofile/2555.

Huang, P., Smock, P. J., Manning, W. D., & Bergstrom-Lynch, C. A. (2011). He says, she says: Gender and cohabitation. *Journal of Family Issues, 32,* 876–905.

Hudson, J. I., Hiripi, E., Pope, Jr., H. G., & Kessler, R. C. (2007). The prevalence and correlates of eating disorders in the National Comorbidity Survey replication. *Biological Psychiatry, 61,* 348–358.

Huesmann, L. R., Moise-Titus, J., Podolski, C., & Eron, L. D. (2003). Longitudinal relations between children's exposure to TV violence and their aggressiveness in young adulthood, 1977–1992. *Developmental Psychology, 39,* 201–221.

Hughes, M., Morrison, K., & Asada, K. J. (2005). What's love got to do with it? Exploring the impact of maintenance rules, love attitudes, and network support on friends with benefits relationships. *Western Journal of Communication, 69,* 49–66.

Hussar, A. D. (2012). *Survey: Most college women want to be married by age 30.* Retrieved from http://www.self.com/blogs/flash/2012/08/survey-most-college-women-want.html.

Hymowitz, K., Carroll, J. S., Wilcox, W. B., & Kaye, K. (2013). *Knot yet: The benefits and costs of delayed marriage in America.* Charlottesville, VA: National Marriage Project.

Jacobsen, W. C., & Forste, R. (2011). The wired generation: Academic and social outcomes of electronic media use among university students. *Cyberpsychology, Behavior, and Social Networking, 14,* 275–280.

Jensen, L. A. (1995). Habits of the heart, revisited: Autonomy, community, and divinity in adults' moral language. *Qualitative Sociology, 18,* 71–86.

Jensen, L. A. (2008). Through two lenses: A cultural-developmental approach to moral psychology. *Developmental Review, 28,* 289–315.

Jeynes, W. H. (2007). The impact of parental remarriage on children: A meta-analysis. *Marriage & Family Review, 40* (4), 75–102.

Johnston, L. D., O'Malley, P. M., Bachman, J. G., & Schulenberg, J. E. (2012). Monitoring the Future national survey results on drug use 1975–2012. Ann Arbor, MI: Institute for Social Research.

Jones, A. (2004). *Review of gap year provision.* University of London, Department for Education and Skills, Research Report RR555. Accessed on April 25, 2013 http://217.35.77.12/archive/england/papers/education/pdfs/RR555.pdf.

Kaye, K., Suellentrop, K., & Sloup, C. (2009). *The Fog Zone: How Misperceptions, magical thinking, and ambivalence put young adults at risk for unplanned pregnancy.* Washington, DC: National Campaign to Prevent Teen and Unplanned Pregnancy. www.thenationalcampaign.org/fogzone/fogzone.aspx.

Keniston, K. (1971). *Youth and dissent: The rise of a new opposition.* New York, NY: Harcourt Brace Jovanovich.

Kessler, R. C., Ruscio, A. M., Shear, K., & Wittchen, H. U. (2010). Epidemiology of anxiety disorders. *Current Topics in Behavioral Neuroscience, 2,* 21–35.

Kett, J. F. (1977). *Rites of passage: Adolescence in America, 1790 to the present.* New York, NY: Basic Books.

Kiernan, K. (2002). Cohabitation in Western Europe: Trends, issues, and implications. In A. Booth & A. C. Crouter (Eds.), *Just living together: Implications of cohabitation on families, children, and social policy* (pp. 3–31). Mahwah, NJ: Erlbaum.

Killen, M., & Wainryb, C. (2000). Independence and interdependence in diverse cultural contexts. *New Directions for Child & Adolescent Development, 87,* 5–21.

Kimmel, M. (2008). *Guyland: The perilous world where boys become men.* New York, NY: HarperCollins.

King, A. (2011). Minding the gap? Young people's accounts of taking a Gap Year as a form of identity work in higher education. *Journal of Youth Studies, 14,* 341–357.

Kirby, D. B. (2008). The impact of abstinence and comprehensive sex and STD/HIV education programs on adolescent sexual behavior. *Sexuality Research & Social Policy, 5* (3), 18–27.

Kirby, D., & Laris, B. A. (2009). Effective curriculum-based sex and STD/HIV education programs for adolescents. *Child Development Perspectives, 3* (1), 21–29.

Kosciw, J. G., Greytak, E. A., Bartkiewicz, M. J., Boesen, M. J., & Palmer, N. A. (2012). *The National School Climate Survey: The experiences of lesbian, gay, bisexual, and transgender youth in our nation's schools.* New York, NY: Gay, Lesbian, and Straight Education Network.

Krahn, H. J., Howard, A. J., & Galambos, N. (2012). Exploring or floundering? The meaning of employment and educational fluctuations in emerging adulthood. *Youth & Society, 44,* 1–22. doi: 10.1177/0044118X12459061.

Larson, R., & Ham, M. (1993). Stress and "storm and stress" in early adolescence: The relationship of negative life events with dysphoric affect. *Developmental Psychology, 29,* 130–140.

Larson, R., & Richards, M. H. (1994). *Divergent realities: The emotional lives of mothers, fathers, and adolescents.* New York, NY: Basic Books.

Larson, R. W., Wilson, S., & Rickman, A. (2010). Globalization, societal change, and adolescence across the world. In R. Lerner & L. Steinberg (Eds.), *Handbook of Adolescent Psychology*. New York: Wiley.

Lasch, C. (1979). *Haven in a heartless world*. New York, NY: Basic Books.

Lask, B., & Frampton, I. (2011). *Eating disorders and the brain*. New York, NY: Wiley.

Lauff, E., & Ingels, S. J. (2013). *Education Longitudinal Study of 2002 (ELS: 2002): A first look at 2002 high school sophomores 10 years later* (NCES 2014-363). US Department of Education. Washington, DC: National Center for Education Statistics. Retrieved from http://nces.ed.gov/pubsearch.

Laumann-Billings, L., & Emery, R. E. (2000). Distress among young adults from divorced families. *Journal of Family Psychology, 14*, 671–687.

Laursen, B., & Jensen-Campbell, L. A. (1999). The nature and functions of social exchange in adolescent romantic relationships. In W. Furman, B. B. Brown, & C. Feiring (Eds.), *The development of romantic relationships in adolescence* (pp. 50–74). New York, NY: Cambridge University Press.

Lee, M., & Larson, R. (2000). The Korean "examination hell": Long hours of studying, distress, and depression. *Journal of Youth & Adolescence, 29*, 249–271.

Lefkowitz, E. S., & Gillen, M. M. (2006). "Sex is just a normal part of life": Sexuality in emerging adulthood. In J. J. Arnett & J. L. Tanner (Eds.), *Coming of age in the 21st century: The lives and contexts of emerging adults* (pp. 235–256). Washington, DC: American Psychological Association.

Leonhardt, D. (2013, September 25). A nudge to poorer students to aim high on colleges. *New York Times*. Retrieved from http://www.nytimes.com/2013/09/26/education/for-low-income-students-considering-college-a-nudge-to-aim-high.html?_r=0.

Levine, A., & Cureton, J. S. (1998). *When hope and fear collide: A portrait of today's college student*. San Franciso, CA: Jossey-Bass.

Levine, A. R., & Dean, D. R. (2012). Generation on a tightrope: A portrait of today's college students. New York: Wiley.

Levinson, D., Darrow, C., Klein, E., Levinson, M., & McKee, B. (1978). *The seasons of a man's life*. New York, NY: Knopf.

Lewis, J. E., Miguez-Burban, M., & Malow, R. W. (2009). HIV risk behaviors among college students in the United States. *College Student Journal, 43*, 475–491.

Lipka, S. (2007, November 9). Helicopter parents help students, survey finds. *Chronicle of Higher Education, 11*, pA1. Retrieved from http://chronicle.com/article/Helicopter-Parents-Help/13578.

Lonsdale, A. J., & North, A. C. (2011). Why do we listen to music? A uses and gratifications analysis. *British Journal of Psychology, 102*, 103–134.

Luyckx, K., De Witte, H., & Goossens, L. (2011). Perceived instability in emerging adulthood: The protective role of identity capital. *Journal of Applied Developmental Psychology, 32*, 137–145.

Lyon, J. D., Pan, R., & Li, J. (2012). National evaluation of the effect of graduated driver licensing laws on teenager fatality and injury crashes. *Journal of Safety Research, 43*, 29–37.

Macek, P., Bejcek, J., & Vanickova, J. (2007). Contemporary Czech emerging adults: Generation growing up in the period of social changes. *Journal of Adolescent Research, 22*, 444–475.

Manago, A. M., Taylor, T., & Greenfield, P. M. (2012). Me and my 400 friends: The anatomy of college students' Facebook networks, their communication patterns, and well-being. *Developmental Psychology, 48*, 369–380.

Manning, W. D. (2013). *Trends in cohabitation: Over twenty years of change, 1987–2010.* (FP-13-12). National Center for Family & Marriage Research. Retrieved from http://ncfmr.bgsu.edu/pdf/family_profiles/file130944.pdf.

Manning, W. D., & Cohen, J. (2011). Premarital cohabitation and marital dissolution: An examination of recent marriages. *Journal of Marriage and the Family, 74*, 377–387.

Marketing Charts Staff (2013). *Are young people watching less TV?* Retrieved from http://www.marketingcharts.com/wp/television/are-young-people-watching-less-tv-24817/.

Marks, N. F., Bumpass, L. J., & Jun, H. (2004). Family roles and well-being during the middle life course. In O. G. Brim, C. D. Ryff, & R. C. Kessler (Eds.). *How healthy are we? A national study of well-being at midlife* (pp. 515–549). Chicago: University of Chicago Press.

Marshall, E. A., & Butler, K. (2015). School-to-work transitions. In J. J. Arnett (Ed.), *Oxford handbook of emerging adulthood.* New York, NY: Oxford University Press.

Martin, C. S., & Chung, T. (2009). How should we revise criteria for substance use disorder in the *DSM-V? Journal of Abnormal Psychology, 117*, 561–575.

Martin, J. A., Hamilton, B. E., Osterman, M. J. K., Curtin, S. C., Mathews, T. J. (2013). Births: Final data for 2012. *National Vital Statistics Reports, 62* (9). Retrieved from http://www.cdc.gov/nchs/data/nvsr/nvsr62/nvsr62_09.pdf.

Masten, A. S. (2001). Ordinary magic: Resilience processes in development. *American Psychologist, 56* (3), 227–238.

Masten, A. S., Obradovic, J., & Burt, K. B. (2006). Resilience in emerging adulthood: Developmental perspectives on continuity and transformation. In J. J. Arnett and J. L. Tanner (Eds.), *Emerging adults in America: Coming of age in the 21st century* (pp. 173–190). Washington, DC: American Psychological Association Press.

Mayseless, O., & Scharf, M. (2003). What does it mean to be an adult? The Israeli experience. *New Directions in Child and Adolescent Development, 100*, 5–20.

McGill, B., & Bell, P. (2013, Winter). The Big Picture. *National Journal*, pp. 14–15. Retrieved from https://docs.google.com/viewer?a=v&q=cache:l1-7jW2fiDcJ:www.allstate.com/Allstate/content/refresh-attachments/Heartland_VII_Editorial_Supplement.

pdf+&hl=en&gl=us&pid=bl&srcid=ADGEESgcebgKUfL61VcFEr-bNYqY_
LNA5LkNr2USdvzdbIudxYpU4xHYi9oHNwthHHmEow7OGX5
SR5fuQYb8DuogbEZA7A-q-I6e7ozbZqe9OVtWa7kVRstVPTn7uXgcJk3O
YweT-Bs4&sig=AHIEtbSlD4q1tDLR8xO2i642fXoue9uAPQ.

McKay, A., & Barrett, B. (2010). Trends in teen pregnancy rates from 1996–2006: A comparison of Canada, Sweden, USA, and England/Wales. *Canadian Journal of Human Sexuality, 19*, 43–52.

Michael, R. T., Gagnon, J. H., Laumann, E. O., & Kolata, G. (1995). *Sex in America: A definitive survey*. New York, NY: Warner Books.

Miracle, T. S., Miracle, A. W., & Baumeister, R. F. (2003). *Human sexuality: Meeting your basic needs*. Upper Saddle River, NJ: Prentice Hall.

Modell, J. (1989). *Into one's own: From youth to adulthood in the United States, 1920–1975*. Berkeley: University of California Press.

Moffitt, T. E. (2007). A review of research on the taxonomy of life-course persistent versus adolescence-limited antisocial behavior. In D. J. Flannery, A. T. Vazsonyi, & I. D. Waldman (Eds.), *The Cambridge handbook of violent behavior and aggression* (pp. 49–74). New York, NY: Cambridge University Press.

Mokhtari, K., Reichard, C. A., & Gardner, A. (2009). The impact of Internet and television use on the reading habits and practices of college students. *Journal of Adolescent & Adult Literacy, 52*, 609–619.

Moore, S., & Cartwright, C. (2005). Adolescents' and young adults' expectations of parental responsibilities in stepfamilies. *Journal of Divorce & Remarriage, 43* (1–2), 109–127.

National Center for Education Statistics (NCES) (2013). *The condition of education, 2013*. Washington, DC: US Department of Education. Retrieved from www.nces.gov.

National Center for Education Statistics (NCES) (2014). *The condition of education, 2014*. Washington, DC: US Department of Education. Retrieved from www.nces.gov.

National Highway Traffic Safety Administration (NHTSA) (2013). *Traffic Safety Facts 2010*. Washington, DC: Author.

National Marriage Project (2012). *The state of our unions, 2012*. Charlottesville, VA: Author.

Nelson, L. J. (2003). Rites of passage in emerging adulthood: Perspectives of young Mormons. *New Directions in Child and Adolescent Development, 100*, 33–49.

Nelson, L. J. (2009). An examination of emerging adulthood in Romanian college students. *International Journal of Behavioral Development, 33*, 402–411.

Nelson, L. J., Badger, S., & Wu, B. (2004). The influence of culture in emerging adulthood: Perspectives of Chinese college students. *International Journal of Behavioral Development, 28*, 26–36.

Nelson, L. J. & Luster, S. (2014). "Adulthood" by whose definition? The complexity of emerging adults' conceptions of adulthood. In J. J. Arnett (Ed.), *Oxford handbook of emerging adulthood*. New York, NY: Oxford University Press.

Neugarten, B., & Datan, N. (1982). Sociological perspectives on the life cycle. In P. B. Baltes & W. Schaie (Eds.), *Lifespan developmental psychology: Personality and socialization* (pp. 53–69). New York, NY: Academic Press.

Neugarten, B. L., Moore, J. W., & Lowe, J. C. (1965). Age norms, age constraints, and adult socialization. *American Journal of Sociology, 70*, 710–717.

O'Connor, T. G., Allen, J. P., Bell, K., & Hauser, S. T. (1996). Adolescent-parent relationships and leaving home in young adulthood. *New Directions in Child Development, 71*, 39–52.

OECD (2010). *Off to a good start? Jobs for youth*. Geneva, Switzerland: Author.

OECD (2014). OECD.statextracts. Short-term labor market statistics: Unemployment rates by age and gender. Retrieved from http://stats.oecd.org/index.aspx?query id=36499.

Olfson, M., Marcus, S. C., Wan, G. J., & Geissler, E. C. (2004). National trends in outpatient treatment of anxiety disorders. *Journal of Clinical Psychiatry, 65*, 1166–1173.

Ollendick, T. H., Shortt, A. L., & Sander, J. B. (2008). Internalizing disorders in children and adolescents. In J. E. Maddux & B. A. Winstead (Eds.), *Psychopathology: Foundations for a contemporary understanding* (2nd ed., pp. 375–399). New York, NY: Routledge/Taylor & Francis Group.

Olson, C. K., Kutner, L. A., & Warner, D. E. (2008). The role of violent video game content in adolescent development: Boys' perspectives. *Journal of Adolescent Research, 23*, 55–75.

Oltmanns, T. F., & Emery, R. E. (2013). *Abnormal psychology* (7th ed.). Upper Saddle River, NJ: Prentice Hall.

Padilla-Walker, L. M., Nelson, L. J., Carroll, J. S., & Jensen, A. C. (2010). More than a just a game: Video game and Internet use during emerging adulthood. *Journal of Youth and Adolescence, 39*, 103–113.

Parker, K. (2012). *The Boomerang Generation: Feeling OK about living with mom and dad*. Washington, DC: Pew Research Center.

Pascarella, E. T., & Terenzini, P. T. (2005). *How college affects students: A third decade of research*, Volume 2. Indianapolis, IN: Jossey-Bass.

Payne, K. K. (2012). *Coresident vs. non-coresident young adults, 2011 (FP-13-01)*. National Center for Family & Marriage Research. Retrieved from http://ncfmr. bgsu.edu/pdf/family_profiles/file124323.pdf.

Peace Corps. (2012). About the Peace Corps. Retrieved from http://www.peacecorps. gov/index.cfm?shell=learn.whyvol.

Perelli-Harris, B., Sigle-Rushton, W., Kreyenfeld, M., Lappegaard, T., Keizer, R., & Berghammer, C. (2010). The educational gradient of childbearing within cohabitation in Europe. *Population Development and Review, 36,* 775–801.

Petrogiannis, K. (2011). Conceptions of the transition to adulthood in a sample of Greek higher education students. *International Journal of Psychology and Psychological Therapy, 11,* 121–137.

Pew Research Center (2010). *Religion among the Millennials.* Washington, DC: Author.

Pew Research Center (2011). *Is college worth it? College presidents, public assess value, quality and mission of higher education.* Washington, DC: Author.

Pew Research Center (2012). *"Nones" on the rise: One in five adults has no religious affiliation.* Washington, DC: Author.

Pinker, S. (2011). *The better angels of our nature: Why violence has declined.* New York, NY: Viking.

Pool, M. M., Koolstra, C. M., & van der Voort, T. H. A. (2003). The impact of background radio and television on high school students' homework performance. *Journal of Communication, 53,* 74–87.

Popenoe, D., & Whitehead, B. D. (2001). *The state of our unions, 2001: The social Health of marriage in America.* Report of the National Marriage Project, Rutgers, NJ. Retrieved from http://marriage.rutgers.edu.

Popenoe, D., & Whitehead, B. D. (2002). *The state of our unions, 2002.* Report of the National Marriage Project, Rutgers University, Rutgers, NJ. Retrieved from http://marriage.rutgers.edu.

Prensky, M. R. (2010). Teaching digital natives: Partnering for real learning. New York, NY: Corwin.

Pryor, J. H., Hurtado, S., DeAngelo, L., Sharkness, J., Romero, L. C., Korn, W. S., & Tran, S. (2008). *The American freshman: National norms for fall 2008.* Los Angeles, CA: Higher Education Research Institute.

Pryor, J. H., Hurtado, S., Saenz, V. B., Santos, J. L., & Korn, W. S. (2007). *The American freshman: Forty year trends.* Los Angeles, CA: Higher Education Research Institute.

Putnam, R. D., Feldstein, L. M. & Cohen, D. (2001). *Bowling alone: The collapse and revival of American community.* New York. NY: Touchstone.

Rainie, L., Smith, A., & Duggan, M. (2013). *Coming and going on Facebook.* Washington, DC: Pew Research Center.

Ravert, R. D. (2009). "You're only young once": Things college students report doing now before it is too late. *Journal of Adolescent Research, 24* (3), 376–396.

Regnerus, M. D. (2007). *Forbidden fruit: Sex and religion in the lives of American teenagers.* New York, NY: Oxford University Press.

Regnerus, M. D., & Uecker, M. (2009). *Premarital sex in America.* New York, NY: Oxford University Press.

Reifman, A., Arnett, J. J., & Colwell, M. J. (2007). Emerging adulthood: Theory, assessment, and application. *Journal of Youth Development, 1*, 1–12.

Richards, M. H., Crowe, P. A., Larson, R., & Swarr, A. (2002). Developmental patterns and gender differences in the experience of peer companionship in adolescence. *Child Development, 69*, 154–163.

Robbins, A., & Wilner, A. (2001). *Quarterlife crisis: The unique challenges of life in your twenties.* New York, NY: Tarcher/Putnam.

Roberts, B. W., Caspi, A., & Moffitt, T. E. (2001). The kids are alright: Growth and stability in personality development from adolescence to adulthood. *Journal of Personality and Social Psychology, 81*, 670–683.

Robinson, J., Sareen, J., Cox, B. J., & Bolton, J. M. (2011). Role of self-medication in the development of comorbid anxiety and substance use disorders. *Archives of General Psychiatry, 68*, 800–807.

Robinson, J. R., & Godbey, G. (1997). *Time for life: The surprising ways Americans spend their time.* State College, PA: Penn State University Press.

Rosenfeld, M. J., & Thomas, R. J. (2012). Searching for a mate: The rise of the Internet as a social intermediary. *American Sociological Review, 77*, 523–547.

Rotundo, E. A. (1993). *American manhood: Transformations in masculinity from the Revolution to the Modern Era.* New York, NY: Basic Books.

Rubin, L. B. (1976). *Worlds of pain: Life in the working-class family.* New York, NY: Basic Books.

Savin-Williams. R. C. (2006). *The new gay teenager.* New York, NY: Trilateral.

Schaefer, R. T. (2006). *Racial and ethnic groups.* Upper Saddle River, NJ: Prentice Hall.

Schlegel, A., and Barry, H. (1991). *Adolescence: An anthropological inquiry.* New York, NY: Free Press.

Schneider, B., & Stevenson, D. (1999). *The ambitious generation: America's teenagers, motivated but directionless.* New Haven, CT: Yale University Press.

Schulenberg, J. E., & Zarrett, N. R. (2006). Mental health during emerging adulthood: Continuity and discontinuity in courses, causes, and functions. In J. J. Arnett & J. L. Tanner (Eds.), *Emerging adults in America: Coming of age in the 21st century* (pp. 135–172). Washington, DC: American Psychological Association.

Schwartz, B. (2000). Self-determination: The tyranny of freedom. *American Psychologist, 55*(1), 79–88.

Schwartz, C. R., & Mare, R. D. (2012). The proximate determinants of educational homogamy: The effects of first marriage, marital dissolution, remarriage, and educational upgrading. *Demography, 49* (2), 629–650.

Schwartz, S. J., Zamboanga, B. L., Luyckx, K., Meca, A., & Richie, R. (2015). Identity development in emerging adulthood. In J. J. Arnett (Ed.), *Oxford handbook of emerging adulthood.* New York, NY: Oxford University Press.

Segrin, C., Woszidlo, A., Givertz, M., Bauer, A., & Murphy, M. T. (2012). The association between overparenting, parent-child communication, and entitlement and adaptive traits in adult children. *Family Relations, 61*, 237–251. doi: 10.111 1/j.1741-3729.2011.00689.x.

Seligman, M. (2002). *Authentic happiness.* New York, NY: Free Press.

Shanahan, M. J., Porfeli, E. J., Mortimer, J. T., & Erickson, L. D. (2005). Subjective age identity and the transition to adulthood: When do adolescents become adults? In R. A. Settersten, F. Furstenberg, Jr., & R. G. Rumbaut (Eds.), *On the frontier of adulthood: Theory, research, and public policy* (pp. 225–255). Chicago, IL: University of Chicago Press.

Shernoff, D. J., & Csikszentmihalyi, M. (2009). Cultivating engaged learners and optimal learning environments. In R. Gilman, E. S. Hebner, & M. Furlong (Eds.), *Handbook of positive psychology in schools* (pp. 131–145). New York, NY: Routledge.

Shulman, S., & Connolly, J. (2013). The challenge of romantic relationships in emerging adulthood: Reconceptualization of the field. *Emerging Adulthood, 1*, 27–39.

Silbereisen, R. K., Meschke, L. L., & Schwarz, B. (1996). Leaving the parental home: Predictors for young adults raised in the former East and West Germany. *New Directions in Child Development, 71*, 71–86.

Silva, J. M. (2013). *Coming up short: Working class adulthood in an age of uncertainty.* New York, NY: Oxford University Press.

Sirsch, U., Dreher, E., Mayr, E., & Willinger, U. (2009). What does it take to be an adult in Austria? Views on adulthood in Austrian adolescents, emerging adults, and adults. *Journal of Adolescent Research, 24*, 275–292.

Smink, F. R. E., van Hoeken, D., & Hoek, H. W. (2012). Epidemiology of eating disorders: Incidence, prevalence, and mortality rates. *Current Psychiatry Report, 14*, 404–414.

Smith. C. (2011). *Lost in transition: The dark side of emerging adulthood.* New York, NY: Oxford University Press.

Smith, C., & Denton, M. L. (2005). *Soul searching: The religious and spiritual lives of American teenagers.* New York, NY: Oxford University Press.

Smith, C., & Snell, P. (2010). *Souls in transition: The religious lives of emerging adults in America.* New York, NY: Oxford University Press.

Smock, P. J., & Gupta, S. (2000). Cohabitation in contemporary North America. In A. Booth & A. C. Crouter (Eds.), *Just living together: Implications of cohabitation on families, children, and social policy* (pp. 53–75). Mahwah, NJ: Erlbaum.

Spataro, P., Cestari, V., & Rossi-Arnaud, C. (2011). The relationship between divided attention and implicit memory: A meta-analysis. *Acta Psychologica, 136* (3), 329–339.

Sperber, M. (2000). *Beer and circus: How big-time college sports is crippling undergraduate education.* New York, NY: Henry Holt.

Staff, J., Messersmith, E. E., & Schulenberg, E. E. (2009). Adolescents and the world of work. In R. M. Lerner and L. Steinberg (Eds.), *Handbook of adolescent psychology*. New York, NY: Wiley.

Steele, J. R., & Brown, J. D. (1995). Adolescent room culture: Studying media in the context of everyday life. *Journal of Youth & Adolescence, 24*, 551–576.

Striegel-Moore, R. H., & Franko, D. L. (2006). Adolescent eating disorders. In C. A. Essau (Ed.), *Child and adolescent psychopathology: Theoretical and clinical implications* (pp. 160–183). New York, NY: Routledge/Taylor & Francis.

Stritof, S., & Stritof, B. (2014). Estimated median age at first marriage, by sex: 1890 to 2012. Retrieved from http://marriage.about.com/od/statistics/a/medianage.htm.

Suarez-Orozco, C., & Suarez-Orozco, M. (1996). *Transformations: Migration, family life and achievement motivation among Latino adolescents*. Palo Alto, CA: Stanford University Press.

Substance Abuse and Mental Health Services Administration (SAMHSA) (2011). Results from the 2010 National Survey on Drug Use and Health: Detailed Tables. Retrieved from http://oas.samhsa.gov/NSDUH/2k10NSDUH/tabs/Sect2peTabs37to46.pdf.

Tamis-LeMonda, C. S., Way, N., Hughes, D., Yoshikawa, H., Kalman, R. K., & Niwa, E. Y. (2008). Parents' goals for children: The dynamic coexistence of individualism and collectivism in cultures and individuals. *Social Development, 17*, 183–209.

Taylor, P., & Keeter, S. (2010). *Millennials: Confident. Connected. Open to change*. Retrieved from http://www.pewsocialtrends.org/files/2010/10/millennials-confident-connected-open-to-change.pdf.

Tillich, P. (2001). *Dynamics of faith*. New York, NY: HarperCollins.

Tosun, L. R. (2012). Motives for Facebook use and expressing "true self" on the Internet. *Computers in Human Behavior, 28*, 1510–1517.

Triandis, H. C. (1995). *Individualism and collectivism*. Boulder, CO: Westview Press.

Turkle, S. (2011). *Alone together: Why we expect more from technology and less from each other*. New York, NY: Basic Books.

Twenge, J. M. (2013). The evidence for Generation Me and against Generation We. *Emerging Adulthood, 1*, 11–16.

Twenge, J. M., Gentile, B., DeWall, C. N., Ma, D. S., Lacefield, K., & Schurtz, D. R. (2010). Birth cohort increases in psychopathology among young Americans, 1938–2007: A cross-temporal metaanalysis of the MMPI. *Clinical Psychology Review, 30*, 145–154.

Twisk, D. A. M., & Stacey, C. (2007). Trends in young driver risk and countermeasures in European countries. *Journal of Safety Research, 38* (2), 245–257.

UNdata (2014). Abortion rates. Retrieved from http://data.un.org/Data.aspx?d=GenderStat&f=inID%3A12.

UNESCO (2013). Tertiary indicators (Table 14). Retrieved from http://stats.uis. unesco.org/unesco/TableViewer/tableView.aspx?ReportId=167.

United Nations (2009). *World fertility report, 2009: Country Profiles.* Department of Economic and Social Affairs, Population Division. Retrieved from http://www. un.org/esa/population/publications/WFR2009_Web/Data/CountryProfiles_ WFR2009.pdf.

US Bureau of the Census (2011). *Current population survey and annual social and economic supplements.* Washington, DC: Author.

US Bureau of the Census (2013). *CPS historical time series tables.* Retrieved from http://www.census.gov/hhes/socdemo/education/data/cps/historical/ fig10.jpg.

US Bureau of the Census (2014). *Statistical abstract of the United States.* Washington, DC: Author.

US Department of Labor (2012). *Number of jobs held, labor market activity, and earnings growth among the youngest Baby Boomers: Results from a longitudinal survey summary.* Economic News Release, Table 1. Retrieved from http://www.bls.gov/ news.release/nlsoy.nro.htm.

Van Doorn, M. D., Branje, S. J. T., & Meeus, W. H. J. (2011). Developmental changes in conflict resolution styles in parent-adolescent relationships: A four-wave longitudinal study. *Journal of Youth and Adolescence, 40* (1), 97–107.

Vazsonyi, A. T., & Snider, J. B. (2008). Mentoring, competencies, and adjustment in adolescents: American part-time employment and European apprenticeships. *International Journal of Behavioral Development, 32* (1), 46–55.

Waite, L. J., & Gallagher, M. (2000). *The case for marriage: Why married people are happier, healthier, and better off financially.* New York, NY: Doubleday.

Walcott, D. D., Pratt, H. D., & Patel, D. R. (2003). Adolescents and eating disorders: Gender, racial, ethnic, sociocultural and socioeconomic issues. *Journal of Adolescent Research, 18,* 223–243.

Wallerstein, J. S., Lewis, J. M., & Blakeslee, S. (2000). *The unexpected legacy of divorce.* New York, NY: Hyperion.

Wang, W. (2012). *The rise of intermarriage: Rates, characteristics vary by race and gender.* Washington, DC: Pew Research Center.

Washington Post (March, 2013). March 2013 Washington Post Poll. Retrieved from http://www.washingtonpost.com/page/2010-2019/WashingtonPost/2013/ 03/18/National-Politics/Polling/question_10009.xml?uuid=qPNlgI_1EeKRc3-Hzac7SQ#.

Werner, E. E., & Smith, R. S. (1982). *Vulnerable but invincible: A study of resilient children.* New York, NY: McGraw-Hill.

Werner, E. E., & Smith, R. S. (2001). *Journeys from childhood to midlife: Risk, resilience, and recovery.* Ithaca, NY: Cornell University Press.

Whitehead, B. D., & Popenoe, D. (2002). Why wed? Young adults talk about sex, love, and first unions. Report of the National Marriage Project, Rutgers, NJ. Retrieved from http://marriage.rutgers.edu/pubwhywe.htm.

Willoughby, B. J. (2009). The decline of in loco parentis and the shift to co-ed housing on college campuses. *Journal of Adolescent Research, 24*, 21–36.

Wilson, J. Q., & Herrnstein, R. J. (1985). *Crime and human nature.* New York, NY: Simon and Schuster.

Wilson, W. J. (1996). *When work disappears: The world of the new urban poor.* New York, NY: Knopf.

World Internet Project (2012). *International report.* Los Angeles, CA: Author.

Xia, Y. R., Ko, K. A., & Xie, X. (2013). The adjustment of Asian American families to the U.S. context: The ecology of strengths and stress. In G. W. Peterson & K. R. Bush (Eds.), *Handbook of marriage and the family* (pp. 705–722). New York, NY: Springer.

Yates, J. A. (2005). The transition from school to work: Education and work experiences. *Monthly Labor Review, 128* (2), 21–32.

Zhong, J., & Arnett, J. J. (2014). Conceptions of adulthood among migrant women workers in China. *International Journal of Behavioral Development, 38*, 255–265.

Zimmer-Gembeck, M. J., & Helfand, M. (2008). Ten years of longitudinal research on U.S. adolescent sexual behavior: Developmental correlates of sexual intercourse, and the importance of age, gender and ethnic background. *Developmental Review, 28* (2), 153–224.

Zuckerman, M. (2007). *Sensation seeking and risky behavior.* Washington, DC: American Psychological Association.

INDEX